Christianity Is Rubbish

John Wall

GN00507673

Mongrel Books

First published in 2004 by Mongrel Books.

A CIP catalogue record for this book is available
from the British Library.

Mongrel Books, PO Box 50712, London NW6 6YZ.

Cover Photograph *Yellow Bulldozer Moving Rubbish In Landfill*
© Francesc Muntada / Corbis.

Printed in Great Britain by Biddles Ltd., King's Lynn, Norfolk

ISBN 0-9548378-0-0

I write it because there is some lie that I want to expose, some fact to which I want to draw attention, and my initial concern is to get a hearing.

George Orwell, *Why I Write*

The pernicious superstition was checked for a moment, only to break out once more, not merely in Judaea, the home of the disease, but in the capital itself, where all things horrible and shameful in the world collect and find a vogue.

Tacitus, *Annals*

But superstition, like belief, must die.

Philip Larkin, *Church Going*

Something wonderful has happened to me. I was caught up into the seventh heaven. There sat all the gods assembled. By a special grace I was granted the favour of making a wish. 'Do you want', said Mercury, 'do you want to have youth, or beauty, or power, or a long life, or the most beautiful girl, or another blessing from the many we have in the treasure chest? Then choose, but only one thing.' For a moment I could not decide. But then I addressed the gods thus: 'Most honourable contemporaries, I choose one thing, that I may always have the laugh on my side.' There was not a god who answered a word, on the contrary, they all began to laugh. From this I concluded that my prayer was granted, and discovered that the gods know how to express themselves with taste, for it would hardly have been appropriate to answer solemnly: 'It is granted to you.'

Soren Kierkegaard, *Either / Or*

Contents

List Of Illustrations

Author's Preface

I'd like to use this space to express my thanks to everyone who offered their support and enthusiasm while I was writing this book – in particular Maria Wronski, Tim Roberts, Michelle Tuft, Andy Lewis, Jan Harvey and Laura Agostini.

I'm grateful also to Shelley Dobson for the cover artwork and to Michael Martin for kindly agreeing to read an early draft and for his encouragement to see it through. A. C. Grayling and Ludovic Kennedy offered some helpful advice and I'm grateful to them for their thoughts. Also thanks to Isabel for lots of photocopying and printing. It is to her and my other two sisters, Marina and Antonita, and to my parents that I dedicate this book.

October 2004

1

The Lord's My Shepherd (I'll Not Want)

Imagine there's no heaven
It's easy if you try
No hell below us
Above us only sky . . .
Imagine there's no countries
It isn't hard to do
Nothing to kill or die for
And no religion too . . .[1]

John Lennon may well have been right when he sang that it was easy to imagine a future world without heaven, hell and all the other appurtenances of religion; but it's another matter altogether to try to conceive how our world might have been had there not been one particular execution by a horribly gruesome method in a far-flung corner of the Roman Empire some 2,000 years ago. T. S. Eliot wrote that 'human kind cannot bear very much reality' and it may be that if a certain Jesus from the otherwise undistinguished town of Nazareth hadn't been nailed to a cross, we would have ended up with some other religion to help us overcome our fear of death and the possibility of there being nothing beyond.

But the world we would've inherited would be completely different: history, philosophy, literature, art, music, architecture, almost all aspects of western life and culture have been dominated and shaped indelibly by the influence of Christianity. Likewise much of our thinking and our responses to many of the most important human concerns are also based to a large extent on Christian teachings. Attitudes towards marriage, sex and divorce in particular have been hugely conditioned by just a few measly words uttered by Jesus on

---

[1]John Lennon, *Imagine*.

1

these matters and only in the recent past have they emerged from under the oppressive weight of Christianity's precepts.

Similarly many of the lesser particulars of our society and everyday lives are tinged with Christian influences: the Samaritans are named after a compassionate character of a gospel story, bank holidays revolve around former Christian holy days, the Red Cross takes its symbol and name from the method of Jesus' execution and so on. And there's no getting away from it; the influences of Christianity, like its god, are omni-present. When the English national anthem is sung at international football matches it's the Christian god[2] we all heartily invoke to 'save our gracious queen', while in the United States you can hardly complete a cash transaction without being reminded by the maxim on the back of every dollar bill that 'In God We Trust'. And as if to end all debate on the matter, even history and time itself are chronicled almost universally by reference to the supposed year of birth of a man known and referred to by hundreds of millions of people as the 'saviour of the world'.

And yet all this began with a lone voice preaching an unworldly, personal vision by the lakeside or in the synagogue to anyone who would listen. The kingdom of heaven, Jesus proclaimed 'is like a mustard seed . . . the smallest of all the seeds on earth; yet once it is sown it grows into the biggest shrub of them all';[3] could he ever have imagined that these words would be used to refer to the global institution founded in his name?[4] Christian compilers of statistics about their religion proudly preface their work with this saying as if to try to persuade us that with so many hundreds of millions of Christians throughout the world, this startling comparison rings true and that

---

[2] There are so many gods. It seems somewhat inappropriate to call the Christian god 'God', thereby going along with the Christian notion that its god is the only god. So I refer to it either as *the Christian god, the Father-god* or *the god*. Where the context is a Jewish one I refer to it by its Jewish name, *Yahweh*. Likewise in his capacity as a god I refer to Jesus as the *Son-god* rather than the more usual Son of God.

[3] Mark 4:31-32.

[4] Or more properly, in the name ascribed to him. Jesus' family name is not known to us, but he can never be said to have been a member of the Christ family. Christ was not originally a name but a title deriving from the Greek translation (*christos*) of the Hebrew word *masiah* (English *messiah*) meaning simply 'anointed (one)' or possibly 'anointed with oil'. *Chrism*, the holy oil used to anoint kings and queens at coronation services, is a related derivation of the word.

Jesus' voice was a prophetic one.

The trouble is, Jesus had in mind the 'kingdom of heaven' whose glorious coming was imminent, a fulfilment that he warned of and eagerly anticipated in the gospels over and over again. But as history records, with Jesus' grand prophecy failing to materialise and the advent of the kingdom indefinitely postponed, what we got instead for the greater part of the past two millennia was the intellectually lousy, misogynistic, war-mongering, power obsessed ideological system called Christianity.

Still, in terms of its widespread dissemination down through so many centuries and across so many countries, one must concede that the simile is an appropriate one. For Christianity has more believers in more countries than any other religion, claiming the souls of almost one third of the world's population. According to the *World Christian Encyclopedia* in the year 2000 there were just under 1.9 billion Christians, a figure expected to grow to some 2.8 billion by the middle of the 21st century.

In comparison, the only religion that rivals Christianity in terms of numbers is Islam, currently with nearly 1.2 billion adherents and projected to increase by over a billion in the next 50 years to form a quarter of humanity. Meanwhile other religions are lesser fish in the vast sea of faith, with 811 million Hindus, 768 million Chinese folk religionists and 359 million Buddhists. Most remarkably Jesus' own religion, Judaism is one of the smaller minnows with only 14 million adherents.[5]

But if a third of the world's souls are claimed by Christianity, this still means that it has failed to convert or persuade most of the world to accept its god and its doctrines, despite its relentless missionary zeal to 'make disciples of all the nations'.[6] Furthermore, the figures in the *Encyclopedia* are almost certainly overstated. It defines a Christian as any person who is a follower of Jesus at any level of commitment. By this measure therefore if you've been baptised you're probably included in these figures as a Christian, a folly we can see most obviously in the

---

[5] *World Christian Encyclopedia 2000,* Vol 1, p 4. The first volume is prefaced with the saying about the mustard seed.

[6] Matthew 28:19. According to Matthew this imperative formed part of Jesus' final instruction before he flew off to heaven.

3

number of Christians it records for the United Kingdom which it considers to be as high as 48.5 million.[7] In a UK population of less than 60 million, this means that over 80% of all people in this country - four out of every five people you know - are professing Christians. The extent of this somewhat inflated claim is confirmed not only by official government surveys, but also by the churches themselves. The *Official Yearbook of the United Kingdom* for example (prepared by the Office for National Statistics and therefore without any Christian bias) records only 6 million Christians in 1998, the discrepancy explained by this record being based on the more accurate and meaningful measurement of active membership of individual faiths. [8]

More ominous for the faith is the relentless and significant decline in Christian belief not only in terms of the numbers of practising members of the various churches but also in the general rejection of or indifference to its principal doctrines and beliefs. According to the *Official Yearbook* cited above, active church membership has fallen by about 35% since 1970, a haemorrhaging that shows no sign of being staunched. Recently for example (in 1997) the number of people attending Church of England Sunday services on a regular basis dropped to below the critical 1 million mark for the first time prompting the Anglican Church to take drastic action.

Accordingly on the same day the news was released, a new method of counting the numbers was announced, using the measure of 'average Sunday attendance' rather than 'usual Sunday attendance'. As a result of this 'more rigorous data collection' Sunday attendance rose dramatically from 0.97 million in 1999 to 1.06 million in 2000 . . .[9] One is reminded of wily government ploys to reduce hospital waiting lists or the asylum seekers total by similar manipulations. So when Dr Carey, the former Archbishop of Canterbury claims that 'the worldwide Anglican Communion, which numbers over 70 million

---

[7] *World Christian Encyclopedia 2000*, Vol 1, p 139.

[8] *Britain 2001: The Official Yearbook of the United Kingdom*, p 235. These figures may also be slightly overstated. For 1998 it records 1.6m active adult Anglicans and 1.8m active adult Catholics. Numbers recorded by the churches are lower: the Church of England records 0.97m active (i.e. attending Sunday services) members for 1999. The equivalent figure for the Catholic Church is 1.06m. Figures from *Church of England Gazette*, Vol. 2, Edition 1 2002 (www.gazette.cofe.anglican.org) and the Catholic Media Office (www.catholic.org.uk).

[9] *The Guardian*, November 13 1999, *Church of England Gazette*.

people, has very great potential as a player on the international scene' one can only smile gently at the extent of his pomposity and delusion.[10]

The situation is similar for the Catholic Church in this country; those attending Sunday mass number just under a quarter of the total (i.e. baptized) Catholic population with actual attendance numbers down from 1.39 million in 1987 to just over 1 million in 2000, a reduction of 27% in just 13 years.[11] Equally alarming for the Catholic Church is the shortage of clergy to conduct its services, with the number of diocesan priests down by almost a fifth over the past 20 years. If the present rate of decline were to continue, by the middle of this century there will only be some 2,300 priests left in the whole country; even so, I don't anticipate long queues outside the confessional box or the rationing of consecrated communion wafers.

With nearly two thirds of all couples preferring to get married without a religious ceremony,[12] despite the obvious and traditional appeal of a church setting and even Christianity's central doctrine, the resurrection of Jesus believed to be a real event by less than half of the *practising* members of the Church of England,[13] the end for Christianity in this country can't be far off. Indeed, the country's leading church statistician, Peter Brierley concluded from a recent survey that church attendance 'may fall to 0.5% of the population . . . within 40 years'.[14]

It's little wonder then that the head of the Catholic Church in England, Cardinal Cormac Murphy-O'Connor should have declared that Christianity in the United Kingdom, as something meaningful 'to people's lives and moral decisions - and to the government, the social

---

[10] *The Guardian*, February 22 2000. The 70m total includes the 26m registered Anglicans in England. But this figure of 26m is made up of all those who have been baptised in the Church of England (most of whom, as speechless infants, would've had no say in the matter) and who are still alive as opposed to genuinely committed members. It's a pity that the Archbishop was unable to make 'more rigorous data collection' a priority in this instance. The claim was made at an address given to the UN General Assembly in 1995.

[11] Figures are for England and Wales only and are taken from the Catholic Media Office website.

[12] *The Guardian,* January 11 2001. Figures were taken from the Office for National Statistics for 1999.

[13] The finding was from a survey conducted by the Catholic magazine, *The Tablet*, April 12 2001.

[14] *The Guardian*, April 24 2000.

life of the country - has now almost been vanquished',[15] a sentiment echoed more recently by his boss the pope, John Paul II who observed that 'in Scotland, as in many lands evangelised centuries ago and steeped in Christianity, there no longer exists a Christian society'.[16]

If Christianity is seen as increasingly irrelevant to the lives of most people, even by those who are among its principal proponents, it's a reasonable and valid observation to make that it no longer has any real value or meaning to contemporary society as a whole. And if this is the case, just as we discard matter that we feel is of no more use or value to us and call it rubbish, so we can consider Christianity in the same way. I shall go on to outline my main arguments in support of this opinion at greater length in due course. But for the moment at this point I can imagine howls of protest from traditionalists that the love and goodness and humility and everything else that goes with our somewhat slushy conception of a handsome and excessively meek blue-eyed Jesus can never be considered as qualities to be rejected by any fair-minded, decent and reasonable person.

To a certain extent I agree with this. The problem is these qualities aren't necessarily and specifically Christian. Being *good* or *decent* or *moral* or even *nice* just isn't the same thing as being a Christian. Jesus may well have taught that we should love our neighbours for example and to show a special consideration for the vulnerable and the poor; but are we to suppose that such compassionate behaviour didn't exist before Jesus[17] or that if he had never lived or hadn't preached these values, we wouldn't demonstrate charity or kindness ourselves to other people? I don't think so. Believing in love and compassion makes you no more a Christian than believing in social justice (a current sound-bite policy of the government) makes you a supporter of the Labour Party; and to reject the Labour Party in no way implies that you reject the notion of social justice. So before I proceed any

---

[15] *The Guardian*, September 6 2001.

[16] *The Guardian*, March 10 2003. A spokesman for the Scottish Catholic Church clarified the pope's remark: 'He singled out Scotland because he was addressing Scottish bishops, but he believes Scotland, like many other western European countries . . . can no longer be called Christian.' The observation was made on the occasion of the Scottish bishops' five-yearly pilgrimage to the Vatican. One suspects that the bishops may well have returned home a little less upbeat than when they set off.

[17] In fact this apparently most Christian of principles - to love one's neighbour as oneself - is a specifically Jewish formula and is found in the book of Leviticus (19:18).

further, it would be helpful to clarify what I do mean by Christianity.

What Is Christianity ?

The parable of the mustard seed might also be usefully employed here to remind us of the enormous diversity of movements and beliefs that have grown from the life and teachings of Jesus. As we shall see, even before the gospels were written there were rival Jesus factions with vying beliefs about what it meant to be one of his followers; and from a single seed has sprouted an overwhelming and unwieldy tangle of shoots and branches growing wildly in all directions, passing down an incredibly wide range of understandings and interpretations. Consequently there are so many different Christian denominations today that it's impossible to consider the individual and sometimes conflicting doctrines of each and every one of them. So instead, as a starting point we might consider that Christianity in its simplest form is based upon Jesus' life and teachings as reported in the New Testament gospels. Few would dispute this, but the problem with this formula is that there are too many Christian doctrines and beliefs that are not to be found in the gospels.

If Christianity is best defined as Christian beliefs and practises, one of the clearest understandings of what constitutes Christianity can be found in a specific statement of its beliefs known as the Creed. Creeds came into being at a very early stage in the Church's development and so have always played an important part in the faith. In the very earliest days of the Church the events of Jesus' life, particularly his death and resurrection, took on an increasing importance for the first Christian communities. Quite soon after his death and under the influence of the apostle Paul, one of Jesus' earliest proclaimers, these began to eclipse his actual teaching to such an extent that an acceptance of these events, and crucially, the interpretation given to them, became one of the distinguishing characteristics and requirements of the new form of worship.

We can see the unfolding and importance of this process in one of Paul's exhortatory letters, written just 20 years or so after Jesus' death. After telling the Christian community in the Greek city of Corinth that the news about Jesus 'will save you *only if* you keep *believing exactly* what I preached', he goes on to share with them what he himself had been taught, so providing us with the first recorded profession of Christian faith. Paul believed 'that Christ died for our sins, in accordance with the scriptures; that he was buried; and that he was raised to life on the third day, in accordance with the scriptures';[18] as his introductory gloss makes clear, it's the belief in this specific interpretation of events rather than following the ethical teachings or example of Jesus or even his call to repentance that provides the key to open the door to salvation.

Gradually these beliefs were formulated into primitive statements or rules of faith which quickly evolved into more precise semi-formal creeds requiring a full and scrupulous compliance from those wishing to join the promising new religion. By the middle of the 2nd century essential beliefs about Jesus had been expanded both in detail and number with the many additional articles of faith that Christianity had adopted, such as the virgin birth, Jesus' divine sonship and his ascension to heaven. It's likely that each church would have drawn up a summary of its own beliefs for the instruction and benefit of those about to undergo the initiation rite of baptism to ensure that they understood and accepted the core doctrines of the faith. So initially in the formative years of the early Church there would have been many variations of this basic creed at the various individual Christian communities. And it was from one of these - the church at Rome - that the earliest formal creed emerged in the closing decades of the 2nd century.[19]

The Roman Creed is significant both for its early origin and because it formed the basis of the Apostles' Creed, so called because it was considered to be a summary of the apostles' faith (and not because it had been formally drafted by the apostles themselves); as such it is highly valued by churches today. By the early 4th century, when order and unity were the most pressing requirements of both church and state, a standard and more comprehensive creed was composed which eventually gained a near universal acceptance. This became known as the Nicene Creed,[20] after the name of the town, Nicaea in north-west

---

[18]1 Corinthians 15: 2-4, (hereafter 1 Cor.), my italics.

[19]Kelly *Early Christian Creeds*, pp 127-130.

[20]The Council of Nicaea took place in 325; however, it wasn't until the Council of Constantinople in 381 that the wording of the Nicene creed was finalised. Despite this, allegiance to local creeds continued for many decades after its introduction.

Turkey where it was formulated and it forms the basis of the Creed which Christians recite at church services today to profess their faith. Christianity therefore may be defined in part as the teaching and acceptance of the twelve articles of faith expressed in this creed; these include the core beliefs in one god, in Jesus, the only son of that god and a true god himself, his birth from a virgin, his resurrection from the dead and ascension into heaven. Again it's worth noting that there are no ethical values or standards of personal conduct proclaimed in this creed; it consists entirely of professions of faith[21] as if to suggest that it is essentially an acceptance of these propositions which first and foremost makes one a Christian.

While the Creed provides us with many of its core beliefs, it's fair to say that contemporary Christianity still means rather more than the total of these articles of faith. For instance the Nicene Creed makes no mention of the doctrines of the Trinity or original sin, usually regarded as essential Christian beliefs. Both of these key doctrines were developed in the 5th century, at least a hundred years after the formulation of the Nicene Creed and are certainly never mentioned at all by Jesus.[22] So the understanding of Christianity that I will be proceeding with consists of Jesus' life and teachings recorded in the New Testament gospels, together with the core articles of faith set down in the (Nicene) Creed and the beliefs and teachings of the Church that have come down to us today.

The problem with the final part of this definition of course, as noted above, is to know which teachings of which church we should refer to. For the purposes of this book I've considered the Roman Catholic Church to be the appropriate authority.[23] This is based primarily on the fact that it claims to have an unbroken succession of bishops from the disciple Peter, named in one of the gospels as the person on whom Jesus founded his church,[24] and because historically

---

[21]The other articles of faith are beliefs in Jesus' crucifixion and death, in the second coming, in the Holy Spirit, in the Church, in the forgiveness of sins, the resurrection of the dead and in an everlasting afterlife.

[22]The doctrine of the Trinity was formulated at the Council of Chalcedon in the year 451. The doctrine of original sin was formulated by Augustine in the early 5th century but wasn't formally adopted until the Council of Orange in 529.

[23]Accordingly when I refer to 'the Church' hereafter, I mean the Catholic Church.

[24]Matthew 16:18 'You are Peter and on this rock I will build my church.' The remark is

other churches are generally recorded as having broken away from it. Moreover, the majority of Christians worldwide (some 56% or just over a billion people if we accept the *Encyclopedia's* data) are Catholics; perhaps all that teaching about the evils of contraception has a meaning and a purpose after all . . .

Recently the Catholic Church has compiled and published a comprehensive and very detailed exposition of its version of the Christian faith, the *Catechism of the Catholic Church*. This massive book, first published in an English translation in 1994, consists of 2,865 articles or paragraphs and sets out its teaching on just about every conceivable matter of Christian belief and worship. It is declared by the Pope, John Paul II to be a 'sure and authentic reference text for teaching catholic doctrine',[25] providing instruction on how one should understand or approach each article of faith set out in the Creed, the ten commandments and the seven sacraments. Additionally it offers guidance for 'Life in Christ' with articles on diverse matters including man's freedom, the morality of the passions, the virtues and - of course - sin, thereby setting out its teaching on a broad range of social and ethical matters.

The *Catechism* offers very few concessions to modernity and is deeply conservative in the position it takes not only with regard to matters of faith but also in respect of day to day behaviour and personal concerns. So for example it declares that reading your horoscope should be avoided since this is tantamount to having a 'desire for power over time' and that 'wearing charms is also reprehensible' (presumably a cross or crucifix doesn't count as a charm).

On a more serious note, under the section relating to the sixth commandment, 'You shall not commit adultery' the Church slips in its very strict precepts on sexuality and sexual morality in general. Gay sex is 'intrinsically disordered' since it is associated with 'grave depravity' and is therefore prohibited; contraception is 'intrinsically evil' (as such it would seem that on the Catholic scale of moral evil, contraception is as wicked and reprehensible as rape which is similarly described as 'intrinsically evil') and divorce is a 'grave offence' made even worse by

---

found only in this gospel. As we shall see, it's unlikely that Peter really was the first head of the community that formed after Jesus' death.

[25] *Catechism of the Catholic Church* (hereafter referred to as *Catechism*), Introductory statement. The *Catechism* can be accessed via the Vatican's web site (www.vatican.va).

remarriage.[26] As deplorable as this is, the *Catechism* is officially sanctioned as a 'presentation of the Catholic faith in its entirety'[27] and accordingly I take the third part of my understanding of what constitutes Christianity from the presentation of the faith in this authority.

Rubbish

This is much easier. As I suggested above, my understanding is that rubbish consists of material that we no longer value or which has no relevance or meaning for us, matter that has no further use. Metaphorically, it also means nonsense or foolishness; a claim or argument or remark is often effectively rebutted merely by throwing out this word with a pleasing measure of contempt. As to why I think Christianity is rubbish, I submit my case around four principal arguments: it is not true, it is non-sensical, it is morally deplorable and it is joyless.

It Is Not True

The first and most important argument that Christianity is rubbish is that its core beliefs are not true. The Christian faith depends on certain beliefs being either *factually true* or, for want of a better expression, *spiritually true*. Factual beliefs are those beliefs which are claimed to be historical in nature: Christianity affirms that certain incidents recorded in the New Testament gospels are actual events in Jesus' life and are indisputably true. They really happened. These are not therefore subjective beliefs dependant on the faith of the individual but a matter of historical record or fact. Nor can they be regarded merely as appendages or fancy trimmings of a legendary nature dreamed up by the evangelists. They include the central incidents of Jesus' crucifixion and bodily resurrection as well as his miracles and virgin birth and in theory at least could be supported by the findings of historical enquiry and investigation.

Beliefs that are spiritually true might also be usefully labelled

---

[26] *Ibid*, 2116, 2117, 2357, 2370, 2356, 2384.

[27] *Ibid*, 18.

theological - literally, *word of god* - beliefs. These are not grounded in history but have been directly revealed or communicated to the Church by the Christian god, usually through the agency of the Holy Spirit. They are generally doctrinal in matter and usually somewhat esoteric and undemonstrable in nature. Frequently they are deemed to be *mysteries of faith*. Examples of these beliefs would include the doctrines of the Trinity and the Incarnation (although to a certain extent these depend on historical foundations: for instance Jesus must have existed historically as a person in order for the Incarnation - the teaching that the Son-god became a human - to be a valid revealed belief) as well as certain teachings such as those concerning original sin or the transformation of bread and wine into Jesus' body and blood, usually known as the Eucharist.

Additionally these word of god beliefs include Christian teachings concerning personal conduct which lack any justification or reasoned support. Some of these have come down from Jesus' teachings (for example on the subject of divorce), others have been proclaimed by the Church (again supposedly under the guiding influence of the Holy Spirit) over the course of centuries and in the present day (teachings about contraception and euthanasia for instance about which Jesus said nothing).

Obviously the whole of the Christian religion depends on accepting the proposition that there is a god in the first place to be true and that this god is the Christian god. According to the *Catechism* it's quite possible to know with certainty of the existence of the Christian god through the faculty of reason alone. Ways of arriving at this certainty are through the means of 'converging and convincing arguments' and two principal arguments are offered: the order and beauty of the world leads one to understand that the Christian god is its origin and creator; and our questioning ourselves about the existence of a god reveals the existence of our souls. The soul can never be reduced to being merely of the material world and so it must be considered a spiritual entity; as such it can only have its origin in the Christian god and therefore the god has to exist.

I don't find these arguments especially convincing, although it must be pointed out that the *Catechism* makes no attempt to present or develop them in any detail. In fact frequently it seems that its purpose is not to persuade or explain but merely to proclaim. So the paragraphs dealing with these matters come across more as an exposition of faith which has already accepted the existence of the god rather than a reasonable and persuasive argument for its existence.[28]

However, I don't want to get bogged down with the abstract and tedious argument of whether or not there is a god and it's not an issue I will be considering. The bottom line is that the existence of one or more gods is a matter that has never been (and one suspects can never be) proven, verified or demonstrated satisfactorily one way or the other. So the Christian claim that certain of its beliefs and teachings are true because they're the word of its god is an invalid and inadmissible one since it appeals to an authority whose existence is not universally accepted and which can't be objectively established.

If we start with this understanding, it is only reasonable to proceed with the principle that we shouldn't dismiss Christian beliefs merely with the formulaic 'there is no god and therefore these beliefs aren't true.' How then might we determine whether such beliefs are true or not true? The most sensible way would be to approach the matter just as we would approach any other belief, by considering the grounds for that belief to be true and then looking for means either to justify and support that judgement or to dismiss it. Of course there might be some Christians who would object to this, maintaining that it's inappropriate to approach religious truths through reasonable enquiry, with a secular mindset; but if Christianity is making historical claims, the most appropriate way to consider these would be just as one would assess any other historical claim or argument. Moreover, as we've just noted, the Church accepts that human reason is an adequate and valid means to approach such matters.[29]

---

[28] *Ibid*, 31-34. In fact if one distils the *Catechism's* arguments to their essentials, free from the religious language, they can be taken as versions of the arguments from cause and design (known in philosophical circles as the cosmological and teleological arguments); while the argument about the existence of a soul is a version of the ontological argument which affirms that the existence of the Christian god can be inferred merely from contemplating the idea of that god. For those who wish to pursue these arguments further, see Martin, *Atheism: A Philosophical Justification* pp 79-153.

[29] *Catechism*, 37: 'human reason is, strictly speaking, truly capable by its own natural power and light of attaining to a true and certain knowledge of the one personal God.' Curiously the *Catechism* goes on to declare that those who lack this intellectual ability are hampered 'not only by the impact of the senses and the imagination, but also by disordered appetites.'

We might begin then by establishing what is usually understood by a belief being *true* and then consider how we would generally substantiate such a claim. First of all I take a belief to mean a theory or proposition to which one has given intellectual (or possibly emotional) assent having used one's reason, judgement and understanding to arrive at a particular conclusion but without having proof for its validity.

A belief may be accepted as true if there are good reasons to accept the validity of its proposition, reasons which can't be obviously and easily refuted. Good reasons would include the obvious logic and coherence of the argument for a proposition and the availability of good quality evidence to support it. Prior experience and common sense might also be influencing factors although a general consensus doesn't in itself make a belief true (that the world was flat and that the sun went round the earth are obvious examples of untrue beliefs which were almost universally accepted in the past). If we accept these principles, it follows that it would be difficult or incorrect to accept a belief as true if the logic of its argument simply didn't make any sense or if there were a significant amount of evidence to refute the case or argue more persuasively to the contrary.

A simple way to understand these basic principles would be to consider how a jury reaches a verdict in a court of law. Suppose we had a case in which Bob was accused of killing Jim; how, in the absence of an admission of guilt, would a jury come to a fair conclusion, beyond reasonable doubt, as the generally accepted principle stipulates (in other words a true belief) as to whether or not the charge were true? It would consider and assess both the prosecution and the defence cases and make a judgement as to which was the more probable based on the arguments and evidence provided.

The prosecution would seek to establish two things: first of all a good argument or motive for Bob to have killed Jim and secondly grounds or evidence to substantiate that argument. So far as motive goes, it always helps a jury to understand why an offence has been committed; but unsupported by any evidence, even the most indubitable motive is unlikely to result in a successful prosecution.

Similarly where the evidence is slight, if the motive itself is incoherent or unable to withstand critical scrutiny, it's unlikely to persuade a fair-minded jury. So to take an extreme example, if our Bob was alleged to have killed Jim because Jim refused to share the lottery winnings on a joint ticket, the motive imputed to Bob could be shown to be a nonsense if it was clear and known by all parties that Jim had never won the lottery or, more preposterously, if there was no such thing as the lottery in the first place. Of course this sounds ridiculous but as we shall see, there are some Christian doctrines whose claims are characterised by an incoherence as great as this; indeed such is the extent of their irrationality that they are even acknowledged by the Church to be 'inaccessible to reason' or beyond 'all human understanding and possibility'.[30]

Next the jury would consider the evidence presented, evidence that would have to be both reliable and persuasive. The testimony of witnesses is crucial to a successful prosecution and depends both on the credibility of the witnesses themselves and the testimony they give. Witnesses usually need to be unbiased and independent to be thought of as reliable. So if the principal witness had sold his story to the press for a huge sum but would only receive payment if a guilty verdict were secured, his personal testimony could well be considered unsafe since he would have a personal interest in a guilty verdict being returned.

Credibility might also be undermined if the defence discovered that the prosecution witnesses had met together beforehand to ensure their evidence agreed. Desperate witnesses might resort to this ploy to try to secure a conviction because it's generally understood that consistency of evidence is usually vital. So if one witness claimed that he saw Bob kill Jim with a knife and another claimed that Jim had been shot, the evidence is conflicting and therefore carries less weight. It might even be impossible to assess on its own without corroboration. Indeed if there were no corroboration or if a post-mortem failed to find the appropriate wounds, then the specific evidence of the two witnesses would be deemed worthless and their overall credibility would be substantially diminished.

Finally the evidence itself would have to be plausible and be in line with general experience. So if a witness claimed that she had been contacted by aliens who had shown her indisputable video evidence of Bob's involvement in the crime but rather unhelpfully hadn't left us their super advanced videotapes to examine, a sensible jury would

---

[30] *Catechism*, 237 on the doctrine of the Trinity; 497 on the virginity of Mary.

dismiss this without too much deliberation. Other more plausible evidence offered by the prosecution of course would need to stand up to the rigorous scrutiny of the defence; it hardly needs to be said, if it is easily refutable, the weight it carries as useful evidence is not going to be great.

It's with the understanding of these basic principles that I will consider the core beliefs of Christianity and argue that they are not true. The historical claims of Christianity concern truly extraordinary events which have never been repeated; indeed, it's likely that in any other circumstances they would be rejected out of hand by Christians and non-Christians alike. It's only reasonable then to proceed with the understanding that they require substantive and compelling evidence to persuade us to accept that they really occurred.

But when we examine the evidence for such matters as the virgin birth, the miracles and the resurrection of Jesus, we find that far from being compelling and persuasive, it's not at all convincing and is fundamentally flawed by the lack of credibility of those presenting it. Over and over again we'll see that all of the basic principles detailed above which we would normally use to help us arrive at a fair and intellectually honest conclusion about a given belief are either breached or cast aside. And when we come to some of the later doctrinal beliefs proclaimed centuries after Jesus' death we will see that the Christianity had become so far removed from reality that it regularly declared its doctrines to be true without any substantiation at all other than the insistence that they had been revealed by its god.

It Is Non-Sensical

We've noted in our court case analogy that a reasonable jury would rightly dismiss testimony that was ludicrously far-fetched and would require credible and convincing evidence to assess a case fairly and responsibly. The response of rationalists and humanists to Christianity has been consistently to reject it along these lines, because of its fundamental implausibility not only in respect of the evidence it offers to support its case, but just as importantly in the nature of the case itself.

But this is not merely post-Enlightenment thinking (as valid as that is) or present day cynicism looking down on a more superstitious age, for we know that Christianity was attacked for being so ridiculous and implausible from its earliest days. One of the first assaults on Christianity for instance - a detailed and incisive work written by a remarkably well informed Greek thinker called Celsus - appeared very early, towards the end of the 2nd century. In fact his treatise against Christianity, *A True Discourse* was considered to be so forceful that 60 years after it was written one of the leading Christian scholars of the age, Origen felt obliged to write a point by point refutation, known simply as *Against Celsus*.[31]

Celsus seems to have formed an intense hatred for just about anything to do with Christianity and he attacked it for many reasons, not all of which we would agree with today. But one of his most scathing criticisms was that it was a stupid belief which was able to spread quickly and widely by preying upon and exploiting the ignorance of the masses. Christians, said Celsus 'take advantage of the lack of education of gullible people [who] do not even want to give or receive a reason for what they believe'. Instead of reasoning and persuasive argument, he observed that they 'use such expressions as "Do not ask questions; just believe" and "Thy faith will save thee."' Catchy slogans are often used by politicians today to sell their (lack of) vision ('Tough on crime, tough on the causes of crime' or, even worse, 'You're either with us or against us') and 'just believe' might well have been a good slogan for a newly emerging sect to gain support and spread its word.

But for Celsus 'just believe' was the only thing that Christianity had to recommend itself and he very soon came to understand that 'just believe' was just so much trickery. People were being duped by the Christians with their fantastic and wildly extravagant stories of Jesus, proclaimed as a new god, born of a virgin and risen from the dead; and it was the vulnerable and easily led, 'the stupid and low class folk' who were most readily hoodwinked into believing.

According to Celsus the Christians could only 'babble about God impiously and impurely'. Perhaps it would have been appropriate he mused if their rallying call had given potential converts fair warning of

---

[31]Celsus' critique appeared originally around 180 CE. It has not survived and is known to us only because Origen's refutation, written around 245, included much of Celsus' text verbatim.

the stupidity of their teachings up front. If they'd been honest, instead of imploring people to believe without question, Celsus ventured that Christian preachers should have fished out suitable candidates for conversion by warning the crowds 'Let no one with education approach, none wise, none intelligent - such things we deem evil. But if there is anyone ignorant, stupid, lacking culture or a fool, let such come with boldness'.[32]

Celsus wasn't just ridiculing the new religion with these words, he was highlighting what he saw to be the case and it's likely that Christianity's earliest followers were generally uneducated and therefore probably quite simple minded or ignorant people. In Paul's first letter to the Corinthians he asks them 'how many of you were wise in the ordinary sense of the word, how many were influential people or came from noble families?' Not many is the expected answer. But this doesn't bother him, because as he pointed out 'God wanted to save those who have faith through *the foolishness of the message that we preach.*'[33] Educated and enlightened people today can see for themselves that Christian beliefs are foolish, but one can feel a degree of sympathy for the simple folk of Paul's time. Many of them may have been slaves or freed men or women, living in a harsh world to whom the assurance of an everlasting life free from the wretchedness of their earthly existence would've had an enormous appeal; and in an unscientific age when miracles, demons and resurrections were far more readily accepted than they are today one can begin to understand.

The trouble is Christianity simply hasn't shaken off these foolish beliefs and it remains as non-sensical today as it was in Roman times when Paul was writing his letters. If anything it has become even more ridiculous not only by *insisting* on these beliefs being literally true, despite the fact that the rest of the world really has moved on, but also by concocting ever more preposterous details and doctrines. Talking

---

[32]Origen, *Against Celsus*, I:9, III:18, IV:10, III:44. Celsus alleged that Jesus was a sorcerer who had learnt his tricks in Egypt and 'full of conceit because of these powers . . . he gave himself the title of god'. He invented the story of the virgin birth to hide his illegitimacy (I:28) and his resurrection was no more than hallucinations experienced by 'a hysterical female and perhaps some other one of those who were duped by the same sorcery' (II:55).

[33]1 Cor. 1:21, 27, my italics.

snakes, magic handkerchiefs, flying spirit creatures organising prison escapes: these might be the trump cards of a Dungeons and Dragons game or perhaps discussion points on the agenda of some nerdy D & D society meeting. But astonishingly these things are also the very stuff of Christianity. Sorcery and spells, turning water into wine and wine into blood is the sort of escapist fantasy you might expect to find in the world of Harry Potter and the Necromancer's Sack of Wind, but surely not in a 21st century world religion which asks us to take it seriously?

Unfortunately the Christian religion thrives on such crazy ideas and is still peppered with patently absurd miracles, visions and nonsense about the imaginary kingdom of its god and the conflict that was waged there long before humanity came into being. To crown it all, in a doctrine of supreme stupidity, Christians worship three separate gods which are mysteriously bonded together with some sort of spiritual superglue to form one indivisible unity. So there is only one god but at the same time there are three gods. Don't understand? Don't worry, you're not supposed to.[34] Just believe.

We can see how absurd Christianity is just by looking at an outline of the faith. As everyone knows, nearly 2,000 years ago the Romans executed a Jewish man using a cruel but by no means unusual form of punishment. But this was a bad mistake on their part because this man was the son of a god and, as would be formally proclaimed nearly three centuries later, was actually a god himself. Along with another god, called the Holy Spirit, which sometimes takes the form of a dove, sometimes a cloud, sometimes fire and sometimes wind, he formed a mysterious trinity with the Father-god, although this was not understood at the time and was only finally established over 400 years later.

Many years after the Son-god was killed, it became clear that it was the Father-god's plan that he should have been killed. The Son-god's death turned out to be a sacrifice to atone for the wickedness and sins of the world which proceeded as the inevitable consequence of the wilful and unacceptable disobedience of the first two humans. The Father-god told the first man and woman that they weren't allowed to

---

[34] As we've already observed, the doctrine of the Trinity is declared to be 'inaccessible to reason' (*Catechism*, 237). Nobody can understand it.

eat the fruit of a particular tree (a) because it said so and (b) because eating this fruit would give them knowledge of good and evil. At first the two humans obeyed. But one of them was successfully tempted by a snake which could talk to eat the magic fruit. The snake was later understood to be a spirit creature called an angel, created by the Father-god and which, in a war in the sky, the dwelling place of the gods and the angels, had rebelled out of jealousy and pride. The Father-god punished the bad angel and all its followers by banishing them from the happy dwelling place to a specially prepared and extremely nasty punishment chamber called hell. Overnight these angels were turned into devils. Piqued and stung by his catastrophic downfall, to try and get even, the devils' leader sought to alienate the humans from the Father-god by getting them to disobey its one command.

When the Father-god found out, it was so angry that its command had been disobeyed, it decided to punish the humans by making life really difficult and nasty and unpleasant for them; as an extra punishment, they would also be subject to death which until then had not existed. And because it was all the woman's fault, the god decided specifically to make the act of giving birth as painful as possible for all women. Finally to make it fully clear just how cross it was, it also decided that any children they might have would inherit their guilt and would have to endure the same punishments, as indeed would all subsequent generations, even though they themselves hadn't disobeyed the god.

Thousands of years later the Father began to feel a bit sorry for the descendants of the first two and therefore decided to give everyone a second chance. But in order to gain this possibility of making up for the original offence and to be restored to favour, there was a price to be paid. The Father-god required a sacrifice, and not just any regular blood sacrifice: cutting the throat of an animal, such as a sheep or goat was never going to satisfy the blood lust of the Almighty. So the Son-god volunteered to become a man and allowed himself to be sacrificed in accordance with his father's wishes. To turn the Son-god into a human, the third god, the Holy Spirit impregnated a woman who was a virgin; and it made damn sure that she remained a virgin until her death so that she wouldn't be tainted by the filthy evil of sex (which is usually a sin). Later it was understood that this woman was so highly favoured that when she died her body was taken up directly to the dwelling place of the gods.

It all went to plan, swimmingly. So it came about that the original execution of the Jewish man was what the Father-god had been planning all along. To prove that this was the case and to demonstrate that the Jewish man really was a god, the Father brought him back to life a couple of days after he was killed. Just before he died the Son-god told his followers to eat him by turning bread and wine into his body and blood with a magic spell. He told them to tell everyone in the world about him; if people believed in him and obeyed his commands, then after they died they would have an eternal life of bliss and happiness in the sky. But if they refused to do so, they would be punished, either by not having the eternal life or by being sent to the punishment chamber where they would suffer forever. Methods of punishment seem to be based primarily around lots of fire.

This essentially is the Christian faith. You don't have to be the most logical person in the world to see how stupid and offensive to your intelligence it is, but anyone with half an ounce of common sense contemplating Christianity is likely to go along with the response often given by the Star Trek computer when given meaningless or irrational data and conclude simply that *it does not compute*. It does not compute: stripped of the pompous and grandiose language of the Church, the body of faith comes across as an imaginative but total nonsense. But churchy language doesn't make any difference to the fact that it's all nonsense, for you can't alter its fundamental absurdity just by selecting different nouns or adjectives to convey the same dotty ideas. If anything such language, which often serves only to mystify and perplex, simply invites further ridicule; sometimes it even seems to be a deliberate exercise in obfuscation. Consider the following for example, taken from the *Catechism* (and remember this is not some archaic, sacred text but was written and first published in 1992):

> St Paul calls the nuptial union of Christ and the Church a great mystery. Because she is united to Christ as to her bridegroom, she becomes a mystery in her turn. Contemplating this mystery in her, Paul exclaims: 'Christ in you, the hope of glory' . . . And holiness is measured according to the 'great mystery' in which the Bride responds with the gift of love to the gift of the Bridegroom. Mary goes before us all in the holiness that is the Church's mystery as 'the

21

> bride without spot or wrinkle'. That is why the 'Marian' dimension of the Church precedes the 'Petrine' . . . The nuptial covenant between God and his people Israel had prepared the way for the new and everlasting covenant in which the Son of God, by becoming incarnate and giving his life has united to himself in a certain way all mankind saved by him, thus preparing for the 'wedding feast of the Lamb'.[35]

What on earth does all this mean? Perhaps like Paul we too are moved to exclaim, but our exclamation is more likely to be along the lines of 'Christ, what the hell's going on here?' What's this mystery business and why does the Church become a mystery? Why does the fact that Mary doesn't have any spots or wrinkles mean that the Marian dimension precedes the Petrine? And why is a lamb going to a wedding? Is the lamb getting married or is it a guest? How can a lamb get married? Or what sort of barmy person would invite a lamb to his or her wedding?

It really is very difficult indeed to take any of this seriously. Of course it might be observed that figurative or poetic language is being used to convey (semi) semi-complex ideas. So the lamb can be understood as a traditional Christian metaphor to express Jesus' sacrificial character and likewise the wedding is a means to convey the union of Jesus to the Church, or something like that. But why use a metaphor that's at least a thousand years out of date? Unless there's a foot and mouth crisis going on, people just don't sacrifice lambs any more, so how can this be in any way relevant to us today? The kindest thing we can say of an excessively flowery passage like this (and there are many like it in the *Catechism*) is that it is *bad* poetry written by a committee of priests with no sense of rhythm and an unfortunate tendency to mix its metaphors; a more critical appraisal might be inclined to dismiss the whole thing, like the faith it means to convey, as meaningless and antiquated claptrap.

It Is Morally Deplorable

Although it is a central article of faith expressed in the Nicene Creed that Jesus came to earth 'for us men and for our salvation', both

---

[35] *Catechism*, 772, 773, 1612.

Jesus and the Church are obsessed with punishment and retribution, often euphemistically referred to as 'divine justice'. In fact salvation and punishment are two sides of the same coin; there can't be one without the other, for what is salvation if it is not to be saved from the fires of hell? For this reason Christianity simply can't bring itself to relinquish its belief in hell, even though teachings about the bottomless pit and its excruciating punishments are often considered to be embarrassing and politically incorrect in our own times.

With the concept of a dungeon of fiery torment outdated and morally offensive as well as somewhat incompatible with the belief in a kind and loving god, more liberal theologians today might try to sell you the idea that hell is merely a place of spiritual isolation. But so far as the Church is concerned, it's still very much a place of suffering and everlasting pain for those who commit even minor offences. If you thought otherwise, consider what the *Catechism* has to say about it: 'The teaching of the Church affirms the existence of hell and its eternity . . . those who die in a state of mortal sin descend into hell, where they suffer the punishments of hell, eternal fire.'[36]

It's true that elsewhere the *Catechism* does make the point that hell is a state of self-exclusion from the god; but note how it seems almost to relish the notion that unrepentant sinners will 'suffer' and endure 'punishments' whose pains are most vividly understood when they are likened to those caused by 'eternal fire'. Does it really need to highlight this last unpalatable detail? One can only reject and feel contempt for so deplorable a system of morality that has caused so much fear and anguish to so many people, and which relies on the threat of violent and everlasting punishment to ensure that its adherents comply with its rules.

It's right of course that if there is to be justice then there must be some form of punishment for those who cause suffering, loss or harm to others and to a certain extent the desire for retribution is an entirely human and understandable one. But enlightened and humane systems of justice pass down sentences or penalties appropriate to the offence and work towards the subsequent rehabilitation of the offender.

Not so with Christianity. Despite what Dante had to tell us about the circles of hell and their ever increasing torments for the

---

[36] *Catechism*, 1035.

progressively more wicked, for those who die in a state of mortal sin, the punishment appears to be uniform for all grave offences. One boiling cauldron fits all and irrespective of whether you've tortured and murdered hundreds of people or have merely committed some lesser though apparently still mortal sin such as theft, the punishment is unvarying in severity, eternal and without any possibility of appeal, remission or rehabilitation.[37]

If only hell was a place of punishment for those whose conduct was so abhorrent and so unforgivable, it might not be quite as objectionable as it is. But as we've noted above, Christianity insists that hell is not only for the wicked but just as much for those who die unrepentant in a state of mortal sin. So what is a mortal sin? Is this the term Christianity gives to absolute wickedness? Is it something so utterly appalling, some crime so heinous that it can only have been committed by a truly evil person thus rendering such punishment fair and appropriate?

Well, no. Unfortunately you don't actually have to be all that evil to earn your place in hell; in fact you don't have to be evil or wicked at all. Mortal sins are simply defined as those transgressions which are grave in nature and which are knowingly and deliberately committed. Grave in nature need not amount to mass murder and is defined merely as 'opposition to God's law'[38] as specified by the ten commandments supposedly given to Moses on tablets of stone thousands of years ago. So if you knowingly steal a paper clip from your employer (thus breaking high command's rule number 7) and were subsequently to die without feeling too cut up about it, in theory at least you could be spending a lot of time participating in a very big fry up in the bowels of the earth or some other horrid place, no doubt wishing you'd gone to confession more frequently.

This is a frivolous example, but the Church does take the sin of adultery (the subject of the sixth commandment) very seriously indeed. Since Jesus forbade divorce absolutely and declared that remarriage after divorce constituted adultery, the Church classifies such actions as a mortal sin. Consequently it condemns divorcees who have established a new loving relationship, declaring that a 'remarried spouse

---

[37]'There is no repentance for men after death' - *Ibid*, 393.

[38]*Ibid*, 1859.

is then in a situation of public and permanent adultery.'[39] Under the Christian moral code then, if a person from a failed or broken marriage tries subsequently to find and give love and happiness in a remarriage and refuses to abandon the new partner or accept any notion of wrongdoing (so remaining unrepentant), he or she is condemned to 'eternal fire'. As the Catholic theologian Hans Kung observed in his history of the Catholic Church, 'There is a long encyclical on mercy, but no mercy is shown over the remarriage of divorced persons'.[40]

But this isn't the worst of Christian teachings on punishment for wrongdoers and sinners. Jesus himself is reported in the Gospel of John to have said 'whoever refuses to believe is condemned already, because he has refused to believe';[41] punishment then awaits those who reject his teachings and his message, a policy that the Church hasn't abandoned to this day. It tells us that 'Jesus often speaks of the unquenchable fire reserved for those who to the end of their lives refuse to believe . . . Jesus solemnly proclaims that he will send his angels and they will gather . . . all evil doers and throw them into the furnace of the fire.'[42] So for the Church, atheists, apostates and anti-Christians who refuse to submit to its teachings are no longer fellow men and women of a different intellectual persuasion worthy of respect, but are now dehumanised through being associated with and labelled as 'evil doers' and accordingly deserve to be punished in the most savage way.

This tends to be the method of the most brutal political tyrannies and in any other circumstances we would rightly consider it abhorrent. Consider for example the Nazi regime which imprisoned and killed its political opponents, the Communists even before it turned its wrath to its racial enemies, simply because they were in a different ideological camp and resisted its doctrines. Responsible and right-minded people

---

[39] *Ibid*, 2384.

[40] Kung, *The Catholic Church*, p 206.

[41] John 3:18.

[42] *Catechism*, 1034. The *Catechism* doesn't state specifically that unbelievers and non-Christians are doomed for the fiery pit. However, under the heading 'Outside the Church there is no salvation', it does declare (846) that 'the Church is necessary for salvation . . . Hence they could not be saved who, knowing that the Catholic Church was founded as necessary by God through Christ, would refuse to enter or remain in it.' It seems then that to refuse to accept the Christian ideology once you have been made aware of it, is to deserve violent and eternal punishment.

throughout the world find the attitudes and practices of such regimes deplorable and unacceptable; yet as soon as the same principle is brought into a Christian context, it suddenly becomes acceptable, desirable even and is allowed to pass without censure. In the UK at least, any political party which formally adopted such a policy would be banned even if it only threatened such actions; yet Christianity, which openly champions this type of intolerance and hatred, is deemed to be acceptable enough to be taught to children in schools. Is this, one wonders, ethical teaching of the most sublime type, or is it part of an ideological code that is morally rotten?

It Is Joyless

There are no jokes in the New Testament and no indications at all to suggest that there's anything approaching a sense of humour or light-heartedness in Christianity. This may sound like a very whimsical or flippant statement, but I'm actually making a serious point. A sense of *joie de vivre* is crucial to the psychological well-being of all of us and one would like to think that it is encouraged by or exists in some form or other in all religious faiths; but this characteristic seems to be wholly absent from the Christian religion. Pleasure, amusement, humour, laughter have no place in its beliefs and practices and if anything are frowned upon. In fact even 'immoderate laughter' at one point is referred to in the *Catechism* as a 'disorder'; irony, something which most of us enjoy and which in the general scheme of things is completely harmless is branded 'an offence against truth' and 'carousing' (which my dictionary defines as having a *merry* drinking spree) is considered a sin.[43] It is very difficult indeed to feel any warmth at all for a religion that is so dour and so resolutely opposed to people having fun or enjoying life.

This is no exaggeration; read the New Testament and you'll find that laughter is conspicuously absent except where it is associated with the wicked and the ungodly and Jesus himself is never described as laughing. Instead the New Testament conveys an overwhelming sense of gloom and doom with its stress on repentance and obedience and

---

[43] *Ibid*, 1856, 2481, 1852. In Paul's letter to the Ephesians (5:4) he announces that 'There must be no coarseness, or salacious talk and jokes.'

26

sacrifice and above all, sin. So depressing is it that it wouldn't be an overstatement to say that early Christianity comes across to us today as a misanthropist's dream come true. And if it is, it's one that is championed by one person above all others: the apostle Paul.

For the Church, Paul is its leading authority after Jesus and one of the most important figures in its history. But for the non-Christian he comes across only as a morbid depressive, a man obsessed with sin and the total unworthiness of humanity. Nietzsche was to call him 'the genius of hatred.'[44] Read the opening pages of his letter to the Romans which has an almost neurotic condemnation of anyone and everyone who chooses not to worship the Christian god and you'll soon see why. Such people, he seems to believe, are rendered almost sub-human in their impiety and depravity because they care only for 'their filthy enjoyments and the practices with which they dishonour their own bodies.'

At this point Paul proceeds to accuse all pagans of a catalogue of offences (ordinary non-Jewish, non-Christian people, according to Paul are all 'addicted to envy, murder, wrangling, treachery and spite') and then for good measure he concludes that they are 'without brains, honour, love or pity.' Their stubborn refusal to repent for this 'monstrous behaviour' only adds to his indignation: 'those who behave like this', he tells his audience 'deserve to die . . . for the unsubmissive who refused to take truth for their guide and took depravity instead, there will be anger and fury. Pain and suffering will come to every human being who employs himself in evil.'[45] As we've already noted, the Christian idea of evil is radically different from that of a reasonable person and seems to consist mostly of anything Christians don't like, especially lack of faith, lack of obedience and sexual promiscuity.

A different lifestyle or contrary set of religious beliefs hardly seems a sufficient justification to label a person as evil. But tolerance of other people's beliefs and habits was clearly too much for Paul, especially if these people appeared to be living happy and fulfilling lives and had no need of the Christian god. So elsewhere in his letters we find a sullen and resentful ill humour, proclaiming that happiness and the pleasures of life are to be despised, expressed most forcefully with his churlish

---

[44]Nietzsche, *The Anti-Christ*, 42.
[45]Romans 1:18-2:10.

and petulant rebuke to the Corinthians: 'those who are enjoying life', he fumes 'should live as though there were nothing to laugh about.'[46] For Paul spreading the good news about Jesus seemed to require him to drag everyone down to his own miserable level.

Of course one man's poison shouldn't contaminate the rest of the world and if Paul's loathings and contempt for human nature had just remained personal animosities, nobody would care too much about such obnoxious opinions. The problem is this bleak and appalling pessimism has filtered down to the Christian belief today which sees the whole of humanity as wretched and unworthy.

More to the point, anything that might be considered pleasurable, fun or desirable is abhorred or condemned by the Church. So to take the obvious example, the Christian teaching on sex is still extremely negative. The Church tries to drag itself into the real world by acknowledging that sex is a legitimate source of pleasure, but the awkwardness of its language betrays an obvious unease: 'The Creator himself . . . established that in the generative function, spouses should experience pleasure and enjoyment of body and spirit. Therefore the spouses do nothing evil in seeking this pleasure.' Well that's good to know. Clearly the reference to evil indicates that it must have been understood formerly that sexual pleasure was considered to be morally reprehensible.

Then, as if it is simply unable to accept fully that there's nothing inherently wrong with sexual pleasure, it just can't help itself and has to qualify its reluctant acknowledgement by insisting that 'spouses' keep within the 'limits of just moderation' (meaning what? Nothing adventurous? Not on Sundays?). Of course, it provides no justification for this reproof. Moreover, even if you are married and keep within these limits (whatever they are), it seems you still can't have sex just for fun, for sex is 'the generative function' and therefore 'it is necessary that each and every marriage act remain ordered per se in the procreation of human life'.[47] One wonders then if infertile married couples are allowed to have sex without feeling that they're engaging in an immoral act. Outside of marriage of course, it hardly needs to be

---

[46] 1 Cor. 7:30. A similar point is made by Jesus himself: 'Alas for you who laugh now; you shall mourn and weep' (Luke 6:25).

[47] *Catechism* 2362, 2366.

said that all sex remains sinful and therefore potentially subject to punishment.

The guidance proffered on sex is more extensive and detailed than it is on other pleasures that life has to offer and the *Catechism* doesn't really have much to say on other positive and joyful human acts and emotions. But we can begin to get some idea of the deeply depressing or indifferent nature of the Church's attitudes to these things by looking at the *Catechism's* subject index.

If we look up 'desires' for example, we find 8 separate references, but *all of them* concern 'disordered' desires, as if to suggest that desire itself is a perversion or some immoral urge. Happiness has 13 entries, most of which focus either on the gospel beatitudes or on the Father-god as the source of happiness ('true happiness is not found in riches or well being . . . or in any human achievement . . . or indeed in any creature, but in God alone'[48]), while joy has only 5 references. Of these 2 are about joy as a fruit of the Holy Spirit and one reminds us of that exciting and unforgettable moment when John the Baptist leapt for joy in his mother's womb when she was visited by the newly pregnant Mary.[49] Friendship has 12 entries, but two thirds of these are about friendship with the Father-god rather than with real people. Amazingly one of the remaining entries refers to the importance of showing friendship to 'homosexuals' to help them overcome their 'grave depravity'.[50] There are no entries for fun, pleasure, humour or laughter. Meanwhile for death there are 81 references and for the Church's favourite topic, sin and the forgiveness of sins, there are a very depressing 148 references.

It's a crude measure, but it does start to give an idea of where Christianity's real concerns and interests lie and suggests just why it is that so many people are deserting the faith in such large numbers: it has nothing bright and sunny to offer and is simply too negative and too miserable about life. The sentiment is perhaps best expressed in William Blake's angry yet beautiful poem, *The Garden of Love*:

---

[48]*Ibid*, 1723. Let's be clear about this. According to the Church true happiness cannot (or should not) be found in your husband, wife, lover, children, parents or friends, nor in anything you do or achieve in your life, but only in the god.

[49]Luke 1:41–45.

[50]*Catechism*, 2359, 2357.

I went to the Garden of Love
And saw what I had never seen:
A chapel was built in the midst,
Where I used to play on the green.

And the gates of this chapel were shut,
And Thou shalt not, writ over the door;
So I turned to the Garden of Love,
That so many sweet flowers bore,

And I saw it was filled with graves,
And tombstones where flowers should be:
And Priests in black gowns, were walking their rounds
And binding with briars, my joys and desires.

Go into this chapel or any other church and you'll find depictions of Jesus and other holy persons (usually Mary, his mother). And in these you'll find a confirmation of just how negative Christianity is. For instance you might come across a statue of Jesus perhaps with his arms outstretched as if imaginary sheep are feeding from his sacred hands or possibly holding up his hand to give one of those cheesy blessings that bishops and priests are fond of copying. But look at the face of the statue or indeed at any picture of Jesus and you won't find a smile. A genuine smile is the most visible and universal sign of kindness and emotional warmth, yet Jesus is never portrayed with this wonderful yet basic human response. Jesus is never presented as cheerful or happy. Instead he usually has a stern, authoritative demeanour or perhaps a melancholy, compassionate look as if he feels nothing but a pitiful sorrow for a fallen humanity.

And much more often than not depictions of Jesus are still more negative and depressing than this. The central Christian symbol has almost always been the cross and in its more repulsive form, the crucifix,[51] the excruciating pain of a man being executed in a slow and barbaric way is not just graphically portrayed but actually celebrated. In fact ultimately the whole of Christian theology revolves around the 'glorification of pain'[52] as one commentator has expressed it; and it's

---

[51]Early Christians felt that crucifixion was such a horrible and degrading punishment that it was not generally represented in Christian art until some 400 years after Jesus' death. See Murray, *The Oxford Companion to Christian Art and Architecture*, p 126.

[52]Kahl, *The Misery of Christianity*, p 30.

the suffering and the agony valiantly endured by Jesus that the Church treasures and reveres most of all. The point of these depictions is that they reinforce the crucial teaching that the suffering Jesus endured was inflicted by all of us and by our misbehaviour; and so-called holy images are just another means to force Christians to face up to their sinfulness and how bad they are and so feel rotten about themselves.

On this point the *Catechism* can hardly be more emphatic. First it tells us (in all seriousness) that the killing of Jesus was 'the greatest moral evil ever committed.' Then in its sour and bloody-minded misanthropy it reminds us that 'the Church has never forgotten that sinners were the authors and ministers of all the sufferings that the divine Redeemer endured', that 'the Church does not hesitate to impute to Christians the gravest responsibility for the torments inflicted upon Jesus' and that 'there is not, never has been and never will be a single human being for whom Christ did not suffer . . . *it is you* who have crucified him and crucify him still, when you *delight* in your vices and sins.'[53]

And so Christianity exercises its nastiest and most powerful hold over the minds of its adherents with its doctrine of perpetual and universal guilt. Even more than the threat of punishment, guilt is the means by which it seeks to break a person's spirit and so bring about a submissive response.[54] Worship, obedience and adoration are taught as the means by which one can respond favourably to the Christian god to make up for the suffering caused to Jesus and for all one's personal sins. But rather than being joyous in nature, Christian adoration comes across as a negative, self-abasing type of behaviour: 'To adore God is to acknowledge, in respect and *absolute submission, the nothingness of the creature.*' Adoration may take many forms but one of the more eminent is 'to offer sacrifice to God'. This sacrifice however must be genuine; and quite disturbingly the *Catechism* lays down the main criterion for a genuine sacrifice: 'the sacrifice acceptable to God is *a broken spirit.*'[55]

Christianity then *wants* its followers to be abject and miserable, to

---

[53] *Ibid*, 312, 598, 605, my italics. It's difficult to understand how the killing of Jesus can be thought of as such an atrocity if it was pre-ordained and understood that he would come back to life again a few days later.

[54] See Smith, *Atheism: The Case Against God*, pp 297-305 for further exposition of this point.

[55] *Catechism*, 2097, 2100, my italics.

endure self-imposed deprivations, to give up the things in life they find pleasurable, to be broken in spirit. By sacrificing the possibilities of happiness and fulfilment in this life, Christians can demonstrate their love and loyalty to the great leader and thereby prove their worthiness for favourable treatment from him after death. As Jesus said, it's the poor in spirit who will get the kingdom of heaven. By the time we get to the writings of Paul this teaching has become still more extreme: those who will be saved will be saved because they 'have been made slaves of God'.[56] And for the Church today, the understanding remains broadly the same: committed believers 'must walk the road Christ himself walked, a way of poverty and obedience, of service and self sacrifice, even to death'.[57] The big question of course is - why? Why do you have to sacrifice your life or be poor to please the Christian god? Why do you have to deny yourself the prospects of happiness and fulfilment in this life? Why do you have to regard yourself as lowly and unworthy? The answer can only be that Christianity, as Nietzsche rightly observed, is founded upon 'A certain sense of cruelty towards oneself', that it is a sickly religion characterised by a 'hatred of the senses, of the joy of the senses, of joy in general'.[58]

The Plan Of My Critique

To summarise then, the course of this book will be to consider and assess Christianity in the light of these four basic arguments. Of course in a work of this length it's not possible to examine every single belief and doctrine; accordingly I shall be concentrating on the core beliefs that usually make up our understanding of the faith. Before looking at these and at various aspects of Jesus' life and teachings, I consider the nature of Christian faith, tracing the development of faith in Jesus in the first Christian communities and try to get a fix on what faith actually means. Like many others, I argue that the concept of a *new covenant* mediated through Jesus was never established by Jesus but was invented by Paul after his death and that it was Paul who proposed the basic Christian exchange that promised salvation in return for faith. My

---

[56]Romans 6:22.

[57]*Catechism*, 852.

[58]Nietzsche, *op cit*, 21.

contention is that Christian faith has three key aspects, all of which the believer is required to accept: *miracle, mystery* and *authority* (Chapter 3).

Following on from this basic understanding of faith, I go on to consider the miracles attributed to Jesus in the gospels (Chapter 4), followed by a more detailed evaluation of the greatest of all Christian miracles, the alleged resurrection of Jesus shortly after his death (Chapter 5).

Next I discuss the Christian use of the concept of mystery and suggest why it is used so extensively in the Church's teachings. Closely related to Jesus' death and resurrection is the redemption mystery - or the Atonement as it is otherwise known - which maintains that through his sacrifice, Jesus was somehow able to provide the possibility of salvation to the world (Chapter 6). After that I consider some of the other central mysteries of faith: the mystery of the Incarnation which maintains that Jesus was both fully human and fully divine (Chapter 7) and those which revolve around Mary, the mother of Jesus such as the virgin birth, her immaculate conception and assumption (Chapter 8).

I then discuss and evaluate some of the ethical teachings of Jesus and of the Church today, arguing that these are not based on morality as we generally understand the term, but on a particularly menacing authoritarianism. I consider that ultimately Christian 'ethics' are no more than a set of stringent rules and requirements for personal conduct rather than a framework which provides the individual with guidance to make moral judgements for himself or herself (Chapter 9). I also use this chapter to highlight some of the double standards of both Jesus and the Church today in this area of their teaching. Finally I consider the Christian idea of sin and show how fundamental and necessary it is to the continued existence of the faith. In particular, I trace the development of the doctrine of original sin, arguably Christianity's most negative and deplorable teaching (Chapter 10).

I offer the case that none of the key beliefs of the Christian religion are true in so far as there are no good reasons to accept that they are, either in terms of compelling evidence or persuasive arguments. I maintain that these beliefs are non-sensical in that if they were put forward for serious consideration in any context other than the Christian one a reasonable person would dismiss them as incoherent and meaningless or little more than fairy-tales. And in respect of Christian ethics or behavioural requirements, I argue that it is not desirable or beneficial to make their harsh prescriptions the basis for living a happy and fulfilling life; in many respects they can be regarded as harmful or detrimental both to the individual and to society as a whole.

But before all that, I begin with an evaluation of the four New Testament gospels, the primary sources which provide us with our knowledge of Jesus' life, his teachings and the strange events that supposedly took place in Jerusalem and Galilee twenty centuries ago and which were to make him the most controversial and influential figure in the history of the world.

2

Pulp Fiction ?

And don't you realise
It's just a story ? [1]

Ask anyone to talk about Christianity and the chances are they'll begin by telling you what they know about the story of Jesus - that he was born of a virgin, in a stable in Bethlehem where he was visited both by wise men who had journeyed from afar to pay homage and by simple shepherds who were tending their sheep in the surrounding fields; that he lived in Galilee, where he became a popular preacher, a healer and apparently a worker of spectacular miracles too.

They may know also that shortly before his death, during a final evening meal with his companions, Jesus told his fellow diners to eat his body and drink his blood and to remember him in this rather macabre fashion. Then, betrayed by Judas, one of his closest supporters, for some reason - perhaps because he was hated and resented by the leading Jews of his day - he was handed over to the Romans to be put to death on a cross. Finally after three days he came back to life, just as he said he would, told his disciples to spread the word about him and soon after went up to heaven where he was reunited with his father.

All of these familiar details, indeed virtually everything we know about Jesus' life and teaching come to us from the four New Testament gospels. These are Christianity's foundation documents and without them it's difficult to see how it could ever have taken its present form, even if we concede that some of the fundamentals of the faith were established not by Jesus but by Paul (as I shall argue in the next chapter).

It's appropriate then that before we try to evaluate anything about

---

[1]The Teardrop Explodes, *Treason.*

Jesus and the religion founded in his name, we should consider the nature and reliability of these source documents. When were they written and why? How can we know - or at least have some confidence - that both the spectacular and the ordinary events in Jesus' life that they record actually happened? Who wrote them? Did these men know Jesus? Did they see all these amazing things for themselves or did they have to rely on earlier witnesses and their testimony? And did they set out to write these recollections (whether their own or those of other people) as a straightforward account of his life or are they trying to push their ideas about Jesus?

For Christians much of the unquestionable authority of the gospels comes about because from an early stage in the Church's history they formed a key part of its holy writings. We will see in the next chapter how, under the influence of Paul, early Christian communities came to understand that through the person of Jesus a *new covenant* with the Father-god had been established. For the Jews the principal means through which their covenant with Yahweh was communicated was the Torah, the first five books of the Old Testament which, together with the books of the prophets and a supplementary collection of miscellaneous writings, formed the Scriptures. As early Christianity began to move away from Judaism and became ever more confident as well as increasingly conscious of itself as a new and separate religion, it felt the need to have its own scriptures through which its new covenant could be proclaimed. As a result a body of writings about Jesus gradually emerged which, by the end of the 2nd century, the Church came to regard as Sacred Scripture. Eventually this diverse collection of writings became known as the New Testament.

The New Testament

The New Testament forms the second half of the Christian Bible and is a miscellany of 27 documents written between 20 and perhaps 100 years after Jesus' death.[2] On the whole these books concentrate on his public ministry, his death and resurrection and how these matters were understood, perhaps re-interpreted and proclaimed by early

---

[2]The earliest and latest books of the New Testament are generally thought to be the first letter of Paul to the Thessalonians (c 49 CE) and the second letter of Peter (c 120-140 CE). See Kummel, *An Introduction To The New Testament*, pp 257, 434.

supporters. It consists of the 4 gospels, sometimes thought of as biographies of Jesus, a quasi-historical account of the very early Church (The Acts of the Apostles) followed by 21 letters written by a small number of his proclaimers either to Christian communities or to individuals, two thirds of which are attributed to the apostle Paul.[3] It closes with a bizarre and extreme, semi-neurotic book presenting a nightmarish end of time vision (The Book of Revelation) which, with its obscure symbolism and relish for hellfire and appalling punishment for the ungodly, few people find accessible or attractive today.[4]

But this is not to say that these were the only early writings about Jesus and the religion that sprung up around him. Although there are only four gospels in the New Testament for example, we know from manuscripts and fragments that have survived and from early references that a considerable number of gospels were written. The gospel of Luke hints at this with its reference to the many others who had written accounts of Jesus' life, a review of which prompted that evangelist to write his own account of the Jesus story.[5]

However, with so many interpretations and versions of events floating around, from quite an early stage the concept of a canon, a body of works officially accepted as Christian, came into being. limiting the 'true' writings about Jesus to those which the Church deemed appropriate. The formation of this canon probably began with the preservation of Paul's letters to form a collection of written teachings which could be read to early Christian congregations as he seems to have intended.[6] Inclusion in the canon soon came to mean

---

[3]This is not to say however that all of these were actually written by Paul; authorship of a number of them, including 2 Thessalonians, Colossians, Ephesians and Hebrews is disputed. Some letters, such as Hebrews or 1 Peter, were not intended for any particular community or individual.

[4]The author of this tract envisages a plague of locusts for instance, 'given the power that scorpions have' sent from heaven to attack the ungodly and 'to give them pain . . . the pain of a scorpion's sting.' (Revelation 9:3-5)

[5]Luke 1:1-4. Luke's assertion that accounts about Jesus' life had been written by 'many others' prior to his own gospel is doubtful - as we shall see, it seems he had only two sources to rely on. However, by the middle decades of the 2nd century there was a substantial mass of Christian literature.

[6]Kummel, *op cit,* pp 478-481. Paul twice orders that his letters should be read to instruct early Christians; his earliest letter closes with the remark 'My orders, in the Lord's name are that this letter is to be read to all the brothers' (1 Thessalonians 5:27) and several

that the Church acknowledged a document to be sacred and inspired and having a value for faith and morality. In practical terms, this meant that a gospel would only be accepted if it was deemed to be of apostolic origin, if it had emerged from one of the great early Christian communities such as those at Rome, Antioch or Ephesus and if it conformed to the Church's fast evolving orthodoxy.

So the Gospel of Peter, dating from around the middle of the 2nd century, was eventually rejected by the bishop of Antioch because it didn't satisfy the final criterion, hinting that in his inability to feel pain while being crucified, Jesus was a divine spirit and not a man (a form of heresy known as Docetism).[7] By the end of the 2nd century then, alongside the letters of Paul and other early Christian writers, there emerged a recognised canon of four and only four gospels with one apologist, the bishop Irenaeus arguing that it was entirely appropriate that there should be four 'since there are four zones of the world in which we live, and four principal winds.'[8] Presumably these were thought to be quite good arguments at the time.

Generally Christians rate the gospels, the first four New Testament books, as its most attractive and important documents. They provide a human interest in the actual person and dramatic story of Jesus and are therefore much more accessible than the rather dry, abstract message of 'Christ crucified' that is the central concern of Paul's letters.

So it comes as something of a surprise to many people to learn that the gospels were not in fact the earliest Christian writings. All of the gospels are predated by the genuine letters of Paul and in this respect their positioning as the opening four books is rather misleading. This order suggests to the uninformed reader that they were the first works to be written about Jesus and therefore the most authentic, the closest to the real man. Indeed, until comparatively recently the gospels were held out and believed to be eye-witness accounts of Jesus' life, written by Matthew and John, two of his disciples; and by Mark and Luke, close companions of Peter (the leader of the disciples and named by Jesus as the founder of the Church) and Paul, next to Jesus and Mary the most important person in Christianity.

---

years later he wrote 'After this letter has been read among you, send it on to be read in the church of the Laodiceans.' (Colossians 4:16)

[7] Elliot, *The Apocryphal New Testament*, p 151.

[8] Irenaeus, *Against Heresies* III. Quoted from *A New Eusebius*, 97.

But the truth would appear to be otherwise; it is generally agreed by New Testament scholars that the authors of all four gospels are unknown, with the names of the evangelists having been ascribed to the works perhaps half a century or more after they had been written. However it suited the early Church to maintain that it had a body of solid, reliable testimony for its historical claims with four separate and apparently independent accounts of eye-witnesses or close associates of Jesus who had recorded the events of his life very soon after they had occurred.

Today the Church's understanding about the composition of the gospels is less compelling and somewhat more whimsical. It continues to maintain that it has this valid testimony, not because it was written by eye-witnesses (modern scholarship has made this stance impossible to sustain) but because the writers of the gospels were inspired by the Holy Spirit, a ghost with a fondness for literary composition: 'Sacred Scripture' the Church affirms, 'is the speech of God as it is put down in writing under the breath of the Holy Spirit.' So now it would seem we have even greater assurance that the details of the events of Jesus' life are true since the Christian god is incapable of deceit and therefore would never lie. Nor indeed, it is presumed, would any of those inspired by the original ghost-writer to do the actual writing, since, being able somehow to read its mind, 'they consigned to writing whatever he wanted written and no more.'

It follows then that pretty much every word in the gospels must be true in one sense or another. The Church throws in a caveat, declaring that Scripture has to be understood in the way that its authors intended it to be; but given that it asserts that it alone has the right to provide an authentic interpretation, authorial intention effectively becomes Church control over how it should be read. So when it tells us that the gospels 'whose historicity she [the Church] unhesitatingly affirms, faithfully hand on what Jesus, the Son of God, while he lived among men, *really did and taught*,'[9] it seems that Christians have to accept the events presented in the gospels, including any incredible or supernatural incidents as being literally, historically or factually true.

Given that many of the gospels stories in any other context would

---

[9] *Catechism* 81, 106, 126, my italics. The term 'historicity' is not defined but it's reasonable to suppose that it implies historical authenticity and accuracy.

be immediately dismissed as ridiculous and unbelievable, it would be unwise for a thoughtful and open minded person to accept without question the Church's claim that the gospels 'faithfully hand on what Jesus . . . really did'. It's only reasonable therefore to consider other means to help us decide whether they can be deemed reliable and trustworthy sources to tell us the truth about Jesus.

This scepticism seems to be justified when the Church's argument is considered more carefully. It claims that Sacred Scripture is the word of its god and that therefore these writings are necessarily and infallibly true. But the problem is, we only know about this supposed infallibility because the Church has pronounced that Sacred Scripture is so characterised. So where does its authority come from to make such a pronouncement?

The *Catechism* informs us that it derives from the apostles of Jesus, who 'left bishops as their successors [and] gave them their own position of teaching authority.'[10] But the only source of information we have that Jesus himself had any authority to pass on via the apostles comes from the writings of the New Testament. So it seems that Sacred Scripture is infallibly true only because the Church has said so; and in turn the only authority that the Church has to make such a pronouncement derives from the very same scriptures. Both traditions are therefore self-referential in their claim to authority or truthfulness. So setting aside this particular claim, how might we come to a reasonable assessment of the reliability of the gospels?

If we feel unable to accept the Church's circular reasoning, one of the more obvious and profitable ways to evaluate the standing of the gospels is to follow the development of critical scholarship and to take on board some of its key principles and findings. This is a discipline whose objective has been to respond to these very concerns, although it is only in the last 300 years or so that this type of study has been vigorously pursued. Perhaps we shouldn't be too surprised at this since for many centuries access to the Bible was highly restricted. It wasn't until 1384 for instance that it was translated into English in its entirety by John Wycliffe and only in the early 16th century did the Great Bible (a revised translation) become available in every English church.[11]

---

[10] *Ibid*, 77.

[11] *The New Jerome Biblical Commentary*, (hereafter referred to as *Jerome*) 68:191, 194.

Once people could read or hear the Bible for themselves however, assumptions began to be challenged. We might even trace this back to Martin Luther who, in his repudiation of the Catholic Church in Rome, held that Christian truth was to be found not in the Church's teaching but in Scripture alone. Luther was a fundamentalist for whom the literal truth of the New Testament was virtually unquestionable. 'The Holy Spirit' he declared, 'is the plainest writer and speaker in heaven and earth, and therefore His words cannot have more than one, and that the very simplest, sense, which we call the literal, ordinary, natural sense.'[12] But with Protestant reformers insisting that the true meaning of the Bible was explained by itself without reference to external dogmatic assumptions, biblical exegesis took on a new and urgent importance; and it was only a matter of time before previously unquestioned fundamentals were to be challenged and refuted.

Early Gospel Criticism

The earliest critical appraisals of the gospels were generally unthreatening, barely departing from familiar and accepted interpretations and began by noting that three of them, Matthew, Mark and Luke had many similarities in structure, language and content, while John was significantly different. This fundamental difference was demonstrated by a Greek edition of the New Testament published in 1775 by Johann Griesbach, a university professor of theology. In this edition he printed the first three gospels together in three parallel columns under the title *A Synopsis of the Gospels of Matthew, Mark and Luke* to facilitate comparisons between them. Consequently they have become known as the 'synoptic' gospels. The Gospel of John, generally acknowledged to have been written later because of its more developed theology, is usually referred to as the Fourth Gospel.

This understanding of the similarity of the first three gospels led to the question of their inter-relationship and dependency, an issue that has become known in New Testament scholarship as the 'synoptic problem'. In many instances the detail of individual stories in these

---

[12]Luther 1521, cited in Kummel, *The New Testament: The History of the Investigation of its Problems*, p 22.

three gospels is so similar that it's clear that they are reworkings of the same material. It's also clear that they couldn't have been written independently of each other. In one of the early miracle stories for example, a woman with a haemorrhage manages to press through the crowd to get close to Jesus to try to be healed by him. Somehow both Matthew and Mark know the woman's innermost thoughts, her belief and longing that if she could only touch Jesus' clothes she would be cured.

Given that the woman remained anonymous, appeared not to have had a follow up interview to detail her encounter and promptly disappeared, it's difficult to understand how one writer - let alone two writers - could possibly have known what her private, unspoken thoughts were. The only reasonable way we can understand how the woman's secret longing - expressed only in her mind - was known by both evangelists and recorded using almost identical words is to accept that this element of the story at least is a dramatic touch inserted by one of the gospel writers and copied by the other.

Similarly in the story of the healing of a paralytic man, Matthew, Mark and Luke were all aware of the unspoken thoughts of the Scribes and record precisely the same thought they have, that Jesus is blaspheming. Moreover all three evangelists record the first part of Jesus' response with exactly the same words and interrupt his speech with a narrative aside at precisely the same point.[13] Numerous passages like this show beyond doubt that two of the evangelists must have based their narratives to a very large extent on an earlier one. So one of the earliest problems for New Testament scholars was to establish which was the original gospel and which were the dependants. Traditionally it was understood that Mark was an abbreviated and later version of Matthew, the first gospel, based primarily on the belief that Matthew was one of Jesus' disciples.

Reimarus And The Great Resurrection Swindle

Around the same time the first really contentious challenge to

---

[13]Matthew 9:1-8, Mark 2:1-12, Luke 5:17-26. In the story of the woman healed by Jesus, Mark (5:28) records that she thought 'If I can touch even his clothes . . . I shall be well again'; Matthew's version (9:21) records her as thinking 'If I can only touch his cloak I shall be well again.'

received wisdom was thrown down with Herman Reimarus' portrayal of Jesus in his work *Concerning the Intention of Jesus and his Teaching.* Reimarus was a respected professor of oriental languages from Hamburg who in secret had written a radical and extensive critique of Christianity which, through his own choice, was published anonymously in fragments after his death in 1774. Indeed with his family fearing for the loss of their good reputation, his identity as the author was not made known until 1814.

The final and most controversial parts of this work were a hostile commentary on the resurrection and a provocative hypothesis about the true motivation of Jesus' disciples. Reimarus alleged that Jesus had never intended to establish a new religion but was a revolutionary who wanted to set up an earthly messianic kingdom in line with the prevailing expectations among the Jews of his time. After his untimely death, his disciples, disappointed by his failure (and disappointed mainly because it meant the end of their own hopes for wealth and high status in the expected kingdom), invented the story of the resurrection.

Reimarus argued that Jesus' central teaching was to repent in readiness for the coming of the kingdom. But the Jews, the disciples contended, hadn't repented enough and so they taught that the messiah had to die to obtain forgiveness on their behalf. As a mark of special favour they claimed that he had been raised from the dead, taken off to heaven and was soon to return in glory to establish the kingdom.

But in order to carry off this deception, just as at a murder scene, 'it was necessary to get rid of the body of Jesus as speedily as possible.'[14] Clearly the production of a corpse would have ruined everything. So the disciples took the risk and stole the body shortly after it was placed in the tomb. Pretending to be astonished when the tomb is discovered to be empty, they held back from proclaiming this resurrection until some 50 days later. By this time they had spirited off his body to the sky so that if anyone asked for the obvious proof, they had the perfect alibi for the risen Jesus: no, you can't talk to him or see him because he's been taken up to heaven. But, they taught, he would return in glory to establish the kingdom 'before this generation has passed

---

[14]Reimarus, *Concerning the Intention of Jesus and his Teaching,* 2:56.

away.'[15] Meanwhile should anyone happen to discover an unclaimed and badly decomposing corpse, 50 days would be more than enough time to ensure that the remains were unrecognisable.

Naturally this provoked outrage from traditionalists, and while the argument was not pursued or taken too seriously it served to establish an absolutely key guiding principle for subsequent investigations (and indeed for anyone approaching the gospels with an open mind), 'to separate what the apostles present in their own writings from that which Jesus himself actually said and taught.'[16]

Reimarus is often regarded as the father of the quest to depict the historical Jesus (as opposed to the Christ of faith) and while he led the way for later scholars to adopt a more rigorous scepticism towards the content, composition and underlying history of the gospels, in his own day he was very much a lone voice. In fact more than half a century was to elapse before the next leap forward with the publication in 1835 of David Strauss' landmark book *The Life of Jesus Critically Examined*. Here for the first time, over 1,400 pages, every incident in the gospels was subjected to detailed scrutiny from a mind open to the possibility that the gospels were not perfectly accurate and reliable accounts.

Strauss And The First Critical Life Of Jesus

Strauss was a young tutor recently graduated from the Protestant seminary at the University of Tubingen. Having studied theology, he was dismayed with traditional interpretations of the gospels which he regarded as antiquated, stupid and incorrect. In Berlin in 1832 he had attended a series of lectures by the theologian Wilhelm Vatke who had shown that it was possible to distinguish the historical from the mythical and the poetical in the Old Testament by adopting a strictly literary and historical approach to the texts, treating them as one would treat any secular text.[17] Aware that such a method could prove fruitful, Strauss set himself the task to investigate the gospels in a similar fashion, free from religious and dogmatic presuppositions.

The success of his labour may be measured by the spectacular

---

[15]Matthew 24:34.

[16]Reimarus, *op cit*, 1:3.

[17]Cromwell, *David Freidrich Strauss & His Place in Modern Thought*, p 42.

impact of the book: hailed as revolutionary, Strauss' *Life of Jesus* was immensely popular in its own time (within ten years it had gone through four editions) and proved to be one of the most influential books of 19th century theology. Not surprisingly it was received very severely by the established Church in Germany and Strauss suffered personally; having been dismissed from his teaching post in 1835 he found himself unable to take up another suitable position for the rest of his life. The leading Protestant German newspaper denounced the work as a 'triumph of Satan' while even the Pope, Gregory XVI, with what he must have thought was the most offensive insult imaginable, called Strauss' book 'demoniacal and devilish.'[18]

But Strauss' intention wasn't devilish. It was to undertake a reasonable inquiry whose objective was simply to investigate the credibility of each gospel story and to assess whether or not it derived from eye-witness testimony or from competently informed reporters. His method was to reject passages which had internal inconsistencies or external contradictions as well as those which were not in accordance with the known laws of nature or which had an elevated or poetical form (such as many of Jesus' lengthy discourses in the Fourth Gospel). Out too went narratives which agreed with prevailing beliefs or expectations of their times since it was likely that these were written in response to theological rather than historical interests.

To argue his case Strauss had to take on and refute the two principal interpretations of the gospels of the day, a task he took on at great length and with some relish. The first and more traditional of these was the supernaturalist response which accepted that the gospels had indeed been written by (or under the inspiration of) the Holy Spirit and therefore had to be infallibly true in every detail. The second, the rationalist response was more progressive and accepted the truth of the gospel stories, but attributed miraculous incidents to misunderstandings on the part of the original witnesses.

The problem for the Supernaturalists, as Griesbach's edition highlighted, was the huge number of inconsistencies between the four different accounts which, if all true, had somehow to be reconciled. For example, all three synoptic gospels contain the story of Jesus bringing back to life a little girl, Jairus' daughter.

---

[18] *Ibid*, pp 15, 86.

For most people the difficulty with this story is accepting that Jesus was able to resuscitate an apparently dead girl; but for the Supernaturalists the real problem was that the accounts did not agree in every tiny detail, with Matthew's version differing slightly from the other two.[19] Their response therefore was to argue that two different resuscitations took place. But since in each account Jesus is accosted by the woman with a haemorrhage on the way, this meant that there also had to be two different women suffering exactly the same condition, both of whom had exactly the same thoughts about being healed and both of whom were restored to health by touching Jesus' clothes without his knowledge. The likelihood of one such co-incidence was small enough; when the number of co-incidences and other implausible explanations was multiplied to account for all inconsistencies, as Strauss demonstrated, this reading became little short of ridiculous.

The dismissal of the Rationalists' arguments was equally effective. While there may be some appeal in a rational explanation for the apparently miraculous episodes of the gospels, the fact that every supernatural detail was given a 'viable' explanation meant that a great deal of conjecture and speculation had to be brought into play. Foremost among the Rationalists and against whom Strauss directed some of his most scathing criticisms, was the German theologian Heinrich Paulus. In his own *Life of Jesus* published shortly before Strauss' work in 1828, he ventured that the disciples' vision of their master walking on water was caused by Jesus walking along the seashore in the mist. And in the calming of the storm, at the very instant that Jesus uttered his command, the boat in which they were sailing gained the shelter of a hill which protected it from the wind, giving the appearance that the storm had subsided and had thereby 'obeyed' him.

This was all very well for one or two incidents, but again for the huge number of supernatural episodes, it was just far too coincidental, stretching credulity to breaking point. Moreover, many of these explanations very often turned out to be as unreasonable as a belief in the supernatural itself; the heavenly voice at the baptism of Jesus for

---

[19]Mark 5:21, Matthew 9:18, Luke 8:40. In Matthew the little girl has already died when the initial approach to Jesus is made by an unnamed official whereas in the other two accounts she is only desperately ill and the official is identified as Jairus.

example was, according to the insight of one imaginative commentator of this school, the explosion of a meteor which just at that moment and at that very spot crashed into the earth.[20]

Instead of such improbable understandings, Strauss proposed a 'mythical' interpretation. The gospels, he argued used extravagant and sensational stories, mostly derived from or modelled on the myths of the Old Testament, to express a particular underlying religious idea. These myths arose in response to the messianic expectations of the age and were presented as actual events in Jesus' career to persuade a relatively unsophisticated audience that he really was the promised messiah.

Consequently the gospels contained very little historical material and their authors could hardly have witnessed or recorded the life of Jesus first-hand. They must therefore have been written some considerable time after Jesus' death, at least a generation later. Although he made no real attempt to date their composition, he agreed with the prevailing critical opinion that all of the gospels had to be written after 70 CE, the year of the destruction of the Temple in Jerusalem to which they clearly referred. Given the degree of accuracy of Jesus' prophecy of this monumental event, which in Luke includes even the detail of Roman fortifications around the city, it could only be seen as a prophecy after the event.[21]

Mark's Secret Agent

While Strauss was probably the most forward thinking biblical scholar of his age, he failed to take on board the findings of other New Testament scholars. Notably he continued to assert the traditional view that Matthew was the first gospel despite earlier hypotheses which suggested otherwise. But by the time of his book's publication this had been more vigorously challenged by Karl Lachmann, a German philologist and editor of a Greek New Testament. By studying the

---

[20]Karl Hase writing in 1829, cited in Kummel, *op cit* (*History*), p 93.

[21]The improbability of Jesus actually having made this prophecy is pointed out by Brandon in *The Fall of Jerusalem and the Christian Church*, p 202: Roman commanders he observes, didn't usually destroy temples. Hence 'a prophecy of destruction so precise as that which Mark ascribes to Jesus . . . would be a temerarious one to make before the event.'

order of each incident in the synoptics Lachmann concluded that Matthew's narrative followed Mark's (and not vice versa) and that therefore Mark was the basic source for Matthew and Luke.

The finding seemed to be confirmed by the primitive nature of Mark not only in its detail (it has the least developed of the resurrection stories for example and omits Jesus' birth and much of his preaching) but also in the roughness of its construction and style. Clearly this presented a new problem to the traditionalists; if the author of Matthew was believed to be the Aramaic speaking disciple of Jesus, and hence an eye-witness to his life, why would he make use of and even copy stories from Mark, a gospel written in Greek, as a source for his own narrative? Why use Mark's often disorderly version of events if he had his own recollections to rely on? The only reasonable answer was that the writer or editor of Matthew could never have been the tax-collecting contemporary of Jesus.

As Lachmann's hypothesis became increasingly accepted among New Testament scholars, critical attention turned to Mark who, if not an eye-witness himself, was somebody who was believed to be very closely associated with the Church in its infancy. Based on the testimony of an early 2nd century bishop, Papias recorded in the Christian historian, Eusebius' later work, the 4th century *History of the Church*,[22] it had long been assumed that Mark was Peter's secretary or interpreter while he was in Rome and that Mark wrote his gospel based on Peter's recollections.

Mark is mentioned in three of Paul's letters; and after escaping from prison in Jerusalem, Acts records that Peter sought refuge in the house of Mary, 'the mother of John-Mark'.[23] The renewal of interest in Mark

---

[22]Eusebius, *History of the Church*, III:39. Eusebius was born in Ceasarea c 260 CE and became its bishop in 313. His two major works are the *History of the Church* and the *Life of Constantine*. The latter is little more than tasteless flattery.

[23]Colossians 4:10, Philemon 24, 2 Timothy 4:11. Acts 12:12. It's unlikely however that the author of Mark was the person who lived in Jerusalem. The author shows an ignorance of Palestine geography on several occasions. He records that Jesus travelled 'from the district of Tyre . . . by way of Sidon towards the Sea of Galilee, right through the Decapolis region.' (7:31) A glance at a biblical era map suggests that this would have been a completely illogical route: Sidon is 20 miles north of Tyre, the Sea is more than 30 miles to the south-east and such a journey would not involve passing through the Decapolis region which itself is further to the south-east of the Sea. Additionally he situates the country of the Gerasenes (5:1) on the lakeside whereas Gerasa is 30 miles to

48

(which had traditionally been regarded as a poor inferior to Matthew) probably arose from the belief that it seemed to offer a straightforward historical presentation of the facts as they may have been related by Peter, suggested by its disorderly structure, unpolished style and apparent lack of authorial interference.

But in due course this willingness to associate lack of literary refinement and historical reliability was questioned and soon came to be seen as much too simplistic an understanding of the work. A critical reading of Mark reveals that despite its primitive style, it wasn't the neutral and artless chronicle that its supporters supposed it to be but a narrative that was suffused with the author's own theological point of view and one which seems to have been broadly influenced by the ideas of Paul.

Mark's gospel is often believed to have been written in Rome for the small Christian community there which had survived Nero's brutal persecution. (The Roman historian Tacitus informs us that Nero unfairly blamed the Christians for the fire in Rome in 64 CE and in revenge had many of them savaged by wild dogs or fastened to crosses and then burned alive to serve as human torches.[24]) This group was also the recipient of Paul's best known and theologically most developed letter written around the year 57. His ideas and teaching therefore would certainly have been known in that circle and it's likely that the writer we call Mark would at least have been familiar with them. Paul's influence can be observed in the editorial position taken by Mark on observance of the Law for example, most notably in the comment that Jesus 'pronounced all foods clean'. Given the controversy about prohibited foods after Jesus' death, so apparent in Paul's letters,[25] it's very unlikely that Jesus could ever truly have made such a pronouncement.

But the biggest blow to the understanding that Mark was a trustworthy history came with the publication in 1901 of *The Messianic Secret* by Wilhelm Wrede. With much closer scrutiny now being given to this gospel, one of its more puzzling aspects required a more rigorous explanation: if Jesus really had come down from heaven 'for

---

the south-east of the lake and refers to Bethsaida (8:22) as a village when in fact it was a large and prosperous town. See Nineham, *The Gospel of St Mark*, p 40.

[24]Tacitus, *Annals*, XV:44.

[25]See for example Galatians 2:12 (hereafter Gal.), 1 Cor. 10:23-30.

us men and for our salvation', why was it that he deliberately kept his identity as the messiah a secret? In Mark's narrative Jesus commands devils and unclean spirits who 'knew who he was' to keep silent about his identity, while some of those who witnessed or benefited from his healings were charged not to tell anyone about them. Later when Peter acknowledges his status, Jesus warns him not to tell anyone and in a key passage, after the Transfiguration, Jesus told his closest disciples 'to tell no one what they had seen, until after the Son of Man had risen from the dead.'[26]

Those who championed Mark as an accurate and reliable account explained this behaviour by claiming that Jesus was concerned that his messiahship should not be interpreted incorrectly - that is, with nationalistic or political hopes and expectations. If we turn to the Fourth Gospel, we read that after the feeding of the 5,000 the crowds were so impressed with Jesus that they wanted to make him their king there and then, a situation that Jesus was desperate to avoid. To prevent this from happening, he only revealed his true status gradually and even then, only to a select group of people, ostensibly to avoid unrest and disappointment.

Wrede dismissed this explanation and argued that none of Jesus' injunctions were historical, that it was only after his death that the secrecy motif was formulated (by the early Christian community) and that it was then developed by Mark and written into his text. But why would this concern for the secret have arisen in the post-resurrection community in the first place? From all the available traditions and stories about Jesus, it must have been clear to Mark that Jesus had never claimed publicly to be the messiah in his lifetime. Only after the resurrection did the early Christian community come to believe that he was this divinely anointed agent. Convinced of this fact, they then went on to believe that Jesus had actually been the messiah all along; but if this were so, how was it that not even his disciples knew he was the oily one? And why did the Jews collaborate in the killing of their messiah? Somehow these awkward problems had to be explained.

Mark's solution was to write the device of the messianic secret into his gospel. The Jews hadn't accepted Jesus as the messiah because he had never allowed his true status to become known to them. And to

---

[26]Mark 1:34, 9:9.

explain why not even the disciples publicly recognised or hailed Jesus as the messiah before his death, despite their loyalty and intimacy with him, Mark depicted them over and over again as being too hard of heart or even too stupid to understand what Jesus taught them about himself. With the messianic secret forming one of the absolutely key themes of Mark's narrative, the obvious conclusion of Wrede's argument was that the whole of this gospel had to be seen as coloured, if not shaped entirely, by the author's own interpretations of the Jesus story. The implications of Wrede's insight then were clear for those trying to get a historical fix on the life of Jesus: Mark's gospel could no longer be taken either as a straightforward biography or as a reliable, objective history.

Form Criticism

If it was understood that the evangelists' narratives could no longer be regarded as eye-witness testimony, it was equally apparent that to discover which details and incidents in the gospels really were authentic recollections of Jesus' life, critical thought would have to shift to determining what the gospels' underlying sources were and how reliable and valid they were. As source criticism (as it was known) developed, it became clear that as well as using most of the material in Mark, Matthew and Luke contained additional material consisting mostly of sayings and teachings common to both but not featured in Mark.

This soon led to the hypothesis that alongside Mark, there must have been another older 'gospel' (now known as Q from the German *Quelle* meaning source) which didn't survive and on which substantial parts of these later gospels were based. Q was likely to have been a teachings or sayings document, lacking a narrative and perhaps written as early as 50 CE.[27] Today there is a near universal consensus among New Testament scholars that both Matthew and Luke made use of Q (as well as Mark). And just as they had used earlier written sources, so it's likely that Mark too had relied either on some earlier and now lost document of sayings and stories or on various smaller collections of disparate pieces of information.

---

[27]Kummel, *op cit (Introduction)*, p 71.

By the first decades of the 20ᵗʰ century source criticism had established the priority of Mark and the identification and use of Q. But by its very nature source criticism was limited to actual or hypothetical written documents and couldn't therefore go any further upstream towards the historical life of Jesus. But much earlier, towards the end of the 18ᵗʰ century one particular insight had suggested that the original source of the gospels had been not a written gospel but one which had been handed down orally, consisting of many individual recollected stories about Jesus.

More than a century later, this was taken up by Karl Schmidt who argued in *The Framework of the Story of Jesus* in 1919 that this rudimentary oral tradition was ultimately behind the gospels' written sources. This spoken 'gospel' would have been in the form of individual 'units' of sayings of Jesus or stories about him around which Mark had constructed a unifying narrative framework. But this frame wasn't based on a real historical knowledge of events but merely on his need to fit the individual stories into a unified and coherent whole. It was therefore imposed by Mark on the available material. Consequently for Schmidt, with the exception of the Passion story, narrative elements were introduced almost at random by Mark without regard for the proper connection of events and providing little genuinely historical information.

The opening chapters of Mark provide a good example of the chaotic form of this imposed narrative. When Jesus first starts to preach with parables for example he's by the lakeside with a huge crowd. Next thing, apparently later, he's alone with his disciples to tell them why he taught in parables and to explain his first parable (of the sower). But he then goes on to tell four more parables suggesting that he's suddenly with the crowd of people again.[28] Each of these is

---

[28]Mark's narrative is very confusing in this passage (4:1-36): after telling the parable of the sower, Jesus is said to be 'alone' but with his 12 disciples and also 'with the others who formed his company.' This group asks him to explain 'what the *parables* meant' (even though only one parable in the whole of the gospel has actually been told so far) and Jesus obliges. It's possible then that the 4 further parables that 'he said to them' immediately after the explanation are recounted to this same group rather than to the crowds. On the other hand, it seems that Jesus told the 4 further parables to the crowds since he specifically said to the inner group 'The secret of the kingdom of God is given to you, but to those outside (i.e. the crowds) everything comes in parables'. And immediately after the last of these parables, when the day is over and Jesus suggests that he and his disciples cross the lake, Mark records their 'leaving the crowd behind'.

introduced with the formulaic words 'He also said' suggesting th
were originally individual sayings which Mark had forced toget
try and give the impression that they formed a coherent body of
preaching taught during a single day.

The clumsiness of Mark's impositions, clearly devices to link stories
and sayings which originally were unconnected with each other, can
also be seen in the chronology of this one day which extends from the
beginning of Chapter 3 to the end of Chapter 4. During a single day
Jesus cures a man with a withered hand in the synagogue, preaches by
the lakeside, climbs up a mountain and appoints his twelve disciples.
He then returns home to eat, but is unable to do so because of the
crowds. So instead he has an argument with the Scribes, a dispute
which is followed by the five parables and the explanations to the
disciples. Finally when evening comes, he crosses the lake and calms a
storm. Was there really such a dramatic, jam-packed day? Or is it more
likely that all these stories were originally unconnected and were fused
together with only a literary justification for doing so?

By removing the often quite obvious editorial links it becomes
possible to break down the gospels into these distinct units, a discipline
which became known as 'form criticism' after the title of a book *The
Form History of the Gospel*, written in 1921 by Martin Dibelius. These
individual units or forms, as they are often called, were now seen as the
basic building blocks of the gospels and enquiring into their individual
origin and history enabled scholars for the first time to get behind the
texts themselves. So for the practitioners of this new method, studying
the gospels was now a matter of understanding the formation,
development and preservation of these units. This involved evaluating
the situation out of which they had arisen and to consider the purpose
of each saying or story. Since the basic principle of form criticism was
that the form of any one unit had been determined by its purpose - in
other words, form followed function - understanding that form would
establish the reason why a particular incident or saying had been
formulated and preserved in the first place and hence would provide
some insight into its historical value.

Dibelius believed that much of the earliest material about Jesus
originated in the disciples' and the early community's preaching after
his death to gain converts and to confirm the faith of the first believers.
Crucial to their preaching was one of the more important forms that

he identified, the pronouncement story or 'paradigm' as he called it. This was a short story, such as the cure of the paralytic man, introduced to illustrate a particular point which originally would have been made in a sermon. This particular story concentrates not on the miracle itself but on the dispute between Jesus and the Scribes over who has the right to forgive sins. Since it was widely believed that illness was a consequence of sin, the removal of the affliction was a sign that the person's sins had also been removed or forgiven. The whole point of the story then is not so much to demonstrate a miraculous cure but to 'prove' that Jesus had the authority to forgive sins and so support the early Church claim that it too had this right. So to present its case more forcefully an imaginative illustration of Jesus' healing ability was incorporated into the sermon.

Alongside preachers, and equally important for spreading the news about Jesus were storytellers. Although Dibelius conceded that there were no sources to corroborate their activity, he believed that the existence in the gospels of stories which are far more descriptive and colourful than the paradigms argues strongly that they played a part in the formulation of certain units. These forms, which he called 'tales' (all of which concern the miraculous), are distinguished by the fact that they are motivated primarily by a pleasure in the actual narrative itself as if they were told to enthral and entertain their audience. So in this category there are the more wondrous miracles, such as the feeding of the 5,000, Jesus' walking on water and the resurrection of Jairus' daughter, stories which would have held their audience spellbound, perhaps in the same way that the film *The Blair Witch Project* (fiction masquerading as supernatural fact) captivated audiences throughout the world a few years ago.

For Dibelius these stories didn't have a didactic purpose and usually concluded not with any doctrinal point but with the amazement of the crowd. But this lack of theological purpose didn't give them a greater assurance of historical authenticity precisely because they evolved as stories specifically conceived to entertain and therefore to win over their audiences. Over a short period of time they would've become more and more sensational so as to continue to captivate and enthral their audiences; so by their very nature they were likely to have been repeatedly embellished by successive story-tellers long before they were written down in Mark.

In his study of the origins of the four gospels, often thought of as the classic exposition of source criticism, the English scholar B. H. Streeter commented on this tendency. The process of imaginative colouring of incidents and stories he argued 'was familiar to the Rabbis in the popular exposition of the Old Testament, so much so that it has a technical name *Haggada*.'[29] Those stories which proved successful and popular in preaching or everyday talk would be remembered; over the years their 'Haggadic' origins would be forgotten and they would eventually become accepted as authentic traditions. In other words imaginative stories told over and over again would gradually come to be thought of as genuine recollections. It's fair and reasonable to assume therefore that this process was almost certainly at work in the development of stories about Jesus as his legendary status grew in the decades after his death.

Developing this method and applying an almost clinical attention to every detail of the synoptic gospels was taken up by Rudolf Bultmann, the leading exponent of form criticism. Bultmann's analysis was much more scientific and rigorous in its approach. Each piece of narrative was minutely examined relative to other literary sources such as the Old Testament, contemporary Rabbinic literature and existing legends and miracle stories either Hellenistic, Jewish or even Buddhist to discover the influences active in its development. Based on this analysis it was possible to assess which actions and sayings of Jesus could be considered authentic and which showed signs of having been borrowed from or modelled on other already existing forms.

Bultmann found that the formation of virtually all gospel material at its earliest stage was shaped by the needs and interests of the infant Church rather than by a desire to preserve an historical record of Jesus' actions and teachings. One of the clearest indications of this he argued, was the existence of a large number of passages which he called 'controversy dialogues' which were broadly similar to Dibelius' paradigms. Like the paradigms these had evolved out the Church's need to resolve its early theological disputes, but this form revolved more around an argument than an action by Jesus. How might it be best for leaders of the primitive community to win an argument about doctrine? By claiming to have Jesus on their side. So these matters of

---

[29]Streeter, *The Four Gospels - A Study of Origins*, p 503.

dispute became transformed into confrontations between Jesus and his opponents, usually the Scribes or the Pharisees, so as to ascribe his authority to a principle or doctrine that the Church itself had adopted such as non-observance of the Jewish Law or the sabbath. In some of these a saying by Jesus may have formed the underlying basis of the story; but to present the principle more graphically an imaginary scene was constructed around it which under close scrutiny can be seen to be highly artificial.[30]

Similarly the construction of the dialogue in these scenes was formulaic, typically following the rabbinic pattern; examples of this manner of argument were abundant in Jewish literature of the period and would have been readily absorbed and understood. The lack of real debate or response from the opponent in these scenes clearly betrays the artificiality of the exchange; often a throw-away remark by Jesus has the unlikely effect of stupefying the well-versed and educated Pharisees into complete intellectual submission. In Mark we find eleven of these hostile encounters with either the Scribes or Pharisees. These maligned groups or individuals always seem to be on hand when some doctrinal point needs to be made; sometimes it almost seems that they were stalking Jesus as he travelled around, even in foreign territory and even on the sabbath. These anonymous, one dimensional opponents may therefore be regarded more as literary props or types rather than real people.

Moreover in many of these incidents it is not Jesus but the disciples who are criticised by the opponent - for not fasting, for plucking corn on the sabbath or for eating with unwashed hands. Obviously it wouldn't have been acceptable for the Church to have had Jesus rebuked, so his own behaviour is portrayed as being beyond reproach in these instances. But if these really were genuine encounters how likely is it that Jesus would have instructed his disciples not to observe a fast (for example) while he himself kept it?

The gospels' central concern however was the proclamation that Jesus was the messiah, demonstrated primarily by the fulfilment of Old Testament prophecies and the working of miracles. Consequently any passages which reported Jesus as fulfilling these prophecies were taken

---

[30]Jesus' encounter with the Pharisees and his teaching about divorce (Mark 10:1-12) is an example of this type of form.

as the work of the early Church rather than a record of actual events while miracle stories were similarly judged as attempts to show Jesus' divine power.

Bultmann allowed that there may have been personal recollections or historical incidents underlying some of these stories. But his painstaking analysis of their detail and construction suggested that the form in which they appeared in the gospels showed that they had been shaped by already existing forms found in literature, folk-tales and legends of the time. It was a frequent element in the stories of the healing of lame people for example that the afflicted man was brought on a stretcher and after being healed was able to carry it away himself as we see in the case of Jesus' healing of the paralytic.[31] Similarly the legends surrounding the birth of Jesus were shown to have very close parallels in the legends of older cult religions: the adoration of the Magi, to give just one example, may have had its origin in an Arabian cult in which the birth of a god from his virgin mother was celebrated with the presentation of gifts such as money, ointments and incense.[32]

Bultmann concluded that very little of the gospel material could be accepted as historical. Even the teaching sayings could not with certainty be accepted as necessarily originating from Jesus since many of them were popular expressions of traditional Jewish Wisdom. The well known formula 'The sabbath was made for man, not man for the sabbath', for example, a saying that we always associate with Jesus, was shown to have a parallel in Rabbinic literature ('the sabbath is given over to you, not you to the sabbath'[33]).

The Gospels As Faith Documents

Bultmann's rigorous approach and uncompromising conclusion, that 'there is no historical-biographical interest in the gospels' and that the gospels are 'completely subordinate to Christian faith and worship'[34] made the chances of recovering a historical life of Jesus all

---

[31] Mark 2:1-12; Bultmann, *The History of the Synoptic Tradition*, p 232.

[32] Bultmann, *op cit*, p 292. He points out that the Cult of Dusares to which he refers may have had a shrine in Bethlehem.

[33] *Ibid*, p 108, Mark 2:27.

[34] *Ibid*, p 372.

the more remote. But at the same time it also placed a new emphasis on the theological motivations of the evangelists. We should remember that the original point of a gospel was first and foremost to provide a particular early Christian community with 'the good news of Jesus Christ.' Here in Mark's opening words we have the assumption from the very beginning that Jesus of Nazareth is the messiah and 'the Son of God'; it follows that anything in this account of Jesus is going to be based around these assumptions. We can begin to see then that a gospel simply can't be regarded as a historically objective or unbiased piece of writing; on the contrary, its very purpose is to help to deepen the faith of those who hear it, to persuade them to accept its message.

Any doubt about this purpose is continually swept aside. Even when Mark appears to provide genuine historical detail, most notably in his account of the events leading up to Jesus' death, he openly states at two separate points that the events in his narrative are 'as the scriptures say' or 'to fulfil the scriptures'. Luke is more explicit, informing his patron Theophilus at the beginning of his gospel 'I . . . have decided to write an ordered account for you, Theophilus, so that your Excellency may learn how well founded the teaching is that you have received', while at the end of the Fourth Gospel, the writer closes his account with a reminder that it was written 'so that you may believe that Jesus is the Christ, the Son of God.'[35]

'That you may believe': it would be difficult to find a more succinct and exact phrase to convey the purpose of ideological propaganda and ultimately the gospels have to be seen as works of this nature. So it's no surprise to discover that the evangelists seem prepared to do whatever it takes to push their message, even if this amounts to distorting historical truth, presenting information that can't be true or manifestly concocting material and passing it off as fact.

These are processes we can observe in all the gospels, but especially so in Matthew, where they are most conspicuous and evident in Jesus' apparent fulfilment of Old Testament prophecies. Scripture for the Jews had a much greater claim to truth than any other form of argument. So when Jesus encounters the Devil in the desert after his baptism, he responds to the Devil's temptations not with reasoned

---

[35]Mark 14:21, 50. Luke 1:3-4; The name means *love of god* and therefore we can't be sure that such a person as Theophilus ever existed. John 20:31.

argument, nor with an intelligent discourse, but instead fends off his attacks with a 'Scripture says' and therefore I win rebuttal, leaving the ruined archangel speechless. In the Fourth Gospel, at his trial Pilate taunts Jesus, asking him: 'what is truth?' Wisely Jesus stays silent (he was not - despite Dubya's imbecile thoughts - a philosopher), but if the question had been posed to the writer of Matthew, he might very well have replied 'Scripture is truth.' And so for all of the evangelists, but for Matthew in particular, the absolute and unshakeable conviction that Jesus really was the messiah could be proven by demonstrating that certain details and incidents in his life had parallels in or fulfilled ancient prophecies taken from the Jewish Scriptures.

The problem with Matthew's prophecy fulfilments however is that the writer tended to ignore the meaning of passages in their Old Testament context and read into them whatever he saw fit for his purposes. Matthew was also inclined to adapt his text to fit in with particular scriptural passages. For example Mark informs us that 'After John [the Baptist] had been arrested, Jesus went into Galilee' where he began his mission. The same passage in Matthew has Jesus returning to the same region, but adds that Jesus went to Capernaum 'a lakeside town on the borders of Zebulun and Naphtali.' Why does he add in this superfluous but very specific detail?

If we read on, we find out, for he tells us that 'In this way the prophecy of Isaiah was to be fulfilled: "Land of Zebulun! Land of Naphtali! . . . on those who dwell in the land and shadow of death a light has dawned."'[36] Matthew's underlying argument therefore seems to be that Jesus definitely was the messiah because by beginning his mission in a particular region he fulfilled a scriptural 'prophecy'. The reality however is that Jesus simply started to preach in a place that happened to border the land of two ancient tribes which just happened to be mentioned in the book of Isaiah in a context that had nothing to do with the expectation of a messiah.

Later Matthew presents us with the preposterous situation that Jesus entered Jerusalem riding two animals, a donkey and a colt *at the same time* so as to fulfil another prophecy from Isaiah.[37] As one very eminent

---

[36]Mark 1:14, Matthew 4:12-16. Zubulun and Naphtali were Old Testament tribes that occupied land in the lower part of Galilee and in the mountainous region to the north-east of Galilee respectively.

[37]Matthew 21:1-7. The prophecy fulfilled is from Isaiah 62:11: 'Look your king comes

New Testament scholar has observed, in Matthew's gospel 'What happened must correspond with "prophecy", as otherwise the proof from Scripture would not be convincing. If it does not correspond with the prophecy found in the Old Testament, Matthew alters the event.' So because Matthew was convinced by his own ideas and was seeking to 'bring others to the same understanding - he considers he is quite justified in correcting history.'[38]

Once In Royal David's City . . ?

To highlight some of the fundamental barriers that prevent us from accepting the gospels as historically reliable accounts, we can turn to one of the best known of all the stories about Jesus, one with which most of us have some familiarity: the story of his birth. While the actual story may be very familiar, less well known is the fact that it is actually made up of two quite separate accounts from the opening of the Gospels of Matthew and Luke.

These were evidently later traditions since neither Mark nor Paul appeared to know anything about the circumstances of Jesus' birth; but they do seem to have evolved at roughly the same time for Luke knew nothing of Matthew's account and Matthew knew nothing of Luke's. As a result, the two stories are quite different to each other, inconsistent in just about every detail except one: both agree that Jesus was born in Bethlehem.

Luke understood that Jesus' parents, Joseph and Mary came from the town of Nazareth in Galilee, some 80 miles to the north of Bethlehem. The main concern of his narrative was therefore to provide an explanation as to how Jesus came to be born so far from the region in which his family were known to have lived. His solution was to link the story of Jesus' birth to a Roman census, an official process that forced the couple to make the arduous journey to Joseph's ancestral hometown to be duly registered. This he records, occurred just at the time that Mary was due to give birth. Fancying himself as something of an historian, or possibly aware that his story was somewhat dubious, Luke attempts to add in some secular historical

---

to you; he is humble, he rides on a donkey *and* on a colt'. The corresponding passage in Mark (11:2-8) has Jesus riding only a colt.

[38] Marxsen, *Introduction To The New Testament*, p 148.

detail to make it more plausible. So we're informed that the census 'of the whole world' came about as a result of a decree issued by Caesar Augustus, that it occurred 'in the days of King Herod' and 'while Quirinius was governor of Syria.' But it's with these very details that Luke begins to dig a hole for himself.

Initially the problem is that there was no census of all people in the Roman Empire at that time. Other than Luke no writer or historian of the period records that such a significant event ever took place. Certainly there was a census at that time, but it was a localised one relating only to the province of Judaea which had recently come under direct Roman control.[39] It also occurred when Quirinius was the Roman legate of Syria, as Luke correctly observes. But Quirinius never held this office during the reign of Herod. Herod was king of Judaea from 37-4 BCE while Quirinius' governorship began only in 6 CE.[40] The two rulers were therefore separated by about ten years or so. Clearly Luke got his facts and dates mixed up - and we might ask, does it really matter?

The answer is yes it does, for huge problems arise when we try to reconcile Luke's narrative to Matthew's. If Luke is correct and Jesus' birth took place at the time of this local census, then Herod can't have been alive. Consequently nearly everything in Matthew's story - which revolves around the jealousy and scheming of the murderous king - can't have taken place. On the other hand, if we're inclined to accept Matthew's account which insists that the birth of Jesus occurred when Herod was still alive, then it can't have occurred at the time of the census for Jesus would have been at least 10 years old when the count took place.

The implications of this of course are disastrous for traditionalists: even if Joseph and Mary did have to travel to Bethlehem, even if the inn was full, Mary could not have been pregnant with Jesus at that time and the best known and best loved detail of the whole story, the folklore birth in a stable with its donkey and ox silently revering the

---

[39] I am greatly indebted to Lane Fox's superb evaluation of the problems posed by the census for much of the discussion that follows. See *The Unauthorized Version*, pp 27-32.

[40] The details of the beginning of Quirinius' rule can be reliably dated to 6 CE. Later in Acts (5:37), Luke associates the date of the census with the revolt of Judas the Galilean. Again this can be dated to around 6 CE.

infant king could never have taken place.[41]

Even if we're prepared to overlook the matter of irreconcilable or problematic dates, further difficulties arise with Luke's story. The census under Quirinius applied to Judaea, but not to Galilee which at the time was not under full Roman jurisdiction. While Judaea became a Roman province, Galilee remained a semi-autonomous kingdom, under the rule of Herod Antipas (son of Herod the Great), mentioned in all four of the gospels. Anyone living in Galilee would not therefore have been obliged to register themselves. So if Joseph did travel to Bethlehem to be counted and assessed under the census, he would have done so voluntarily. But why would he have done this? Why go to all that trouble if he had not been bound to do so?

Joseph's voluntary compliance is all the more difficult to understand when we take into account the purpose of the census. It's very unlikely that the Romans were interested in conducting a trends and social attitudes survey among the newly subjected people so that their interests could be catered for and the services they most wanted be provided accordingly. The census would have been conducted for one reason only: to assess the population of a region for the tax that could be raised from their property.

So why would Joseph have volunteered to be assessed for tax? And why would the officials administering the process have insisted on moving people from one town to another causing an enormous and potentially unmanageable upheaval? What on earth was the point of removing people from their homes to faraway places where details of their property and livelihoods could never be verified? Why should they have been in the least bit interested in ancient Jewish genealogies? How would the Roman authorities know of the ancestral town of every man in Judaea anyway? Did they have a register? And finally why would an unmarried woman in such a late state of pregnancy accompany her betrothed on such a long journey? Why didn't she return to her own home town if she had to go anywhere at all?[42]

---

[41]The animals are not mentioned anywhere in Luke's narrative. They seem to derive from Isaiah 1:1-2. In this passage it's clear that the donkey and the ox are mentioned for their stupidity and stubbornness rather than for any privileged insight or reverence they might have had, being compared with the Jews' hard heartedness and refusal to listen to the Lord.

[42]Lane Fox (*op cit,* p 31) notes 'We know from the evidence of Roman tax censuses in

None of this matters to Luke. The important thing is that Jesus has to be born in Bethlehem and for the 'historically' minded Luke, writing some 80 years after the event probably for a largely uneducated audience, perhaps far removed from Judaea and unlikely to have the means or indeed any interest to verify his account, a census is as good a stratagem as any to achieve his purpose. Clearly it's a literary device designed to bring about the birth of Jesus in Bethlehem. But why did Luke go to such extraordinary lengths to have Jesus born there in the first place?

The answer can be found if we turn to the other version of events in the gospel of Matthew. The Jews believed that Bethlehem had long been prophesied as the place where the messiah would be born. In fact Matthew even works a prophecy into his story to ensure his readership gets the point and to add to his argument that Jesus really was the messiah: 'And you Bethlehem, in the land of Judah . . . out of you will come a leader who will shepherd my people Israel.'[43] Of course Jesus had to be born somewhere and Bethlehem is as good a place as any, even if it was somewhat unlikely for one whose family was known to have settled in Galilee. But once we become aware of and take the prophecy into account, the claim that Jesus was born in David's royal city starts to become rather suspect since it appears to be motivated by the interests of theology rather than by the concerns of historical accuracy.

So important was this idea that Matthew considered that Jesus' family *must have* lived in Bethlehem at the time of the birth. There was no need therefore to resort to a census or any other means to get the holy family to be in Bethlehem at the crucial time. Now if Joseph and Mary normally resided in Bethlehem, the chances are they had their own house and so there would've been no reason at all for Mary to have wandered off to a stable to give birth. In fact if we read Matthew's gospel carefully we see that he records that Joseph did have his own home and that Jesus was born there: 'When Joseph woke up he did what the angel of the Lord had told him to do: he took his wife *to his home* and . . . she gave birth to a son.' Later on, when the Magi

---

Egypt, still surviving on papyrus, that one householder could make the return for everyone in his care' and that therefore 'there was not a legal need for Mary to go.'

[43]Matthew 2:6, citing Micah 5:2 and 2 Samuel 5:2.

come to visit the new-born king, Matthew says that 'The sight of the star filled them with delight, and going into *the house* they saw the child.'[44] Incidentally, it's worth noting that even if we accept Luke's account of the birth, there is no mention of a *stable* in the whole of his story. The idea was inferred from the narrative which tells us merely that there was no room at the 'inn' and that Mary laid her child in a 'manger'. However, as Marina Warner observed in her study of Mary, *Alone of All Her Sex*, the Greek word translated as 'inn' - *katalemna* - actually means 'an upper room' and was translated as such when Luke re-used the same word in a later episode.[45]

It seems then that the reality in Luke's story was that there was no room for Mary and Joseph in the upper (and presumably more comfortable) room of the house where they stayed and so they were obliged to stay on the lower floor which perhaps opened out to a courtyard where animals may have been kept for the night. Not having their own crib, the practically minded owners of the house might quite sensibly have suggested that they use an animal feeding box. The story of the desperate couple being turned away by a heartless innkeeper 'in the bleak midwinter' and being forced to sleep in a stable, Warner concludes 'is all the collective inheritance of western fantasy.'[46]

If Matthew's holy family lived in Bethlehem to begin with, he still had the same problem that Luke had, except in reverse: how was he to get them back to Galilee where Jesus was known to have lived? His solution is no less contrived but much more fanciful and the whole of his narrative after the birth is a consequence of his having Bethlehem as the family's original hometown. Ultimately all of the legendary details in Matthew's story after the birth that we so associate with Christmas -

[44]Matthew 1:24, 2:10-11, my italics. Even if Joseph did not yet have his own home and was living in the family home, it seems very unlikely that his parents would have forced Mary to go and give birth to their grandchild in a cow shed.

[45]Warner, *Alone of All Her Sex*, p 13; Luke 22:12, 'The man will show you a large upper room furnished with couches.' In this incident Jesus is instructing his disciples to find a room to celebrate the Passover meal. Elsewhere Luke actually refers to an inn (in the parable of the good Samaritan, 10:34), but he uses a completely different word - *pandocheion*.

[46]*Ibid*, p 14. We might also note that the actual date of Jesus' birth is unknown and there is only a 1 in 365 chance that it was December 25. This date was considered to be the birthday of Jesus only in the 4th century, probably because it was the birthday of the pagan god, Sol Invictus, whom the emperor Constantine associated with Jesus.

the star, the Magi, the slaughter of the innocents and the flight to Egypt - can be seen as parts of an extended literary device whose main purpose was to return the family back to Galilee.

First of all we have the fairy-tale star of Bethlehem which is so bright and so precise in the way that it can direct its light that it is able to guide people to the very spot where Jesus was born. Clearly this star was no ordinary star, for 'it went forward and halted over the place where the child was.'[47] Of course stars simply can't move like that and we have to ask how likely is it that there was some sort of magic star, able to shine in a specific place from a distance of millions upon millions of miles?

While the star is brought into the narrative as a sign in the heavens to associate the birth with a spectacular cosmic significance, its primary purpose is as a device to further the plot. For the star brings about the arrival from the east of the Magi (usually thought of as wise men but perhaps more appropriately they should be regarded as sorcerers or astrologers; they certainly weren't kings) who follow its light, believing that it will lead them to the birth place of a new Jewish king. Quite how they deduce that it heralds such a birth and exactly why they might be so interested in it to make their journey is never explained. Nor is the fact that at first the star guides them to Jerusalem. However, if we're willing to respond critically to the text and see the story as just that, a story and not an authentic, historical account, we can soon see that this rather erratic guidance also turns out to be part of the plot. For it is with the astrologers' arrival in Jerusalem that the villain of the piece, King Herod makes his entrance and first learns of the birth of a rival king.

Although the astrologers agree to inform Herod of the precise whereabouts of the royal birth, they are warned in a dream not to return to him, for Herod's intentions were far from friendly. Dreams play an essential part in Matthew's nativity story (in fact there are four dreams, each one a warning or message) without which it is very difficult to see how the narrative could be carried forward and developed. Somehow Matthew was aware of all four. It's often difficult to remember one's own dreams from the previous night let alone from many years beforehand; how was it then that Matthew, again writing

---

[47]Matthew 2:9.

his account at least 80 years after the birth, was able to know the dreams of men whom he had never met and whose identities were unknown, who returned to the east and who were never heard of again? Did they write them down? Did they tell some of the local people who somehow remembered and then passed on this vital intelligence to their children and grand-children? Did the Jews of Bethlehem even speak the same language as these eastern strangers?

If we think these suggestions are ludicrous, how else might he have come by this information? If no plausible explanation can be furnished, ultimately we have to accept that Matthew never truly had this knowledge; and the only tenable understanding of this detail is that the dreams were a product of the imagination, either Matthew's own or that of his source. Matthew may well be a teller of fantastical stories but clearly he is not a reliable historian.

As a result of the dream, the star-gazers don't return to Herod who is so incensed that he decides to kill all infant boys in the vicinity. Along with the star, shepherds, angels, wise men and the stable, the slaughter of the innocents, as it has become known, may be very appealing to children at Christmas time and a thrilling part of their nativity plays; but in the grown-up world it is an incident that no other writer or historian corroborates. In particular, the Jewish historian Josephus, writing in the last decade of the 1st century, recorded many of Herod's blackest deeds,[48] but seemed to know nothing of this atrocity. One might wonder why Herod simply didn't have the astrologers followed if he was so perturbed about a rival king, or why his agents were unable to locate the place of Jesus' birth if a star had hovered over it.

The answer would seem to be that Matthew wanted to have a massacre so that Jesus' birth could be paralleled with the birth of Moses

---

[48]Josephus was born around 37 CE and died in the year 101. He was an educated Pharisee who initially supported the Jewish war against Rome. After surrendering to Vespasian, he befriended the emperor, travelled to Rome after the war and became a Roman citizen. His major works are *The Jewish War* and *The Antiquities of the Jews*, an ambitious history of the chosen people in 20 books from the creation to the start of the war. In this latter work, completed by 94 CE, he recorded that Herod had his wife Miriamne murdered (XV, vii, 4) and his son, Antipater killed (XVII, vii, 1). He also recorded the chilling and bizarre story of Herod's concern that he wouldn't be mourned when he died. As a result the bitter and demented king rounded up men from all over his kingdom whom he ordered to be butchered when he died so that the whole of Israel might be plunged into mourning at the time of his death (XVII, vi, 5-6).

and the subsequent massacre of Israelite children by the Egyptian Pharaoh. What is improbable historically makes sense theologically. Naturally he considers that both the slaughter and the flight to Egypt fulfil Old Testament prophecies, thereby further adding to his 'proof' that Jesus was the messiah, so again we might be additionally sceptical about whether these events really took place.

Finally some years later, after the death of Herod, Joseph is advised in a dream to return from Egypt; intending originally to return to Judaea, the province in which Bethlehem was located, he is advised in yet another dream to go to Galilee. So, like some ridiculous shaggy dog story, it seems that the whole purpose of the star, the astrologers, the murder of infant boys and the emigration to Egypt is simply to bring about the eventual resettlement of Jesus' family in Galilee. At this point Matthew goes into overkill and can't resist another prophecy fulfilment, for by living in Nazareth, 'the words spoken through the prophets were to be fulfilled: "He will be called a Nazarene".'[49] What's interesting about this particular claim is that nobody has ever been able to find the source for this so called prophecy. In his over enthusiasm or desperation to drive home the fact that Jesus is the messiah, Matthew resorts to pure invention and appears to make up a prophecy.

In these narratives then we can find all the issues and problems that make it so difficult for us to accept the gospels as a solid, reliable foundation for the historical claims of Christianity (of which the birth in Bethlehem is one of the most widely and readily accepted). It's not simply a matter of their attempts to convince us that an improbable, unlikely event occurred; it's the manner in which they try to pass this off as fact that so undermines their credibility. We see clear evidence of fabrication in the census, of childish folklore in the star and the intellectual dishonesty of the writer in the matter of divine revelation being made known through dreams.

But the greatest problem is the fact that the narratives are driven not by a desire to record historical events faithfully but by theological concerns, to proclaim from the very beginning and with every incident possible that Jesus was the messiah. We see this most apparently in the shaping of material to 'fulfil' prophecies, with Bethlehem as the place of birth being the most obvious example and the slaughter of children

---

[49]Matthew 2:23.

the most offensive.[50]

So how should we regard our four gospels? We started off by observing that they are sometimes thought of as biographies of Jesus and therefore might be expected in some measure at least to be factually true. By now however we should be able to understand that this is a misconception and that while there may be some historical events underlying individual gospel stories and sayings, they simply can't be read as reliable historical or biographical documents.

And yet Christianity continues to insist that all the key events in the life of Jesus as presented in these faith documents are historically true. 'Jesus was born in a humble stable' the *Catechism* affirms; and 'the magi's coming to Jerusalem in order to pay homage to the king of the Jews . . . in the messianic light of the star of David', the flight into Egypt and the massacre of the innocents,[51] these too were all real events so far as the Church is concerned today. Our brief review of the background to the nature and composition of the gospels might suggest otherwise. But historicity is so absolutely essential to the message and perpetuation of Christianity that it has to be defended in its entirety and at all costs. As we will see when we come to evaluate some of the gospels' more extravagant claims - the virgin birth, the miracles attributed to Jesus and most important of all, the resurrection - this absolute defence of historicity is one that just doesn't stand up.

---

[50]Paradoxically Christians have to hope that this aspect of the story isn't true. For if it is true, then the Christian god bears much of the responsibility for the carnage: if it was able to warn the astrologers in a dream not to return to Herod, why couldn't they have been warned before they arrived in Jerusalem not to speak to him? Why couldn't it have 'fixed' the star so that it guided them directly to Bethlehem? And if Joseph was warned in a dream to depart, why couldn't other parents have been similarly advised?

[51]*Catechism*, 525, 528, 530.

3

New God, New Deal

Prepare yourself, you know it's a must
Gotta have a friend in Jesus
So you know that when you die
He's gonna recommend you to the spirit in the sky[1]

Before we come to assess the key aspects of Jesus' life and the main doctrines and claims of Christianity in detail, it's worth spending some time to consider a couple of crucial but often overlooked questions about the faith as a whole, the most important of which is this: *what is the point of Christianity?* Even if there is a god living in or beyond the sky, why was it necessary for Jesus, a new and unknown god to come to the earth and be sacrificed on a cross? What is the meaning of salvation? Why do people need to have faith to be saved? And just what does faith consist of anyway? Anyone who wishes to understand and assess Christianity will make little headway without first addressing these fundamental concerns.

Answers to the first question tend to follow a similar theme and have almost become meaningless clichés themselves. What's the point of Christianity? The Christian god so loved the world that he sent his only son to redeem us, Jesus came to save us from our sins, through Jesus we should once again be reconciled with the Father-god and so on and so on.[2] But if we're prepared to press a little deeper and explore Christianity beyond these tired and rather bland platitudes, we come to something altogether darker and more disturbing. Although not often

---

[1]Norman Greenbaum, *Spirit in the Sky*.

[2]See for example *Catechism* 51, 457, 458: 'It pleased God, in his goodness and wisdom, to reveal himself . . . His will was that men should have access to the Father through Christ . . . The Word became flesh for us in order to save us by reconciling us with God, who loved us and sent his Son to be the expiation for our sins . . . that whoever believes in him should not perish but have eternal life.'

69

expressed, according to Christian teaching it would seem that Jesus' mission was planned by the Father-god because the whole of humanity was deemed to be so irreparably sinful and so offensively disobedient to his will that, left to itself and without the intervention of Jesus it would have been damned for all eternity and deservedly so.

Of course this aspect of Christian teaching is rarely expressed today because it comes across as so negative about our common humanity and too shocking and offensive to our sensibility. That said, occasionally one can still detect traces of this old school Christianity in today's *Catechism*, suggesting that the Church can never quite wash away its fundamentally pessimistic regard for mankind. 'Sick, our nature demanded to be healed; fallen, to be raised up; dead, to rise again' is how it characterises the human condition for instance - sick, fallen, dead. And just as disturbingly it speaks of 'one man's trespass [which] led to condemnation of all men' and of the 'faithlessness of men's sin and *the punishment it deserves*.'[3]

However, Christianity today tries to be slightly more user-friendly (to use the jargon) and accordingly gives this traditional view a more positive spin. So the main emphasis of its message for our own times centres not so much around hellfire, condemnation and paying for your sins, but around *salvation*. As we've noted, the Nicene Creed affirms that Jesus came down from heaven 'for us men and for our salvation.' But what exactly is this thing, salvation?

For many of us, constantly searching for a lasting and meaningful happiness for our lives, and aware with absolute certainty that our time is limited and that its end is inevitable, salvation is generally thought of in terms of a happy afterlife that somehow will provide us with the sense of purpose we so desperately seek. In Albert Camus' play *Caligula*, the fundamental absurdity of life that was at the heart of that author's entire oeuvre is neatly summed up by the deranged and troubled emperor in just a few words: 'Man dies and he is not happy.' Christianity, like many other religions, holds out the prospect of dealing with the existential angst born of this sense of the absurd with its promise of salvation, a perfectly fulfilling afterlife, a sort of spiritual antidote to all the suffering and pain to be endured in our lives and which will compensate us for all the injustices of this world; to the

---

[3] *Ibid*, 385, 402, 211, my italics.

transience of life and to the fear of death.

The trouble is, unless we're prepared to accept that there is actually something from which we will be saved, the concept of salvation is a redundant and essentially meaningless or illogical one. What that something is, as we've already discovered, is the punishment of hell. Whether or not there is an actual hell with sulphurous fires and devilish torments is irrelevant. Even if we can't reconcile the thought of fiery punishment with a kind and loving god, and consider that those who are unworthy or unbelieving simply don't get an afterlife, this deprivation is still a punishment. So salvation must involve being *saved from some form of punishment;* whether the punishment consists of the fires of hell, spiritual isolation from the Father-god or simply a complete and final extinction after death instead of the opportunity of a second life is neither here nor there. The fundamentally important thing in the Christian belief is that there are some who will be saved from being punished and there are some who will not.[4] And according to Christian teaching, the best way (and for some fundamentalists the *only* way) to get into the right camp after your final sunset is to embrace the Christian religion, to make sure that Jesus is on your side and that he will look favourably on your case when the terrible Day of Judgement finally dawns.

But why do we need to be saved in the first place? Why should there be this menacing threat of everlasting punishment? If there is an afterlife, why can't all people enjoy it? According to Christian teaching, following on from the original sin of Adam and Eve, the Father-god decreed that all of their descendants, that is all members of the human race, should share their fault and are born equally condemned. I shall have more to say about this understanding in a later chapter, but for the moment we need to go along with the Church's argument that the whole of humanity is justly condemned for the rather paltry transgression (eating a special fruit and thereby disobeying the god) of the first two individuals. The judgement may be harsh and troubling to our minds, perhaps incomprehensible; but we can take comfort from the abundance of the Father-god's love for us. Because

---

[4]If this were not so, if it were the case that *everyone* was saved, no matter what they did or believed during their lifetime, there would be no need for Christianity or to be a Christian at all.

his love and mercy are so immeasurably great, he later decides freely to enter into a series of agreements or deals with Adam and Eve's descendants, holding out the possibility of a reprieve. These deals are known as covenants and they provide the key to understanding both the Jewish and Christian religions.

Dealing With The Lord

The first of these covenants is struck between the Lord god and Noah after one of the better known stories of the Old Testament, the great flood, told in the book of Genesis. Enraged by the universal wickedness of mankind, the god decides that the most appropriate course of action is to wipe out the whole of humanity except for one righteous man, the 600 year old Noah and his family. So Noah is instructed to build a boat of very specific dimensions in which he and his family and some animals were to take refuge when the watery retribution was visited upon the earth.[5] Once the waters receded, Noah offered a pleasing sacrifice to the Lord (thereby wiping out one of the remaining species he had taken such care to save?), presumably to thank him for not having been drowned. In return the Lord god, perhaps feeling somewhat remiss for having brought such destruction to the world promises never again to take such drastic action: 'I now establish my covenant with you and your offspring to come . . . I will maintain My covenant with you: never again shall there be a flood to destroy the earth.'[6] At this point Noah is not considered to be a Jew and so the Church teaches that this covenant extended to all peoples and remained valid until the time of Jesus.

Later covenants with the chosen people of Israel were to be more elaborate. The first of these was made with Abraham, the greatest of all Jewish patriarchs. In return for following the ways of the Lord god,

---

[5]The story of Noah of course is best remembered for its concern for animals, especially when told to young children. The senseless slaughter of the human race tends to be overlooked or ignored. Ask anyone to tell you what she knows about this story and the chances are the genocide won't get a mention. It is very troubling to reflect that the Lord god of Jewish scripture, who eventually became (and is the same as) the Christian god, thought that innumerable men, women and children were so irredeemably wicked that they all deserved to be drowned without mercy. The *Catechism* refers to this episode (56–58) but doesn't mention the mass murder.

[6]Genesis 9:9-11.

Abraham is promised that his wife will bear him a child, despite her being 90 years old, and that his destiny is to become the father of many nations. Divine favour would continue to accrue to his descendants down the ages so long as they kept the sign of the covenant, the circumcision of all males.

Shortly after this we come to the disturbing story of Yahweh's command to Abraham to sacrifice this same child, Isaac for no good reason other than to test his faith so that Abraham might prove his worthiness. Without any hesitation Abraham obeys the commandment and makes the appropriate preparations for the ritual murder, journeying with the unsuspecting boy for three days to Mount Moriah, later identified by a Jewish tradition as the site of the Temple in Jerusalem.[7]

At the last minute, just as he is about to cut the throat of his young and defenceless son, the Lord god intervenes through an angel to inform him that he was only fooling around and that an animal sacrifice would suffice. As a consequence of Abraham's trust and obedience, of his faith in the Lord, the promise is renewed and enhanced. Now Abraham is promised that his descendants will be 'as numerous as the stars of heaven and the sands on the sea-shore.'[8] As we shall see, centuries later this appalling episode was to have enormous resonance in the development of Christian thought.

The second key event in the formation of the Jewish religion was the covenant made through Moses. Having delivered his people out of Egyptian slavery (believed to have occurred around 1250 BCE) and while leading them over the course of 40 years through the desert to the promised land, Moses is promised that he and his people will live under Yahweh's blessing and protection if they agree to live by his Law. The best known part of this Law is the ten commandments, but the Torah, to give it its correct name (which is perhaps better translated as 'wisdom' or 'teaching') strictly speaking covers the whole of the teaching in the first five books of the Old Testament. Those who obeyed the Law and were faithful to the Torah received Yahweh's love and favour; those who transgressed roused his anger. Over the centuries the expression of this anger came to be seen in the

---

[7]Vermes, *The Changing Face of Jesus*, p 84.

[8]Genesis 22:17.

misfortune that fell to Israel; catastrophes for the Jewish people such as the Babylonian captivity in the 6th century BCE or the Roman occupation in the times of Jesus were often interpreted as divinely imposed punishments for the collective sins of the nation.

According to Christianity however, such deals were merely the preparatory understandings in anticipation of the long planned arrangement that would be set into being by Jesus. The life and sacrificial death of Jesus are taught by the Church as being the establishment of a new and everlasting covenant superseding all others and now providing the true path to salvation. At its heart therefore Christianity is a covenant religion with a deal that offered salvation in return for faith. This was a radical and innovative departure from the ancestral beliefs of Judaism and almost in an instant proclaimed a thousand years or more of Jewish worship to be invalid or inadequate.

Moreover it changed the very nature of faith; instead of observance of the Torah, believers now had to have faith in the person and sacrifice of Jesus who was eventually proclaimed to be a god. So extreme was this new teaching that those who didn't recognise him as such were soon told that they would be punished after death for this reason alone. But how did such a revolution come about? What were the characteristics of the new faith? Was this something that Jesus himself preached or was it a subsequent interpretation of his life and death? To find answers to these questions we need to turn not so much to the gospel lives of Jesus but to other New Testament documents, those which provide us with some understanding of the earliest Christian teachings and communities in the first two to three decades after his death.

In the very earliest days of the Church, the Way, as the religion of Jesus was originally known, was characterised by intense rivalry and bitter infighting (as indeed it has been for much of its history). In the middle decades of the 1st century two distinct factions emerged, each preaching a contrary gospel with its own understanding of Jesus and each headed by a new, dominant and forceful personality.

According to Church tradition leadership of the new movement fell to Peter, the disciple presented in the gospels as foremost among the Twelve and, alongside an unnamed 'beloved disciple' frequently mentioned in the Fourth Gospel, the most intimate with Jesus. It was Peter who was generally believed to have had the first experience of the risen Jesus and it was he who appears to have been the most eloquent and enthusiastic of the group. Furthermore according to Matthew, Jesus himself seemed to favour him and even told him that he would be the rock upon whom he would build his Church. Tradition has it that towards the end of his life Peter travelled to Rome to found what was to become the universal Catholic Church.

Whether Peter did actually establish or even visit the Christian community at Rome is far from certain. What is known however is that quite soon after Jesus' death Peter's leadership was eclipsed by two personalities not mentioned - or mentioned only in passing - in the gospels: the apostle Paul and a vague, shadowy figure who remains largely unknown to Christians today called James.

James And The Jesus Movement

While the New Testament has four gospels about Jesus' life and mission, we have only one book that tells the story of the infant Church immediately after his death. This is The Acts of the Apostles, the sequel to Luke's gospel, generally accepted as having been written by the same author about a decade later, appearing around 85-90 CE.[9] Some of the events related in Acts are corroborated by references in the much earlier letters of Paul; but Paul's intention was never to provide us with a history of the development of the Church and these matters are quite incidental to his evangelising purposes. Moreover, the Christian communities to whom Paul wrote were based in gentile territory, far removed from Jerusalem both geographically and culturally. Ultimately Paul's perspective can only be that of an outsider. So if we want to discover and consider the very beginnings of the Jesus movement (a term that is perhaps more appropriate than 'infant Church'[10]) it is to Acts that we are obliged to turn.

The problem is, while the author set out to write an 'ordered account', a basic history, as the prologue to his gospel would suggest, it's widely recognised that this later narrative cannot be taken as an accurate and reliable chronicle. Acts is highly selective both in the

---

[9]See Kummel, *Introduction To The New Testament*, pp 185-186.

[10]The word 'church' derives from the Greek word *ekklesia* meaning a community. However this word has such strong Christian connotations today that it is inappropriate to use it in this context.

events it reports and the way in which it reports them. Just as in his gospel Luke rewrites or even fabricates certain details (such as the story of the census and birth of Jesus in Bethlehem) to fit his theological purposes, so we see him distorting the likely course of events and subjecting it to his pro-gentile ideological bias in similar ways in his follow-up work.[11] Acts is big on legends and miracles and in presenting us with an idealised picture of the early Christian community with the added drama of unjust (but thrilling) persecutions and divinely aided triumphs; but in the final analysis, it is sloppy with history.

Even so, occasionally there are glimpses of the beliefs and practises of Jesus' initial followers that may be based on genuine recollections. So for instance we may take the report of Peter's earliest, unsophisticated preaching to the crowds about Jesus, 'a man commended to you by God by the miracles and portents and signs that God worked through him' as a fair and plausible indication of the disciples' post-resurrection understanding and proclamation of Jesus as the messiah. Here we see that Peter's concern is simply to preach that Jesus the Nazarene (he hasn't yet acquired his Christian name of Jesus Christ) as a descendent of King David, so fulfilling strictly Jewish hopes and expectations. It is because of this royal descent and the fact that 'God raised this man', that he is proclaimed to be the messiah, Yahweh's anointed one, chosen to inaugurate his coming kingdom. There is no thought at this very early stage that his death was regarded as a sacrifice for the sins of the world or that it 'has made salvation possible for the whole human race' as Paul would later proclaim. Nor is there any hint that he is a god or even the only son of the one true god.[12]

We also see the group remaining true to some of Jesus' more probable teachings in their everyday lives, living in a simple community and continuing with traditional Jewish forms of worship: 'The faithful all lived together and owned everything in common; they

---

[11]Historical inaccuracies include a reference by a Pharisee, Gamaliel to a small rebellion by a certain Theudas. The rebellion occurred in the year 45, but Gamaliel's speech is made before the conversion of Paul, i.e. at least 10 years before the rebellion took place. The ideological bias is reflected in the idyllic growth of the Church, in the way that Paul becomes its glorified and undisputed champion and in the attempts to gloss over and harmonise any differences between Peter and Paul. See Brandon, *op cit*, pp 206-212.

[12]Acts 2:22, Titus 2:11.

sold their goods and possessions and shared out the proceeds among themselves according to what each one needed. They went to the Temple every day but met in their houses for the breaking of bread; they shared their food gladly and generously.'[13]

Little is said about the leadership of the group and it is assumed (but never explicitly stated) that Peter emerged as its natural leader. Certainly in the opening chapters he's the only character permitted to speak at any length. However, as the narrative unfolds, another figure emerges whose authority appears to exceed Peter's. He is first mentioned very briefly after Peter is forced to flee from Jerusalem having just escaped from prison (with the apparent assistance of an angel of the Lord). Before fleeing the city he urges his companions to 'tell James' of his miraculous deliverance. For Peter then, James seems to be a person of some significance, but we're not told who he is. It's clear however that he can't be one of the Twelve mentioned in the gospels for the narrative tells us that the disciple called James had already been arrested and beheaded.[14] Unfortunately the writer provides no further information about the identity or status of James and initially the reader can only assume that he is a secondary and inconsequential figure.

But James doesn't disappear from the narrative and he returns some time later as a more central and much more authoritative character. Following a serious controversy about whether gentile converts should be circumcised and whether or not they needed to adhere to the Torah, the key players in the Jesus movement assemble for a meeting in Jerusalem to debate and resolve the matter. Paul and his assistant Barnabas arrive to argue the case for non-observance and they appear to be supported by Peter. Yet even he, the rock of the Church and first among the disciples is soon over-ruled by this unknown and somewhat elusive figure. James is the last to speak and although he is given no formal introduction, it's clear from his language and tone (he expresses his opinion - or rather his judgement with a magisterial 'I

---

[13] Acts 2:44–45.

[14] In fact there are two disciples called James in the gospels - the son of Zebedee (who was beheaded) and James, son of Alphaeus. Whenever this latter disciple is mentioned in the New Testament, he is always referred to as James, son of Alphaeus and is therefore distinguished from the James in question. No reason or details are given for the execution of James, son of Zebedee.

decree') that he has a presiding role.

We also know from Paul's letters that whoever he was, James was one of the community's leading figures. In his letter to the Galatians written around the year 54, some five years after the assembly, Paul reluctantly acknowledged him as one of the three pillars of the movement (the other two being the disciples Peter and John). Furthermore Paul referred to James before the other two suggesting that it was generally understood that he was the community's leading figure. Outside of the New Testament Eusebius, relying on earlier Jewish and Christian sources, also confirmed that leadership of the movement passed to James who, he wrote 'was the first . . . to be elected to the episcopal throne of the Jerusalem Church'[15]

So who was James and how could he have emerged above Peter as the leader of the movement? While the gospels record that James played no significant part in Jesus' ministry during his lifetime, a careful reading reveals that he is none other than Jesus' younger brother. Since the Church has nearly always taught that Jesus was Mary's only child, this may come as something of a surprise to traditionalists; but it is an understanding based purely on the dogmatic belief in Mary's 'ever virgin' status (which I shall consider in greater detail later on) rather than one which has any reliable historical foundation. Ignoring this belief, which was formulated centuries after the gospels were written, there's no reason to suppose that Mary did not have a number of children; for mainstream Judaism had none of the hang-ups about sex that Christianity was later to develop and tended to regard large families as a blessing.

In fact a large family - five brothers, including Jesus and at least two sisters - is confirmed by the gospels themselves which mention Jesus' siblings several times. Mark for instance refers to his 'brothers and sisters' twice and on the second occasion, when the locals of Nazareth marvel at how a simple carpenter has turned out to be such an astonishing man, they even name one of his brothers as James: 'What is this wisdom that has been granted him, and these miracles that are worked through him? This is the carpenter, surely, the son of Mary,

---

[15]Eusebius, *op cit,* II:1. Eusebius' sources were Hegesippus, a 2nd century Jewish Christian and Clement of Alexandria, an early 3rd century Church father. Eusebius' terms - *episcopal, throne* and *Church* are historically inappropriate.

the brother of James and Joset and Jude and Simon?'[16]

So it seems it was the family connection that gave James the right to assume the leadership of the movement, quite possibly from a very early stage after his brother's death. His rise to prominence might have come about not only because of his great piety - he was highly revered in his own age, so much so that he became known as James the righteous - but also because the risen Jesus was reported by Paul to have appeared to him. Furthermore one tradition, the non-canonical Gospel of Thomas, discovered quite by chance near the Egyptian town of Nag Hammadi in 1945, actually has Jesus himself appointing not Peter but James as his successor: 'The disciples said to Jesus, 'We know you will depart from us. Who is to be our leader?' Jesus said to them, 'Wherever you are, you are to go to James the righteous, for whose sake heaven and earth came into being.''[17]

However, while James was clearly a thoroughbred in his own times, next to Peter and Paul, usually regarded as the two leading figures in the establishment of the Church, his status today is closer to that of an also-ran. In fact James has turned out to be something of an embarrassment for the Church, somehow to be excused or explained away. So he is recognised neither as Jesus' actual blood brother - so as to preserve the doctrine of the perpetual virginity of Mary, nor as the Church's first true leader so as to preserve its apostolic status and the primacy of Peter (and by extension, of the Roman Church). But perhaps the greatest obstacle that led to James' demise in mainstream Christianity was the nature of the beliefs held by himself and the closely-knit community he led.

From the sparse amount of reliable historical information we can usefully extract from Acts, we can surmise that Jesus' original followers

---

[16]Mark 6:2-3.

[17]Gospel of Thomas, 12. The gospel is introduced with the claim 'These are the secret words which the living Jesus spoke' and consists only of sayings (some of which are similar to those in the New Testament gospels) and a small amount of dialogue between Jesus and his disciples. It is primitive in style, without any narrative element or overall structure and with the sayings repeatedly introduced by the simple phrase 'Jesus said.' Scholarly opinion is divided about the dating of this gospel; traditionalists maintain it was written in the 2nd century while more radical critics argue for a date before Mark. As with all of Jesus' recorded words, whether he actually issued this instruction has to be considered with great caution. But the saying indicates that there was a strong and possibly very early tradition that regarded James as Jesus' natural successor.

were practising Jews rather than primitive Christians. They probably continued to observe the Torah, as suggested by the controversy about circumcision and certainly worshipped alongside their fellow Jews in the Temple, perhaps even participating in its sacrificial ceremonies.[18] Within its walls they preached daily, but while they proclaimed that Jesus was the messiah and were unwavering in spreading his call to repentance in anticipation of the coming kingdom, there's nothing to suggest that in these early days Jesus was proclaimed or worshipped as a new deity.

It's difficult of course to reconcile this to the questionable teaching of the Church today which affirms that at the feast of Pentecost, when the Holy Spirit supposedly descended on the apostles, the Christian Trinity was fully revealed.[19] If the Trinity really was revealed on this momentous occasion, why wasn't Jesus acclaimed and worshipped as a god from that moment on? Why, we might wonder, did Peter preach immediately afterwards (when supposedly he had just received the Holy Spirit and when presumably he was at his most inspired) that Jesus was merely 'a man commended to you by God'?

The simple and traditionally Jewish worship of this original Jesus community is confirmed elsewhere in the New Testament, specifically in the letter of James, one of only a handful of documents in the canon that appears to derive from a Jerusalem tradition. That the letter was actually written by James is disputed today (the doubt is based mainly on the excellence of its Greek which would probably have been beyond the abilities of a Galilean Jew of modest education); but its straightforward, practical teaching probably reflects the spirit and piety of James and his congregation. Not surprisingly the epistle has long been regarded as the least 'Christian' of all New Testament documents: often seen as a rebuttal to the faith centred theology of Paul, it hails the

---

[18]Vermes (*op cit*, p 130) points out that Peter and John went to the Temple at the ninth hour (i.e. 3 pm), the time when the afternoon sacrifice, the *Tamid* was offered (Acts 3:1).

[19]*Catechism* 732. The *Catechism* also proclaims that at the Transfiguration, when Jesus ascended to the top of a mountain, 'the whole Trinity appeared: the Father in the voice; the Son in the man; the Spirit in the shining cloud' (555). It is somewhat perplexing (to say the least) to consider that one of the Christian gods believed that the most appropriate way to reveal itself was in the form of a random mass of water vapour which would have been indistinguishable from any other cloud through which the sun was shining. In this respect the Holy Spirit seems to be reminiscent of the 'tree spirits' and 'thunder gods' of more primitive religions.

Jewish Law to be 'the perfect Law of freedom'[20] rather than the dark, oppressive force that Paul considered it to be.

More importantly it has no reference to a new covenant established by Jesus, it fails to mention the central Christian ritual of the Eucharist and gives no indication that Jesus was recognised as a new saviour god. Even the earthly historical figure of Jesus remains largely in the background, almost irrelevant to its preaching. So instead of an innovative Christ-centric theology we find a more traditional religion that emphasised practical morality and good works above faith. With its denunciation of wealth and regard for temperance, its concerns reflect some of the values that may have been taught by Jesus. Yet despite appearing to continue the authentic teaching of Jesus, the letter was accepted into the Christian canon only at a very late stage[21] and its essentially Jewish character continued to trouble fundamentalist Christians down the centuries; most notably it was denounced by Luther in his 1552 preface to the New Testament as nothing more than an 'epistle of straw.'

So in the early chapters of Acts and in the moral exhortations of a letter supposedly penned by James, we catch a glimpse of the lives and devotions of the original group of Jesus' followers, of those who were most closely associated with him during his lifetime. All the indications are they remained Jews and initially at least there was little to distinguish them from their Jewish brethren other than their belief that Jesus had been raised and exalted as the messiah. None of the key doctrines and practices of the Christian religion – the divinity of Jesus, his virgin birth, faith in the redeeming nature of his sacrificial death, the sacrament of the Eucharist – appear to have been adopted or known by this group. If Jesus had instituted or taught these beliefs and practises, it's hard to understand why his immediate disciples failed to practise or preach *any of them* in the years following his death.

Initially the Jerusalem community formed the heart of the Jesus movement and had it survived, it's unlikely that Christianity would have developed into a new and separate religion. But in the second half of the 1st century two key events rocked the community and

---

[20]James 1:25.

[21]It was finally recognised as part of the New Testament at the end of the 4th century. See Kummel, *op cit*, p 405.

shifted the centre of gravity away from Jerusalem to rival groups at Rome or Antioch. The premature death of James in 62 (killed at the instigation of Hanan, the high priest) enhanced his own saintly reputation but it deprived the Jerusalem community of a charismatic and widely revered leader and severely weakened its authority.

But the more fatal blow was to come with the catastrophic defeat of the Jewish revolt in 70 CE, culminating in the sack of Jerusalem and the destruction of the Temple. Those who survived the Roman onslaught were scattered and as messianists, eagerly awaiting a new king, were actively persecuted by the Romans. Though they regrouped in small numbers, eventually to form a sect called the Ebionites, they never regained the authority they held before the war and were unable to exercise any restraining influence over gentile Christianity. Continuing to observe the Torah, these Jewish 'Christians' lived a life of poverty and worldly detachment. They held on to the belief that Jesus was the messiah, their champion who would come again to inaugurate the kingdom, but could never acknowledge his divinity or virgin birth; inevitably they became increasingly marginalised from the mainstream church.

In part this was due to doctrinal differences; but with the rebellious Jews having become reviled throughout the Empire, it suited gentile Christianity to distance itself from its Judaic roots. In the highly charged political atmosphere of the day any association with Jewish messianism would have been seen as dangerously anti-Roman and disastrous for a newly emerging sect. It was only a matter of time then before these descendants of the original Jesus movement were to be declared heretics by Christians whose faith, under the influence of the apostle Paul, had taken a radically different direction.

Paul Of Tarsus: An Angry Young Man

Generally known to church-goers throughout the world as Saint Paul and universally regarded as both the leading theologian and greatest missionary of the Christian faith, Paul is often credited with being the true founder of Christianity.[22] We can readily understand

---

[22]*A Dictionary of Comparative Religion* (p 491) declares that he 'laid the foundations of Christianity as a universal salvation religion'; *A New Dictionary of Religions* observes (p

that without Jesus there would never have been a Saint Paul; but it's also fair to say that without Paul we would probably never have heard of or known anything about Jesus. By establishing or influencing small Christian communities in towns and cities such as Thessalonika, Corinth and most notably Rome and, more importantly, by preserving his thoughts and ideas about Jesus in a series of letters to them, almost single-handedly Paul transformed a marginal Jewish movement first into something of a mystery cult appealing to lower class gentiles and eventually into a radical new religion that for centuries was to dominate the culture, politics and everyday life of the western world.

Paul was of Jewish birth and was originally called Saul, a name he shared with the first king of ancient Israel, from whose tribe he claimed descent. According to Acts, but never confirmed by Paul himself, he was also a Roman citizen by birth and originated from the city of Tarsus. Located in the south east of Asia Minor (modern day Turkey), Tarsus was the busy capital of the Roman province of Cilicia. Although the city was a thriving centre of Hellenistic philosophy and culture, for a devout Jew like Paul it was something of a religious backwater compared with Jerusalem. Always anxious to impress both his supporters and detractors with his impeccable religious credentials, perhaps this may explain his reluctance ever to mention the place of his upbringing.

From an early age, even before he'd heard of Jesus, religion seems to have been the most important thing in Paul's life. From his own testimony we can see that in his youth and early manhood he was an intensely ascetic man, wholly committed to a strict observance of the Jewish Law: 'as far as the Law can make you perfect', he later wrote with evident pride, 'I was faultless . . . I stood out among other Jews of my generation.'[23] But his near fanatical devotion had a dark and ugly side and in his early years for some unknown reason he developed a fierce, almost pathological hatred for Jesus and his followers.

Paul is first introduced in the early chapters of Acts with a touch of drama, brought into the story as a young man present at the stoning of Stephen. Generally thought of as the first 'Christian' martyr, Stephen

---

374) that 'He is suitably regarded as the founder of Gentile Christianity.' Jewish, or non-gentile Christianity of course has not survived.
[23] Philippians 3:6, Gal. 1:14.

was a Hellenist who had joined the Jesus movement at a very early stage, perhaps within a year or two of Jesus' death. He had been condemned by the Sanhedrin, the Jewish council, for blasphemy, but his death seems to have been more at the hands of an over zealous mob. Paul is not reported to have taken part in the actual stoning, but, if we accept the testimony of Acts, he took a keen interest in the affair and 'entirely approved of the killing.'[24] If this event took place within a few years of the crucifixion and a young man is taken to be aged in his early 20s, Paul's year of birth would have been around 10-15 CE.

Paul claimed on numerous occasions in his letters that he was a Pharisee and Acts adds that he was also the son of a Pharisee. Luke's narrative seeks further to enhance his credentials by contending that he was brought up in Jerusalem and studied under the Pharisee Gamaliel, 'a doctor of the Law and respected by the whole people.'[25] This last claim seems somewhat unlikely, for if true it's hard to understand why Paul, a man frequently inclined to boast of his accomplishments and religious upbringing, failed ever to mention it himself. The doubt is only increased when we note that the same Gamaliel is reported in Acts to have advised that Jesus' followers should be treated leniently and left to themselves, a recommendation that Paul went out of his way to flout. If there really had been some connection between the two, one would hardly expect the teachings of an esteemed mentor to have been so vehemently opposed.

Acts provides no explanation as to why Paul felt such a violent and obsessive hatred for Jesus' supporters - we're told only that immediately after the killing of Stephen, acting like some self-appointed inquisitor, he went from house to house to arrest and imprison other members of the group. A little later, 'still breathing threats to slaughter the Lord's disciples'[26] we find him applying to the high priest to authorise him to travel to Damascus to arrest any further supporters he might find there. Luke may have exaggerated Paul's fanaticism in order to make his later u-turn all the more dramatic, but from Paul's own account of himself, we can see that he certainly

---

[24]Acts 8:1. It's unlikely that Paul really was present at the stoning - see for example Bornkamm, *Paul*, p 15, *Jerome* 44:50 which maintains that Paul's presence is merely part of Luke's 'exquisite literary design'.

[25]Acts 5:34, 22:3.

[26]Acts 9:1.

claimed to have been a 'persecutor of the Church' and that he'd been 'merciless' in his harassment of its members. Unfortunately, he too omits to provide any explanation for his ugly behaviour and justifies it merely by pointing out 'how enthusiastic I was for the traditions of my ancestors.'[27] So why might he have been so consumed by such a bitter and unreasonable grudge against the Nazarenes?

Many explanations for Paul's attitude and behaviour have been offered over the years. A. N. Wilson argues that the seeds of Paul's hostility lay in his conviction that Jesus had undermined the strict legalism of the Pharisees.[28] In the gospel story of the tax collector and the Pharisee, Jesus proclaimed that it was not the virtuous Law abiding Pharisee who received Yahweh's favour, but the tax collector, a sinner so aware of his faults and his lowliness that he didn't dare 'even to raise his eyes to heaven.'[29] So far as Jesus was concerned, what mattered was an acknowledgement of and repentance for one's sinfulness together with a recognition of utter dependence on Yahweh's infinite mercy and forgiveness.

But virtue in the form of a scrupulous observance of the Torah (and pride in that observance) formed the very backbone of Paul's religious belief and practise. Now he was confronted by a radical new doctrine, spreading like wildfire, which taught that such righteousness was neither here nor there, that indeed, it counted for very little. If repentant sinners were considered equally justified before the Lord, what was the point of keeping the Law so assiduously in the first place? Wilson believes that Jesus' opinions and teaching would have horrified and infuriated Paul; it would have made a mockery of the whole of his life as a devout and strictly observant Jew. A volatile and highly-strung character, with an intense religious consciousness, Paul was simply unable to help himself. And rather than allow it to tear him apart, he was driven to take matters into his own hands to stamp out such a dangerous and offensive doctrine.

For the Jewish scholar Hyam Maccoby, Paul was never a Pharisee,

---

[27]Gal. 1:14.

[28]A. N. Wilson, *Jesus*, pp 29-33.

[29]Luke 18:9-13. The same principle, that repentance rather than a rigid observance of the Law, finds greater favour, is similarly made in the better known parable of the Prodigal son.

merely 'an adventurer of undistinguished background'[30] who aspired to, but failed to join the Pharisaic movement. Rejected by the Pharisee community probably in Jerusalem, Paul chose the next best option and allied himself to their political and spiritual opponents, the Sadducees. This was the party of the high priest which had reconciled itself to collaborating with the Romans so as to preserve its position of economic and social privilege. All of the gospels indicate that it was the high priest and his sect who were responsible for handing Jesus over to Pilate to be tried and condemned. It's plausible then that in the years following his death this same party sought to clear up any remaining threats of trouble coming from his supporters. Indeed when we read Acts carefully we see that it was none other than the high priest who was responsible for the arrest and imprisonment of Peter, John and various other apostles.

Anxious to make a name for himself, Maccoby argues that Paul was an ambitious Temple police officer[31] who volunteered to carry out these underhand assignments. But cleansing the synagogues and Temple precincts in Jerusalem of these undesirables wasn't enough to satisfy Paul's fervour. And so we find him in Acts applying to the high priest for authority to journey to Damascus to arrest any of Jesus' supporters who might have found asylum there.

The trouble is, as Maccoby and numerous other commentators point out, Damascus at that time didn't fall within the jurisdiction of the Jerusalem high priest. Damascus lay in the kingdom of Nabataea, then under the rule of Aretas IV, an independently minded king who in all probability would not have complied with Jerusalem based extradition requests. The forcible return of wanted dissidents therefore wouldn't have been a lawful one and Maccoby sees Paul at this point in his life as little more than a small time undercover agent on an illicit mission to kidnap 'any followers of the Way, men or women that he could find.'[32] Indeed when we read Paul's own account of what happened in Damascus, it seems that it was he himself who was considered to be a dangerous and unwelcome troublemaker by its

---

[30]Maccoby, *The Myth Maker: Paul and the Invention of Christianity* p 15. Maccoby argues that Jesus himself was a Pharisee.

[31]Luke's gospel (22:52) confirms the existence of 'captains of the Temple guard' who were called upon to arrest subversives or potential troublemakers like Jesus.

[32]Acts 9:2.

authorities. Writing many years later he boasted that on his return to Damascus some time later, Aretas' governor was actually seeking to arrest *him* (rather than any of Jesus' followers) and that he was only able to escape by being lowered from the city walls in a basket.

The Damascus Trip

But Paul never fulfilled his dark commission, for on the legendary road to Damascus something happened to him that changed the course of his life and the history of the world. Traditionally this is thought of as his 'conversion' to 'Christianity', or if that term is anachronistic, at least to the Way or persuasion of Jesus. Whereas Christians see this event as miraculous in nature, those not inclined to believe in divine interventions comment that Paul seems to have experienced a nervous collapse, possibly manifested in a seizure of some sort.

We know from Paul's own testimony that he was prone to having visions and he associates these with an unknown illness, 'a thorn in the flesh',[33] as he called it. This has led some commentators to venture that he may have suffered from epilepsy and that his 'divine' revelation in reality was one particularly powerful ecstatic fit.[34] If this is the case, one might venture that the whole of Paul's religious conviction and missionary drive were based ultimately on unusual or abnormal brain chemistry rather than on a series of truly divine communications.

However, we have to accept that precisely what happened to him on that fateful day is something we can never know: he himself says very little about it in his letters while the second-hand reporting in Acts (there are actually three separate accounts of the event), written at least half a century later, has been so elaborated with legendary detail and so subjected to Luke's theological reflection and requirements that as purported history it is virtually worthless.

According to Acts Paul is struck down by a brilliant light from

---

[33] 2 Corinthians (hereafter 2 Cor.) 12:7. In the same passage he claimed also to have been taken up to the highest heaven where he 'heard things which must not and cannot be put into human language.'

[34] The case is argued by Klausner, *From Jesus To Paul*, pp 322-330. He bases his case on the blinding flash of light, ecstatic feelings often experienced by epileptics, Paul's reference to his disease which could arouse contempt and disgust (as epilepsy tended to do) and the fact that in Acts he was recorded as having fallen to the ground (in Hebrew epilepsy was known as the 'falling sickness').

heaven and is spoken to by a voice that identifies itself as Jesus. Temporarily blinded, he is commanded by the voice to continue his journey to Damascus where he'd be given further instructions about what his future mission would be. Three days later another disciple living in the city, one Ananias also receives a heavenly vision and is ordered to minister to Paul. Ananias protests, aware of Paul's dismal record as a persecutor, but is told in no uncertain terms by the Lord that he must tend to Paul 'because this man is my chosen instrument to bring my name before pagans and pagan kings and before the people of Israel.'[35]

Meanwhile Paul is now expecting his arrival, having rather conveniently received a further vision of Ananias coming to take charge of him. As soon as Ananias lays his hands on Paul, his sight is miraculously restored and within days the new preacher is out and about, proclaiming in the local synagogues that 'Jesus is the Son of God.' The narrative then goes on to relate that Paul went back to Jerusalem to join the disciples, thereby giving the impression that he became a member of the original community very soon after his 'conversion', so providing a continuity of tradition from Jesus to Paul.

Paul's own recollection of events however is much less fanciful. He doesn't refer directly to his experience but merely appends it to what seems to be a pre-established list of appearances of the risen Jesus. According to a tradition passed on to Paul, Jesus appeared to Cephas (Paul usually referred to Peter by his Aramaic name) and to the twelve disciples, to James and to various other followers. To this Paul adds 'and last of all he appeared to me too.' In another letter, where he provides the fullest account of his spiritual journey from zealous persecutor of the gospel to its most enthused proclaimer, he simply observes that 'God . . . chose to reveal his Son in me.' In neither of these accounts does he mention being blinded, hearing heavenly commands or being tended to by Ananias.

Nor does he say that he went straightaway to Jerusalem to receive instruction from James or any of the other disciples, or even to share his extraordinary experience with them. On the contrary he wants it to be known that he resolutely maintained his independence from the Jerusalem community. So far as Paul was concerned his revelation was

---

[35]Acts 9:15.

a strictly private affair and he recorded that he travelled elsewhere, presumably to reflect privately upon its meaning: 'I did not stop to discuss this with any human being, nor did I go up to Jerusalem to see those who were already apostles before me, but I went off to Arabia *at once*'.[36]

Paul's account of himself after his change of heart reveals that he wasn't at all concerned to discover and learn more about the teachings of Jesus or the background to his life from those who knew him in the flesh. A proud and headstrong character, 'lacking in humility, exceedingly confident of himself, and boastfully condescending' in the words of one biographer,[37] he had a powerful sense of destiny that derived to a large extent from his numerous personal revelations. These he believed were vastly superior to any knowledge of the earthly Jesus. And to his mind his heavenly visions were given not to galvanise him into following the Way established by James, Peter and the other disciples who carried on in the tradition of Jesus, but to inspire him to journey down the theological road of his own making. Accordingly it was only after a period of three years that Paul saw fit to pay a brief visit to Jerusalem to meet Jesus' original followers. There he met only James and Cephas but from the tone of voice in the letter that records this meeting one senses that even this was something of an embarrassment or irrelevance to him.

For whatever reason Paul was unwilling to play second fiddle and just a fortnight after first meeting these closest associates of Jesus he was off, anxious to preach his version of the gospel to both Jews and gentiles in Syria and his home region of Cilicia. But increasingly the Jerusalem apostles viewed Paul's mission with a sense of dismay and suspicion. In the words of Hugh Schonfield, they regarded him as a 'presumptuous upstart'[38] who set himself above their authority. How could this unknown man who had never spoken to or even listened to Jesus in his lifetime presume to know more than they about the teachings of their master? Such presumption might not have been so galling and so impertinent had Paul been singing from the same hymn sheet; but his teachings were seen by these original followers as

---

[36]1 Cor. 15:8, Gal. 1:15-16, 16-17, my italics.

[37]Klausner, *op cit*, p 424.

[38]Schonfield, *Those Incredible Christians*, p 63.

contrary to theirs and, more importantly, contrary to those of Jesus himself.

How can we tell that this was the case? We know because while Acts tries to harmonise the two differing sets of teaching and glosses over any sense of disagreement, Paul himself openly refers to a 'different version of the Good News', different that is to his own version. And it was one to which, to his consternation and dismay, some of his followers in the region of Galatia in central Asia Minor had switched allegiance. Frustratingly for Paul, this lack of loyalty to his gospel and to his authority was not a one off. To his followers at Corinth for instance he also complained 'any newcomer has only to proclaim a new Jesus, different from the one that we preached . . . or a new gospel, different from the one you have already accepted - and you welcome it with open arms.'[39]

Alarmed at Paul's corruption of the true message of Jesus, it seems that James and his supporters sent out envoys to those communities that Paul had established or visited to correct their understanding of Jesus. They must have made some headway thanks presumably to their actual knowledge of the real, earthly Jesus (an intimacy that Paul lacked and which the Jerusalem apostles obviously used to their considerable advantage), for he was clearly rattled by the interference of these 'troublemakers', as he called them. 'These people are counterfeit apostles', he fumed, 'they are dishonest workmen disguised as apostles of Christ.' And to another of his communities in the city of Philippi, which had evidently received a visit from head office, his response was still more bitter: 'Beware of dogs! Watch out for the people who are making mischief. Watch out for the cutters. We are the real people of the circumcision.'

For Paul the preaching of another gospel to *his* followers must have seemed like an act of great treachery. And to fight it off he was given to adopt a more extreme and authoritarian stance, one that was not minded to tolerate dissent: 'let me warn you that if anyone preaches a version of the Good News different from the one we have already preached to you, whether it be ourselves or an angel from heaven, he is to be condemned.'[40] By this stage it seems that Paul had such a high

---

[39]Gal. 1:6, 2 Cor. 11:4

[40]2 Cor. 11:13, Philippians 3:2-3, Gal. 1:8. In this letter Paul's invective reaches its

opinion of himself, or was so incensed by others muscling in on his territory and undermining his authority that, quite bizarrely, he was intimating that his preaching was superior even to that of 'an angel from heaven.'

But it was this preaching, *his* version of the gospel rather than that of the Jerusalem community which emerged to become the foundation of Christian theology and which has come down to us today. We've noted that it was sufficiently different from that of the original Jerusalem apostles and, from their point of view, sufficiently corrupting to cause them great alarm. Accordingly it seems they took steps to correct this misrepresentation by sending out their own agents to repudiate Paul's authority and to preach the true message about Jesus. What this original preaching and understanding was, Paul does not report. But the Christ of his gospel is strikingly different from the Jesus of the Jerusalem community and, crucially appears to have originated from himself, or if we're inclined to take him at his word, from his revelations: 'The fact is . . . the Good News I preached is not a human message that I was given by men, it is something I learnt only through a revelation of Jesus Christ.'[41] What then were the main features of Paul's theology and how much of it really derived from the teachings of Jesus?

Paul's Brand Of Christianity

Much to the disquiet of the Jerusalem apostles, after taking leave of them Paul marched off to become the self-styled apostle to the gentiles. Although undeniably successful, throughout his missionary career he was frequently hampered by his status as an apostle. In the opening chapter of Acts the writer relates that after the death of Judas the remaining eleven disciples gathered together to elect a further member to their number. From the earliest days of the post-resurrection community it was clear that there was one principal qualification to becoming an apostle: according to Peter, Judas' replacement had to be somebody 'who has been with us the whole

---

lowest point - he tells his supporters to tell the Jewish apostles that 'I would like to see the knife slip', i.e. he hopes that those undergoing circumcision will have a very unpleasant accident.
[41] Gal. 1:11.

time that the Lord Jesus was travelling around with us, someone who was with us right from the time when John was baptising.'[42]

This of course would have excluded Paul who had never known Jesus and who would always have been seen as an outsider. To overcome this shortcoming Paul's solution was to proclaim that his appointment to the apostleship was a divine one and therefore more exalted than any human election. But his lack of personal knowledge of and intimacy with Jesus during his earthly life was also to have a huge impact on the character and development of his mission. Unable to preach what Jesus himself actually taught, Paul ignored the human and historical figure almost entirely. Virtually everything that Jesus did and said during his ministry in Galilee and Jerusalem was irrelevant to Paul's gospel. The only things about Jesus that had any significance for Paul were his death (and in particular the manner of his death on the cross) and his resurrection, as he openly declared to his followers in Corinth: 'the only knowledge I claimed to have was about Jesus and only about him as the crucified Christ.'

What was important to Paul was not Jesus, the man of flesh and blood from Nazareth, but the exalted Christ 'revealed to us through the Spirit' whose origins were heavenly. 'Even if we did once know Christ in the flesh', he wrote 'that is not how we know him now.'[43] Accordingly the person of Jesus underwent a radical transformation in his hands. In the synoptic gospels Jesus frequently (and somewhat enigmatically) refers to himself as the 'son of man'[44] but by the time Paul has finished with him, he has evolved into being the 'son of God', now more of a quasi-divine figure than a human one. Likewise he turned the title of 'messiah' given to Jesus by his followers into a name, Christ. And at times Paul even refers to Jesus as 'Christ crucified', thereby having the effect of depicting him more as an abstract concept at the centre of his blood and cross theology than as a real person.

But how was such a radical move away from the original

---

[42] Acts 1:21-22.

[43] 1 Cor. 2:2, 1 Cor. 2:10, 2 Cor. 5:16.

[44] Vermes (*Jesus the Jew,* pp 137-165) argues that 'son of man' was used by Jesus as a recognised circumlocution to refer to himself (see for example Matthew 8:20). On two occasions (Mark 13:26, 14:62) the 'title' has a messianic connotation, where Jesus specifically alludes to the Book of Daniel. But Vermes concludes that there is no argument that these uses can be traced back to Jesus himself.

understanding of Jesus possible and why did it come about? To a large extent it can be explained by the audience to whom Paul was preaching. This consisted not of Jews but gentiles and his 'gospel to the uncircumcised', as he called it, was adapted to suit their needs and circumstances. Two aspects of this teaching were fundamental in the appeal to the gentiles and the divergence from the original Jewish conception of Jesus: his new and highly individual interpretation of Jesus' death and resurrection and his response to the Torah.

For the Jews the long awaited messiah was seen above all as a kingly deliverer, a nationalistic figure who would liberate Israel from foreign oppression and whose mission therefore would always have a political dimension. As in Elizabethan England, the Poland of the 1980s and sadly the Palestine of today, politics and religion were inextricably interlinked in 1st century Judaea. But for the evangelists, particularly Mark who was probably writing in Rome, it was essential to present Christianity as a faith unthreatening to Roman rule, particularly in the aftermath of the Jewish revolt. So the more sensitive and more dangerous concern of Jewish nationalism was largely written out of the New Testament gospels. Even so from time to time we can still find clues of how Jesus might originally have been perceived and what the disciples genuinely understood about his mission. In the gospel of Luke for example, at his trial Jesus is brought before Pilate as a 'political agitator' and soon after his death one of his followers, Cleopas remarks that 'Our own hope had been that he would be the one to set Israel free.'[45]

But for the gentiles of Paul's communities in Greece and Asia Minor, far removed from the culture and politics of Palestine and perhaps not as antagonised by Roman rule, such hopes had little meaning or relevance to their lives. So not surprisingly Paul's teaching about the resurrection and promised second coming of Jesus and its consequences differed radically from the understanding held by the Jerusalem apostles. Like them he was convinced that they were living

---

[45]Luke 23:14, 24:21. It's also worth noting that in Acts when Gamaliel defends the early apostles, he compares Jesus not with any religious blasphemers but with two political rebels, Theudas and Judas the Galilean. Judas led a revolt against the imposition of tax on Judaea following the census under Quirinius and is usually cited as being the founder of the Zealots, an anti-Roman political / guerrilla movement. Theudas, as we've already noted (see above, footnote 11) led a small rebellion in 45 CE.

in the last days and that Jesus' return from the sky was at hand. Again and again he told his people to prepare themselves for this glorious return which, like 'a thief in the night' might come at any time. In fact he was so persuasive in conveying the certainty and imminence of the end of the world that among some of the believers in the Greek port of Thessalonika, to whom the first of all Paul's surviving letters was sent, a rumour went around that it had already happened.[46] However, for Paul the effects of Jesus' return would have less to do with the liberation of Israel from its foreign and ungodly oppressors and much more to do with the personal salvation of the individual.

This salvation would take the form of a resurrection from the dead or, for those still living, would involve an instantaneous transformation from the perishable flesh to a glorious spiritual body not susceptible to death. The victory over death had come about, Paul believed, because through baptism Christians had secured a mystical union with Jesus, an idea that he conveyed through the metaphor of the body. The bodies of those who believed in Jesus were 'members making up the body of Christ'; as a consequence of this union they shared in his experience of death and resurrection. Indeed for Paul himself this union in death was so intimate he was even able to claim 'I have been crucified with Christ.' Yet far from being a gloomy, death-obsessed fixation, for Paul this association was a positive and life affirming privilege. For if Christian believers endured the suffering of Jesus and shared his death mystically, then they would also be raised with him: 'If in union with Christ we have imitated his death, we shall also imitate him in his resurrection.'[47]

While this idea of dying and rising with a saviour was a doctrine that was unknown in Jewish belief (and almost certainly not held by the Jerusalem apostles), it was a central feature of many of the pagan mystery religions of the age and would have been very familiar to a gentile audience. Like Christianity, the Mysteries (the cults of Eleusis or Attis for example) were personal religions that concerned themselves with the salvation of the individual and which thrived in response to the spiritual yearning of those who found little satisfaction in the

---

[46] 2 Thessalonians (hereafter 2 Thess.) 2:1-3. It seems that those who believed that the end was happening saw no point in bothering to work. Paul had to advise the community that those who refused to work should not be given any food (3:6-12).

[47] 1 Cor. 6:15, 2 Cor. 4:10, Gal. 2:19, Romans 6:5.

existing 'state' or 'public' religions. Then, as now, people were much more concerned with the well-being of their own souls than with the good of the community or the state as a whole (which was the primary interest of the 'official' religions). So while these brotherhoods had no developed systems of theology they did offer their followers a saviour god who answered their personal religious needs, gaining in popularity because they sought to bring their members into closer communion with the gods through an acceptance of their beliefs and ritual.

One of the principal occasions for worship in these religions was the initiation ceremony for those who wished to join any such brotherhood. Often this took the form of a sacramental drama in which the novice was required to enact the dying and rising experience of the cult deity, a rite designed to evoke an ecstatic response so as to bring about a mystical union between the two. This re-enactment and celebration of the god's death and resurrection was believed by its devotees to make them eligible for immortality themselves. In the mysteries of Attis for example and in the related cult of Cybele, the great mother goddess, the novice underwent a symbolic death by being buried literally up to his neck in a trench or grave; from this state he was then acclaimed to have risen to a new life in the faith.[48]

The beliefs behind this ceremony are highlighted by Sir James Frazer's description in *The Golden Bough* of the annual spring festival commemorating the death and resurrection of Attis. Following ceremonies which re-enacted and mourned the death of the god, he recounted how 'when night had fallen, the sorrow of the worshippers was turned to joy. For suddenly a light shone in the darkness: the tomb was opened: the god had risen from the dead; and as the priest touched the lips of the weeping mourners with balm, he softly whispered in their ears the glad tidings of salvation. The resurrection of the god was hailed by his disciples as a promise that they too would issue triumphant from the corruption of the grave'[49]

---

[48]See Angus, *The Mystery Religions and Christianity*, pp 95-97; Klausner, *op cit*, pp 106-107; James, *The Origin of Sacrifice*, p 134. Perhaps the fear experienced as a result of being almost completely buried would have induced an hysterical response which may have been interpreted as an ecstatic manifestation of divine seizure or union.

[49]Frazer, *The Golden Bough*, V, ii, 1. It's interesting to note that Attis was a shepherd (just as in the gospels Jesus is called 'the good shepherd') and was believed to have been born

Could Paul have been influenced by these mystical rituals and beliefs? Scholarly opinion is divided with Christian critics, not surprisingly, reluctant to acknowledge any association. If it's unlikely that Paul consciously set out to develop a new mystery cult, it's almost impossible to suppose that he had no knowledge or awareness of the ceremonies and teachings of these brotherhoods. Tarsus, the place of his birth and upbringing, to where he returned after meeting James and Cephas in Jerusalem, was an important centre for many of the Mysteries, as was Ephesus[50] where Paul believed there was a big opportunity for his mission. We may even venture that some of those attracted to Paul's preaching belonged to some of these movements and that his association with these pagans increased his awareness of their forms of worship.[51]

Nor is it impossible that Paul subconsciously borrowed from their ceremonies and beliefs. When we look at Paul's ideas about baptism for instance, we can begin to see some suspiciously similar traits. In the gospels baptism, as practised by John the Baptist on the banks of the river Jordan, is depicted as a rite of purification and repentance, a symbolic washing away of former sins.[52] Paul's ideas about baptism however were far removed from this simple ceremony and seem much closer to the initiation rites of the mystery cults. Through baptism the believer in Paul's communities now immersed himself in the death and resurrection of Jesus, thereby sharing his experience: 'when we were baptised in Christ Jesus we were baptised in his death . . . when we were baptised we went into the tomb with him and joined him in death, so that as Christ was raised from the dead by the Father's glory, we too might live a new life.'[53]

---

of a virgin. He died by bleeding to death after castrating himself but was commonly depicted as the 'hanged god' (the myth evolved that his body was hung from a pine tree to allow his *blood* to fertilise and so give life to the fields). Paul also referred to Jesus as having been hung from a tree: 'Christ redeemed us from the curse of the Law by being cursed for our sake, since scripture says: *Cursed be everyone who is hanged on a tree*' (Gal. 3:13).

[50]Maccoby, *The Sacred Executioner*, p 114, Kennedy, *St Paul and the Mystery Religions*, p 73.

[51]Kennedy, *op cit*, p 79.

[52]Josephus (*Antiquities* XVIII, v, 2) commented that John's form of baptism was 'for the purification of the body when the soul has been cleansed by righteous conduct' - that is, an outward symbol of repentance that had already been offered.

[53]Romans 6:3-4.

The second aspect of Paul's branching away from the Jewish conception of Jesus was his repudiation of the covenant. As we've noted, it seems the Jerusalem community led by James, and having those who were intimate with Jesus during his lifetime in its ranks, maintained a strict observance of the Torah, hailing it as 'the perfect Law of freedom.' So their intense opposition to Paul's teaching about disregarding the Law (which threatened to bring their movement into disrepute among their Jewish brethren) probably arose not only from their own beliefs as devout Jews, but also from what they knew of Jesus' own response to the Torah. Perhaps they recalled Jesus' words from one of his sermons, perhaps one he preached to crowds gathered on a hillside, urging them to understand that he wholeheartedly endorsed it: 'Do not imagine that I have come to abolish the Law or the Prophets . . . I tell you solemnly . . . the man who infringes even one of the least of these commandments and teaches others to do the same will be considered the least in the kingdom of heaven.'[54]

Why then did Paul take such an adverse stance against the Law and preach such a radical non-observance? The traditional Christian interpretation of course is that in a blinding flash of light, the truth about Jesus came to Paul: that as a new saviour god Jesus himself had established a new covenant through his sacrificial death and hence the Torah was not only redundant but ineffectual.[55] However, if we're disinclined to accept the reality of one to one communications from heaven, it might be more instructive to consider the influence of Paul's youthful religious character and experience on his later thought.

As we've seen, in his early manhood Paul was devout to the point that he seemed to be possessed by what today we might call an intense Puritanism. His spiritual pride in the strictness of his commitment would have been clear to his contemporaries and one senses that in matters of devotion he was something of a perfectionist. But perfectionists are rarely able to achieve that sense of inner peace and satisfaction they so desperately crave. For Paul the frustration would have been made all the worse by his equally intense awareness of himself as a sinner. As a Pharisee (either a genuine one or an aspiring

---

[54]Matthew 5:17. It's possible however that these words were ascribed to Jesus by Matthew as a denunciation of Paul's antinomianism.

[55]Paul taught that 'no one can be justified by keeping the Law' (Gal. 2:16).

one) one of his primary religious concerns would have been a strict application of the Torah to his everyday life.

But while Paul may have regarded the Law as sacred and just and good, it seems also that he felt it to be a terrible burden, one which threatened to overwhelm him and crush him completely. For it was his belief that to keep the Law one had to keep it in its entirety: 'Those who rely on keeping the Law are under a curse' he was later to reflect, 'since scripture says: "Cursed be everyone who does not persevere in observing everything prescribed in the book of the Law."' In the face of such severe absolutism it was inevitable that the perfection he struggled for so earnestly would never be within his reach, that the only consequence of this pursuit would be a sense of failure and despair. Indeed when we come to one of the more autobiographical passages in his letter to the Romans we find that he confesses as much: 'Once when there was no Law, I was alive; but when the commandment came, sin came to life and I died: the commandment was meant to lead me to life but it turned out to mean death to me.'[56]

It meant death to him. If this was the case then the teaching and example of Jesus might well have seemed like a lifeline thrown out to save him from his extreme inner turmoil and spiritual despair. Although it seems clear that Jesus and his original supporters upheld the Law, Paul might well have been aware of Jesus' association with the tax collectors and sinners of Galilee and of the emphasis he placed on repentance rather than on ceremonial observances and formal compliance. Perhaps he too, like so many of those in Galilee, gave in and responded to the persuasion of Jesus and his message of mercy and forgiveness.

Or wanted to. For his headstrong character and spiritual pride may well have prevented him from embracing this attractive new teaching until he was close to the point of collapse. Unable to bear his sense of guilt and failure any longer and under the pressure of some sort of nervous seizure, which to Paul's troubled mind was a manifestation of the risen Jesus, he fused together a belief in the death and subsequent resurrection of Jesus and the idea of an unconditional forgiveness of sins that made adherence to the Law redundant. Keeping the Law was a curse and if the Law was a curse, then one man's undeserved death

---

[56]Gal. 3:10, Romans 7:9-10.

on a cross took away that curse, transferring the burden to the condemned man himself. So powerful and appealing was this idea for Paul that he was even able to develop a quirky, nonsensical interpretation of Scripture - from one of the books of the Torah - to 'prove' that this was so: 'Christ redeemed us from the curse of the Law' he argued, 'by being cursed for our sake, since scripture says: "Cursed be everyone who is hanged on a tree."'[57]

The New Deal: You Gotta Have Faith

Whether this sense of release came to Paul immediately or whether it developed over the years he spent by himself in Arabia is something we can never know. But as time passed he distanced himself ever further from long established Jewish customs and beliefs. During Paul's last visit to Jerusalem for instance, sometime around the year 58, by which time his ideas about Jesus had fully developed, he was berated by James for having abandoned the Jewish religion. According to Acts James alleged that Paul instructed 'all Jews living among the pagans to break away from Moses, authorising them not to circumcise their children or to follow the customary practices.'[58] Of course this divergence from ancestral Judaism must have been due to his innermost religious feelings and convictions; but it might also be explained - or was perhaps was given an additional impetus - by his mission to the gentiles.

Unlike the Jews, the gentiles to whom Paul preached responded positively and enthusiastically to his message of 'Christ crucified' and the redemption his sacrifice offered. We've seen that in part this success might be attributable to Paul's ideas about Jesus as a saviour figure, similar to the gods or semi-divine figures of the mystery religions and to which the pagans would have warmed. But just as

---

[57]Gal. 3:13, quoting Deuteronomy 21:23. Like Matthew, Paul frequently used and interpreted Scripture to fit his own purposes. In fact the concern of Deuteronomy was simply that a hung body should not be left to hang overnight since this was considered to be an affront to Yahweh. We might also consider that many thousands of Jews were crucified by the Romans; if Paul's argument is valid, any one of them could be thought of as removing the curse of the Law.

[58]Acts 21:21. James' speech also revealed that there were 'thousands of Jews' living in Jerusalem who had become believers and who were all 'staunch upholders of the Law', thus indicating clearly that there were two different versions of Christianity.

likely to have won them over were the inherent attractions of Judaism itself: its antiquity, its purity with its unwavering loyalty to one true god, its high moral standards and its Scriptures. Now, according to Paul, the prospect of salvation promised by the highly esteemed Jewish god to his own people could be theirs also. Yet it could be won without their having to fulfil any of the arduous and forbidding customs that were required of the Jews, namely the adoption and practise of the Torah, with its mass of complex ceremonial observances and (for the men) the painful operation of circumcision. All that seemed to be required of them was to believe in the death and restoration to life of a new saviour called Jesus Christ whose life and death had been foretold in ancient scriptures.

The problem for Paul was how to disregard the Torah, the foundation of the Jewish religion for over a thousand years and given to Moses on Mount Sinai from heaven. Paul had two solutions. First, without any scriptural warranty, he affirmed that the Torah had been given to Moses not by Yahweh but by angels and was given only as a temporary measure.[59] That this appeared to go against the grain of Jesus' teachings was neither here nor there. Paul didn't know much about the real Jesus and his reluctance to take instruction from Cephas, James and the other apostles suggests he didn't want to know. So Jesus' endorsement of the Law found no place in his gospel for it was quite irreconcilable with the position that Paul adopted, that 'the Law has come to an end with Christ.'[60]

Next, he introduced a more developed argument that focused around the patriarch Abraham, from whom the Jews traced their descent as the chosen people. Paul stressed that Abraham received Yahweh's promise of a special destiny, to be the father of many nations, solely on account of his faith. Effectively the promise made to Abraham was a 'free gift' for which Abraham did nothing except put his trust in the Lord, to believe him when told he would have a son, despite the fact that both he and his wife were over 90 years old. Not only did this promise precede the Law (which by Paul's reckoning was given 430 years later), but just as crucially for his gospel to the gentiles, it was made even before the establishment of the covenant with

[59]Gal. 3:19, 24.
[60]Romans 10:4.

Abraham, and therefore before the requirement to be circumcised arose. Abraham therefore was justified before he had been circumcised and, according to Paul's logic 'in this way [he] became the ancestor of all uncircumcised believers, so that they too might be considered righteous'.

For Paul therefore, it was Abraham's faith alone which brought about the promise that would justify or save him and his line: 'The promise of inheriting the world was not made to Abraham and his descendants on account of any Law but on account of the righteousness which consists in faith.'[61] Moving on from this, Paul would readily have understood the later story about the intended sacrifice of Isaac as a test of Abraham's faith that brought a renewal of Yahweh's promise.

It is very disturbing to note that the Church today continues to regard this willingness to carry out the ritual murder of a child as an admirable and praiseworthy quality. The *Catechism* points out that the adequate response to its god is faith, and that 'by faith Abraham offered his only son in sacrifice.' Consequently Abraham is hailed as the model of Christian faith.[62] But perhaps after a moment's reflection we shouldn't be too taken aback or horrified by this - after all killing one's son forms the very basis of the Christian religion. For just as Abraham was willing to sacrifice Isaac, so Yahweh - who by now was fast evolving into the new Christian god - was preached as willing to sacrifice his own son as a sign of his commitment to his chosen people.

That this episode had a particular resonance for Paul might be better appreciated in the light of an illumination put forward by the distinguished Jewish scholar Geza Vermes. In his case for understanding Paul's theology, Vermes identified a reinterpretation of the story that was current in the inter-testamental period - roughly from about the 2nd century BCE. In this version Isaac was not a helpless child, but an adult who was aware of his impending fate. Yet instead of resisting, he willingly consents to the sacrifice and runs to the altar, offering his neck to his father. A further Jewish tradition, again familiar to 1st century Judaism, portrayed the event as happening on the date that would eventually become the Passover date. Vermes

---

[61]Romans 4:11, 4:13.

[62]*Catechism,* 142, 144, 145.

suggests that in Jesus' apparently willing sacrifice at the time of Passover, Paul would readily have seen 'the perfect fulfilment of the redeeming self-offering of Isaac' the consequence of which would have been a renewal of the original promise given to Abraham.[63]

So the deal that Paul taught was on offer was salvation in return for faith. We've considered what Christianity understands by salvation; for Paul it was a victory over death and a right to participate in a heavenly afterlife, an understanding probably shared by most Christians today. But what was meant by faith?

For the Jews faith was a matter of loyalty to the covenant; the deal with Yahweh had been struck and their side of the bargain was clear. There was no need to be concerned with intellectual aspects of theology, what they should or should not believe; their concern was simply with keeping the Law of Moses. As Hyam Maccoby puts it, 'All Jews lived within the Covenant, and did not have to worry about anything so basic as salvation. What they had to worry about was to fulfil the conditions of the Covenant, and even this was not a great worry . . . for individual sins could be wiped out by repentance.'[64] But the Christian concept of faith, under the influence of Paul's theology, very quickly became something quite different, revolving around very specific beliefs concerning the increasingly god-like figure of Jesus.

My contention is that Christian faith has three core components without which the religion can't be sustained. First of all it requires a belief in or acceptance of miracles worked by Jesus. Although Paul didn't know of, or perhaps didn't care about the gospel miracles of Jesus, and although there are many Christians today who are disinclined to accept the reality of these same miracle stories (such as Jesus' ability to walk on water, control the weather or re-animate a badly decomposing corpse[65]), the whole of the Christian religion necessarily revolves around one key miracle, generally reckoned the greatest of them all: Jesus' coming back to life on the third day after he had been killed.

So fundamental is the resurrection of Jesus to Christianity that without this key belief, it's difficult to understand how many of its

---

[63]Vermes, *The Changing Faces of Jesus*, pp 84–86.

[64]Maccoby, *The Sacred Executioner*, p 105.

[65]Mark 6:45–51, 4:35–41, John 11:17–44.

other doctrines could be sustained; why, for instance should one believe that Jesus is a god if he didn't really rise from the dead? And if Jesus isn't a god, the whole doctrine of the Trinity immediately collapses. Perhaps the last word about the supreme importance of the resurrection – and hence about the absolute necessity of at least one miracle for Christian faith – should be left to Paul himself: 'If your lips confess that Jesus is Lord', he told the Romans 'and if you believe in your heart that God raised him from the dead, then you will be saved.'[66]

The second requirement of Christian faith is a willingness to submit one's intellect to accept certain propositions that can't be reasonably explained or which are altogether beyond logical coherence. Once again this characteristic would appear to derive not so much from Jesus but from the more esoteric teachings of Paul. In everyday terms the core of Paul's teaching really was nonsense, a fact that he himself acknowledged. Having announced that 'the language of the cross [was] illogical', he insisted that the believer shouldn't look to human reasoning – or 'philosophy' as he called it – to receive (one hesitates to use the word 'understand') his message about Jesus. Faith, he declared 'should not depend on human philosophy but on the power of God.' As a result the only way that the 'hidden wisdom' of his gospel could be grasped was 'spiritually': 'we teach, not in the way that philosophy is taught, but in the way that the Spirit teaches us . . . an unspiritual person . . . sees it all as *nonsense*; it is beyond his understanding because it can only understood by means of the Spirit.'[67] Unfortunately he never spells out precisely how one is to understand something by such a means.

For Paul the most arcane doctrine in the hidden wisdom of his preaching was the redemptive power of Jesus' death, something that philosophically or in terms of reason simply could not be explained. In the centuries after Paul the Church followed his lead and taught that many more of its fundamental truths, such as the doctrines of the Incarnation and the Trinity, were also spiritual or revealed truths and as such, were only accessible through faith. These propositions or beliefs became known as 'mysteries' (a term that Paul himself used frequently

[66]Romans 10:9.
[67]1 Cor. 1:17 – 2:14, my italics.

in his letters) or 'mysteries of faith'. As with Paul's teaching about the illogical language of the cross and the atoning properties of Jesus' death, when subjected to reason these mysteries, the essential 'truths' of the Christian faith, either make no sense at all or have nothing to substantiate their extravagant claims. The only way that the Church can maintain that its core beliefs are 'true' is to teach that they must be believed spiritually or through faith. Reason, common sense and basic human intellect must therefore be cast aside for the sake of dogmatic, irrational or meaningless propositions.

Understanding 'by means of the Spirit' would therefore seem to consist of accepting Paul's esoteric ideas wholeheartedly, without thinking about them and happily jettisoning one's rational objections. So through its wide use of mystery the Church is able to secure from its members the response it seeks and prizes most of all: a blind or unquestioning acceptance of its teachings which believers don't even want to subject to critical or reasonable scrutiny. As Celsus perceived at a very early stage, the guiding maxim of Christianity was 'just believe'; the concept of mystery that promoted and encouraged this response soon became and indeed remains a core component of Christian faith.

An acceptance of mystery goes hand in hand with the third component, a submission to the Church's authority. From the very earliest days of the Church, the importance of *obedience* was repeatedly drilled into the first Christians. In his letters Paul insisted that Christians should always obey the existing state authorities: 'You must all obey the governing authorities. Since all government comes from God . . . anyone who resists authority is rebelling against God's decision, and such an act is bound to be punished'[68] In part this insistence to conform with the civil authorities may have been made so as not to give the Romans any excuse to persecute the new faith; later it would prove to be very helpful in cementing the political union between Church and state. Those who caused trouble for or protested

---

[68]Romans 13:1-2. Paul even went so far as to say that civil authorities 'are there to serve God: they carry out God's revenge by punishing wrongdoers.' Unfortunately this would seem to suggest that Jesus was justly condemned. Other New Testament writers took a similar line. The author of the second letter of Peter urged that 'For the sake of the Lord, accept the authority of every social institution: the emperor as the supreme authority . . . God wants you to be good citizens' (2 Peter 2:13-15).

against either ecclesiastical or secular authorities were made to understand that their dissent was a sin as well as a civil offence and that even if they got away with it in this life, they would always have to answer for it in the next.

But it seems also that Paul had something of the authoritarian in him. He cherished the 'virtue' of compliance and the importance he attached to this ideal soon came to form part of the very fabric of the new religion. As we've seen, Paul was frequently having to defend his position from the interference (as he saw it) of the Jerusalem apostles. It was absolutely essential for him therefore to assert and enforce his own authority to maintain the loyalty of his communities. The principal means of doing this was to control what his converts should and should not believe. Only *his* gospel and what he proclaimed would do: 'the gospel will save you', he insisted 'only if you keep believing *exactly what I preached* to you - believing anything else will not lead to anything.'[69]

So a standard or orthodoxy of precisely what to believe became fundamental to Christianity from a very early stage. Since only the authorised (i.e. Paul's) version of the truth about Jesus would save souls and since Christianity had a duty, apparently handed down by Jesus, to disseminate its message of salvation to the whole world,[70] any deviation from this orthodoxy was wrong and had to be suppressed. Paul made his position clear in a chilling passage which introduced the concept of *thoughtcrime* to Christianity: 'every thought is our prisoner, captured to be brought into obedience to Christ. Once you have given your complete obedience, we are prepared to punish any disobedience', while anyone deviating in the teaching of *his* truth (and subsequently the Church's truth) was 'to be condemned.'[71] As history shows, with the systematic and unspeakably violent persecution, torture and murder of dissidents over the course of many centuries, these words have not been taken lightly.

In much the same way Paul felt obliged to stamp his controlling authority on his converts in matters of morals and personal conduct.

---

[69] 1 Cor. 15:2, my italics.

[70] Matthew 28:18-19: 'All authority in heaven and earth has been given to me. Go, therefore, make disciples of all the nations.'

[71] 2 Cor. 10:5-6. Thoughtcrime in Christianity is better known as *heresy*.

Because he taught his followers that they had been saved and had gained the promise of an eternal life simply by believing that Jesus had risen from the dead, some of them came to believe that their behaviour, whether good or bad, made no difference to their happy prospects when the end of the world arrived, prospects, according to their teacher, that were guaranteed. Now Paul may have insisted that through baptism and faith they had been released from the slavery of sin; but with human nature as it is and not always predictable, it appears many of them conducted themselves with a rather different understanding of this new-found freedom.

So we find that Paul was often outraged by the immoral and indecent behaviour of some members of his communities. In Corinth for example, the conduct of some Christians was so scandalous that according to Paul it would have shocked even the ungodly pagans, while in Galatia those who indulged in 'fornication, gross indecency and sexual irresponsibility . . . drunkenness, orgies and similar things'[72] had to be warned that they would never inherit the kingdom if they carried on with this unseemly behaviour, whether they believed or not. Very quickly Paul appreciated that some sort of moral authority had to be introduced to control indecency and that adherence to certain standards had to be an integral part of the faith. Christians may have been released from the Torah that Paul believed had enslaved the Jews; but they soon became subject to the 'law of Christ' which ultimately was to evolve into the code of canon law, an authority which continues to govern the Church today and to whose innumerable precepts the faithful are equally enslaved.

So let's take stock of what we've discovered so far about the fundamentals of Christianity. Since we're told that Jesus came to the earth 'for our salvation' we can fairly infer that the main point of believing in him and hence the main point of being a Christian is to be saved after death. The whole of humanity has been condemned by the Christian god because of the initial disobedience of Adam and Eve. But, after a series of preparatory deals arranged with the Jewish people or their forefathers, the Christian god was willing to offer a full reprieve to mankind by sending his son, Jesus to establish a new covenant. Through this deal the prospect of being saved from

---

[72]Gal. 5:19-22.

punishment after death was offered, a prospect brought into play and paid for by the free and willing sacrifice made by Jesus on a Roman cross.

This then is the Church's line. But if we read the New Testament critically and carefully we can see that not much of this survives close scrutiny. We can tell that after his death Jesus' closest disciples and original followers, those who knew him best, did not themselves preach to their fellow Jews anything about a new covenant. There are important clues in Acts to suggest that quite to the contrary they remained loyal to the existing covenant, the Torah and that they continued to practise traditional Jewish forms of worship revolving around the Temple. In doing so they were undoubtedly following their master's lead. The concept of a new covenant established by Jesus must therefore have originated with Paul; if it were otherwise, why don't we see Peter proclaiming this understanding at the feast of Pentecost when supposedly he had just been inspired by the tongues of fire of the Holy Spirit? And why did Paul claim that the central ideas of his gospel, ideas about Jesus as a new saviour god, were revealed to him directly and not through any human agency?

We have only Paul's word to substantiate the understanding that he received such intelligence through a divine revelation. Naturally Paul fiercely defended his claim that Jesus had truly appeared to him, for the whole of his authority was completely dependent on this event (and therefore he could never admit to it being a subjective experience or a hallucination).

But in the possibility of a nervous collapse, precipitated by an ecstatic fit or seizure, there is a far more plausible - and hence more likely explanation for this undeniably powerful experience. Moreover, there is a strong suggestion from Paul's own words that he was inclined to fabricate or exaggerate the incidence of revelations in his life (when summoned to Jerusalem by James to explain himself for instance, he later claimed it was a revelation that inspired him to go, presumably to convey to his supporters that he wasn't subordinate to James' authority). As a consequence of these dreams and visions, over the next two decades Paul formulated a new theology which had at its heart the doctrine of faith in Christ which had little to do with the actual person of Jesus himself. And according to Paul this was now the only means by which one might be saved from 'the anger of God'.

What faith in Jesus consists of is never precisely and fully articulated by Paul; but we can argue that through faith Christians are required to accept the reality of miracles worked by Jesus, to submit their reason and intellect to unreasonable propositions called 'mysteries' by the Church and to accept its authority (which it claims derives from Jesus himself) in terms of the propositions one must believe and the requirements of personal conduct. To distil this further to the formulation used by Dostoevski's Grand Inquisitor, we may venture that Christian faith revolves around *miracle, mystery, authority*, the three forces according to the terrifying old tyrant that can conquer and forever hold captive the minds of the weak. These then are the three main themes that I shall be considering in my evaluation of Christianity.

4

Miracle

I believe in miracles, where're you from, you sexy thing?
I believe in miracles since you came along, you sexy thing.
How did you know I needed you so badly?
How did you know I'd give my heart so gladly? [1]

If the writers of some of the less well-known gospels are to be believed, Jesus in his childhood was just as remarkable as he was in his adult life. According to the Infancy Gospel of Thomas as a youngster Jesus was able to amaze and terrify all those who encountered him. Like his dad (the heavenly one that is) he could take soft clay and mould it into living creatures, in one instance turning mud into twelve sparrows just by clapping his hands. Earlier, aged just three he took a dried, salted fish and ordered it to breath again, whereupon it was restored to life. 'Reject the salt you have' Jesus tells the lucky fish, 'and go into the water.'[2]

Playful and amusing as these pranks were, it wasn't all harmless party tricks for the infant deity. Two years later, aged five, he causes another child to shrivel up like a withered tree for messing up the puddles of water he was playing with, calling him an 'insolent, godless ignoramus.' Immediately afterwards, still in a sulk, he tells a boy who accidentally bumped into him that he won't go any further, whereupon the unfortunate child instantly collapses and dies. Like the Devil, whom Jesus later described in the Fourth Gospel, it seems as if 'he was a murderer from the start.'[3] When the distraught parents confront Jesus for having killed their child, unfortunately they find no comfort in the Lord. In fact their anguish is only made worse when he

---

[1] Hot Chocolate, *You Sexy Thing*.

[2] Infancy Gospel of Thomas, 2 (Greek A text), 1 (Latin text), Elliott, *op cit*, pp 67-83.

[3] John 8:44.

curses them and then causes them to go blind. Eventually things get so bad that his exasperated father (this time the earthly one) has to tell Mary that for the good of the community the devil-child Jesus can't be allowed out of the house, 'for all those who provoke him die.'[4]

In another infancy gospel Jesus' magical abilities are matched only by his enmity and sheer nastiness; indignant when some children run away (understandably they don't want to play with him), he approaches the house where they've hidden and asks some women if they know where they are. The women have obviously wisened up to the fact that Jesus is danger-kid and pretend they don't know. When he asks who is in the archway, they tell him that it's just some goats, whereupon the mischievous young Lord bids the children 'Come out O goats to your shepherd.' To the women's horror the little boys have all been turned into goats and are only restored to their human form after the women have grovelled and begged him sufficiently.[5]

This is all a world away from the more familiar 'wondrous childhood' in which Jesus, in the words of an overly sentimental Christmas carol, is presented as a role model for children who 'should be mild, obedient, as good as he.' Of course one suspects that these magical adventures were the stuff of the adult fantasy channel of antiquity, as it were, rather than genuinely biographical material; and if they were in the Bible only a complete imbecile would believe that they had really happened.

But this begs the question – why would a Christian today reject these clearly legendary, improbable miracles of Jesus' childhood yet accept that as a man he could walk on water and could rustle up enough food out of thin air to feed 5,000 people? Are these later supernatural tricks that we're more familiar with somehow more credible than the bizarre and really quite frightening childhood miracles? Was Jesus only capable of miracles in his adult life, and only benevolent ones at that? Or could it be that since these childhood miracles aren't in the Bible, they're not considered to be true, implying that those which are in the New Testament gospels actually happened simply because the Church says so? Or might a believer today explain

---

[4]Infancy Gospel of Thomas, 3, 4, 14 (Greek A text).

[5]The Arabic Infancy Gospel 40, Elliott, *op cit*, pp 100-107. This is the only story in the whole of Christian writing that has made me laugh. However, I doubt it was intended to be funny so it doesn't count as evidence of humour in Christianity.

that she didn't really believe in the New Testament miracles but nevertheless was still willing to accept Jesus as a god?

This last possible response leads us to consider the place and significance of Jesus' miracles in the Christian faith today, which until the Enlightenment some 300 years ago, were regarded as one of the surest indications of its truth. In our own times however, like the polished bones of ancient saints, they're more likely to be regarded as embarrassing relics of a superstitious, bygone age. So are they still meaningful and relevant for Christianity today? Does the Church still teach that they actually occurred?

The answer is rather backwards looking. The Church continues to endorse miracles, proclaiming that 'the miracles of Christ and his saints . . . are the most certain signs of Divine revelation' and that 'his deeds, miracles and words all revealed that in him the whole fullness of deity dwells bodily.'[6] In other words, Jesus' miracles prove that he is a god; and presumably since he's a god, we can feel confident that they really did happen. There's a bit of circular reasoning going on here; but let's not get bogged down with minor detail, because no matter how absurd or circular the argument, the Church has to persist doggedly in its belief that Jesus really did work the most stupendous miracles.

For miracles in Christianity simply aren't dispensable because the entire religion is ultimately based on a miracle, the big mother of all miracles that is, which usually we know as the resurrection. If a man can come back to life after having been dead for nearly two days, why shouldn't he be able to walk on water? Why shouldn't he be able to raise other people (or fish) from the dead or be able to turn water into wine or even children into goats if the fancy so possessed him? If you can believe that Jesus returned from the dead then there's absolutely no reason not to believe almost anything about him, the crazier and more improbable it is in fact, the better.[7]

The flip-side of this however is if you're disinclined to accept the reality of Jesus' miracles, why believe that he came back from the

---

[6]*Catechism*, 156, 515.

[7]The argument of some Christian apologists seemed to be that nobody would be so stupid as to make up a miracle that was so incredibly amazing it wouldn't be believed. Hence such miracles had to be true. The paradox is best (and most absurdly) expressed by the formulation of the 2nd century Church father, Tertullian about the resurrection of Jesus: 'Because it is impossible, it must be true.'

dead? Why believe in this one miracle and no other? It follows then that if it's unlikely that any of the gospel miracles really occurred or if they can be understood in non-miraculous terms, then it's reasonable to question whether the miracle of the resurrection itself ever took place; and once this has gone, the validity of much of the Christian religion goes with it.

Signs Are Taken For Wonders. We Would See A Sign !

Immediately after his baptism, the synoptic gospels record that Jesus stayed in the desert for 40 days where he was tempted by the Devil. In Matthew Jesus is challenged to perform miracles - such as turning stones into loaves of bread and throwing himself off the parapet of the Temple to see if he would be saved from death - to prove that he was the big guvnor's son. But Jesus was adamant that no miraculous signs would be given to confirm his status; and making sharp use of the authority of Scripture he reminds the arch-fiend that 'You must not put the Lord your God to the test.'

Mark doesn't contain the detail of the temptation, but about halfway through his gospel, the Pharisees (depicted almost as devils in another form) try to test him in the same way, asking for a heavenly sign. Naturally Jesus tells them that no sign will be given. In Matthew this response is sharper, almost vicious when Jesus condemns his entire generation as 'evil' for having the temerity to question him and ask for such a sign. So it's difficult to reconcile this with what is immediately striking in Mark's opening pages, the sheer number and impact of miracles suggesting that Jesus was only too ready to oblige. It is harder still to reconcile his reluctance to give signs with the Fourth Gospel miracles which were consciously performed as signs and through which, we are told, 'he let his glory be seen'[8]

Mark begins his gospel with a brief account of Jesus' baptism and then plunges into an extended sequence of miracles with most of the early chapters devoted to them. Jesus is soon casting out devils and unclean spirits and healing the sick including a leper, a paralytic and many others suffering from all sorts of unspecified diseases. As if this were not enough to establish his credentials, he demonstrates his power

---

[8]Matthew 4:7 (quoting Deuteronomy 6:13); John 2:12.

over the forces of nature, calming both the wind and the sea. Even better, for no apparent reason except to show off, he later walks across the sea. Matthew and Luke add in even more instances of miracle cures. And in the Fourth Gospel there may be fewer examples of healings, but it's here that we find the most sensational miracles of all, including the raising of Lazarus who had been dead for four days. Take away miracles then and you remove a very significant part of the gospels.

So our gospel Jesus is evidently a man of miracles; but as the insights of the form critics suggest, this probably tells us more about the gospel writers and their original audiences than it does about the true, historical Jesus. Clearly it was a time of magic and miracle workers, when people genuinely believed in such things just as today we might wholeheartedly believe in 'miracles of technology' or in the possibility of miraculous cures brought about by a wonder drug or gene therapy. People then believed in spells and the practise of magic and some possessed valuable books to guide them in their arts. In The Acts of the Apostles (where this detail is recorded) we also encounter a small number of figures associated with sorcery. Naturally all of them are disreputable, but we get an insight into how commonplace and accepted such figures and their practices were in Biblical times.

So we have two magicians, Simon who 'practised magic arts in the town and astounded the Samaritan people'; and a Jewish magician in Cyprus called Bar-jesus. Of course as soon as the apostles turn up everyone is won over to the Christian persuasion, including even Simon himself who is astonished at the still greater powers that the name of Jesus commands. But when Paul meets Bar-jesus it is a much darker encounter resulting in Paul cursing him as the 'son of the devil'[9] and then blinding him in the name of the Lord for being an enemy of all true religion. Interestingly the accusation of sorcery was a charge made against Jesus himself. His opponents, the Pharisees believed that he was possessed by Beelzebub, the prince of devils. And as we've noted, Celsus alleged that having learnt sorcery in Egypt, Jesus was able to perform miracles only through the practise of this dark magic.[10]

---

[9] Acts 19:18, 8:9-11, 13:6-12.

[10] Origen, *op cit,* I:28: 'because he was poor he hired himself out as a workman in Egypt and there he tried his hand at certain magical powers . . . he returned full of conceit because of these powers.'

Sorcery was regarded as a black art, often to be feared and the idea of Jesus as a magician would've been firmly rejected by early Christians. But if Jesus was regarded more as 'a doer of wonderful works',[11] as he is described by Josephus, it's clear that he wasn't the only miracle worker known to the age. Apollonius of Tyana, a Greek sage who lived slightly later than Jesus, but still in the 1st century, was credited with numerous miracles including resurrecting a young woman from the dead. And the emperor Vespasian, according to Tacitus was also able to effect miraculous healings.[12]

Moreover in Jewish literature, as we shall see, there was a tradition of holy men known for their ability to heal and perform other marvellous works. None of these however could touch Jesus when it came to miracles in terms of the number, the variety and the sheer astonishment they are recorded as having caused. In this respect Jesus was in a league of his own, excelling at all types of miracles. These included exorcisms of unclean spirits, healings of physical symptoms, resuscitations from the dead and powers over the forces or laws of nature.

The Exorcist

For most of us exorcism is little more than superstitious nonsense which barely has any meaningful existence today outside the realm of Hollywood. It may seem redundant even to consider the matter, so foreign is it to our general experience. So it comes as something of a shock to learn that for the Church both the principle and the practice of exorcism, an invocation made in Jesus' name for protection against 'the power of the Evil One . . . the expulsion of demons or . . . the liberation from demonic possession', continues to be taken seriously. Like it or not, Satan isn't some vague, figurative entity which epitomises the concept of evil, but is a real, living being, continually on the prowl and from whose dominion all Christians need to be protected. In its exegesis on the final petition of the Lord's prayer, 'deliver us from evil' the *Catechism* affirms that 'in this petition, evil is

---

[11]Josephus, *op cit*, XVIII, iii, 3.

[12]Philostratus, *The Life of Apollonius of Tyana* 5:45; Tacitus, *The Histories*, IV, 81. Like Jesus, Vespasian apparently restored the sight of a blind man with his spittle and healed a man with withered hands.

114

not an abstraction, but refers to a person, Satan, the evil one, the angel who opposes God.'[13] And Church ritual to 'deliver' Christians from Satan's grip, far from being extremely rare, is very much an everyday occurrence.

Becoming a Christian today, as always, involves undergoing the rite of baptism. Believers usually regard baptism as a sacrament to welcome a new person, usually an infant into the Church. Non-believers are more inclined to see it merely as a naming ceremony. But for the Church it's a ceremony not only of initiation but also of exorcism. 'Since Baptism signifies liberation from sin and from its instigator the devil', it declares, 'one or more exorcisms are pronounced over the candidate . . . [who] explicitly renounces Satan'. Admittedly this refers to adult baptism but alarmingly, even with infant baptism this understanding is part of the ceremony: 'exorcism is performed at the celebration of baptism' because 'children also have need . . . to be freed from the power of darkness'.[14] In other words your new-born needs to be protected from the evil designs of Satan or, even worse, your baby has demons.

Elsewhere, in a publication more recent than the *Catechism*, the Church has reaffirmed these beliefs even more emphatically. The Devil, it has proclaimed 'goes round like a roaring lion looking for souls to devour.' Presumably it was the terrifying reality of this scenario that led the Vatican to publish its new manual for exorcism *De Exorcismis et Supplicationibus Quibusdam* in January 1999 in which this comparison of Satan with a hungry lion can be found.[15] Prepared under the supervision of a sort of Ghostbuster General, Cardinal Jorge Arturo Medina Estevez (whose name alone, one feels, is chilling enough to smoke out the hardest of the hardcore), the manual is written entirely in Latin and is therefore somewhat inaccessible to just about anyone outside of Club Vat. Perhaps that was the intention, for exorcism isn't intended to be a spectator sport as *De Exorcismis* makes clear, forbidding any outside or media presence during a gloves-off fight with the Devil.

Indeed the Church seems to be strangely reticent about the whole

---

[13]*Catechism*, 1673, 2851.

[14]*Ibid*, 1237, 1250.

[15]*The Guardian*, 27 January 1999.

subject of exorcism. In his biography of the Devil, Peter Stanford points out that it is 'distinctly reluctant' even to reveal the name of the priest in each diocese who can perform exorcisms and that while the present Pope, John Paul II has himself conducted such a ritual, no details were ever made available.[16] Similarly the *Catechism* isn't minded to promote this potentially embarrassing subject having only one paragraph on the matter which, apart from the distressing news about baptism, focuses on the importance of distinguishing illness, psychological or otherwise from the 'presence of the Evil One'.

Today we may be inclined to dismiss claims about 'the Evil One', but in Jesus' day these were taken extremely seriously. The world was filled with demons and devils and the task of the exorcist, to expel these unclean spirits from those they possessed, was very much a real one, widely and fervently believed in. Geza Vermes points out that 'in inter-testamental Judaism expelling demons was common practice', that the Pharisees were known for such practices[17] and that even the secular historian Josephus took the practice of exorcism seriously enough to record that the Jews were known for their expertise in such matters.

For Jesus too exorcism was a vital practice, its significance reinforced by the widespread belief that the establishment of the messianic kingdom would be preceded by a final war against Satan and the forces of evil.[18] The fight against these devils, whose existence was manifested in the forms of mental disturbances and illnesses, therefore heralded the coming of the kingdom and was a sign of its imminence. Indeed, so momentous was this battle that the first of Jesus' miraculous works in the synoptic gospels is not a healing but the casting out of an unclean spirit from a man in the synagogue at Capernaum.

Following on from this, we learn that Jesus travelled throughout Galilee to 'cast out many devils' and Mark records three further specific exorcisms including perhaps the best known of all, that of the Gerasene demoniac. This story tells of a man unfortunate enough to be possessed by so many devils of such power that when Jesus forced them out, they were able to bargain with him to be allowed to possess a herd of

---

[16]Stanford, *The Devil: A Biography*, p 214.

[17]Vermes, *op cit*, p 160. See for example Matthew 12:27.

[18]Nineham, *op cit*, pp 44–45.

2,000 pigs. Perhaps the moral of the story is if you're an evil spirit don't try to cut a deal with the saviour; immediately afterwards the pigs themselves become hysterical and plunge off a cliff into the sea where they drown. The devils, it is presumed, lose their new home and are themselves destroyed. So how should we regard these startling affairs? Since exorcism was a widespread custom and the gospels repeatedly insist that Jesus was very preoccupied with devils (so much so that his opponents thought that he was possessed by one), we can venture that the real Jesus was a genuine exorcist and that actual incidents underlie these gospel stories.

But this is not to say that the devils themselves truly existed, despite the elaborate way in which these stories have been developed to convince us they did. For if we read carefully we can see that legendary details have been written in to enhance Jesus' status, to persuade us that he was much more astonishing than he really was. A close scrutiny also reveals that the devils existed not so much in real life but merely in the minds of the gospel characters and writers. Our suspicions are first aroused by the devils' awareness of Jesus' true identity: 'I know who you are: the Holy One of God' shouts the first devil driven out by Jesus, while the Gerasene demoniac asks him 'What do you want with me Jesus, son of the Most High God?' Elsewhere we're told whenever he encountered devils 'he would not allow them to speak, because they knew who he was.'[19]

So how do they know who Jesus is? We've seen that Jesus' secret messianic identity is a very prominent theme in Mark's gospel and initially his messiahship wasn't even known by his disciples let alone by the people. But according to the exorcism stories, long before anyone (including the disciples) knew about it, the devils recognised him as 'son of the Most High God.' Anxious to protect his true identity, Jesus forbade them to talk about it, just as later he ordered Peter not to reveal it to anyone.

Now there's only a limited number of possibilities to explain exactly how this identity is known by the devils. Either the afflicted people really were possessed by devils which had a supernatural insight not shared by humans; or the possessed were informed beforehand by the crowd who Jesus was; or finally these comments about his identity

---

[19]Mark 1:25, 5:7, 1:34.

were never really uttered but are later literary interpolations. We can discount the second possibility since (according to Mark) Jesus didn't reveal his status to the disciples until much later, so it's extremely unlikely that he would've told any other individual earlier than this. Furthermore, it's not plausible to suppose that the crowds would then have informed the tormented demoniacs; as the case of the Gerasene demoniac suggests, they were probably far too disturbed to be capable of understanding such news.

Now if we allow the first possibility, that the devils are genuine, invisible spirits, roaming the earth like hungry felines looking for a human body or soul to take over, to be the true explanation, then we have to accept that the symptoms the afflicted people show are not symptoms of any mental derangement or illness but are the direct consequence of having one's body and soul taken over by a devil.

However, in a later exorcism story a man pleads with Jesus to cast out a very powerful devil from his son. The manifestations of this devil are vividly described in particular detail: 'when it takes hold of him it throws him to the ground, and he foams at the mouth and grinds his teeth and goes rigid', the desperate father explains to Jesus. Then, after Jesus commands the spirit to leave the boy, it throws him into 'violent convulsions . . . and the boy lay there so like a corpse that most of them said "He is dead."'[20]

From this graphic description we can see that the boy is not possessed by demons, devils or evil spirits at all, but in all probability is an epileptic suffering from an attack.[21] Most commentators agree that this is the case and usually refer to the child as 'the epileptic boy'. If this assumption is correct, it appears that in this instance possession by devils for Jesus and his contemporaries, however earnestly believed in, was nothing more than an explanation for a medical condition they simply couldn't understand and whose alarming symptoms greatly disturbed or frightened them. As Vermes puts it succinctly, 'in the

---

[20]Mark 9:18, 20.

[21]One commentator, Edwin Yamuchi points out that the symptoms 'correspond with the following stages of epilepsy: 1) aura or premonitory stage, 2) unconsciousness, 3) tonic stage of muscular rigidity, 4) clonic stage of muscular jerking, 5) flaccid stage of unconsciousness, and 6) recovery.' *Magic or Miracle? Diseases, Demons and Exorcisms*, p 129 from *Gospel Perspectives: The Miracles of Jesus*, ed Wenham / Bloomberg. See also *Jerome*, 41:59: 'the 'speechless spirit' [which] seizes the boy is usually explained as an epileptic seizure.'

popular belief of Jews living in the age of Jesus, devils were acknowledged as the cause of all spiritual and bodily evil.'[22] It's often said that ignorance and superstition go hand in hand and the reaction of Jesus and the crowd to this incident is a clear example of this principle. In this instance then it seems very unlikely that the supposed devils had any reality outside of the minds which conceived them and this therefore places considerable doubt on the genuine existence of the devils in earlier exorcisms.

Now if we've discounted the first two possibilities, this means that the only remaining explanation is that the devils' apparent knowledge of Jesus' identity wasn't historical but was a detail added to the story much later and retained by the evangelists, by Mark in particular. But what would have been his motive for doing so? If Mark was trying to keep Jesus' identity as the messiah a secret, why draw attention to it?

The answer lies in understanding that in this respect at least, Mark was an accomplished story-teller. First of all, it begins to build up a certain dramatic tension: in the days of the infant Church it would have been very satisfying for the first audiences (those hearing or reading the gospel) to start to figure out for themselves that Jesus is the messiah. With evil spirits recognising and paying reluctant homage to Jesus, it's clearly signalled that he is an extraordinary figure, something the audience can appreciate long before any of the characters in the narrative. It's called dramatic irony.

A similar ploy to convey information is often found in storytelling of our own times, especially in Hollywood supernatural films. In this genre generally it's an animal - usually the family pet dog - that can detect a supernatural or evil presence long before the main characters who never seem to catch on until they're in great danger.[23] This is a signal to the audience (which understands and accepts the convention that animals are regarded as more sensitive to spiritual presences than humans) that something nasty or creepy is about to happen, increasing the tension and sense of dread. It's the same with the gospels except that a benign presence is being announced, thus arousing the audience's sense of expectation.

---

[22]Vermes, *op cit*, p 232.

[23]Perhaps the best example of this is the scene from *The Omen* in which the devil-child, Damien is taken to visit the safari park.

Secondly, in this context, knowledge of an opponent's name was of great importance and was believed to give one power over an adversary.[24] This too is a convention that continues in popular storytelling today: in the film *Die Hard* for instance Bruce Willis' character, the hero John Mclane seems to flummox his terrorist opponents when he reveals that he knows the name of their leader, Hans as well as those of several of his bonehead thugs. For the Jews names were almost weapons in themselves: the name of their god, Yahweh was so powerful and held in such awe that they were forbidden to and dared not utter the word. And when Jesus teaches his followers to pray, the first entreaty is that their god's *name* should be revered.[25]

So it would appear that by identifying and naming Jesus the devils were trying to obtain some advantage over him so as to defend themselves; and in doing so revealed and acknowledged a messianic power not yet appreciated by the crowds. So, given that the naming of opponents was a standard literary feature of exorcism stories and the understanding that devil possession was probably a medical or neurotic affliction, it's much more likely that the devils' insight enabling them to identify Jesus came from the mind of the writer (or his sources). And if this is so, how can we be sure - or even feel confident - that the devils had a real and objective existence outside of the minds of the gospel writers and characters?

In the best known story of Jesus' exorcisms, that of the Gerasene demoniac, there may well have been a basic historical source underlying the story, but its structure and detail betray the elaboration of the writer or his source. This encounter takes place in gentile territory, a prerequisite for the presence of the pigs and so Mark has Jesus crossing the lake to the country of the Gerasenes. As soon as he steps ashore he is accosted by the rabid, howling man who was so demented that he ran around naked and had to be restrained with chains; but not even these chains were enough to prevent him from breaking free and injuring himself with stones. These vivid and distressing details may point to an historical origin but it doesn't take long for the literary conventions to take over.

---

[24]Nineham, *op cit*, pp 75-76; Bultmann, *op cit*, p 232.

[25]Matthew 6:10: 'Our father in heaven, may your name be held holy.'

This is signalled first of all by the emphasis on where the encounter took place, near some tombs (mentioned three times) considered then, as now as a spooky place where evil spirits were likely to lurk and hang out. Then, as Bultmann observed in his analysis of this story, the rest of the narrative is constructed according to the form typical for a confrontation between an exorcist and the demons he is about to expel: the initial meeting, followed by a description of the dangerous nature of the derangement, the recognition of the exorcist by the demons, the exorcism itself and finally a demonstration of the departure of the demons.[26]

It's the devils' departure of course, via the herd of pigs that has made this story so memorable and which presents the real challenge to our credulity. The Rationalists of Strauss' day attributed this bizarre repercussion to the supposed howlings of the man during the actual exorcism which, frightening the pigs, caused them to stampede over the cliff. But given the geographical and topographical inaccuracies (the town Gerasa is some 30 miles south east of the Sea of Galilee which itself is not noted for its high cliffs[27]) it's more likely that the detail concerning the pigs is a legendary addition written in to reflect the beliefs of the time.

This detail would actually serve two main purposes. First of all the whole point of the story is to confirm the power of Jesus over even the most powerful of devils. We already know from the man's frenzied behaviour that these devils are particularly virulent. That they can take over an entire herd of pigs and cause them to go wild confirms this strength and thereby signals the still greater power and victory of Jesus, just as in the previous story he had mastery over the storm at sea.

Secondly, it was a recognised feature of exorcisms that there should be some sign that the demon really had departed from the possessed man. A number of commentators cite the story in Josephus' *Antiquities of the Jews* of how a certain exorcist, Eleazar, requiring the expelled demon to prove that it had departed, commanded it to knock over a cup of water placed some distance away.[28] Thus the detail that the

---

[26]Bultmann, *op cit*, p 210.

[27]Nineham (*op cit*, p 153) ventures that the small town of Kersa may be the true location of this incident. He notes however that 'it has no cliffs overhanging the lake.'

[28]Vermes, *op cit*, p 235, Bultmann, *op cit*, p 231, both citing Josephus, *op cit* VIII, ii, 5.

devils went into the pigs was a sign that they had yielded to the irresistible power of Jesus. That they should go into other living creatures is best explained by Jesus' own words on the matter: 'when an unclean spirit goes out of a man it wanders through waterless country looking for a place to rest, and cannot find one. Then it says, "I will return to the home I came from."'[29] If this was a prevailing belief about the domestic habits of devils, then clearly the earliest traditions would hardly have wanted such an impressive victory over Satan to be a temporary one. So to ensure that the devils cannot return to the same man and that there is no re-match, they have to be manifestly housed elsewhere or, even better, destroyed.

As to why pigs happened to be the unfortunate creature of choice, perhaps it was deemed fitting that unclean spirits should enter into unclean animals. But it's also worth considering the observation of Edwin Yamuchi who notes that in the treatment of demonic illnesses in Mesopotamia 'a common magical praxis was to place a clay figure or an animal, such as a suckling pig or kid, upon the patient in order to transfer the illness to the substitute, which was then destroyed.'[30] Of course this belief originated hundreds of years before Jesus' time; could it have survived over such as long period? Perhaps it had continued down to his time in much the same way that people today often exclaim 'bless you' after a person has sneezed because hundreds of years ago a sneeze was believed to be the first sign of having caught the plague?

Curing All Kinds Of Diseases And Sickness

Although Mark distinguishes between exorcism and healing, recording that people 'brought to him all who were sick and those who were possessed by devils', there was often a fine dividing line between the two. On healing Simon's mother-in-law from a fever for example, we're told that 'the fever left her', which recalls the language used to report the departure of a devil. In Luke the same incident has a

---

[29]Matthew 12:43-44.

[30]Yamuchi *op cit*, p 103. He goes on to point out (p 118) that 'The development of demonology in the later period of the Old Testament is often attributed to Iranian influences' and that 'the conquest of Mesopotamia in 539 BCE by Cyrus certainly did expose the Jewish exiles to Iranian culture.'

closer affinity: here Jesus specifically 'rebuked the fever' just as in the exorcism of the epileptic boy he 'rebuked the unclean spirit.' If devils were believed to be responsible for torments and mental disturbances, physical illnesses were often regarded by the Jews as divinely ordained punishments for one's sins. So it wouldn't have been considered offensive or absurd for the disciples, after encountering a blind man, to ask Jesus 'Rabbi, who sinned, this man or his parents for him to have been born blind ?'[31]

Likewise the earliest readers of Acts were more likely to have been impressed than shocked to note that a man and his wife collapse and die after lying to the Holy Spirit; instead of outrage we learn that this sinister incident 'made a profound impression on the whole Church.' And in one of Paul's letters the connection is more or less unequivocal when, after a sharp reproach for their liturgical failings, he tells the Corinthians: 'that is why many of you are weak and ill and some of you have died. If only we recollected ourselves, we should not be punished like that. But when the Lord does punish us like that, it is to correct us.'[32]

It is a matter of great regret that the Church has not abandoned this connection between sickness, sin and punishment. In its teaching on the sacrament of the anointing of the sick the *Catechism* recalls this association, reminding us that 'It is the experience of Israel that illness is mysteriously linked to sin and evil.' It's true that it doesn't say that this is its understanding of illness today, but why make the point except to draw attention to this relationship? What has the experience of ancient Israel, whose response to illnesses often consisted of sacrificing animals or fretting about devils, got to do with us today? It continues with the more explicit observations that 'on the cross Christ . . . took away the sin of the world *of which illness is only a consequence*' and that suffering, like death 'is a consequence of original sin'[33]

Elsewhere, with disconcerting insensitivity to the pain and distress caused by terminal illness and with its usual bleakness, the Church tells

---

[31]Mark 1:32, John 9:2. For decent and compassionate people today, Jesus' response to this question is almost offensive: 'Jesus answered "he was born blind so that the works of God might be displayed in him"'. In other words, the unfortunate man had to endure years of disability simply to enable Jesus to show off.

[32]Acts 5:11, 1 Cor. 11:30-31.

[33]*Catechism* 1502, 1505, 1521, 1008, my italics.

us that its god appears to take a perverse satisfaction from human suffering. In its *Declaration on Euthanasia* of 1980, the Sacred Congregation for the Doctrine of the Faith (which in earlier centuries went under the ominous name of the Inquisition) affirmed that 'According to Christian teaching . . . suffering, especially suffering during the last moments of life, has a special place in God's saving plan.'[34] It is very difficult indeed to understand how anyone experiencing either physical or emotional pain arising from serious illness or impending death can find such harsh teaching to be of any comfort whatsoever.

This association of illness and sin is established in one of Jesus' first healings, of the paralytic man who, unable to get close to him because of the crowds, was lowered on his stretcher through the roof. When Jesus first sees him he merely tells him that his sins are forgiven, understandably provoking the anger of the Scribes and he hardly seemed interested in healing him. When eventually he does so, it is not out of any concern or compassion for the man but only to trounce his opponents, 'to prove to you that the Son of Man has authority on earth to forgive sins'.[35] As we've already observed because the belief at the time associated sinfulness and illness, taking away one went hand in hand with taking away the other. So when the infant Church preached after Jesus' death that he (and by extension, the Church itself) had the right to forgive sins, the principle was demonstrated in the more visible form of a miraculous healing. And so over time the story probably arose that a miracle genuinely happened.

Soon after we see another miracle being used to resolve a similar dispute, with Jesus healing a man with a withered hand on the sabbath. Again the healing itself is secondary to the religious principle, whether Jesus had the right to heal on the sabbath. So it may be that the story was constructed around a saying attributed to Jesus about observance of the sabbath which evolved into a confrontation with the Pharisees and

---

[34]*Declaration on Euthanasia*, 5 May 1980. Sourced from www.vatican.va. I owe this reference to Kennedy, *All In The Mind*, p 260. The declaration goes on to say that one should not be surprised 'if some Christians prefer to moderate their use of painkillers, in order to accept voluntarily at least a part of their sufferings and thus associate themselves in a conscious way with the sufferings of Christ crucified.' The message would appear to be the more you can suffer, the more you will be looked upon with divine (or Church) approval.

[35]Mark 2:10.

which then had a miracle introduced to 'prove' the point being made.

But for these stories to have been plausible, just as the exorcisms probably had historical incidents underlying them, so there must have been a tradition of actual healings and Jesus must have acquired a reputation as an effective healer. The activity of healers of course, like that of exorcists, was not unknown in the period. In his study *Jesus the Jew*, Vermes sees Jesus following in a tradition of Jewish holy men known as *Hasidim* two of whom - Honi the Circle Drawer and Hanina ben Dosa - lived either shortly before or at about the same time as Jesus.[36]

These were popular and respected figures, distinguished by their piety and unworldly lifestyle. Like Jesus they too were credited with the ability to perform miracles which included controlling the weather and withstanding the bites of poisonous snakes. But it was their abilities as healers that made them popular figures of their day. We should remember that this was an age when there were no hospitals or health services to fall back upon and, as the experience of the woman with a haemorrhage suggests (she had seen doctors for 12 years without any success), when the expertise of physicians was not especially beneficial. Good health was considered then, as now, the greatest blessing. So if a healer with a reputation to be able to cure effectively were to turn up, it's likely that he would have been highly esteemed.

This high regard may explain Jesus' apparent ability to heal that most biblical of all diseases, leprosy. This condition is known today as Hansen's disease after the Norwegian who identified the causative bacillus, *Mycobacterium leprae* in 1872; but as numerous commentators, both biblical and medical,[37] have observed it's unlikely that this is the disease depicted in the gospels. It's believed that leprosy originated in India and travelled to Europe and the biblical region with the troops of Alexander the Great returning from the Indian campaign of 326 BCE. Hansen's disease is characterised in its more malignant form by skin

---

[36]Vermes, *Jesus the Jew*, pp 50-63.

[37]*The Companion Encyclopedia of the History of Medicine* maintains 'there are major difficulties in showing that the biblical and medieval leper suffered from the same disease identified clinically and pathologically as leprosy today' (p 531); *Black's Medical Dictionary* (p 530) observes 'The term [i.e. leprosy] is used in the Authorised Version of the Bible, but experts differ as to whether this is the correct translation of the Hebrew word *Tsaraath*.' See also *Jerome* 76:105. The details of Hansen's disease are taken from *Black's*.

manifestations such as lesions or nodules and extensive damage to the nerves which untreated can lead to the deformities such as the loss of fingers or toes for which leprosy is commonly known. It wasn't until the discovery of the modern drug, *Daphone* in 1941 that the disease in this form became clinically treatable.

Biblical leprosy however seems to have been some other malignant skin condition, possibly psoriasis or eczema,[38] characterised by flakiness of the skin or blistering causing redness to affected areas. This understanding of the true nature of biblical leprosy derives from the Bible itself, specifically the Old Testament book of Leviticus, dating from around the 6th century BCE. In an extended and detailed commentary it describes a number of lesser skin disorders under a generic term translated as leprosy. None of the symptoms it specifies, such as 'a white swelling in the skin' or 'a boil that has healed and in the place of the boil . . . a white swelling or a reddish-white spot'[39] can be regarded as clear manifestations of Hansen's disease. Moreover, it appears from the text that these varying types of 'leprosy', unlike Hansen's disease, were readily cured or tended to heal naturally.

Despite its observations, Leviticus is not an ancient medical text but a holy book prescribing the practical application of Jewish Law and ritual. Detailing these symptoms was made not for therapeutic reasons but to determine whether or not the person afflicted was considered ritually unclean. Those declared unclean were obliged to live apart from the community for up to two weeks after which they returned to the priest. Acting as an interpreter of the Law rather than as a physician, he declared the sufferer clean or unclean; if declared clean, then after the appropriate animal sacrifices were made, the newly cleansed person was permitted to rejoin the community.

So in the story of Jesus and the leper, it may be that the leper, aware of Jesus' reputation as a healer and of the high esteem he enjoyed, was cleansed or pronounced clean by him and wasn't actually healed of his condition.[40] Given that leprosy was very closely associated with ritual uncleanness but wasn't a grave health risk, as soon as he is

---

[38] As suggested by Davies, *Jesus the Healer,* p 68.

[39] Leviticus 13:10, 18-19.

[40] Taylor, *The Gospel According to Mark,* p 185 points out that the Greek verb used can mean to declare clean.

pronounced clean by Jesus, he is effectively (i.e. from the legal standpoint) no longer leprous. So it's not surprising to learn that 'the leprosy left him at once' for this is precisely the effect of being declared clean. Had it been a priest that made the same pronouncement the result would also have been that the leprosy left him at once. In this context being declared clean has no medical connotations. It simply brings about the situation that one is no longer considered leprous or ritually unclean. So it seems that either Jesus was illicitly taking on the priests' responsibility which may explain why he subsequently orders the cleansed man to tell nobody about this incident; or alternatively, since he says to the leper 'go and show yourself to the priest and make the offering for your healing' he may simply have been providing an 'expert opinion'.[41]

Of course the infected man, declared clean, goes and tells everyone. Presumably Jesus' reputation, as a respected authority and man of the people willing to declare people cleansed, is enhanced. Shortly after this we encounter the woman with the haemorrhage. Although not specifically stated, it's likely that this woman was suffering from persistent menstrual bleeding. As a result, she too would have been declared unclean and her chronic condition would have made her life insufferable under the oppressive regulations of the Law: 'When a woman has a discharge of blood which is her regular discharge from her body, she shall be in her impurity for seven days, and whoever touches her shall be unclean until the evening. And everything upon which she lies during her impurity shall be unclean; everything also upon which she sits shall be unclean . . . And if any man lies with her, and her impurity is on him, he shall be unclean seven days . . . if a woman has a discharge of blood for many days . . . all the days of the discharge she shall continue in uncleanness'.[42]

Clearly very few people would have wanted to be in contact with so unfortunate a woman, effectively making her an outcast from society. Perhaps she had heard that there was a holy man and a healer of great repute who declared people clean without too strict an observance of the Law, and decided to approach him in the hope of being cleansed. As this story was told and retold over the course of 30

---

[41] Mark 1:42, 44.
[42] Leviticus 15:19-20, 24, 25.

or 40 years, we can venture that this pronouncement of being clean gradually evolved into a full and immediate healing as Jesus' legendary status grew. That the original incident was embellished or exaggerated is clearly suggested by the dramatic elements typical of a healing encounter added to it: the painful yet fruitless treatment under various doctors, the instantaneous cure and the subsequent reluctant confrontation with Jesus; and most obviously, the woman's ever so slightly melodramatic secret longing which has the effect of revering Jesus "'If I can touch even his clothes", she had told herself, "I shall be well again"'[43]

Understanding Jesus' Exorcisms And Healings

If we accept that underlying these stories there were historical incidents which, if not so dramatic as the gospels suggest, yet caused people to believe that Jesus had cast out devils or had effected a miraculous cure, how are we to understand what happened? How might Jesus have brought about these healings? One of the noticeable features of many of these encounters is the authority that Jesus shows. Frequently he commands in a loud voice, rebukes a devil or fever, or speaks sharply to his patient. One commentator, Ian Wilson has suggested that Jesus was a hypnotist whose authoritative presence induced the possessed into a trance thus promoting a calming effect and so giving the appearance of a release or cure.[44] Other exorcists of the time were recorded as performing incantations to expel devils[45] suggesting that rhythmic chant may have served to tranquillise the afflicted person. It may be that Jesus too employed some form of erratic behaviour to induce a trance. Mark's gospel even suggests this possibility: his family for instance were worried that he was mad while the Pharisees thought his behaviour was so frantic that he was actually possessed by a devil himself.

If this is the case, the types of illnesses Jesus was dealing with, which his age attributed to demonic possession or divine punishment, may well have been forms of what we now term hysterical disorder.

---

[43]Mark 5:28.

[44]Wilson, *Jesus: the Evidence*, pp 86–95.

[45]Vermes, *op cit*, p 47.

Today this condition is a recognised and well documented type of psychiatric illness. Conversion disorder (as it is technically known) is defined as a condition which displays physical symptoms but for which no physical explanation can be discovered. The American Psychiatric Association describes the complaint as 'an expression of a psychological conflict or need . . . not under voluntary control [whose] symptoms resemble the symptoms of neurological diseases such as paralysis, aphonia, seizures, coordination disturbance . . . blindness',[46] symptoms which tally with those shown by many of the people Jesus healed. These symptoms, it continues, have a symbolic value that represent an underlying psychological conflict. So to remove the symptoms one must address and remove that subconscious conflict.

If we are reluctant to acknowledge the reality of such disorders, we may feel more comfortable if we substitute *conversion disorder* with the better known term *shell shock*, the popular name given to the hysterical illnesses suffered by thousands of soldiers of the First World War whose symptoms are preserved in the grainy and distressing footage of England's war hospitals.

In his study of war and neuroses,[47] Eric Leed highlights and analyzes some of the symptoms (and their causes) shown by shell-shocked troops: 'The symptoms of shell shock were precisely the same as those of the most common hysterical disorders of peacetime . . . hysterical neuroses with gross physical symptoms of paralysis, spasm, mutism, blindness and the like . . . predominated in the ranks.' Some progressive doctors and analysts treating the afflicted soldiers recognised that these symptoms were neurotic in origin and that neurosis was a flight into illness or sometimes a coping mechanism to help the soldier deal with the trauma of the battlefield. One British doctor's analysis from 1917 for instance observed that there was often a simple connection between the symptom and its cause: 'hysterical blindness follows particularly horrible sights; hysterical deafness appears in men who find the cries of the wounded unbearable'; while a German counterpart understood that 'mutism and speech disorders were the most common symptoms of war neurosis . . . [because] the soldier was

---

[46] *The Diagnostic and Statistical Manual of the American Psychiatric Association,* 1980, p 247, quoted in Wolman, *Psychosomatic Disorders,* p 217.
[47] Leed, *No Man's Land: Combat And Identity in World War I,* pp 163-192.

required to be silent, to accept often suicidal edicts of authority and to hold back or severely edit any expression of hostility.'[48]

Consequently for these more enlightened doctors, hypnosis offered a much more practical and successful method of treatment than the inhumane electrical therapy favoured by others. Today it is recognised that hypnosis, while not fully understood, can often provide a very effective means to address these conditions. Practitioners of this therapy have explained their understanding of its success by observing that hypnosis is

> an altered state of consciousness in which it is possible to focus the attention in a particular direction and thus easily achieve a state of muscle relaxation. During this procedure it is possible to change a subject's experience of pain, cold, heat and other sensory perceptions. This kind of altered consciousness could also occur in patients with conversion symptoms. Patients feel their legs are paralysed and behave like someone whose paralysis has a physical cause. They see that they are paralysed and feel paralysed. Under hypnosis, disorders such as those seen in conversion patients can be evoked and made to disappear again in very suggestible subjects.[49]

This last point about 'suggestible subjects' is revealing. The authors of this study go on to observe that patients suffering from conversion disorders have been shown to be 'exceptionally suggestible'. But what has this to do with Jesus' healings? In this context suggestibility implies that the patient is receptive to the influence or word of the hypnotist and can be led to understand that his apparently physical complaints have been removed. This isn't very far removed from the concept of 'belief' or 'trust' in the healer's abilities; and this of course was an essential aspect of many of Jesus' healings, the only difference being that instead of the secular, psychological term 'suggestibility', Jesus used the word 'faith'.

In Jesus' healings the importance of faith is frequently emphasised: he heals people when he can see their faith (as with the paralytic man)

---

[48] *Ibid*, pp 163-178 citing Salmon, *The Care and Treatment of Mental Diseases and War Neuroses in the British Army*, 1917 and Simmel, *Psychoanalysis and the War Neuroses*, 1918.

[49] Hoogduin / Roelofs, *Conversion Disorders*, p 162 in the *International Handbook of Clinical Hypnosis*, ed Burrows / Stanley / Bloom. The authors report cases of 'paralysis of one side of the body, paralysis of both legs, blindness . . . inability to speak and assorted disorders relating to the senses and pain' at the psychiatric unit where they practice.

and on one occasion he even asked a blind man 'Do you believe I can do this?' In the case of the desperate woman with the haemorrhage, it may be that as his mission progressed and his fame became known, his reputation alone was enough to suggest to her that she might be cleansed or possibly even healed. In this story the narrative claims that Jesus sensed 'the power' had left him via his clothes, but his response 'Your faith has restored you to health'[50] is much more illuminating. It would appear that the healing arises not from any magical properties within Jesus' outfit, but from the belief in the woman's mind.

In medical practice today it's well known that genuine belief in the body's ability to heal itself, as demonstrated by the use of placebos, can bring about improvements to a complaint. Equally revealing is the occasion when Jesus returned to his home town, Nazareth where, unable to heal anyone at all, 'he was amazed at their lack of faith.'[51] Perhaps those who knew Jesus more closely were not so enthralled by him as strangers appear to have been. In these and other instances if we use the word 'suggestibility' instead of 'faith', we can venture and understand that these healings probably had more to do with the workings of the mind than with the workings of a supposed deity.

Could conversion disorders and hysterical disturbances be behind the afflictions of those who were healed by Jesus? Contemporary case studies and clinical observations found in medical textbooks suggest that this may at least be a possibility. For example, in his study of psychosomatic disorders, Benjamin Wolman notes that 'hysterics may experience the most severe pain in almost every part of the organism'.[52]

This may provide some understanding as to why the wild and uncontrollable Gerasene demoniac, prone to self-mutilation and unrestrained howling, was in so grievous a state. One contemporary case study details a patient whose condition and symptoms were strikingly similar to those of this unfortunate man. The patient, a psychotic woman in early adulthood was admitted to hospital 'with symptoms of confusion, hallucinations, belligerent behaviour and generally inappropriate behaviour including; smearing her faeces,

---

[50]Matthew 9:28, Mark 5:34.

[51]Mark 6:6.

[52]Wolman, *op cit*, p 216.

crawling on her hands and knees and taking off her clothes.' The study goes on to give details of a programme of hypnotherapy which over the course of 15 months resulted in the successful reintegration of the woman into a responsible life. [53]

While this shows certain similarities with the gospel demoniac, the most obvious difference between the two cases is the amount of time taken to bring about a cure. Jesus' healings and exorcisms are all achieved almost instantaneously. Of course it may be that the gospel writers knew nothing of the actual Jewish ritual of exorcism and therefore couldn't detail the process, as Vermes suggests.[54]

However, as we've observed, there's almost definitely some literary licence in the telling of these stories which may well have extended into the time taken to effect a cure. After all, if the gospels had reported that *after another four hours the man was still howling, so Jesus tried one last time to expel the devil* they would hardly have been so compelling for their first audiences.

Moreover, the evangelists are telling the story of the anointed one of the supreme and all-powerful god, so it would've been somewhat inappropriate to portray Jesus as having to struggle in any way against the devils. And lastly, we don't know what the long term effect of these healings was. Certainly there are no instances of people returning to Jesus to complain or ask for a refund, but on the other hand, there are no case notes to tell us what happened to these people either. It may be that once the calming effects of an induced trance wore off, the symptoms returned. Indeed Jesus' words about wandering spirits seeking to return to the body from which they had been expelled strongly suggests that the effects of exorcism and healing may well have been only temporary.

Of course all of this is speculative only and it's impossible for us to say now what actually happened - nothing can be verified or tested. All we can do is suggest possible explanations which have some plausibility and which we feel are less improbable than divinely worked miracles.

---

[53]Jobsis, *Personality and Psychotic Disorders* pp 171-186 in the *International Handbook of Clinical Hypnosis*.

[54]Vermes, *op cit*, p 7.

Promoting Jesus To The Super League

Our next consideration is to try to understand how Jesus' miracles evolved from these simple and sometimes plausible exorcisms and healings to the definitely implausible supernatural acts which included resurrecting people from the dead and controlling or overcoming the forces of nature.

As we've seen, the gospels were written not so much by individuals but were compiled out of existing stories or traditions formulated and preserved orally before being written down. In his enquiry into the origin of these traditions, Bultmann sought to discover the influences active in their formation and to understand the laws which governed their transmission. One of his methods was to observe how material from Mark (and to a lesser extent from the other source, Q which scholars have been able to reconstruct) was adapted by Matthew and Luke. If any patterns or laws could be detected, Bultmann argued that these would probably have been operative on material even before it was fixed in Mark and Q. In other words, if Matthew and Luke had adapted their sources, it was likely that Mark too had adapted his source material in similar ways. In theory then, by applying these basic principles to the text of Mark, one could read back to the earliest stages of the tradition to discover or hypothesise what the original form of material might have been before it was first written.

A good example to illustrate this principle would be the increasing idealisation of Jesus with each succeeding account. Indicators of this are numerous. After he walked across the sea, in Mark the disciples are not astonished but perplexed. But in Matthew the disciples worship Jesus and declare that he is 'the Son of God'. And as such Matthew's Jesus can't have any faults. So while Mark records that Jesus' immediate family thought that he was mentally disturbed, Matthew and the other evangelists omit this detail.

Similarly Mark is the only gospel that describes Jesus' baptism without any sense of embarrassment or unease. Matthew has a contrived dialogue inserted, highlighting the Baptist's reluctance to baptise Jesus since it suggested that Jesus was his inferior. Only grudgingly (and inexplicably), because it is what 'righteousness demands', does Jesus allow himself to be baptised by John. Luke deals with the matter in just four words ('Jesus *after his own baptism* was at prayer'[55]) and doesn't even mention that John performed the rite (in fact he tells us immediately beforehand that John is banged up in prison).

By the time we get to the Fourth Gospel, Jesus isn't baptised at all (even though there is an encounter between Jesus and John), presumably because John's baptism was known to be one 'of repentance for the forgiveness of sins.' Anyone coming to John to be baptised therefore must have regarded himself as a sinner. Indeed, Mark noted that 'as they were baptised by him in the river Jordan they confessed their sins.'[56] But by now Jesus has been idealised to such an extent that he's not just the messiah; he has now evolved to being the Son, the bread of life, the true vine, the good shepherd, the lamb of god, the light of the world and so on. He is holiness personified. Effectively he is way, way too righteous and too perfect ever to have sinned. So to maintain that Jesus needed to undergo a baptism of repentance becomes embarrassing and redundant.

If Bultmann's contention is valid, we can argue that although Mark sought to underplay and keep Jesus' messianic identity secret, he too idealised Jesus, elevating his status and reputation. So this idealising tendency can be applied backwards from Mark to earlier material to suggest that the closer one gets to Jesus' actual lifetime, the more likely it is that he was regarded as a normal human person. Thus during his lifetime Jesus' contemporaries probably regarded him as an exorcist, a healer, a teacher, perhaps even a pious hot-head or a charismatic holy man as Vermes argues. But they wouldn't have identified him as a god in his own right, the light of the world and, as Wrede's hypothesis suggested, probably not even as the messiah.

The same process can be discerned in his miracles. As we move further from Jesus' historical life, miracles become both more numerous and increasingly sensational. Material in Mark is either worked over, expanded or, where it doesn't suit their purposes, occasionally omitted by the subsequent evangelists. Thus before the feeding of the 5,000 Jesus has pity on the crowds in Mark because they were so helpless; but in Matthew's version Jesus' pity is a cue to write in a few more vague and unspecified healings. Similarly, even when he

---

[55]Matthew 3:15, Luke 3:21, my italics.
[56]Mark 1:4-5.

is mad with rage, chasing out the money dealers from the Temple, somehow Matthew's Jesus still has the time and presence of mind to calm down and cure a couple of blind and lame people, medical services that Mark knows nothing about. And in Luke at his arrest Jesus regenerates the ear of the high priest's servant, a detail missing from Mark, perhaps to demonstrate not only a rejection of violence, but also his powers even in a time of crisis.

Are The Dead Restored To Life ?

This increasing sensationalism can also be seen in the resurrections of dead people. There are three occasions when Jesus resurrects people, one common to all of the synoptics, one in Luke only and the last only in John. The first story concerns the young daughter of Jairus, the synagogue official. If we accept Mark's version of events, the day when this occurred had been a hectic but nevertheless very productive one for Jesus; having exorcised the Gerasene demoniac, returned across the lake and healed the bleeding woman, he then felt he had enough power left in him (after being touched Jesus feels 'the power' draining away) to do a quick resurrection. So as some commentators like to observe, during the course of a single day Jesus demonstrated his ascendancy over Satan, sickness and death, naturally conquering all three. Not bad for a day's work but not likely to be historically true either.

The little girl is first described as desperately sick and shortly after she apparently dies. There's some uncertainty here since Jesus says she isn't dead but merely sleeping - presumably the girl slipped into unconsciousness. Matthew ups the stakes and definitely reports the girl as dead with her father imploring Jesus to restore her to life. Quite why he believed that Jesus could do so is inexplicable since, according to Matthew, he had never before performed this type of miracle. For Luke there may still have been the lingering suspicion that this was not a genuine resuscitation but merely the healing of a high fever; accordingly when he introduces another resurrection he takes care to show that the character really is dead by having him in his coffin, about to be buried. Finally in the later Gospel of John we come to the most sensational resurrection of all with the raising of Lazarus who had been dead for four days and whose body had begun to decompose.

Clearly, restoring a putrefying corpse back to life is much more impressive than reviving a child who may only have been unconscious.

What should we make of these stories? The raising of Jairus' daughter may have had its origin in the healing of a girl who appeared to be so close to death that, over the course of time, this element of the story was dramatically exaggerated. If over the 30 years or so between the appearance of the gospels of Mark and John stories about Jesus raising people from the dead had become so much more sensational, it's quite possible that the enthusiasm of the time between Jesus' actual life and the first gospel (some 40 years) could have coloured the historical event underlying this story. In fact it would have been during this period, before stories about Jesus had been fixed in writing that the imaginative element would have been most at work.

As in the case of the bleeding woman whom Jesus encountered on the way, this is a story with many melodramatic touches: the initial meeting with Jairus who falls at his feet, the cool, self-assured wisdom of Jesus when told that the girl is dead, the unrestrained weeping and the mockery when he proclaims that she is only sleeping are all designed to tug at our heartstrings and then to evoke the greatest astonishment and admiration for Jesus (who revived the girl even though everybody was laughing at him). All of this suggests that the original incident has been embellished or exaggerated as a result of being told over and over again.

So was the little girl really dead? The crowds definitely think so. But we've seen already in the case of the epileptic boy that most of the people present thought he was dead when in fact he was only unconscious. And later on, some years after Jesus' death, we encounter a young man who fell asleep during one of Paul's (evidently long and boring) sermons and having fallen out of a window to the ground three floors below is pronounced dead.[57] But he too turns out to be unconscious only. It would seem that from the evidence available, the crowds are hardly experts when it comes to distinguishing between the dead and the seriously ill.

In the story unique to Luke however, there seems to be no doubt

---

[57]Acts 20:7-12. According to Acts the sermon 'went on till the middle of the night'. Paul himself never claims in his letters to have brought anyone back to life.

that the man is dead. Here Jesus encounters a funeral procession and, feeling sorry for the dead man's mother who is also a widow, commands him to come back to life. This is clearly an exceptional miracle, so great in fact that everyone is astonished, Jesus is hailed as a great prophet and this news and opinion of him spreads all over the country. It is equally astonishing therefore that it wasn't recorded by any of the other evangelists, especially since (if we accept the chronology of Luke's 'ordered account') it occurs before Jesus raised up Jairus' daughter. If this miracle had *really* happened and news of it spread so far and so quickly, how on earth could they not have known about it or have declined to include it in their own narratives?

Furthermore, when we consider the context of this story, we might begin to suspect that it was written in to the narrative by Luke. In Christianity today John the Baptist is presented as Jesus' immediate precursor, the last of the prophets humbly preparing the way for him. But the historical reality was probably very different as the embarrassment surrounding John's baptising of Jesus suggests. It's likely that John was seen by early Christians as a rival of Jesus, one who had attracted a large following which lasted many years after his death[58] and who probably didn't recognise Jesus as the messiah. If John was considered to be a rival, this helps to explain why he is made so subservient to Jesus in the gospels, apparently confessing that he's not fit even to undo Jesus' shoe. The evangelists couldn't expunge him from their narratives since details about him were too well known; so instead they reduced his significance to a bit-part level.

But rewriting history creates problems. Jesus' baptism is marked by a heavenly sign with the Holy Spirit, in the form of a dove descending on him as he rises from the water and a voice that proclaims him as 'the beloved'. In Mark the voice addresses itself directly to Jesus and only he sees the heavens open and the dove from above, suggesting more a visionary, subjective experience rather than an actual event.[59]

---

[58] In Acts for example it's noted that some of the Jews at Ephesus were baptised 'with John's baptism' (19:4) suggesting an early influence at least equal to that of Jesus.

[59] Of course this presents us with the problem of how Mark knew what Jesus saw and heard; the only possible explanation is that Jesus himself told people about it. But given that throughout Mark's gospel Jesus is extremely reluctant to reveal his messianic identity, it seems very unlikely that he would have bragged about such signs of divine approval.

Matthew removes any misunderstanding by having the voice address everyone present, speaking of Jesus in the third person. But problems arise as a consequence of this enhancement. In his absolute determination to demonstrate that Jesus was the messiah and, equally importantly, that this was conceded by John, later on he introduces a story about the Baptist who by now is languishing in prison. From his cell we're told that John sent out his own disciples to establish whether Jesus really was the messiah or an impostor.

But Matthew obviously failed to cross reference and reconcile this story to his earlier story of Jesus' baptism; for had the voice from the sky been a real one there would've been no doubt in John's mind in the first place. To try and settle the matter once and for all, both Matthew and Luke decide to show that Jesus was the messiah by having his miracles pointed out to the Baptist. Accordingly they have Jesus declare 'Go back and tell John what you have seen and heard: the blind see again, the lame walk, the lepers are cleansed, and the deaf hear, *the dead are raised to life*.' As well as informing John about Jesus' miracles, this remark also alludes to a prophecy 'proving' that Jesus is the messiah through its suggestion that prophecies are being fulfilled in him.[60]

However, as we've discovered, whenever an apparent fulfilment of a prophecy arises, we should pause and consider whether the fulfilment truly occurred. And in this instance we should be wary of accepting that Jesus really had performed all of these miracles prior to this point, even though the evangelists had no such difficulty. In fact they've been very careful to detail these signs, so much so that the whole sequence of miracles comes across as artificial and contrived. Matthew was careful enough for example to ensure that there was a healing of two blind men prior to this saying, a healing which doesn't exist in Mark.

But the artifice is most apparent in Luke where the arrangement of his material meant that he didn't actually have a resurrection story at this point (he places the episode of Jairus' daughter after this message to the Baptist whereas Matthew was smart enough to remember that it had to precede it if Jesus' retort were to be credible). So in order to justify Jesus' boasting, Luke has to ensure that there's a prior

---

[60]Matt 11:4, Luke 7:22, my italics. The prophecy is from Isaiah 26:19, 29:18-19, 35:5, 61:1-2.

resurrection story in his narrative and very suspiciously it occurs *immediately* before the message to the Baptist. Consequently one can't help being rather sceptical as to whether the raising of the widow's son really occurred, particularly so when we consider that this story is modelled very closely on an Old Testament miracle.[61]

Miracles Outside The Gospels

As we move further away from the life of Jesus and into the post-resurrection period, miracles attributed to the apostles become even more impressive (or unbelievable) than Jesus' miracles. In the Acts of the Apostles we find the magic handkerchief which only has to touch Paul to be charged with healing properties so as to cure the sick. In fact by now healings from all sorts of diseases are so common that those who are sick are cured simply by having Peter's shadow pass over them.

Acts is also known for the descent of the Holy Spirit soon after Jesus went to heaven. Settling on the disciples' heads like 'tongues of fire', this spirit gives them the apparent ability to speak in foreign languages. Here we can see that some 50 to 60 years later the writer has given free rein to his imagination, not letting reality get in the way of a good story; for we know from Paul's letters that the gift of speaking in tongues didn't consist of speaking in foreign languages at all. On the contrary it amounted to nothing more than a fervent but meaningless babble. 'If your tongue doesn't produce intelligible speech, how can anyone know what you are saying?' he asks the Corinthians when discussing this 'gift'; 'I would rather say five words *that mean something* than ten thousand words in a tongue'[62] he concludes. That the disciples were talking twaddle is made clear by remarks attributed to bystanders who think the disciples are drunk; but why would they believe they were drunk just because they were talking in a foreign language? Think about it - isn't it much more likely that you'd think somebody was drunk if he were talking incoherent gibberish as

---

[61] 1 Kings 17:8-24. The miracle in question is the raising of a *widow's son* by the prophet Elijah who was renown for being a miracle worker. Luke actually lifts the words he 'gave him to his mother' directly from the Old Testament and the crowd hails Jesus, like Elijah, as a 'great prophet'.

[62] 1 Cor. 14:9, 19, my italics.

opposed to speaking intelligible French or German?

We then get to some later works, the non-canonical gospels and apostolic accounts which as we've seen contain some of the most unbelievable miracles of all. Best of all perhaps (and one of my personal favourites) is a story in the Acts of Peter, written around the end of the 2nd century,[63] which recounts how Peter arrives in Rome to confront our old friend the wicked magician, Simon. Having lured Christians away from the faith, Simon refuses to receive Peter at the house of Marcellus, a Roman senator; so Peter sends along a big dog which, presumably by the power of Jesus, is able to talk. Standing on its hind legs the dog denounces Simon as a 'wicked and shameless man' and amazingly starts to preach to him causing huge astonishment (of course) and the eventual and predictable conversion of Marcellus. Unfortunately once the dog has completed its mission and reported back to Peter and before anyone can talk to it and actually discover some genuinely interesting information (such as what's it like to be a dog?), it immediately falls at his feet and dies.

Clearly as we move further away from the actual life of Jesus, Christian miracles become increasingly legendary in character. But what about miracles attributed to Jesus as we move in the other direction and get closer to his lifetime? Here our only source of information is the apostle Paul. But as we've seen, Paul is almost totally silent in his letters about the real Jesus. He says nothing of Jesus' birth or parentage or where he lived; he barely mentions any of his teachings. Nor are the key incidents that led to his death, the disturbance in the Temple, the betrayal by Judas and the trial before Pilate mentioned or even alluded to. More to the point he says nothing about any of Jesus' miracles. We know that he had little concern or interest to learn more about Jesus, but his failure to mention the miracles is especially baffling, for it would clearly have been in his interests to tell his audience about them.

It must be the case that Paul either knew about Jesus' miracles and chose not to mention them at all or he didn't know about them. Let's consider the first possibility. If he knew about the miracles, why might he have omitted to confirm them or to use them in his preaching? We can venture that he did so because he felt they were irrelevant, perhaps

---

[63]Elliot, *op cit*, p 392.

because he didn't believe in miracles himself and doubted they were true or because he didn't actually value miracles as a means to persuade people to accept his teachings about Jesus.

But there's nothing in his letters to support these hypotheses; on the contrary, Paul did appear to believe in miracles and appreciated their value for preaching purposes. He speaks for example of 'the gift of healing' and 'the power of miracles' alongside the gifts of preaching and faith, suggesting that he regarded these gifts as equally natural and common phenomena. And he reminds his converts that they themselves had seen 'all the things that mark the true apostle . . . the signs, the marvels, the miracles.'[64] Now if he believed that a true apostle could perform miracles, it seems he would almost certainly have believed that Jesus himself had such an ability. Why should he have doubted Jesus' own miraculous powers? So had Peter informed him about Jesus' miracles at one of their meetings, he would've had no reason to disbelieve or reject them.

But would he have made use of Jesus' miracles to win converts had he known about them? Again, his own words suggest that he would. Frequently in his letters Paul gives the impression of being so passionate about his mission that there was nothing he wouldn't do to ensure its success. He was prepared to endure considerable hardship, imprisonment, floggings and on one occasion a stoning; his dedication and conviction are unquestionable. 'I have made myself the slave of everyone,' he wrote proudly, 'so as to win as many as I could. I made myself a Jew to the Jews, to win the Jews.'

It seems then that if Paul could've found some means to persuade the Jews to accept his message, then in all probability he wouldn't have hesitated to make use of it. In fact there was one such means which we've already seen in the gospels and which he even highlighted in the same letter: 'the Jews demand miracles'[65] he tells his community at Corinth. So why didn't he tell them (or anyone else) about Jesus' miracles? It can only be that he knew nothing of them, an ignorance that can be explained either by the fact that he wasn't told about them by Peter who, according to the gospels was the star eyewitness to all of the miracles, or they simply didn't happen.

---

[64] 1 Cor. 12:9-10, 2 Cor. 12:12.
[65] 1 Cor. 9:19-20, 1:23.

So the next question to consider is why wouldn't Peter have told Paul about these astonishing stories? If it really had been the case that Jesus resurrected people from the dead, walked on water and fed thousands of people with just a handful of loaves, it's almost inconceivable that Peter wouldn't have told Paul about such astonishing signs. It's in human nature to share knowledge of unusual, inexplicable or wondrous phenomena and there is no satisfactory explanation as to why Peter would have refused to inform Paul of Jesus' miracles. After all, Paul seems to have been told about Jesus' resurrection. Moreover, the gospels stress again and again his great fame which spread throughout the land as a result of his miracles: was Paul the only person never to have heard of them?

We're asked to believe then that astonishing miracles took place, were known throughout the land, and yet the key witness and leading follower of Jesus decided inexplicably to say nothing about them to Paul. Or if he had told Paul about them, Paul dismissed them as worthless for preaching purposes when it's clear they would have strengthened his case. It is much more probable that at this very early stage in the development of the Jesus movement, these stories simply hadn't yet evolved. Far from being historical, it would seem then that the supernatural miracles are the result of rumours and traditions which in excitable times became increasingly legendary and sensational in character as a consequence of repeated story-telling.

Some Incredible Showing Off

The miracles over nature are among the best known of all Jesus' works and are much more dramatic than his healings. Jesus satisfied thirst and hunger by turning water into wine and by feeding thousands of people on two occasions with an impossibly small number of loaves and a couple of fishes. As if this were not enough to astonish the multitudes, he could also control the weather and even defy gravity by walking across the sea. And possibly recalling the petulance of his childhood days from the later Infancy gospels, we're told that he cursed a fig tree, causing it to wither just because (being out of season) it didn't have any fruit for him to eat.

These marvellous acts add to the sense of astonishment and wonder associated with Jesus. So after the feeding of the 5,000 in the Fourth

Gospel, Jesus is so admired by the crowds that they want to make him their king there and then. And as we've already noted, in Matthew when Jesus walks across the sea he is acclaimed and worshipped by the disciples as 'the Son of God' for the first time. It seems very strange then that Jesus should have been so wholly rejected by the people and even abandoned by his disciples if he really had given these ample demonstrations of his status and powers. Along with other arguments, such as Paul's silence noted above, this unexpected and wholescale desertion of Jesus adds to the case that these miracles never actually took place as the gospels depict.

If this is so, how and why did these stories arise? Is there some theological concern or are they just the result of imaginative storytelling? I would argue that as with many of Jesus' healings, there's a didactic purpose at work in these miracles and it's this purpose which provides some clues to understanding how they may have come about.

The feeding of the 5,000 is one of the more significant miracles, being the only one recorded in all four gospels. It must therefore have been highly regarded. In this story it is Jesus' supposed pity and compassion for the crowds following him which brings about the free food. But in Mark's account, Jesus' pity is aroused not because of any hunger pangs the people might have had, but because they are 'like sheep without a shepherd'.[66] Consequently Jesus decides that the ideal solution is to start preaching to them again 'at some length.' It's actually the disciples who first express concern for the crowd's welfare to which Jesus appears initially to be indifferent, telling the disciples to deal with it themselves. He then relents and after the available food is brought to him, he says a magic spell and begins to break the loaves and fishes, continually handing the broken pieces to the disciples to distribute to the people. Afterwards, when everyone has had enough to eat, there is such an excess that the disciples collect twelve baskets of scraps and leftovers.

Matthew and Mark record that shortly after Jesus worked a very similar miracle, except that fewer people were fed and only seven baskets of leftovers were collected. In both cases the structure and detail of the stories are virtually identical including the disciples'

---

[66]Sheep eat grass, not handouts provided to them by the keeper of the flock, so there's no indication that Jesus is concerned about the physical hunger of the crowd.

bewilderment as to how to deal with the crowd's hunger. But if both feedings were actual events, on the second occasion how could the disciples have been so thick that they couldn't recall that Jesus had previously performed a feeding miracle? Why didn't they simply ask him to do the magic again rather than whinge about how far they were from the nearest village? Clearly these two episodes are variants of the same story at different stages of development, an argument that most commentators accept, with the later feeding of the 4,000 presumed to be the earlier tradition since it is less impressive in terms of numbers.

As with so many of the miracles, once you start asking simple yet obvious questions about this story and scrutinise the details closely, it begins to lose plausibility. Where did the baskets, in which the excess bread and fish were collected, come from for example? Was there a disciple who carried twelve baskets just in case such a situation ever arose? Or did each disciple have his own basket specifically to collect scraps that people left behind? Of course one might argue that they were itinerant preachers who naturally would carry some sort of bag on their travels. But this would've been in direct contravention of Jesus' specific instruction issued to them beforehand – 'to take nothing for the journey except a staff – no bread, no haversack'[67] – and in Mark the feeding occurs directly after the disciples have returned hotfoot from these first missions.

More perplexing however is to wonder about the action of the miracle. Did the loaves and fishes divide themselves in Jesus' hands like giant bacteria on speed to replicate and form copies of themselves? Or was it the case that when he broke a fish in half, it somehow regenerated the part that had been torn off to re-form as a whole fish? Or did the food somehow well up from the ground beneath him? We shall never know. Unfortunately (but perhaps wisely) the gospels are silent about this and it seems that none of the dimwit disciples were sufficiently curious to look to see precisely how all this food was being produced. But reasonable or sensible people today *would* want to know; and a reasonable person would have considerable doubt as to

---

[67]Mark 6:7. Mark actually records that there were 'twelve basketfuls' (as opposed to 'baskets') of scraps; but if there were no actual baskets, how did he know that there were precisely 'twelve basketfuls' and, later on in the second feeding, 'seven basketfuls' of scraps? The numbers are relevant for Jesus' subsequent comment on the feedings.

whether this feeding miracle really happened, especially when it can be understood in non-miraculous or literary terms.

When we consider the details and the overall context of this story we can begin to find some clues to help our understanding. In Mark and Matthew the location of the feeding is described three times as a 'lonely place' or 'deserted place'[68] suggesting that it took place in the wilderness or desert. But it is not so remote that the crowds from local towns and villages can't get there before Jesus arrives; and his reference to the 'green grass' indicates that it can hardly have been the desert that the evangelists would like us to think it is. Why then is this incongruous detail emphasised?

It's because Mark and Matthew want us to believe that the feeding took place in the desert so as to recall the Old Testament manna, the miraculous bread of heaven provided through Moses to the Israelites wandering in the desert. It was through this heavenly food that Yahweh rescued and saved his people, an act of deliverance which, in the words of one commentator on Mark, became 'the basic foundation of Israel's history'.[69]

If this seems far-fetched, we should remember that the evangelists are trying to convince their earliest audiences that Jesus is on a par with Moses (at the Transfiguration Peter suggests making three tents - one each for Jesus, Moses and Elijah). They want us to understand and accept Jesus as the mediator of a new covenant, his blood, as he claimed at the Last Supper, being 'the blood of the covenant'[70] which does away with the old Law. So if the new covenant is to replace the existing one established by Moses, Jesus must be portrayed as at least equal to Moses in stature and authority. And what better way to endow Jesus with such authority than to impute to him miracles similar to or greater than those worked by Moses?

In John the desert location is missing but the connection is made explicitly in a discussion between Jesus and the crowds the next day. After Jesus has told them that they must believe in him, they ask him for a sign, reminding him 'Our fathers had manna to eat in the desert.'

---

[68]Nineham points out that the literal meaning of the Greek word used - *eremos* is desert, *op cit*, p 182.

[69]*Ibid*, p 178.

[70]Mark 14:24.

When Jesus tells them that this came not from Moses but from his father, they ask him to give them bread always, to which Jesus responds: 'I am the bread of life. He who comes to me will never be hungry'.[71]

Now people hearing these words in John's gospel would have just listened to a wonderful, uplifting story supposedly telling of a real event (and one which would've been much more readily believed by the community for which the gospel was written than it is today), 'proving' that those who come to Jesus are nourished and provided for. Having heard this 'proof', these listeners would be much more receptive to the theological idea or message underlying the miracle, that Jesus is as great an authority as Moses. All who come to him and believe in him will find satisfaction for their hunger, spiritual or otherwise. We can see then that the feeding miracle becomes a graphic illustration of a theological idea, a story which over time was transformed to become an actual event. It is also very reminiscent of the Christian Eucharist in which the bread of life, Jesus' body is given to the congregation; again it can be seen as a vivid, easy to grasp representation of the underlying idea behind the Christian ritual.

Immediately after this feeding we come to the story of Jesus walking across the sea. Jesus sends the disciples on ahead of him in their boat, not joining them because he wants to pray by himself. This seems like a fairly lame excuse to send his disciples on by themselves, especially when the lateness of the hour is considered, but the important thing for Mark is to get them out to sea without their master. However, the connection between the feeding miracle and this one is extremely tenuous as indicated by the hopelessly mixed up chronology.

At the beginning of the feeding miracle we're told twice that it is 'very late', even before the distribution of food begins. Fast food wasn't even a concept in those days and to feed 5,000 people (and possibly up to 10,000 or even 15,000 in Matthew, for he boasts that the 5,000 is 'to say nothing of women and children', exaggerating once again) when it seems that only twelve people are handing out the food is going to take some considerable time, a couple of hours perhaps. When the meal is over Jesus sends the disciples and the crowd away,

---

[71]John 6:28–35.

146

by which time one might reasonably suppose that it is night. And yet even after the time taken to row far out on the lake, Mark tells us that Jesus sees them 'when evening came' as if to suggest that when the crowd had been sent home it was only late in the afternoon. Again we can see here two individual stories or units clumsily strung together to try to present a justification for the disciples to be separated from Jesus.

In John the story is different, with the crowds so impressed by the feeding miracle that Jesus thinks they want to make him their king. One would have thought that if he'd wanted to avoid being mobbed by the crowd he would've got into the boat with the disciples since this would have provided a much better escape route than going off to the hills where he could be easily pursued. In fact earlier in Mark Jesus foresaw the possibility of being assailed and specifically asked the disciples to have a boat ready to allow for this.[72] It seems then that getting away by boat would've been much more practical. But sensible behaviour isn't followed because again the only thing that matters is that the disciples should be in a boat without Jesus so as to allow this miracle to take place.

As if to confirm how contrived these stage directions are, strangely enough, when Jesus encounters the very same crowd the next day it has completely lost its enthusiasm to make him king. Was Jesus suffering from delusions or was the crowd's fervour simply a literary device to bring about the separation of the master from his disciples? That we should be suspicious that this event really took place is therefore immediately signalled by the artifice by which the two main accounts contrive to bring about the situation in which the disciples are in a boat without Jesus.

Some time later through the darkness and (according to John) from a distance of about four miles Jesus is somehow able to see that the disciples are worn out with rowing and that the wind was against them. It was only then, very late into the night with the crowds long gone, that he decided to walk across the sea, a feat witnessed therefore only by the disciples. Is this truly sufficient or compelling evidence for believing that such an astonishing event *really* happened?

If we feel that the grounds for accepting this claim are insufficient, we might wonder how and why this story came about. Again we can

---

[72]Mark 3:9

begin to understand by considering that as with the feeding of the 5,000, this incident was born out of the illustration of a theological idea perhaps arising from a parable or saying and evolving through a number of stages eventually to become a supposedly historical event in Jesus' life.

That such a process may have occurred can be seen if we look at another unlikely miracle, the cursing of the fig tree. In this episode for no good reason Jesus curses a fig tree causing it to wither away. In Mark, when the disciples marvel at this on the following day, Jesus' response simply doesn't fit in with the situation: 'Look rabbi' they say to him, 'the fig tree you cursed has withered away' to which Jesus responds 'Have faith in God'[73] But what on earth has faith got to do with his earlier petulance? This was hardly a miracle which required faith so why does Jesus make a reply wholly inappropriate to the situation?

Matthew, perhaps mindful that the form of the story received from Mark was unsatisfactory, writes in an explanation to try and make some sense out of it by having Jesus declare clumsily 'if you have faith and do not doubt at all, not only will you do what I have done to the fig tree, but even if you say to this mountain, "Get up and throw yourself into the sea", it will be done.'[74] In Luke the miracle doesn't occur. Instead there's a parable about a fig tree in which a man, dissatisfied with his tree because it hasn't given any fruit for three years, wants to cut it down. But he is persuaded to leave it for one more year by the gardener who pledges to tend to it carefully. If after a further year it bears no fruit, he agrees that it should be cut down.

Now this parable occurs directly after Jesus has been preaching his usual message of doom and gloom - 'unless you repent you will all perish.' It seems therefore that the parable is an illustration of his teaching about the punishment to come to those who don't repent, to those who remain unfruitful by not accepting his teaching (earlier, John the Baptist used exactly the same image of an unfruitful tree to emphasise the urgent need to repent[75]). Or to put it in a slightly

---

[73]Mark 14:24. In Matthew's version of the story the fig tree withers immediately before their eyes, again demonstrating increasing sensationalization.

[74]Matthew 21:21.

[75]Luke 13:5, Matthew 3:9.

different way, those who don't believe or have faith in Jesus and his message will suffer the consequences. Thus the apparently incongruous response - 'have faith' that we found in Mark becomes explicable if we understand that this miracle is a developed variant of the original parable which gradually evolved into an actual miracle story and which Mark seems not to have fully understood.

In the same way then the story of Jesus walking across the sea can be seen as an illustration of the need to have faith and probably evolved out of a parable or saying similar to the one about moving mountains through faith. It's often suggested that in the Church's earliest days, when it was suffering sporadic persecution, the story was originally a parable with the boat representing the Church and Jesus coming to its aid in times of trouble, when it would have seemed to the early Christians that they were continually rowing against the wind. As soon as Jesus is with them and speaks to them the wind drops and troubles disappear.

In Matthew the idea is more explicit with Peter, the rock on whom the Church was founded, trying to join Jesus on the water. His faith is inadequate, but even so Jesus is there to save him: 'Then Peter got out of the boat and started walking towards Jesus across the water, but as soon as he felt the force of the wind, he took fright and began to sink. "Lord save me!" he cried. Jesus put out his hand at once and held him. "Man of little faith," he said "why did you doubt?"'[76]

If we think this use of fantastic stories to convey ideas is a slippery ploy to attract only the foolish and gullible, perhaps we should pause to consider how prevalent this form of persuasion is in our own times. Advertisers for instance are aware of our receptivity to being reached in this way and have long communicated the underlying value of products through vivid, easily understood but clearly impossible scenarios and illustrations.

For example a woman fights against a *giant* living cigarette to show that with nicotine patches you can overcome the *huge* craving to smoke. A car emerges totally unscathed after being driven over by a huge monster truck to prove how strong it is, while other, lesser cars are crushed. A vacuum cleaner is so powerful that it can suck in a

---

[76]Matthew 14:29-31.

menacing tornado.

And just as some of the gospel stories are designed to evoke a sense of astonishment and wonder to enthral the audience, so in our own times we have a variant on this, the ad conceived to attract us to the product or the brand by entertaining us. So we see lizards talking about having lost out on a major beer contract or a piano-playing dog that can talk to plug a particular brand of vodka. It's cool, it's cheerful, it's captivating; it becomes a talking point and maintains our awareness of the product being sold. And so we 'buy into' (or, depending on your point of view, are sucked into) the brand.

Human psychology and emotions don't change that much over time and one might venture that the writers of the gospels - the creative and marketing directors of Christianity - were using a broadly similar technique (probably subconsciously), appealing to the same human responses to sell their own product, Jesus Christ, a new, improved way to worship. According to Matthew Jesus told his disciples that they would become 'fishers of men'. In a culture and age in which divine miracles were the supreme trump cards that could tune into and give hope to the deepest longings of a needy and often desperate people, people who might indeed be willing to give their hearts so gladly, perhaps it was these fantastic stories that gave the disciples and evangelists the hook to help them land their catch.

So should we believe that Jesus really did perform miracles such as walking on the sea and bringing dead people (including himself) back to life? Essentially Christianity uses two key arguments to support its claims about Jesus' miracles. Firstly, Jesus is a god and therefore he *could have* performed miracles; and secondly, the gospels record that he did perform miracles and therefore he *must have* done so.

But these arguments are based on an endlessly circular reasoning. How do we know that Jesus *could have* performed miracles? Because he's a god. But how do we know that Jesus is a god? Because of his miracles. How do we know that Jesus' life *was* characterised by miracles? Because the gospels tell us that it was. How do we know that the gospels are true and accurate in their reports about such phenomena? Because, like all of Sacred Scripture, they were written by writers inspired by the Christian god and therefore they must be true. So how do we know about the Christian god? From the teaching and revelation of Jesus. But why should we accept the word and teaching of Jesus? Because he's a god. And so on and so on.

Moreover, as we've seen, it's almost impossible for an impartial observer to accept the gospels as wholly accurate and reliable accounts of the events in Jesus' life, a fact that becomes all the more apparent when we come to look at the greatest of all Jesus' miracles, his own resurrection.

5

Easter's Morning Glory

Now he's got morning glory
Life's a different story
Everything going jackanory . . .[1]

It's fair to say that for most of us in Britain today the celebration of
Easter means not very much more than brightly covered chocolate
eggs for the children, a couple of days off work (and a good
opportunity to visit the sea-side, Ikea or the local gardening centre)
and the occasion for some quality sporting fixtures. Commemorating
ancient resurrections however, doesn't seem to figure too prominently
in 21st century bank-holiday plans. Yet despite this general indifference
to the true spirit of the Easter holy-day,[2] the idea of the resurrection of
Jesus is so familiar to the collective western consciousness that it hardly
strikes us as at all strange (or ghoulish) that the religion of millions of
people should revolve around the 'resuscitation of a corpse',[3] as Rudolf
Bultmann once referred to the original Easter event.

For Christians the death and resurrection of Jesus are at the very
heart of their faith and are undoubtedly the most important events in
the gospel lives of Jesus. Without the resurrection, Christianity would
never have arisen in the first place and only a handful of scholars of
ancient Jewish literature or Roman history might ever have heard of

---

[1] Blur, *Country House.*

[2] A recent survey conducted by MORI found that 43% of the UK population didn't
know what Easter celebrates (*The Guardian* April 13 2001). Of the remaining 57% of the
population, it seems unlikely that all (or even a majority) of them would rate celebrating
the resurrection of Jesus as the most important aspect of the bank holiday weekend.

[3] Bultmann, *New Testament and Mythology*, quoted from Fuller, *The Formation of the
Resurrection Narratives*, p 1.

Jesus today, perhaps as a charismatic healer, perhaps as a seditious trouble-maker in a distant province of the Empire. So it is with the resurrection, 'the crowning truth of our faith in Christ' as the *Catechism* hails it,[4] that the Christian religion stands or falls, a point that the apostle Paul bluntly acknowledges: 'if Christ has not been raised then our preaching is useless and your believing it is useless.'[5] In other words, if it transpires that Jesus didn't *really* come back from the dead, then it would be fair to say that Christianity is useless, that it's rubbish.

How might we assess what really happened? So many centuries after the event we can never know anything for certain and nothing can be proven one way or the other; but we can show that there are not good grounds for believing that a bodily resurrection took place. By this I mean that the weight of available evidence and the balance of probabilities are not sufficiently compelling to persuade us that the extraordinary Christian interpretation of events, a literal resurrection, is justified. Here, more than anywhere else perhaps, it's worth keeping in mind the 'court case' principles that I outlined in the first chapter as we try to assess the reliability and validity of the testimony we have.

According to the *Catechism*, the reality of this 'crowning truth' has been established by the documents of the New Testament. We've noted already that it has endorsed the 'absolute historicity' of the gospels. When it comes to the matter of the resurrection, just to ensure there's no doubt, it is even more emphatic: 'Christ's resurrection is a real event with manifestations that were historically verified as the New Testament bears witness . . . Christ's resurrection cannot be interpreted as something outside the physical order, and it is impossible not to acknowledge it as an historical fact.'[6] As an historical fact then, it can only be appropriate to investigate it using historical methods and (more importantly) historical standards of criticism.

Despite the fine words and confident assertions, the (historical) fact remains that there were no witnesses to the actual resurrection itself, to that vital moment when the life force returned to the inert corpse and the sacred heart began to beat again. What we do have are *reports* written several decades later and based on oral traditions about an

---

[4] *Catechism,* 638.

[5] 1 Cor. 15:14.

[6] *Catechism,* 639, 643, 644.

empty tomb and of strange, unexpected and elusive appearances of Jesus to some of his followers. We also have the word of a single eyewitness, Paul who claimed that Jesus *appeared* to him some years after his death. It is on these particulars and these alone that the Christian claims of a bodily resurrection are founded. So let's consider the written testimony we have to see if it stands up to critical scrutiny and to consider the validity of the argument or belief drawn from those particulars. Of course the gospels are the best known sources for the resurrection belief and provide virtually all of the detail we know today; but we'll begin with the earlier but less detailed and less well known account provided by Paul, written some 10 to 15 years before the first gospel.

The Appearance To Paul

Some time around the year 56 Paul wrote a letter to a diverse group of people living in the Greek city of Corinth, 'the holy people of Jesus' as he called them, a group which under his guidance had formed one of the earliest Gentile Christian communities. In part the letter seems to have been a response to some of the issues the community had raised about matters of faith and personal conduct. Corinth had something of a reputation for its sexual license and the middle part of the letter deals with one particular sexual scandal (a case of incest) and with prostitution in general.

But some of the group had questioned whether there really was going to be an end of time resurrection of the dead, as Paul had taught. So the letter also contained Paul's beliefs and understanding about this general resurrection, together with a brief indication of his own encounter with the risen Jesus as part of his response to those doubts. As such this forms the earliest written record of the resurrection and is therefore one of the more important passages in the New Testament:

> in the first place I taught you what I had been taught myself, namely that Christ died for our sins, in accordance with the scriptures; that he was buried; and that he was raised to life on the third day, in accordance with the scriptures; that he appeared first to Cephas and secondly to the Twelve. Next he appeared to more than five hundred of the brothers at the same time, most of whom are still alive, though some have died; then he appeared to

James and then to all the apostles; and last of all he appeared to me too[7]

What can we reasonably accept from this passage? What's noticeable about it, apart from its brevity and possible unfamiliarity (the appearances both to James, Jesus' brother and to the five hundred don't feature in any of the gospels) is the way that it comes across almost as something of a formula, with its impersonal tone and fourfold repetition of 'that'. It's quite apparent that Paul has no first-hand knowledge of these resurrection appearances and he can only pass on what he himself had been told, presumably at one of the several meetings he'd had with James or Cephas. And while this may be the most comprehensive record of Jesus' post resurrection appearances, all it really amounts to is just a list, reported by a third party. Even so, one of these appearances – to the five hundred – is especially perplexing. If so many people saw the risen Jesus all at once this suggests that the resurrection was not a subjective faith experience but a real and verifiable event in history. So can we consider this as valid and reliable evidence for the resurrection?

Well, not really. Who for instance are these five hundred and when and where did this happen? Unfortunately Paul doesn't elaborate, although he points out that some of these people were still alive, as if to suggest that their personal testimony might still be sought by anyone who didn't believe him and who was prepared to make the long and arduous journey to Jerusalem. But few people took to the road over matters of religion as readily as Paul did and he must have known that it was extremely unlikely that anyone in the community would've even thought of travelling so far to verify his claim. Ultimately the implied invitation to check his word is disingenuous and provides no additional assurance.

Still, one would have thought that the appearance of a man who really had risen from the dead before so many people would have aroused considerable excitement, perhaps attracting the attention of some of Jesus' opponents, the priestly hierarchy or the Roman authorities for example. Yet no other source, Christian, Jewish or Roman makes any reference at all to this mass appearance. And for one

---

[7] 1 Cor. 15:3-8.

who insisted so vehemently on the reality of the resurrection, it's very odd that Paul should never mention it again. If this appearance really had taken place, why didn't the disciples and other apostles, men who were prepared to risk their lives to spread the word about Jesus, make use of this astonishing story? Why doesn't it feature in *any* of the gospels?

The obvious and most probable conclusion is that it simply didn't occur, or at least not as a genuine encounter. A single uncorroborated sentence just doesn't provide sufficient (if any) assurance that such an extraordinary event as this really happened. It might be that this appearance story originated with Paul, desperate to convince his supporters, or that it was recounted by James or Cephas (or was just one of many rumours) which he believed uncritically. Either way, his credibility as a trustworthy reporter of the resurrection is diminished and our confidence in the reliability of his statement as a whole is weaker as a result. Yet incredibly enough, it is this passage, so sparse in detail, so lacking in colour and proclaimed with almost clinical detachment, that the *Catechism* cites as its supporting testimony when it insists that it is impossible not to acknowledge the resurrection as 'an historical fact'.

We then move on to Paul's personal experience: 'and last of all he appeared to me too.' This is included as the last in the sequence of appearances suggesting that Paul regarded it as being in the same league as the first appearances in Jerusalem or Galilee. But it seems quite incorrect to suppose that the appearance to Paul was of the same type that is related in the gospels. We will see that the gospels insist that the resurrection of Jesus was very much a physical one. However, at the very beginning of the Acts of the Apostles, Luke records that the resurrected body of Jesus was taken off into the sky (on a cloud if we accept this particular ascension story[8]) an event that occurred well before Paul's encounter. If Christians accept the specific article of faith concerning the ascension, unless Jesus decided to make a quick return trip to the earth, Paul can't have seen the same resurrected body of Jesus that the gospels claim the disciples saw.

As with his understanding of the resurrection appearances Paul is

---

[8]Acts 1:9. In Luke Jesus is taken up at night on the same day that he emerged from his tomb. In Acts, also written by Luke, the writer had second thoughts and Jesus moved on after hanging around for 40 days. The cloud reminds me of a flying carpet.

strangely reticent about his own encounter with Jesus and doesn't elaborate further about this life changing event. There's no description of what he saw or of the circumstances. Although he provides no location or occasion, traditionally the appearance is believed to have taken place while he was on the road to Damascus, journeying there to kidnap or arrest early followers of Jesus. However, we only have this understanding second-hand, from Luke's account of it in Acts, written some 50 to 60 years later.

Acts provides three separate accounts of Paul's experience and there are significant discrepancies between them.[9] Initially Paul is struck down by 'a light from heaven all around him' and hears a voice which reveals itself as that of Jesus. Paul gets up and finds himself blind, unable to see, eat or drink for three days. His companions apparently heard the voice but couldn't see anyone. This of course is clearly inconsistent with the idea of a true bodily resurrection, something that is part of the 'physical order'.

Much later Paul describes the event to his opponents, the Jews in Jerusalem who are out for his blood. In this version his companions 'saw the light but did not hear his voice'; while still later, defending himself in front of Agrippa, the king of Judaea, the dazzling light strikes not just Paul but the others also, causing all of them to fall to the ground. Even if we're prepared to overlook the inconsistencies, from all three accounts it seems much more likely that what was experienced was a personal vision of blinding light rather than a physical encounter that a bodily resurrection would entail. It simply doesn't follow therefore that this provides any substantive evidence for a bodily resurrection.

But what about Paul's own version of what happened? This specifically claims that it was Jesus the person rather than a blinding light that appeared to him. So far as we know Paul had never met Jesus so it's difficult to understand how he recognised that it was Jesus who appeared to him (there is no self-identifying voice); but ignoring this, what can we make of his testimony? Undoubtedly he genuinely believed that he'd had some encounter with the risen Jesus; but this doesn't mean that his subjective experience must be taken as being objectively true. As we've already considered, it might be the case that

---

[9]The story is told in Acts 9:1-9, 22:6-11 and 26:12-18.

the experience was a hallucination, the result of a fit or seizure of some sort which Paul and his companions were simply unable to understand and which he, in his enthusiasm attributed to divine intervention.

We need also to consider Paul's motives at this point; why does he highlight his personal experience here when throughout the rest of his letters he is almost silent about the matter? The context of this passage in fact is very significant and this part of his letter has two specific concerns. Firstly, as we've noted, he is responding to earlier doubts about whether or not there will be a general resurrection of the dead. Essentially his argument is that there will definitely be such an event because he himself had seen Jesus, a man who *really had* been raised from the dead. Paul's whole mission depended entirely on the resurrection of Jesus, so it's not surprising that he should defend it so vigorously.

Secondly, as ever, Paul is being very defensive about his status and authority as an apostle. Throughout his letters there are hints of a latent but nagging inferiority complex when he compares himself with James, Cephas and John, 'the arch apostles' as he calls them, men who were more closely associated with Jesus than he was. For example immediately after this passage he lets slip that he sees himself as 'the least of the apostles' hardly worthy of the calling; on another occasion he falls into a resentful self-abasement: 'Though I am a nobody, there is not a thing these arch apostles have that I do not have as well.'

Yet for the earliest Christians, perhaps the most important thing an apostle might have had was a personal connection with Jesus, as evidently James, John and Cephas had. Paul was painfully aware of this requirement and insists that he too measures up: 'I am an apostle and I have seen Jesus our Lord'[10] he protests. But the truth is he never *knew* Jesus when he was alive and he simply couldn't claim such an intimacy. Instead his authority has to rest solely on his claim that he saw Jesus after he had died, that he was marked out by a special appearance. Not surprisingly then, once he overcomes his reticence about his revealing his past experience, Paul plays this card for all its worth.

---

[10] 2 Cor. 12:11, 1 Cor. 9:1. A. N. Wilson (*op cit*, p 205) suggests tentatively that Paul's claim to 'have seen Jesus' (as opposed to his other claim to have received an appearance) was based on him having been present (as one of the servants or guards of the high priest) when Jesus was arrested.

Paul's personal testimony therefore comes across not as an impartial recollection of his experience but one that is motivated by the interests of his mission and driven by his desperate need to assert and maintain his credibility and authority. This was a critical time for Paul. From other parts of the same letter we can see that he wasn't the only Christian preacher to have visited Corinth and that in his absence some of his rivals were increasing their influence to his detriment. In fact their progress was so significant and so disturbing to Paul that in his next letter to the Corinthians he berates the community for transferring its allegiance to an alternative gospel preached by 'counterfeit apostles . . . dishonest workmen disguised as apostles of Christ',[11] as he scornfully calls them. In the circumstances, his insistence that he really had seen the risen Jesus starts to become a little suspect and we need to be wary of his boasting.

Paul almost certainly had some sort of intense mystical, visionary or psychological experience, powerful enough to change the course of his life; he may have been absolutely convinced that Jesus appeared to him. But a claim to have received an appearance, from a man prone to having visionary experiences, is very different from a genuine, physical encounter with a man risen from the dead; and there's nothing in Paul's testimony to substantiate the latter.[12]

Jackanory: The Gospel Resurrection Stories

If we had only Paul's testimony, we would know next to nothing about the immediate aftermath of Jesus' death and the first resurrection appearances. But over the course of the following 40 years or so, increasingly elaborate stories about the resurrection began to appear, beginning with Mark's gospel, generally thought to have been written around the year 70 and ending with John's, some 20 to 30 years later.

---

[11] 2 Cor. 11:13.

[12] In fact Paul seems to regard Jesus' resurrection more a spiritual one than a bodily one. When he considers the questions that the Corinthians probably asked about the (general) resurrection, such as 'How are dead people raised, and what sort of body do they have when they come back?' his response is abrupt and dismissive: 'They are stupid questions . . . flesh and blood cannot inherit the kingdom of God' (1 Cor. 15:35, 36, 50). The *Catechism* calls the appearance to Paul an 'apparition' (659), a word that can mean an appearance but which (more usually) has spiritual or ghostly connotations. It is difficult to use this word without being aware of such connotations.

These narratives divide into two basic types of stories: those about the discovery of the empty tomb of Jesus and those about his appearances in the days that followed. Taken as a whole they provide the detailed reports of the resurrection with which we are more familiar today.

However, there are numerous problems with these accounts. They are almost bursting with inconsistencies and often glaring contradictions to the extent that it has become impossible to know what the true course of events really was, if indeed it was as any one of the gospels makes out. This would not be such a problem for a more everyday type of event such as the baptism of Jesus for example; but given that his alleged resurrection is often regarded as the most extraordinary event of all time and, according to Christianity, forms the pivotal moment in human history, one might have expected testimony more compelling and more consistent (especially since the authors of Sacred Scripture were supposedly inspired by the Holy Spirit).

But this isn't the only stumbling block. The problem is exacerbated by the fact that some of the details in these narratives (like Paul's claim of an appearance to the five hundred) are simply not plausible, even for believers, or are not substantiated in any way. And we must bear in mind that these stories, some of which come across as clearly fictitious, were passed down through oral traditions (and thus repeatedly subject to exaggeration or embellishment) and then distilled through a theologically minded and ideologically motivated writer. As a result, it's difficult to feel confident that either the reporters of the resurrection or the traditions they proclaim are especially reliable or trustworthy.

Mark And The Empty Tomb

The first issue to address is the empty tomb: how did the body of Jesus come to disappear from the tomb in which it was supposedly placed? This ever perplexing, ever unanswerable conundrum and the circumstances surrounding it form the whole of Mark's resurrection narrative. Mark's account is by far the shortest, with only eight verses[13]

---

[13]Almost all New Testament scholars agree that verses 9-16 which include stories of the risen Jesus were added on subsequently by a later, different writer.

and, as one might expect, it is the least developed with the risen Jesus failing to make an appearance.

Nevertheless, Mark establishes the absolutely key theme of the missing body. The evangelists insist that Jesus' resurrection was a physical one and this part of the story provides the foundation for that belief. For had there not been an empty tomb or a missing body, a belief in a physical resurrection from the dead would simply have been impossible to sustain. Not surprisingly the later evangelists follow this lead and devote a significant part of their own narratives to this part of the story.

With Paul completely silent about the actual crucifixion, Mark provides the earliest report of what happened immediately after Jesus' death. Once the grisly method of killing was concluded, the body was taken down by Joseph of Arimathea, a 'prominent member of the Council' and placed in the tomb. Presumably this is the same Jewish council, the Sanhedrin that handed Jesus over to the Romans. It seems slightly suspect then that one of its members should now be so concerned about providing a decent burial for Jesus, especially since Mark records that '*all* [of the Sanhedrin] gave their verdict: he deserved to die.'[14]

Matthew and John address this problem by claiming that Joseph was a secret disciple. According to Mark, Jesus had been either abandoned or denied by his closest disciples from the moment of his arrest. So again it's very odd that a secret disciple, unwilling to 'come out' or even to voice his opinion in the Council to save Jesus, should suddenly make so public a display of allegiance at this potentially dangerous moment. With the disciples having run away, probably in fear of their lives, the only close associates of Jesus to witness the crucifixion were three of his female companions, Mary of Magdala, Mary the mother of Joset, and Salome. Together they look on from a distance when the body is laid in the tomb by Joseph. Unable to anoint the body because the sabbath was falling, the women return to the tomb at dawn on the day after the sabbath to complete the burial rites, only to find that the stone sealing the entrance has been rolled

---

[14]Mark 14:64, my italics. Of course it's possible that the unanimous condemnation of Jesus by the Sanhedrin is part of Mark's anti-Jewish polemic, in which case the intervention of Joseph of Arimathea is at least plausible. But at the same time this would compromise Mark's credibility as an impartial and trustworthy reporter.

away and that the body has vanished.

There are only a limited number of possible explanations for this disappearance, one of which is that Jesus really did rise from the dead. Other possibilities, while speculative, can only be less improbable than this. Some commentators have suggested that Jesus wasn't actually dead when he was taken down from the cross and that he was subsequently revived in the calm and peaceful atmosphere of the tomb, perhaps aided by the mixture of myrrh and aloes that John records being placed there. Apart from the fact that the gospels unambiguously record Jesus as having died, it's difficult to reconcile this conjecture with the experience and competence of the Romans, 'the world's most efficient executioners' as Ian Wilson calls them.[15]

That Jesus' body was secretly removed from the tomb has long been considered as an explanation for its disappearance, although Reimarus' argument that the disciples stole the body to stage a fake resurrection now seems far-fetched. But this appears to have been a genuine concern at the time and, as we shall see, Matthew devotes much of his narrative to dealing with this allegation. More plausibly perhaps, the body may have been taken by a third party unknown to Jesus' disciples and friends; his family for instance may have wanted to bury him privately in a family tomb in Galilee. Earlier in Mark we find a hint of antagonism or even resentment between Jesus and his family; convinced that he's out of his mind, 'they set out to take charge of him.'[16] Clearly they did not succeed. Perhaps after being snubbed by Jesus they despaired or washed their hands of him and left him to follow his own inclinations.

But now that the consequences had proved disastrous and their son and brother had paid for his convictions with his life, perhaps they felt a degree of personal responsibility and remorse. In the circumstances the only practical response and the final act of love would have been to provide a proper burial for him. And if his disciples and followers had abandoned him at his moment of need, why should they be informed? This hypothesis becomes more plausible when we consider that as a convicted criminal, Jesus' body might well have been placed in a common grave or burial pit, perhaps alongside the two men crucified

---

[15]I. Wilson, *op cit*, p 115.

[16]Mark 3:21.

162

at the same time. If so, then the slightly suspect intervention of Joseph of Arimathea can be readily understood as a later, unhistorical tradition introduced to try to cover up a dishonourable burial.[17]

It's also fair to speculate that the women may have gone to the wrong tomb, if indeed they did go there in the first place. All of the evangelists use their narratives not just to tell the story, but also to refute various early objections to the resurrection belief; and for Mark it seems that this was one of the most contentious issues to address. Accordingly he deals with it by emphasising that the women carefully noted where Jesus was laid and by having the young man they encounter in the tomb specifically confirm that they had come to the correct place. However, there is a hint in the Fourth Gospel that Jesus was buried hastily and that the tomb where he was laid was only a temporary one;[18] if this is the case, it's possible that his body was moved before the women arrived.

But what are we to make of these women, especially Mary of Magdala, the central figure of this affair and the only one present at the tomb in all four gospels? According to Matthew and John, she is also the first to see the risen Jesus, even before Peter or any of the other disciples. Not only does she appear to have been a close follower of Jesus, she is also someone who had been exorcised by him. From Luke we learn that Jesus had cast out not one but *seven* devils from her (who was counting?), a point reiterated in the longer ending to Mark's gospel.[19]

So it would seem that the principal witness of the empty tomb was a woman who, perhaps like the Gerasene demoniac that we've previously encountered, appeared at one time to be so disturbed or mentally unstable that she was thought of by her contemporaries as being possessed by seven devils. Having just gone through the enormous distress and horror of seeing her beloved mentor and friend being crucified, who can say what was her state of mind? Arriving with the other women so early in the morning, just as dawn was breaking, she may well have been desperately tired and confused, perhaps

---

[17]The point is argued by Ludemann in *The Resurrection of Jesus*, pp 40–43.

[18]John 19:42: 'Since it was the Jewish Day of Preparation and the tomb was near at hand, they laid Jesus there.'

[19]Luke 8:2, Mark 16:10.

emotionally exhausted or even traumatised. Perhaps the devils returned to unsettle her once again? Later on in the Fourth Gospel we see the same Mary broken down in tears, so distraught that she appears to accuse a complete stranger of having taken the body. In the circumstances, it's at least possible that she went to the wrong tomb and in her distress or panic she initiated fantastical or hysterical stories about a missing body.

On the other hand, it's equally possible that this whole episode is not historical at all and that the story was either written into the narrative by Mark or (more likely) evolved as one of the many earlier oral traditions. Werner Kummel suggests that 'in view of the Palestinian climate, it is not conceivable that the women intend to anoint a corpse on the third day after death' and he observes that it was not the custom of the Jews to make such an anointing with spices in the first place.[20] So why introduce this story? As we've noted, for a physical resurrection belief to be valid, the body of Jesus cannot be allowed to remain in the tomb: it *must* be reported as missing, otherwise the disciples would be open to the charge that they had merely seen a ghost or vision of Jesus. So once the resurrection belief began to spread, stories of the women visiting the tomb on the third day and finding it empty may have begun to circulate.

We can venture that these stories emerged quite late, certainly some time after the appearances belief took hold, since Paul seemed to know nothing about the empty tomb or Mary of Magdala. Commentators have often objected to this hypothesis on the basis that if this episode were fabricated, women would never have been used as credible witnesses for so crucial a discovery. But it may be that the ignominious (if understandable) desertion of Jesus by his disciples was already too well established to be disregarded. Hence the only remaining close associates who witnessed the crucifixion and burial and who would have had a reason to return subsequently were the women.

On entering the tomb the women are amazed to find a young man in a white robe who tells them that Jesus has risen and was proceeding to Galilee where he would meet his followers. No one knows who this man is, no one questions what he was doing there. Sometimes he is

---

[20]Kummel, *The Theology of the New Testament,* p 100. His conclusion is that this story of the visit to the tomb is not historical and 'undoubtedly developed only later' (p 102).

thought of as being the same mysterious man who ran away naked when Jesus was arrested, sometimes an angel; but he might just as easily be nothing more than a literary device planted there to convey information. From this moment on effectively the women are stunned: overwhelmed by the discovery that the body is missing and by the sudden and disturbing news that Jesus is not dead, they run off in fear, unable even to tell anyone about their experience. And there Mark's short narrative abruptly ends with no satisfactory denouement. For 'what happened next' in the resurrection drama we must move on to the later gospel accounts.

Matthew's Resurrection Muddles

Matthew takes up Mark's narrative and generally follows its sequence of events. But we must remember that this isn't a completely independent account but one which is almost certainly based on Mark's text. However, perhaps aware that it wasn't entirely satisfactory, with no actual appearance of the risen Jesus, Matthew substantially expanded and reworked the original narrative, adding in a number of new elements and changing some of the details. But in doing so his resurrection story starts to become hopelessly mixed up and implausible, suffering both from serious discrepancies from Mark and from material that is simply not credible or coherent.

That we should be deeply sceptical about the whole of Matthew's resurrection story as a reliable history is signalled at the outset by a spectacular detail added in just prior to the burial. At the very moment of Jesus' death, with a strange and ominous darkness covering the land, Matthew claims that there was an earthquake and, as if this were not dramatic enough, that 'the tombs opened and the bodies of many holy men rose from the dead.' But he suddenly realises that this is a big mistake since it really should be Jesus who is the first person to come back from the dead, not anyone else. Consequently he writes in a quick afterthought to try and correct his blunder: 'and these, *after his resurrection*, came out of the tombs, entered the Holy City and appeared to a number of people.'[21]

---

[21]Matthew 27:52-53, my italics. Matthew hardly succeeded in repairing the damage since it was still the case that these people came back to life before Jesus did. The

165

Once again it seems as if Matthew has let his imagination and enthusiasm run away with his better judgement and he has created severe problems for himself. If this general resurrection of the many happened, it is surely much more sensational than Jesus' own resurrection (just one man) and would've had dozens of witnesses. In fact Matthew specifically says that the newly arisen dead 'appeared to a number people.' Yet inexplicably this astonishing episode, like Paul's appearance to the five hundred, went *entirely* unreported in all of the other gospels and in Jewish writings of the time. Matthew also called these men 'holy', suggesting that he must have had at least some awareness of their identity (how else could he have known whether they were holy or unholy?). But we're not given any names or further information about who they are or even about the people to whom they appeared.

Nor are we told when they died. One might reasonably suppose that some of them had been dead for some time. Their remains therefore would have been in advanced stages of decomposition; tissues and entire organs, hearts, livers, lungs and so on, would have to have been instantaneously regenerated. Brains, starved of blood and oxygen for weeks, months or even years and probably completely shrivelled or disintegrated would suddenly have bloomed and started to function again, recovering all of their former memories. Yet having been so miraculously restored to life, what do these men do? Do they go to the Temple to praise and give thanks to the Lord? No. Do they set out to be reunited with family and friends? No. Do they go to keep vigil outside Jesus' own tomb so they could worship the new god whose sacrifice had brought about the triumph over death? No.

Instead *all of them*, without exception, decide to hang around in their tombs for a further 36 hours or so before coming out. But why would they do that? Observing the sabbath? Or were they under starter's orders as it were, awaiting an instruction from the Almighty for the right moment to go? One would have thought that after being dead for so long a person suddenly restored to life would be desperate to get out of his tomb as quickly as possible, if only to get a breath of fresh air or something to eat or drink. But these holy men apparently felt otherwise. Unfortunately for Christians it just doesn't add up and

---

earthquake is not elsewhere recorded.

every detail of this story comes across as silly and unbelievable. And when we consider that the story is based solely on a throwaway claim by a single writer (and one that we know is prone to exaggeration and fantasy) we cannot but dismiss it as an extravagant and embarrassing fiction.[22]

For much of the rest of his narrative, Matthew's main concern is to defend the resurrection against the later suspicion of the Jews that Jesus' disciples stole his body to stage a fake resurrection. So to try to show that it would've been impossible for them to have taken the body, he introduces the story of the soldiers sent (at the request of the usual suspects, the chief priests and our friends the Pharisees) to guard the tomb so as to foil this unlikely plot.

But this whole episode comes across as psychologically implausible. Even though the gospels report Jesus as repeatedly prophesying that he would rise from the dead, it's hard to believe that the disciples truly expected this to happen. None of them for instance drew any comfort from the possibility of a resurrection after Jesus was arrested and killed, nor were they inclined to believe the women's reports about an empty tomb. To excuse this lack of expectation, throughout the gospel the disciples are presented over and over again like a gang of village idiots, too stupid to understand or remember their master's earlier prophecies about rising from the dead, despite the fact that such a belief was not uncommon at that time.[23] Could they really have been so uncomprehending or so forgetful? Or is it more likely that Jesus never actually made any such 'prophecies' and that these words were ascribed

---

[22]Biblical commentaries written by Christians pass over this incident with inane comments such as 'these verses answer the mockery [of Jesus] and begin the process of divine vindication: Jesus' death is life giving' (*Jerome* 42:163); or 'The entry of the faithful of the OT into the holy city of Jerusalem ushers in the messianic era. The Jerusalem here envisaged is not primarily the earthly but the heavenly city' (*A Catholic Commentary on Holy Scripture*, p 951). The *Catechism* (647) seems to be embarrassed about the whole story and fails to mention it even though it comments specifically on other characters in the gospels (Jairus' daughter, the son of the widow of Nain and Lazarus) who had been raised from the dead.

[23]Mark records that it was only the aristocratic, priestly sect, the Sadducees 'who deny that there is a resurrection' (12:18); moreover, earlier there was a rumour going round that John the Baptist had risen from the dead (6:14). The popular imagination appears to have had no difficulty in understanding the concept in this instance. Perhaps the disciples understood, but couldn't remember? If this is the case it's extraordinary that Jesus' opponents, the chief priests and Pharisees were able to recall his prophecy (Matthew 27:62-63) yet his disciples experienced a massive collective amnesia.

to him subsequently?[24]

If this is the case, and if neither the disciples nor indeed anyone else expected Jesus to come back to life after being killed, they would've had no reason to want to steal the body in the first place. So why would they go to so much trouble to pull off such a stunt? And given their fear and dejection, demonstrated by their desertion of Jesus when he was arrested, how likely is it that within a day or so they would have found the courage or mental reserves to conceive the plot and then actually steal the body?

Even so, Matthew takes this charge seriously enough to devote nearly half of his narrative to refute this allegation.[25] The story even includes private conversations between the Roman governor, Pilate and the chief priests and between the priests and the soldiers. But how could Matthew (or his source) possibly have known about these details? Would the Pharisees and chief priests have admitted their underhand dealings to him or to some other party? Again, this whole episode, not reported in any of the other gospels, has all the hallmarks of being fictitious.

The story begins with Pilate willingly responding to the chief priests' request for soldiers to guard the tomb: 'You may have your guard' he says nonchalantly, as if he hadn't a care in the world and had dozens of men to spare, despite the fact that Mark records there was rioting and an uprising going on at the time.[26] When the women arrive at the tomb, the tension is further heightened with another violent earthquake and the transformation of Mark's young man inside the tomb into 'the angel of the Lord.'[27] Descending from the sky and with

---

[24]The artifice of Jesus' supposed prophecies is most apparent on the night of his arrest. When Jesus predicts that his disciples will lose faith, he is reported as saying 'after my resurrection I shall go before you to Galilee.' (Mark 14:28) But if he really spoke these words at such a critical time, why couldn't any of the disciples remember them just a few days later? Still more inexplicable is the fact that none of them made any comment on this astonishing prophecy at the time: instead of arranging a convenient rendezvous or even asking Jesus what he meant by his resurrection, Peter simply says 'Even if all lose faith, I will not.' The 'prophecy' interrupts the flow of the narrative and is clearly a later interpolation.

[25]After the burial of Jesus, there are a further 25 verses in Matthew's gospel; 10 of these deal with the sub-plot about the guard (27:62-66, 28:11-15) and a further 8 verses concern the discovery of the empty tomb (28:1-8).

[26]Mark 15:7

[27]Matthew 28:2-3. In Luke, at first there are 'two men in brilliant clothes' appearing to the women, but later on they are transformed into 'a vision of angels.' In John there is

a face like lightning, the angel terrifies the soldiers. It then proceeds to roll away the stone sealing the tomb, explaining to the women that Jesus has risen.

But here we discover Matthew's second major unforced error and his story starts to become seriously muddled: for the tomb is already empty. This must mean that Jesus rose from the dead prior to this and moved the stone himself (or another angel descended beforehand and moved it) and then, most bizarrely, rolled it back into place. But why on earth would Jesus or the angel bother to do this? Matthew declines to provide any explanation.[28]

Meanwhile the soldiers have been so frightened by the angel that they're like 'dead men' and they run away to tell the chief priests what has happened. Despite their fear and the extraordinary nature of their experience they are easily bribed by the supposedly devious priests to lie and say that they fell asleep while on duty and that the disciples stole the body.[29] Now Matthew really starts to lose the plot. For this must mean that they were not asleep and therefore if Jesus really did emerge from the tomb they must have witnessed it. So if they saw him leave, why didn't they arrest him and bring him before their commander or even the chief priests? Alternatively, if they thought Jesus was a ghost and were too frightened to challenge him, why did they stay at the tomb until the women arrived? And if their line is that they fell asleep, how could they possibly have expected anyone to believe their story about the disciples coming to steal the body? How could they ever have known it was the disciples of all people if they had nodded off to sleep?

Moreover, it is almost inconceivable to think that trained, professional soldiers of an occupying power would report this incident

---

no one either near or in the tomb when Mary and the disciples first arrive, but subsequently Mary sees and converses with two angels sitting inside.

[28] Of course it's possible for Christians to claim (ridiculously) that Jesus passed *through* the rock, just as later he would pass through other physical barriers as recounted in John's resurrection narrative. The Church claims that Jesus' body was transformed as a result of the resurrection and was therefore able to behave in this way. But this doesn't explain why the stone is already moved in all of the other gospels. Moreover one feels that such a response has something of the 'make it up as you go along' about it.

[29] The possibility of the disciples stealing the body was the very thing the priests feared and sought to prevent in the first place; yet suddenly they instruct the soldiers to spread the story that the disciples *did* steal the body. It just doesn't add up.

to a bunch of priests rather than to their own commander and then readily agree to admit that they fell asleep while on guard, one of the worst derelictions of duty a soldier can make. Lastly, the fact that the priests bribe the soldiers with 'a considerable sum of money' suggests that they themselves believed the soldiers' story to be true, otherwise they would have surely dismissed it without further ado.

So it seems that according to Matthew the first witnesses of the resurrection were Roman soldiers and the first believers were the ungodly chief priests who, astonishingly believed without having seen the risen Jesus and indeed, before any of the disciples had seen him. In the end this sub-plot is so muddled that it becomes unintelligible to the point of being incoherent and therefore lacking any plausibility. It's hard to avoid the rather obvious conclusion: so far as history is concerned this story has no value at all.

So far we haven't considered any of the actual appearances of the risen Jesus. Mark concerns himself solely with the empty tomb and Matthew spends most of his narrative on much the same matter, arguing furiously but ineptly about unlikely tomb-raiders. All his chicanery would be wasted however if there were no appearances of Jesus and accordingly he records two such encounters. The first is with Mary of Magdala and the other Mary (as she is called), just after they leave the angel at the tomb. This appearance specifically contradicts Paul's account which records Jesus appearing first to Cephas and is at odds with Mark who has no such meeting in the vicinity of the tomb. In fact it interrupts the flow of the story and seems to be forced into the narrative, with Jesus unnecessarily reiterating the angel's message about returning to Galilee where he would meet the disciples.

Matthew's understanding that the appearance to the disciples took place in Galilee meant that several days would have to elapse to enable them to travel back to their villages. Perhaps this is why he inserted the appearance to Mary to allow him to have an appearance on the third day, thus 'proving' that Jesus really did rise on the third day to fulfil his earlier prophecies. His gospel closes with Jesus appearing to the disciples on a mountain. It's a crucial but unconvincing and unsatisfying scene, sparse in detail and lacking in colour. And with a mountainside setting, recalling the Sermon on the Mount, the Transfiguration and the passing of the Old Testament covenant from Yahweh to Moses on Mount Sinai, the whole scene is crudely painted, theologically rather than historically. Consequently the actual appearance of Jesus becomes wholly secondary to the proclamation of the Easter message.

It's Jesus' words however that really give the game away. Apart from the claim to have been given 'all authority in heaven and on earth' and the general (and predictable) instruction that the disciples must teach everyone to *obey* his commands, Jesus makes only two remarks, neither of which can be taken as authentic. First he tells the disciples that they are to preach to all nations and next that they must baptise people.

But these instructions seem to go against the grain of Jesus' teaching before his death. Not once in Matthew's gospel did Jesus mention the necessity or importance of baptism and he stressed that his mission was 'only to the lost sheep of the House of Israel.' To his disciples he even said 'do not turn your steps to pagan territory, and do not enter any Samaritan town.'[30] So why should he suddenly stress these two issues at such a crucial moment? The truth is the voice doesn't belong to Jesus but is a proclamation of the infant Church some 50 years after the episode to justify its adopted practice of baptism and its missionary activity in foreign territory. If this is so then we can't feel confident that this appearance really happened as reported and once again Matthew's credibility as a fair and reliable reporter is critically undermined.

Luke And John: Grilled Fish And Ghostly Visions

Matthew's apparent ignorance of any first-hand recollections of the risen Jesus shows itself in the contrived nature of his appearance scenes; his risen Jesus is not so much a real character, but a voice of proclamation of the Christian mission. In the more elaborate appearance stories in Luke and John however, Jesus isn't simply a mouthpiece but more an actual character, with human traits and responses, one that engages with the disciples and their concerns. But in their attempts to be faithful to the true resurrection traditions, both evangelists create significant additional problems.

---

[30]Matthew 28:18, 10:6. If Jesus really had given his disciples this last instruction about preaching to the Gentiles there would hardly have been the fierce theological disputes on this matter between James and Paul so evident in Acts and in Paul's letters.

Both Luke and John provide three additional appearance scenes. Although they differ, they share certain key characteristics, raising questions about the nature and status of the risen Jesus. Both begin with Mark's empty tomb, again to emphasise the physical nature of the resurrection. In Luke there's no appearance near the tomb, but in the Fourth Gospel Jesus appears to Mary of Magdala. This scene is one of the more moving of all the resurrection appearances, with Mary utterly distraught about the disappearance of the body. Twice she is asked why she is crying, first of all by the two angels which have suddenly turned up inside the tomb and subsequently by an unknown man whom she takes to be the gardener. Believing that it is he who has removed the body, she implores him to tell her where it is. His response is to call her by her name whereupon she suddenly recognises that the gardener is in fact Jesus.

In Luke's first appearance story this surprising lack of recognition of the risen Jesus is also one of the key motifs. On the same day, two of Jesus' followers, Cleopas and another (who remained unnamed) are walking to a village, Emmaus some seven miles from Jerusalem. On the way, their spirits downcast, they discuss 'all that had happened', expressing their bitter disappointment that Jesus had not set Israel free as they had once hoped he would. As they walk, they are joined by a mysterious stranger. At first he seems to know nothing about Jesus but then proceeds to correct their understanding of him, explaining why it was necessary for the messiah to suffer. As evening draws in they invite him to stay with them at the village and as they share their bread, 'their eyes were opened and they recognised him'. But at this very moment of recognition, Jesus vanishes from their sight.[31]

The pair rush back to Jerusalem in a state of excitement to tell the other disciples about their experience. They find them assembled together but unfortunately they're trumped with the news that Simon (Peter) had also seen the risen Jesus. This vital story is included almost as an aside with no further detail, strongly suggesting that Luke had no actual knowledge of this appearance. Perhaps he felt obliged to write it in to his narrative so as to harmonise his account with the older tradition of Paul who recorded that the first appearance was to Cephas.

---

[31]Luke 24:13-35. Unfortunately Luke seems to have thought that Jesus' crucial explanation of why the messiah had to suffer wasn't worth preserving.

As they discuss the strange events of the day (and in complete contrast to Matthew who records the first appearance to the disciples in Galilee), Jesus quite suddenly appears among them and all think they are seeing a ghost. Jesus assures them that he is flesh and bones and to make the point more forcefully, Luke contrives to have him eat a piece of grilled fish before their eyes. Presumably it was the common understanding of the time that spirits were unable to eat food.

Similarly in the final resurrection appearance by the sea of Galilee, recounted in a later appendix to the Fourth Gospel, Jesus stands on the shore, unrecognised by several of the disciples who have returned to their trade as fishermen. Having failed to catch anything during the night, they are advised to cast their nets again, whereupon an unusually large (and precise) number of fish are caught. None of the disciples dare to ask who this helpful stranger is, yet at the same time 'they knew quite well it was the Lord.' Sharing their bread and fish for breakfast, cooked over a charcoal fire, Jesus demonstrates again that he is not a spirit. But from the previous appearances to the disciples in Jerusalem one might have thought precisely the opposite. On two separate occasions they are within a closed room yet twice Jesus suddenly appears among them. Each time it is noted that 'the doors were closed' and on the second occasion John even sets up a contradiction - 'the doors were closed *but Jesus came in*'[32] - suggesting that it is recognised that Jesus is a spirit able to pass through physical barriers.

What's going on here? On the one hand, the evangelists insist that there has been a physical resurrection and that Jesus has a body which can digest food and be touched. Most famously in John there is the story of 'doubting Thomas' who is invited to touch Jesus' wounds to satisfy himself that it is the same crucified body. Given the attention to this aspect of the resurrection, it may be that these details are a response to another early objection to the Christian belief, that what the disciples saw were visions or the spirit of the dead Jesus. On the other hand, perhaps to be faithful to the oral traditions handed down to them, Luke and John record Jesus' behaviour after the resurrection very much like that of a spirit. As we've seen, he appears variously under different forms and passes unrecognised; he appears and

---

[32]John 21:1-14, 20:19-29, my italics.

mysteriously disappears without explanation and can walk through closed doors. Quite how the Church is able to maintain that these two contradictory states can co-exist in one person is something we will come to in the next chapter.

Just Believe

What then may we conclude about these enigmatic and conflicting narratives? As we noted earlier, the gospels were written primarily to strengthen the faith of the first Christian communities. The resurrection narratives form a key part of that call to faith and from their very nature they can't be relied upon to provide impartial and historically accurate accounts of the events surrounding the death of Jesus. The evangelists' priority would have been purely doctrinal, to proclaim Jesus as the risen Christ, in whose name 'repentance for the forgiveness of sins would be preached to all the nations.'[33] Consequently their principal concerns, as I've argued above, are with the rebuttal of early objections, the proclamation of the belief with angels, earthquakes, fish suppers, anything in fact to cajole people into believing, and with the strengthening of this early faith with appeals to the authority of Scripture. But they would not have been especially concerned with historical accuracy.

So far we haven't considered the appeal to scriptural authority, which for the Jews of the age would have been like an appeal to reason or to video evidence in our own times. At times this appeal is very contrived and is clumsily forced into the narrative. Luke for example writes in two separate (and probably quite tiresome) RE lectures given by Jesus to the disciples in which he explains that all Old Testament prophecies are fulfilled in him, while in John there's an awkward editorial comment on how they had failed to understand 'the teaching of scripture, that he must rise from the dead.'[34]

However, scriptural authority has probably shaped the whole of the resurrection story in a much more indelible way. In all four gospels the first appearance of the risen Jesus (or the understanding that he had risen in the case of Mark) was on the third day, Easter Sunday in the

---

[33]Luke 24:47.
[34]John 20:9.

Christian calendar. Yet clearly three days had not elapsed from his death on the day before the sabbath (i.e. Friday); in fact it was less than two full days between these two events. Christians explain this by saying that the day of the crucifixion counts as one whole day. But this is simply not what Jesus said. In Mark for example he said on three separate occasions that 'after three days' he would rise again. Matthew spotted the problem and tried to correct it by changing the wording so that Jesus now prophesied that he will be raised 'on the third day.' But Matthew was careless and elsewhere, in response to the Pharisees' request for a sign, Jesus specifically says that just as Jonah was in the whale for three days, 'so will the Son of Man be in the heart of the earth for three days and three nights,'[35] a comment that is usually taken as a reference to his death and resurrection. And in the Fourth Gospel Jesus is recorded as having said that 'in three days' he would raise up 'the sanctuary that was his body'.[36] Why then is there this obsession with the third day?

This formula is found first of all in Paul's proclamation: 'he was raised to life on the third day, *in accordance with the scriptures.*' Paul's understanding then was that the resurrection on the third day had been foretold in some prophecy or other scriptural passage. It is not certain however whether this understanding came from Paul himself or from an earlier tradition which he was merely reporting. Nor is it certain precisely which passage in the Scriptures is referred to. In Acts Peter's earliest preaching quotes Psalm 16 'you will not abandon my soul to Hades, nor allow your holy one to experience corruption' as a scriptural prophecy (and hence proof) of the resurrection. This may suggest that it was understood that the resurrection took place before decomposition first began which the Jews believed was after the third day.[37]

---

[35] Mark 8:31, 9:31, 10:34; Matthew 16:21, 17:23, 20:7, 12:40.

[36] John 2:19-22. In this gospel Jesus is killed on the Passover day (i.e. Thursday); hence according to John he did remain in the tomb for three days (Thursday, Friday and Saturday) before emerging at daybreak on Sunday. However, traditionally the Church maintains that Jesus was executed on (Good) Friday.

[37] Acts 2:27. The passage is also cited by Paul in a later sermon in Acts (13:35). We must remember however that Acts itself is a late work (written c 85-90 CE) and isn't historically reliable. It's very unlikely that the third day belief emerged as early as Peter's first preaching. The fact that Acts uses the Greek LXX translation of the Psalm (given away by the use of the word 'Hades') suggests that this sermon and use of Scripture was a

However, Paul's understanding of the resurrection seemed to be that it did not involve the physical, earthly body. For Paul the resurrection event somehow transformed the physical body into a spiritual body (something of a contradiction in terms): 'whatever you sow in the ground has to die before it is given new life and the thing you sow is not what is going to come . . . the thing that is sown is perishable but what is raised is imperishable . . . flesh and blood cannot inherit the kingdom of God'.[38] Since resurrection from the dead was a relatively new doctrine for the Jews,[39] it may be that any scriptural authority which appeared to sanction this belief would have been enthusiastically embraced. And the only text which suggested a resurrection, from the prophet Hosea, simply couldn't be separated from the third day formula.

Often cited as the relevant passage 'In the third day he will raise us up',[40] this appears at first to be a precise prophecy of Jesus' third day resurrection. However the use of the first person plural rather than a reference to one specific person is problematic, as is the context and poetic form of the prophecy which concerns the raising of Israel as a nation after it has been *wounded* (by Yahweh in the form of a lion) rather than the literal raising of just one man *from the dead*. And of course as with so many other apparent fulfilments of prophecies, one must ask did the passage actually prophesy the event or was the event formulated or rewritten to fit in with the prophecy?

Finally we can see how important the call to faith was in what is probably the best known and most dramatic of all the resurrection stories, the appearance to the disciple Thomas found in the Fourth Gospel. This story is so remarkable and so memorable that if true one can't imagine how the earlier evangelists knew nothing about it or why they chose not to include it in their own narratives. The fact that they didn't do so suggests that it was a later tradition or, more probably, a moving and imaginative fiction originating with the writer of this gospel. The whole point of this story of course is the requirement to have faith with Thomas's doubt having come down to

---

later literary construction. In the story of Jesus raising Lazarus from the grave it is pointed out that 'by now he will smell; this is the fourth day' (John 11:39).

[38] 1 Cor. 15:36–50.

[39] Vermes, *The Changing Faces of Jesus*, pp 170–171.

[40] Hosea 6:2.

us today as a sign of weakness while its opposite, faith - belief without any evidence - is portrayed as the supreme virtue.

But Thomas is simply being sensible and responds entirely reasonably, unwilling to believe in something so extraordinary until he can see with his own eyes and touch with his own hands. When Jesus reappears to them, eight days later, he is somehow aware of these doubts and invites Thomas to touch him. Thomas' response is to recognise Jesus as 'My Lord and My God' to which the saviour responds 'You believe because you can see me. Happy are those who have not seen and yet believe.'[41] The message to the early Christians is clear: the resurrection was a real event (not just a matter of faith) which convinced even non-believers. And if even the most sceptical of the disciples came round to believing in Jesus' resurrection, then all followers of the new movement should likewise believe and believe without question.

So what remains if we remove the apologetic and sensationalising chaff from the narratives to try to reach a historical kernel? Obviously nothing can be known for certain, but from Mark we have the strong possibility that there were a number of women who witnessed the crucifixion. At some point, not necessarily at dawn on the day after the sabbath, one or more of them *may have* set out to see where he had been buried. Additionally from Matthew we can usefully surmise that an objection to the belief in the resurrection - that the disciples stole the body - did not arise in the days immediately after Jesus' death. Such an objection only emerged later and the story of the guards is a clumsy attempt to rebut that *later* belief.

Some days after the crucifixion, the disciples would've returned to Galilee perhaps to try to pick up their former lives as fishermen. Here one of them (probably Peter) seems to have had some sort of visual experience of a risen Jesus. If this first appearance occurred in Galilee and the disciples remained in Jerusalem until the day after the sabbath (as all of the gospels maintain) it is impossible that this could have happened on the third day. Similarly, from Luke we can guess that two more of Jesus' followers may have had a similar visionary experience of Jesus while travelling on the road, but again not on the third day. From John all we can usefully accept is the possibility of enigmatic and

---

[41]John 20:29.

elusive visions and his insistence on the supreme importance of faith.[42]

What Might Have Happened ?

Despite the lack of hard evidence we can venture that there must have been something behind the profound convictions of a risen Jesus that the disciples began to feel soon after his death. Of course it's impossible for us today to know precisely what happened. But it is possible to put forward a plausible hypothesis which, unburdened by the weight of religious faith, can yield a more reasonable and therefore more probable explanation.

One of the more cogent and comprehensive attempts to get to the historical truth of the events soon after Jesus' death and to try to explain what may have been the underlying causes for those early beliefs has been put forward by the German professor of theology, Gerd Ludemann. Believing that 'the historical question is one of the decisive questions' concerning the resurrection, Ludemann set out to argue a 'reasonable, human'[43] and non-supernatural understanding of the story, but one which nevertheless was able to explain the inner transformation of the disciples. His method was a purely historical investigation into the resurrection texts with the objective of reaching a hypothesis that had the fewest obstacles and which resolved the most difficulties so as to reconstruct the *probable* course of events.

Ludemann's argument and conclusions are that the first appearances did not take place at the tomb since this episode, as outlined above, seems to be a later, unhistorical story that emerged in response to Jewish concerns about the body of Jesus. The first appearances he maintains took place shortly after the disciples had returned to Galilee and therefore could not have occurred on the third day. It was Peter, he believes who first saw the risen Jesus, but this was a vision produced by his own mind rather than by a genuine bodily resurrection.

When Jesus died, Peter's world collapsed. In a state of profound

---

[42]In fact according to one theologian, Willi Marxsen 'The only thing that is historically accessible is Simon's faith'. He then goes on to ask the vital question 'Can one deduce the resurrection of Jesus as a factual event from the existence of faith? The answer is an unequivocal no', *The Resurrection of Jesus of Nazareth*, pp 96, 110.

[43]Ludemann, *op cit*, p 180, p vii. The book was adapted for a less academic readership under the title *What Really Happened to Jesus?*

distress, his bereavement was intensified by his denial of Jesus immediately after his arrest. After having boasted about his loyalty, Peter denied knowing him repeatedly, probably because he feared for his life had his association with Jesus become known to the authorities. Jesus died while he lived because of his cowardice and lack of loyalty. For Judas this feeling of guilt arising from his own betrayal was too much to bear and led to his suicide. Peter, as Ludemann sees him, experienced a similar severe guilt complex and was in a state of 'unsuccessful mourning', in which he simply couldn't reconcile himself to his loss.

In support of his argument Ludemann cites contemporary research into the psychology of bereavement which found that sudden death, an ambivalent attitude toward the dead person associated with feelings of guilt and a dependent relationship were all factors which could hinder the process of mourning. In some extreme instances, unable to deal with the reality of the situation, the unconsciousness creates a 'pseudo-satisfaction' for itself, leading the bereaved to 'see' the dead person or to feel his presence.[44]

This, Ludemann argues, was the underlying psychological trauma that caused Peter, unable to bear his mourning, to experience one or more genuine visions which, in the absence of any understanding of psychology or neuroses, he earnestly believed to be the risen Jesus. The key effects of this experience were twofold: firstly it aided the mourning process and so eased the pain and guilt that Peter was feeling. Consequently the appearances or apparent resurrection of Jesus became associated with a feeling of freedom from guilt or, in religious terms, the forgiveness of sins. Secondly, the other crucial element of the Easter faith was the belief that in death Jesus had not been abandoned by the Father he so loved; death had been overcome to allow him to return to the world. Effectively then he had opened the gateway for a general end of time resurrection - a time, according to Jesus, that was soon in coming.

When news of this appearance or repeated appearances spread, a chain reaction of events was set into motion. The likely transformation in Peter's spirit, from being depressed and guilt-ridden to being visibly overjoyed and ecstatic would have been enough to persuade his closest

---

[44] *Ibid*, pp 97-100.

companions of his sincerity and of the authenticity of his experience. In a culture relatively unsophisticated in terms of psychological understanding, but profoundly earnest in religious terms - and one that was inclined to believe in angels, visions and literal resurrections - the disciples would readily have conjectured or accepted that this was a sign from heaven that Jesus was favoured and blessed. Enthused by the messianic expectations of the time, it was then an obvious step for the disciples to come to regard and proclaim Jesus as the 'anointed one', perhaps prompted by Jesus' own messianic consciousness. And so belief or faith in him, and more specifically in his 'resurrection' (or perhaps more appropriately his exaltation) soon became the all important doctrine through which everyone, like Peter could find forgiveness for their sins and participate in the coming of the holy kingdom.

This initial appearance probably acted as a catalyst to spark further visions either real or claimed in others thrilled and caught up in the volatile and easily combustible messianic enthusiasm of the age. There may even have been a 'herd mentality' whereby the other disciples, not wanting to feel left behind, also claimed to have seen the risen Jesus. In the gospels we see them bickering with each other when Jesus was alive as to who among them was the more favoured;[45] such a competitive attitude might well have continued to prevail after his death. The subsequent appearances to larger groups of people (to the twelve or the five hundred as claimed, but not witnessed by Paul) Ludemann suggests were the result of a mass ecstasy or hysteria aroused by the recollections and previous visions of a small number of individuals preaching in an excitable and spiritually intoxicating atmosphere.[46]

This hypothesis is certainly able to explain many of the problems we've discovered in the gospel narratives. Earlier we saw that Jesus mysteriously appears and vanishes, apparently able to pass through solid walls or doors. But if these stories are actually about fleeting visions that one or more of the disciples experienced (probably not at the same time) then these bizarre details start to make sense. Hallucinations, by

---

[45]Mark 9:34 ('they had been arguing which of them was the greatest'); 10:35-37 ('James and John, the sons of Zebedee approached him . . . They said to him, 'Allow one of us to sit at your right hand and the other at your left in your glory''); Luke 22:24 ('A dispute arose also between them about which should be reckoned the greatest').

[46]Ludemann, *op cit*, pp 173-179.

their very nature are transitory and unexpected and like dreams are not altogether coherent; many of Jesus' brief and sudden appearances are similarly characterised.

So it may be that these aspects of the appearances that we see particularly in the Fourth Gospel were the authentic 'resurrection' experiences and were more or less faithfully preserved. But just as the miracle stories became increasingly elaborate and removed from their historical kernel, so these authentic *appearance* traditions became more and more extravagant, until at some point they were transformed into stories of a *bodily* resurrection, an event that found a credulous and enthusiastic audience. As if to confirm this, when we return to the earliest testimony provided by Paul we find no mention of an empty tomb and the emphasis of his personal experience and resurrection belief is on the 'spiritual' form rather than on a bodily one.

Finally once the physical aspect began to dominate the whole affair, the story of an empty tomb was introduced, perhaps even based on a real or aborted visit to Jesus' burial place or some genuine confusion about the whereabouts of his body.

A Modern Day Parallel ?

Of course all of this is conjecture only and none of it can be proven one way of the other. We all believe what we want to believe, whatever suits us best. We may even find it difficult to accept this hypothesis of guilt or grief induced visions and hysteria related beliefs. But if we recall a death similar in certain circumstances to that of Jesus which occurred in our own times and consider our responses to it, we may be able to appreciate that this is not such a ludicrous idea after all and in fact may even be taken as quite plausible.

When Diana, Princess of Wales was killed in a car crash in 1997 there were many striking parallels with the death of Jesus. Like Jesus, Diana was a well known, popular and highly charismatic figure; as Jesus may have been regarded by some as the messiah and therefore of royal blood, so Diana made known her wish to be considered as 'queen of people's hearts.' Popular acclaim was central to the standing of both these figures and in part it was earned through healing the sick and caring for the needy. Jesus' reputation and abilities as a healer we have already considered; Diana too was noted for this 'gift' during her lifetime and more particularly so after her death. Just one day after the fatal accident for instance, the Catholic peer, Lord St John of Fawsley observed that 'she had a real and charismatic gift for healing' while journalists toyed with the idea of possible cures in her name in the not too distant future.

Jesus and Diana were also anti-establishment figures who came to be seen as potential threats to the established order. This reputation came about not only through their association with the marginalised and those at the bottom of the pile, but also in their opposition (whether explicitly articulated or not) to the stuffiness and remoteness of the elitist institutions that maintained the status quo. And throughout their public careers both were hounded: Jesus (according to the gospels) by the Pharisees and Scribes who seemed to be plotting his downfall and death at every turn and from the very outset; Diana by the media and paparazzi whose constant faultfinding and disparagement or whose intrusive photos were referred to by her brother, Earl Spencer in his funeral address as 'a permanent quest . . . to bring her down.'[47]

Both died young, very unexpectedly and violently. If we accept the gospel accounts of Jesus' last days, his trial and condemnation were as swift as they were sudden. While Jesus himself may have had some terrible inkling of his fate, it's unlikely that this premonition was shared by his disciples; still less could his supporters in the streets, who had greeted his triumphal entry into Jerusalem just a few days earlier, have foreseen such a catastrophe. With Diana too death came just as dramatically and without warning. The fatal car crash may confer iconic status on today's celebrities, as it has ever since the death of James Dean, but it's in the nature of such tragic events to be quite unexpected. One normal Saturday evening she was there, the next, as the nation got up on Sunday morning, she was forever gone and the world was thrown into a state of shock. Perhaps as a spontaneous reaction to the sudden death of popular and charismatic figures rumours and stories quickly evolve and spread as if people simply can't take in or accept the shocking news. In the age of Jesus angels, earthquakes and an empty tomb were the order of the day while in our

---

[47] *The Independent* 8 Sept 1997, *The Guardian* 8 Sept 1997; Earl Spencer's funeral address, Sept 6 1997, Associated Press.

182

Adam and Eve condemned and expelled from the garden of Eden [Masaccio]. Their fallen state was to be passed on to all humanity as the consequence of disobedience, Christianity's original and most intolerable sin.

Abraham, about to cut the throat of his son Isaac [Rembrandt]. Because of his obedience, to the extent that he was prepared even to murder his own child, Abraham is considered to be a model of Christian faith.

The annunciation [Murillo]. A flying spirit creature, Gabriel tells Mary, the mother of Jesus that the Holy Spirit (represented by a dove) will come upon her and that she will conceive a child. The Church understands this to mean that there was no sexual act in the conception of Jesus and that the Holy Spirit was sent to sanctify her womb and 'divinely fecundate it.'

The birth of Jesus [Campin]. Nowhere in the New Testament is there any mention of Jesus being born in a stable. To the right of Mary is Salome who, disinclined to believe in the virgin birth, is about to have her hand consumed by fire.

Christian theology revolves around 'the glorification of pain.' The agony of a cruel and painful death is vividly depicted by Grunewald's altar piece. According to *The Oxford Companion to Christian Art*, 'No other crucified Christ in all Western art exceeds this one as an expression of the full ghastly horror of Christ's terrible death.'

The gospels record that Jesus was able to raise people from the dead on three separate occasions. Here he restores the daughter of Jairus, the synagogue official back to life [Polenov].

Another crucifixion scene [Van Eyck], this one depicting Jesus' death not so much as 'the perfect sacrifice', but for what it really was – an execution.

Jesus taken down from the cross [Massys]. The Church believes 'it is you who have crucified him and crucify him still when you delight in your vices and sins.'

The risen Jesus [Garofalo]. According to the Church the bodily resurrection of Jesus was a real event and 'it is impossible not to acknowledge it as an historical fact.'

The Trinity [Raphael]. The Holy Spirit in the form of a dove is placed between the four gospels to indicate that they were written under its inspiration.

The conversion of the apostle Paul on his way to Damascus to kidnap or arrest the earliest followers of Jesus [Michelangelo]. According to Acts Saul was struck down by a blinding light from heaven to be transformed from persecutor to Paul, the gospel's most enthused proclaimer.

Detail from Michelangelo's Last Judgement in the Sistine Chapel. One of the clearly terrified condemned souls is dragged down to hell for everlasting punishment by a pair of demons.

The Emperor Constantine receives a vision of the cross shortly before the battle of Milvian Bridge [Raphael]. His victory would lead eventually to the triumph of the faith throughout the Empire. Next to the cross is the heavenly instruction to Constantine to 'Conquer by this'.

own time dozens of conspiracy theories, perhaps a modern day equivalent of supernatural rumours, circulated at internet speed.

More importantly, both Jesus and Diana underwent a mythical transformation soon after their death. Within hours Diana was officially proclaimed to be 'the people's princess' by the Prime Minister, Tony Blair, a figure of great authority and respected by all the people *at that time,* as a modern day evangelist might describe him. And just as Jesus acquired the title messiah, the Christ, which eventually became his name and epitomised his very being, so the title that Diana had ventured for herself, 'queen of people's hearts' which had once seemed so laughable and so embarrassing, overnight became the most fitting epitaph, defining her life and her 'mission' perfectly.

It didn't take long for this transformation to take on a quasi-religious character. Given the enormity of the grief and dejection that people felt, unable to reconcile themselves to the loss, perhaps this was the only response that could bring some consolation out of the tragedy. So on the following day a tabloid headline read 'Born a Lady, Became a Princess, Died a Saint'. But even this near instantaneous secular canonisation was not enough to ease the pain of the nation's collective consciousness and soon there followed more extravagant proclamations and musings: 'If Jesus was God's only son, then who was Diana?' was one person's desperate question and by the day of the funeral a week later, effectively she had achieved a resurrection of sorts with one national paper proclaiming 'Diana, Princess of Wales is dead; but Diana, Queen of Hearts, yet lives.'[48]

Yet in the weeks and months leading up to her death, attitudes to Diana were ambivalent; often satirised, she came perilously close to becoming a figure of ridicule. Unable to pull it out as the appalling news of the crash came in, *The Observer* for instance went to press on the day with a satirical article, *Mrs Blair's Diary* in which a fictitious PM's wife poured scorn on Diana's naive political musings, 'the witterings of a woman who, if her IQ were five points lower, would have to be watered daily.'

But it was the press intrusions into her personal life and conduct that were most damaging and, as it was felt at the time, ultimately it

---

[48] *The Mirror,* 1 Sept 1997, *The Independent on Sunday* 7 Sept 1997, *The Guardian* 6 Sept 1997.

was the paparazzi who were judged responsible for her death. Such was the general hysteria and the need to find a scapegoat that journalists were as bad as murderers and Earl Spencer's reaction on the following day, that the press had 'blood on its hands' captured the immediate popular sentiment. Yet it was this same public that had created and sustained the demand for pictures and which fuelled the celebrity gossip machine. Perhaps there was a terrible but unacknowledged sense of collective remorse or even guilt: as one journalist wrote 'Now we have Diana the martyr . . . She, who died for our sins, because we had to buy the newspapers that printed the photographs . . . We therefore crucified her with our strange appetite for celebrity . . . we know that it is really our fault that she died.'[49]

In such a charged and difficult time it didn't take long for people to begin reporting seeing visions of the dead princess. As mourners queued for up to ten or eleven hours to sign the books of condolence in St James' Palace some claimed to have seen her face in the top right hand corner of Edward Bonner's portrait of Charles I. 'It was Di . . . Seriously . . . It's the photo with her hands clasped . . . It's just there' claimed one young man, while another witness said that she saw it 'As clear as day. You know the pose the one with her head cupped in her hands. She's got the tiara on as well.' Another woman who emerged in a flood of tears even claimed to have seen that Diana had a red dress on.

Naturally we may think that these apparitions are poor comparisons to the gospel appearances of Jesus. But we must remember that we don't have the actual details of what those first eyewitnesses saw in the days and weeks after the crucifixion; and it's very likely that the reports and stories of Jesus' appearances were exaggerated as they were told and retold over and over again, particularly so in that they couldn't be explained or even thought of except by reference to divine intervention and to the supernatural.

Since then the world has moved on and we now have a much better understanding of such phenomena as not uncommon symptoms of mourning. So the media-friendly clinical psychologist Oliver James offered an explanation for visions of Diana on the following day, suggesting that they were 'an extreme manifestation of a recognised

---

[49] *The Observer* 31 August 1997, *The Independent* 1 Sept 1997.

184

phenomenon among the recently bereaved. One response in some people is to see the dead person all around them. They smell them, hear them, sense them everywhere. In extreme cases, people have hallucinations and it can be very infectious.'[50]

Visions of recently deceased people then would appear to be a recognised and well-documented phenomenon.[51] If people in an age far more secular and aware than that of 1st century Judaism responded involuntarily to the violent and sudden death of a public figure in such a fashion, it's quite reasonable to consider that the death of Jesus evoked a similar response from some of his own supporters. And it's likely that the visionary experience would have been much more intense for his closest associates than for those who 'saw' Diana since these mourners were not especially intimate with her. We do not genuinely *know* what those experiences were; but whatever Jesus' followers saw, if alternative, more plausible explanations for their experiences can be ventured, then divine intervention and a bodily resurrection can no longer be considered as the most probable interpretation of events, particularly when that interpretation is so poorly supported.

As we've seen, the report of the only eyewitness, Paul, is undermined by its extravagant and uncorroborated claims as well as by the fact that it is driven by his need to assert his authority and prove his argument that there really was going to be a general end of time resurrection. Even ignoring these factors, his personal testimony conveys little more than a subjective vision as opposed to a true physical encounter.

Then we've looked at the narratives of the resurrection *reporters* (not witnesses) and seen that they are so inconsistent they simply cannot give us a reliable historical fix for a supposedly historical event. And we've seen that the evangelists themselves can't be thought of as impartial and trustworthy reporters. Not only are their narratives, in the words of Willi Marxsen, 'sermons to sustain the Church',[52]

---

[50] *The Independent* 4, 5 Sept 1997.

[51] See for example the *Handbook Of Bereavement Research* (ed. Stroebe et al, published by the American Psychological Association, 2001), pp 435-436, Sanders, *Grief: The Mourning After*, 1989, pp 70-71, and Littlewood, *Aspects of Grief: Bereavement In Adult Life*, 1992, p 47.

[52] Marxsen, *op cit*, p 165.

formulated as the story of doubting Thomas shows, to bring about uncritical, unquestioning belief; but they also show clear evidence of often harebrained fabrications written in to try to persuade us to believe. In the end one may either believe or not believe; but in the words of one eminent scholar's conclusion on the resurrection narratives, they 'can no longer be read as direct accounts of what happened'.[53]

So is it really still tenable to consider the bodily resurrection of Jesus as an indisputable historical fact as the Church maintains? Or might an impartial observer find it more reasonable to conclude that if, over the course of centuries it has not been turned to dust, somewhere in Jerusalem or Galilee a special set of bones remains to be discovered?

---

[53]Fuller, *op cit*, p 172.

6

Mystery

*And blind acceptance is just a sign
of stupid fools who stand in line* [1]

So far we've considered Jesus' death and resurrection as an event
and a miracle without considering their theological significance, the
redeeming power unleashed by the sacrifice, and the triumph over sin
and death achieved by the resurrection. The Church rarely refers to
the resurrection as a miracle, preferring instead to call it a 'mystery'.
Mystery has become one of Christianity's central and most important
concepts (the whole of the second section of the *Catechism* for example
is entitled *The Celebration of the Christian Mystery*) and many of its key
doctrines are called 'mysteries of faith'; so what does it mean by this
term and why is it so widely used?

Mystery seems to have a threefold use. In everyday secular use the
word is used to express the unknown and enigmatic: we might speak
of the mysteries of the deep or the mysteries of the universe for
example when contemplating the hidden depths of the oceans or when
trying to understand the extent or origins of the universe. The Church
also uses mystery in this simple sense to convey that we can never
presume to know everything about its supreme being, the Father-god.
So he - or it - is proclaimed as mystery itself, 'the inexpressible, the
incomprehensible, the invisible, the ungraspable.'[2] Mystery in this
simplest sense then is something elusive that baffles and perplexes,
something that essentially is unknown or unknowable.

---

[1] The Sex Pistols, *EMI*.

[2] *Catechism* 42. Perhaps on reflection this isn't so straightforward as first appears: how for
instance can the Church *know* anything about its god if it is *incomprehensible*? The
Catechism goes on to declare (370) that the god is 'neither man nor woman . . . [but] is
pure spirit in which there is no place for the differences between the sexes.'

However, the Church's use of mystery undergoes a subtle change; from denoting something that we do not or cannot understand, it becomes the principal means of rebuttal to refute obvious flaws or otherwise unanswerable objections to the Christian belief. *God works in mysterious ways* is the well-worn cliché that epitomises this intellectually lousy response.

So for instance if the Christian god wants all people to be saved through the mediation of Jesus, one might legitimately ask why immediately after his resurrection did Jesus appear only to his close supporters? Why didn't he appear to all people, including his opponents such as the unbelieving high priest and the Pharisees? Why not to the Roman authorities? Surely that would have brought more people around to the Christian faith? Why doesn't Jesus appear to non-believers today? Why can't he appear in a demonstrable and verifiable way that would satisfy all sceptics and silence all critics?

To this the *Catechism* responds that while the resurrection was an historical event, it was at the same time 'at the very heart of the mystery of faith' and hence 'this is why the risen Christ does not reveal himself to the world but to his disciples.'[3] This isn't much of an explanation, in fact it's no real use at all, being little more than an empty rhetorical statement without any logic or argument to substantiate it and one that fails to address the issue. Clearly it's not a response with which one can reasonably argue and so it actually forms a very effective means of stonewalling.

Consequently mystery becomes a rather handy ploy to get the Church out of all those difficult corners and tight spots: if there is a devil, why does the Christian god allow it to continue to cause so much suffering and evil (arguably the greatest conundrum of the faith)? 'It is a great *mystery* that providence should permit diabolical activity.' How can a sin committed by one person be passed down to all humanity? 'The transmission of original sin is a *mystery* that we cannot fully understand.' Why was it necessary for the Father-god to send his son to die to redeem the world and how can Jesus' death achieve this anyway (the big questions with which this chapter is mostly concerned)? 'The Father accomplishes the "*mystery* of his will" by giving his beloved Son and his Holy Spirit for the salvation of the

---

[3] *Ibid*, 647.

world.'[4] And so on and so on.

In fact the *Catechism* is so fond of and so immersed in mystery that it soon starts to become quite overwhelming and tiresome, meaningless in fact. Virtually anything can be (and is) deemed to be a mystery. So because of the Incarnation, because the Son-god became a man, 'Christ's whole life is mystery' and strangely every minor detail and incident in it, from the swaddling clothes at his birth (why?) to the vinegar offered to him on the cross is 'a sign of his mystery.'[5] Indeed so excessive is its use of mystery that inevitably there are certain paragraphs that descend into being impenetrable, esoteric gibberish, as the example in the opening chapter showed.

But Christianity uses mystery in a more profound and disturbing sense than this for many of its key beliefs: the doctrines of the Incarnation, the resurrection, the Eucharist and above all the Trinity are all expressed as 'mysteries of faith'. There's no specific article which defines mystery in this respect but we do get some understanding of what the Church means by it in the *Catechism's* exposition of the Trinity, 'the central mystery of Christian faith and life' and 'the source of all the other mysteries of faith.' The Trinity, we're told, is a mystery of faith in the strict sense, because it is one of those key beliefs that 'can never be known unless they are revealed by God', and which are 'inaccessible to reason alone.'[6] Undemonstrable illumination from above, usually through the agency of the Holy Spirit and apparent unintelligibility would therefore appear to be the two principal characteristics of Christian mysteries.

Mental Cheating: Mystery And Irrationality

But why complicate things and insist on beliefs that are inaccessible to reason if, as the *Catechism* maintains, 'human reason is . . . truly capable by its own natural power and light of attaining to a true and certain knowledge'[7] of the Christian god? And why might such beliefs be inaccessible to reason in the first place? The best way to answer this

---

[4] *Ibid*, 395, 404, 1066, my italics.

[5] *Ibid*, 515.

[6] *Ibid*, 234, 237.

[7] *Ibid*, 37.

and to understand the Christian use of mystery is to turn to an unlikely source to consider a similar and equally sinister ideological stratagem: the use of *doublethink* in George Orwell's bleak satire *1984*.

Like a sceptic or an outsider trying to make sense of the mysteries of the Christian revelation, Winston Smith, the narrator of Orwell's masterpiece, is also a seeker, a sometimes defiant and half-heroic everyman as his name suggests, struggling to understand the prevailing ideology which controls his world. Winston's instinct is to hate and reject the Party whose dark machinations he is only too aware of. Throughout his brief period of rebellion he is constantly troubled by one of the principal disciplines Ingsoc uses to maintain its authority over society: the practice of doublethink.

Doublethink, he understands, is a mode of political or ideological thinking whereby one is obliged 'to know and not to know, to be conscious of complete truthfulness while telling carefully constructed lies, to hold simultaneously two opinions which cancelled out, knowing them to be contradictory and believing in both of them'. Doublethink, as the word implies, is two thoughts, essentially 'the power of holding two contradictory beliefs in one's mind simultaneously, and accepting both of them,'[8] a more succinct definition that Winston later reads in the forbidden book of the Party's arch-heretic, Emmanuel Goldstein.

Now when we consider Christian mysteries of faith, we can see that they too tend to be based around an internal contradiction; the believer is required simultaneously to accept two contradictory propositions which obviously goes against all logic and explains precisely why these beliefs are inaccessible to reason. Mysteries of faith by their very nature simply *cannot* be reasonable or coherent propositions.

With the doctrine of the Trinity, Christians are obliged to accept that there are three separate and distinct gods, but at the same time that there is only one god. With the Incarnation Christians must think that Jesus was simultaneously *fully* human and *fully* divine, a teaching which of course is conceptually impossible because of the contradiction arising from a dual nature (try to think of a piece of material which at the same time is 100% steel *and* 100% wood - or 100% steel and 100%

---

[8]Orwell, *1984*, pp 35, 183.

not steel - to appreciate the absurdity). With Mary, the mother of Jesus we see the contradiction expressed in terms of a natural, biological impossibility: she is a virgin and yet at the same time she cannot be a virgin.[9] And in the 'Sacred Mysteries' of the Eucharist the bread and wine become 'in a way surpassing understanding, the Body and Blood of Christ . . . mysteriously made present';[10] and yet the bread and wine themselves are never demonstrably changed. Mystery then, if you think in terms of ideology, in its purest form is a type of theological doublethink; if you take the down to earth approach it can only be described as irrational gobbledegook.

The next question to ask is - why did this situation develop? In part, mystery was forced on the Church from its legacy from both the Old and New Testaments and was the only practical or possible response. This was certainly the case in the development of the mystery of the Trinity for example. As we shall see in the next chapter, in the Hellenistic milieu in which early Christianity thrived, cut off from its Jewish roots, Jesus was soon acclaimed and worshipped as a god in his own right. However, in the gospels he frequently refers to his heavenly father as a separate god. So it came about in the early 2nd century there were two Christian gods, joined much later by a third, the Holy Spirit.

The problem was, with its fondness for ancient writings and the prophecies they contained, crucial for Jesus to have been proclaimed as the messiah, Christianity appropriated the Jewish Scriptures as its own. But these were writings which were adamant that there was only one god which could be worshipped. It was impossible for Christians to abandon either of these beliefs (that there was only one god and that Jesus was another god distinct from the Father); but it was also just as impossible reasonably to maintain both. The only way out of the impasse was to declare that both gods (eventually joined by the Holy Spirit), while separate and distinct, were at the same time one god. The fact that this made no sense didn't matter; it was now a 'mystery of faith', inaccessible to reason and the believer wasn't expected (or required) to understand. Truth had been revealed and the faithful were

---

[9]Obviously today it's technically possible for a woman to have a fertilised egg inserted into her womb and then to go on to become a mother without ever having had sex. Such a procedure of course was impossible in biblical times.

[10]*Catechism*, 1333, 1357.

expected simply to accept and believe.

But there are darker reasons for the Church to have brought mystery to the centre stage and make it so prominent a feature of the faith. Because mysteries are accessible only to faith and not to reason, the believer cannot legitimately subject these beliefs to any form of intellectual scrutiny. Consequently one believes (and should believe, perhaps even must believe) uncritically and unquestioningly; effectively mysteries require and oblige the faithful to respond with an unseen or blind acceptance. The point is neatly made by Karen Armstrong in her book *A History of God* with the observation that the word mystery derives from the Greek verb *musteion*, meaning to close the eyes or the mouth.[11] As the story of doubting Thomas suggested, a willingness to accept beliefs so contrary to reason and experience without seeing and without understanding soon became an eminent virtue and key requirement of the early Christians, a response that is just as important for the Church today. 'Happy are those who have not seen and yet believe.'

We may venture then that those who can be steered into not even wanting to see or understand are still more highly regarded. For if the faithful cannot or will not subject a proposition to intellectual scrutiny, they accept and recognise the authority of the institution (i.e. the Church) that is proclaiming that proposition, thereby empowering it further. Consequently these people yield to or subject themselves to that authority rather than rely on their own judgement and resources; and little by little that authority, using the formula that 'God's will' is this or that, becomes increasingly difficult to challenge, to the extent that eventually it can govern and determine both thought and behaviour. Hence the crucial point to understand about mysteries of faith is that they help to form a very effective instrument of control; if the believer can be led into accepting irrational doctrines without question, then the authority behind those doctrines is all the more respected and firmly entrenched and can't be easily challenged.

We can see these dark consequences if we return to Orwell's *1984* and consider the insight offered by one of Winston's colleagues, Syme, the intellectual working on the 'Newspeak' dictionary. Newspeak is the Party's official language and the dictionary is being compiled not to

---

[11] Armstrong, *A History of God*, p 244.

define and clarify language but systematically to reduce and destroy it so as to 'narrow the range of thought' and make freedom of thought and expression virtually impossible. In his perverse enthusiasm for his work Syme shares his vision of how the world will be in a depressing yet comic lunchtime conversation with Winston. In the future he says with an absurd yet grim relish, 'there will be no thought as we understand it now. Orthodoxy means not thinking, not needing to think. Orthodoxy is unconsciousness.' What the Party wants, as Winston subsequently learns in unspeakable agony as he's being tortured, is unconscious faith, a complete and voluntary submission to its way of thinking, to its control, without any question or hint of doubt.

To achieve this it requires and insists (like the Church) that it alone has an absolute infallibility; according to O'Brien, Winston's ruthless tormentor and Ingsoc's own Grand Inquisitor, 'Whatever the Party holds to be the truth, is truth.' And in its determination to maintain this infallibility one of its principal methods is to twist the laws of reason with the technique of doublethink so that two and two really can equal five or three or even both of these at once. Doublethink, Winston comes to realise, is 'a vast system of mental cheating' which exists only so that those in authority can maintain their status and power: 'if the High, as we have called them, are to keep their places permanently – then the prevailing mental condition must be controlled insanity.'[12]

Mystery too is a form of 'mental cheating' and its purpose and the consequences arising from its use are broadly similar. Just as orthodoxy for Ingsoc meant 'not thinking, not needing to think', so mystery in Christianity discourages or tries to prohibit its adherents from thinking about its most important doctrines. Through mystery, its own version of 'controlled insanity', the Church is able to get people to believe in and accept propositions that clearly make no sense at all, that are literally *non-sense*. This can only be achieved by teaching that as mysteries, these irrational and nonsensical beliefs must be approached through faith. Consequently common sense is denigrated and faith, in the form of a willing subjection of the self to authority, is proclaimed to be the 'adequate response' to the Christian revelation, valued far

---

[12]Orwell, *op cit*, pp 50, 214, 184, 185.

above reason and intelligence: 'what moves us to believe is not the fact that revealed truths appear as true and intelligible in the light of natural reason: we believe because of the *authority* of God himself who reveals them.'[13]

For Christians the price to be paid is a heavy one and the consequences are little short of disastrous. Effectively reason has to be sacrificed, for faith isn't simply a matter of vague belief but a surrender of reason and indeed of personal intellectual freedom: 'By faith man *completely submits his intellect and his will* to God. With his whole being man gives his assent to God.'[14] And if by faith one willingly and wholeheartedly accepts irrational propositions such as two and two make five or three or, in the case of the Trinity, that three ones are not three but one, then this more than anything else is an unequivocal confirmation of that surrender. Faith props up mystery; but mystery also helps to ensure that faith (which, as the example of Abraham shows, ultimately means little more than obedience and which can lead to the most appalling practical consequences) remains the most important and most valued response a Christian can give.

But how do Christians in our own times know about these revealed truths and the divine will? The days of a loud voice emanating from the sky or Jesus appearing in a blinding light are long gone and revealed truths are communicated today not by the god itself but by the somewhat more earthly authority of the Magisterium, the teaching office of the Church. So when this supreme body proposes doctrines for belief 'as being divinely revealed, and as the teaching of Christ' it insists that these too '*must be adhered to with the obedience of faith.*'[15]

In practice this means that by submitting one's will and one's intellect to the god, the Christian allows his or her mind to be guided by those who have set themselves up as revealers, proclaimers and interpreters of the god's word, that is, the priestly hierarchy. The consequence then is to bring about a less questioning and therefore less critical, more docile body of supporters which can be more readily

---

[13]*Catechism*, 142, 156, my italics. The *Catechism* appears to contradict itself over this matter: first it tell us that mysteries – defined as revealed truths – are '*inaccessible to reason*' (237), but now it claims that 'revealed truths appear as true and *intelligible* in the light of natural reason'.

[14]*Ibid*, 143, my italics.

[15]*Ibid*, 891, my italics.

194

controlled and manipulated by those in authority. Let us recall again Paul's dismal and chilling words on the matter. Once reason and one's better judgement are willingly surrendered, one has virtually turned oneself into a moral and intellectual captive. Those who have committed themselves to Christ he says 'have been made slaves of God . . . every thought is our prisoner, captured to be brought into obedience to Christ. Once you have given your obedience, we are prepared to punish any disobedience.'[16] And with the Church as the earthly representative of the god, obedience to the Church and to the pope becomes an obligatory consequence of faith. So we should hardly be surprised to find that when it speaks of 'sinning against faith', the *Catechism* still includes even today the sin of *schism*, 'the refusal of *submission* to the Roman Pontiff.'[17]

The Deity's New Clothes

The resurrection of Jesus is described as a 'mystery of faith' and in one particular aspect we can see this contradictory principle operating in the narratives of Jesus' appearances. In the previous chapter we left unresolved the matter of the nature and status of the risen Jesus in the accounts of the later evangelists, Luke and John. On the one hand they insist that a physical resurrection had taken place and that Jesus' body, with its open wounds and ability to consume food, was the same earthly body as that which had been crucified. But they also record the risen Jesus behaving like a spirit, able suddenly to appear and disappear and to pass through physical barriers. Clearly it's not possible to maintain both propositions – (1) that the body of the risen Jesus is the same human body that was crucified and placed in the tomb and (2) that the risen Jesus is able to act like a spirit, unlimited by the constraints of flesh and bones – at the same time: human bodies simply cannot defy these principles.

It's obvious that there's a contradiction here and it's one that the *Catechism* has to address. Not surprisingly, the Church wants it both ways: 'he is not a ghost . . . the risen body in which he appears . . . is the same body that has been tortured and crucified . . . Yet at the same

---

[16]Romans 6:22, 1 Cor. 10:5-6.

[17]*Catechism*, 2089, my italics.

time this authentic, real body . . . [is] not limited by space and time.'
The fact is however that real bodies *are* limited by space and time. So if
Jesus could fly around and vanish, his body simply can't be the same in
nature as any other human body or even his own, pre-resurrected
body. But if his body isn't the same crucified body, then it could be
that the risen Jesus seen by the disciples was a spirit, and hence the
whole of the resurrection belief is undermined. The only way out is to
turn what the Church has previously called an historical event into a
mystery, something that can be taken on board only through faith.

So Jesus' body is proclaimed as having been transformed and now
has 'the new properties of a glorious body.' Even though it has been
asserted that 'Christ's Resurrection can't be interpreted as something
outside the physical order', the resurrection is now a 'transcendent
event.' As such, it's not 'perceptible to the senses' and presumably isn't
accessible to reason either, being something that is 'at the very heart of
the mystery of faith'.[18] Most reasonable people will be able to see that
there's an element of 'mental cheating' going on here to get round this
manifest contradiction; and it's only by defining the resurrection as a
mystery which must be approached through faith - through blind
acceptance - that the Church can hold its line.

Unfortunately sorting out one problem just creates another and in
this instance simply leads to an ever more ridiculous state of affairs. Let
us accept for the moment the Church's assertion (to call it an
explanation suggests that it can be reasonably understood) that Jesus'
body was gloriously transformed by the resurrection. We now have a
problem with his clothes. None of the gospels record anything unusual
about Jesus' appearance or state of dress, so we can fairly assume that
the risen Jesus didn't walk the earth naked and was probably clothed in
much the same way as his disciples were.

Now if Jesus' 'glorious body' could suddenly appear and vanish,
pass through physical barriers and move about unconstrained by space
and time, then it must be the case that his clothes also had such

---

[18] *Ibid,* 645, 647, 643. Of course it's possible that within the physical order entities can be
transformed. For example water is turned into ice, a solid below 0° Celsius and into a
gas above 100° Celsius. In these different states the water has different properties but
remains essentially the same (the same elements of hydrogen and oxygen). But it can't
have the differing properties at the same time. Water or ice cannot be both liquid and
solid simultaneously. The Church claims that Jesus' body has the physical properties of a
normal body and spiritual properties of a transformed body at the same time.

properties. For if only his body vanished into thin air as he was having supper with two of his followers at Emmaus, as Luke records, a small heap of clothes would have been left at the table. And if he suddenly appeared to his disciples in a room, as both Luke and John reported, then his clothes too must have appeared just as miraculously or must have been able to pass through physical barriers.

But exactly what was Jesus wearing as he emerged from the tomb? The problem arises because Jesus' own clothes were recorded by all four evangelists as having been divided out among the soldiers who carried out the execution. The only other material that could have covered him as he emerged into the fresh air was the burial shroud that the gospels mention. But John notes specifically that these 'linen cloths' remained in the tomb. So what was Jesus wearing and where did he get these clothes from so early in the morning ('it was still dark when Mary of Magdala came to the tomb')?[19] Was there a wardrobe to die for upstairs in heaven from which an appropriate robe was hastily sent to cover him? Or did Jesus have to acquire his resurrection clothes from a more down to earth source? Perhaps he borrowed them from the gardener that Mary mistook him for?

Whatever the explanation, these clothes also would have to have acquired 'glorious' properties; normal clothes unfortunately, like earthly bodies, simply cannot appear and vanish or pass through mud or stone walls. And so we get the ludicrous situation that just as Jesus' body was transformed, so too must have been his resurrection outfit. But the transformation of the clothes must have occurred separately since he simply didn't have them at any point between his death on the Friday and his appearance on Easter Sunday (unless they came from heaven). So this means that there must have been a second 'transcendent event' to account for the transformation of normal clothes, whether they were acquired from the gardener or a pre-dawn Jerusalem market, into magic clothes with matching 'glorious' properties. Once again, the whole situation becomes comical and ridiculous, absurd beyond belief. In trying to overcome one impossibility with a nonsense assertion about a 'glorious body', the Church simply creates another problem and its interpretation of events

---

[19]John 20:5-7, 1. It's likely that this detail was mentioned to demonstrate that the tomb had not been visited by grave robbers and that therefore Jesus' body hadn't been stolen. The other gospels don't mention whether or not the shroud remained in the tomb.

becomes ever more unsustainable.

As in the children's fable of the vain and deluded emperor, it only takes a little bit of common sense to see through the finery of the Church's spin. One suspects that this is hardly an issue that the Church would ever condescend to address. Presumably the believer shouldn't ask awkward questions like this but, through faith, should just blindly accept the Easter mystery. But the more fundamental issue to consider is this: why are Christians so willing to suspend critical judgement, to cast reason and common sense aside and 'just believe' these untenable, non-sensical teachings?

It's The Redemption, Stupid

The answer to this question is to be found by considering the theological significance claimed for Jesus' death and resurrection. While the New Testament doesn't say explicitly why the Son-god had to die in such violent circumstances, the Nicene creed, the basic profession of Christian faith states that 'for our sake he was crucified. . . suffered death and was buried.' The *Catechism* expounds on this, affirming that 'when the time had fully come, God sent forth his Son' and that 'Jesus' violent death was . . . part of the mystery of God's plan . . . Christ's whole life is a mystery of redemption. Redemption comes to us above all through the blood of his cross.'[20] So it would appear that in some way Jesus' death (especially its more bloody aspects) and resurrection 'redeems' the whole of humanity. But what does this mean and how and why has such an understanding come about? How can the death of one man, or even the death of a god redeem all those who are prepared to accept Christian teachings? Why was the shedding of blood necessary? Why would an all powerful god have to resort to killing its son to enable this redemption to take place?

The *Catechism* provides no real answers to these questions, but instead is content to reiterate the proclamation of a redemption mystery that has three key aspects: first, the execution of Jesus is acclaimed as a sacrifice; then, through this sacrifice the sins of the world are somehow removed and mankind is reconciled to the Father-god; and finally, this reconciliation with its benefit of being saved is

---

[20]*Catechism*, 422, 599, 517.

made only with those who have faith in Jesus. For most Christians this forms the core of their religious belief and the tantalising prospect of being saved is the whole point of the faith; so clearly these are fundamentally important ideas. But can they be thought of as being true? What grounds do we have for accepting these propositions and is the argument for this doctrine intelligible? Was this teaching really divinely revealed, as the Church maintains, or is it possible that it was merely concocted by fervent religious imaginations shortly after Jesus' death to try and make sense of the loss?

Jesus The Suffering Servant

Quite soon after the crucifixion Jesus' earliest supporters came to see his execution as some sort of sacrifice. Of course anyone killed by a hostile occupying power stands a good chance of being proclaimed a martyr; but the status accorded to Jesus' death by the first Christians went far beyond this. How then, and why did this first crucial step in the evolution of the redemption doctrine come about?

We noted that after the death of Diana, Princess of Wales conspiracy theories and rumours of dark forces at work soon began to circulate in response to her sudden death, as if people were simply unable to accept the terrible blow dealt by a such a tragic accident. It is psychologically very likely that the disciples, close followers and friends of Jesus who had abandoned their former lives and had placed all their hopes in him, would have been similarly devastated by his shocking and violent end. So likewise they too probably would've tried to make sense of the whole situation and see his unjust and untimely death as being meaningful in some way.

This basic human need to try to find something positive out of even the greatest calamity would've received an additional impetus and taken on a much greater urgency when Peter and possibly one or two of the other disciples began to experience unexpected appearances of their master. In our review of the resurrection story we left off with the understanding that the appearances would've been enthusiastically interpreted as a sign of divine favour and would've brought about a complete transformation in the disciples' spirits. Far from his life and mission ending in disastrous failure, it would have seemed to them that Jesus had been divinely vindicated and exalted by the Father.

As a result of this apparent glorification they evidently came to believe that Jesus really was the long awaited messiah who had come if not to deliver Israel, then to herald the new kingdom whose imminent coming he had eagerly and continually proclaimed before his death. In Acts the messianic status of Jesus comes across as one of the central themes of Peter's earliest preaching, given immediately after the disciples were inspired by the tongues of flame that descended from the sky at Pentecost. In this very first Christian sermon Peter's main concern is to persuade his fellow Jews that Jesus really was the promised descendant of King David.[21]

The problem was, Israel's messiah was popularly thought of as a powerful and glorious kingly figure, the chosen instrument who would finally liberate Israel from its enemies and who would inaugurate the holy kingdom and reign of Yahweh. But who in their right mind would support a dead or defeated pretender? Jesus' life had ended not in triumph and glory but in scandal and failure, on a Roman cross leaving nationalistic hopes unfulfilled and almost automatically cancelling any messianic pretensions he may have had. Not only had Jesus died before delivering Israel from its ungodly oppressors; he had even been humiliated by having to endure an ignominious death at the hands of those very enemies that the messiah should have vanquished in the first place.

In order to persuade their contemporaries that Jesus was the messiah, the disciples would have to convince them that Jesus was neither dead nor defeated. Their absolute conviction that he hadn't been abandoned in death but had been raised and exalted was proven by their resurrection faith and experiences. But how could they explain the suffering and shame he'd had to endure before being raised up? Why would Yahweh have allowed his anointed one, his messiah to have his life ended in such a catastrophic way? In trying to understand this most puzzling issue and how it could have been the Father's will, it would've been natural for them to have turned to the Scriptures for enlightenment. Just as the evangelists sought proof and guidance from the prophets, so too might have the disciples. And sure enough, their eyes and ears might have been opened when they considered the

---

[21]Acts 2:22-36: 'Brothers, no one can deny that the patriarch David himself is dead . . . But . . . God had sworn him an oath to make one of his descendants succeed him on the throne . . . what he foresaw and spoke about was the resurrection of the Christ.'

prophet Isaiah's foretelling of a Suffering Servant, a type that seemed to fit their needs and the circumstances of Jesus' death almost perfectly.

Towards the end of the book of Isaiah in a series of moving poems the prophet speaks of an unidentified servant, a chosen one in whom the Lord (i.e. Yahweh) delights and on whom his spirit is bestowed. But the servant is also called upon to endure torments and humiliation, to be despised by all; and in doing so, to take on the burden of guilt of the wicked: 'he was pierced for our transgressions, tortured for our iniquities . . . The Lord laid upon him the guilt of us all . . . he submitted to be struck down . . . he was led like a sheep to the slaughter.' Despite the terrible extent and injustice of his suffering, the servant willingly submits to the brutality and ignominy of his fate and his reward is not to be abandoned in death; on the contrary, after his presumed demise he is duly glorified and prophesied to find the highest favour: 'my servant shall prosper, he shall be lifted up, exalted to the heights . . . after his disgrace he shall be fully vindicated.'[22]

We may begin to see just why this text appealed to Jesus' earliest post-resurrection supporters.[23] If Jesus was the messiah, then 'the full message of the prophets' had not been properly understood, that it was 'ordained that the Christ should suffer.'[24] But it wasn't just suffering that was to be the servant's lot; crucially the final poem tells of the voluntary and sacrificial nature of his death, not only in the image of the sheep being led to the slaughter, but in the specific recognition that he made himself 'a sacrifice for sin . . . he bore the sin of many and interceded for their transgressions.'[25]

It seems then that the disciples' belief that Jesus was the messiah would have been confirmed by the scriptural revelation that Yahweh's anointed one was destined to be not the nationalistic deliverer of popular expectation, but a lowly, humble servant, unrecognised in his own lifetime, but exalted after death. Consequently the disaster of Jesus' death could be seen as being in harmony with the Father's will; and with this new found confidence it was given a positive spin,

---

[22]Isaiah 52:13-53:12.

[23]Hengel (*The Atonement: The Origins of the Doctrine in the New Testament,* p 60) notes that the Isaiah 53 passage is one of the most quoted (or alluded to) in the New Testament.

[24]Luke 24:25-26.

[25]Isaiah, 53:10, 4.

transformed from a shameful Roman execution into a glorious self-sacrifice freely given for 'the sin of many'. So when Paul cited his profession of faith about Jesus, that 'Christ died for our sins, in accordance with the scriptures',[26] it may be that it was this earliest understanding that was being alluded to.

Jesus The Goat

Earlier we noted that one of the likely key effects of Peter's resurrection experience was his feeling of release from the enormous guilt he suffered as a consequence of denying and abandoning Jesus. During his lifetime Jesus had stressed not only the urgent need for repentance, but also that forgiveness would be freely given to all those who did repent. Now, after his death, Peter was feeling the abundance of that forgiveness for himself. Even though he'd deserted Jesus, the pain and guilt that had been tearing him up inside as a result of his cowardly weakness had been taken away. The slate had been wiped clean and his greatest sin, his denial of his master, who by now was thought of as the messiah, had been forgiven.

We can venture then that if Jesus' death had come to be thought of as a sacrifice, this experience would have suggested or confirmed to the disciples that the clearest practical consequence of that sacrifice was the forgiveness or taking away of sins from those who repented in his name and who accepted him as the risen or exalted messiah. And so it may have been that the disciples found their conviction to preach in the synagogue or Temple that believing in Jesus as the messiah, or faith in Christ (as Christians later began to proclaim this doctrine) and in his resurrection in particular took away 'the sin of the world' for the genuine and newly repentant sinner.

There may have been some radical and innovative thinking going on here, but such teaching was nevertheless based firmly on Jewish traditions and beliefs. Sacrifices were part of the customary Temple worship in Jerusalem and sin offerings would have been nothing new for the Jews of that age. These individual and personal sacrifices might be made at any time and Jesus' action to evict the money changers and merchants selling cattle, sheep and pigeons from the Temple suggests it

---

[26]1 Cor. 15:3.

was a thriving practice. But the supreme sin offering was that which was made once a year on Yom Kippur, the Jewish Day of Atonement when the high priest made special sacrifices to Yahweh for the sins of all Israelites.

In this solemn ritual dating back hundreds of years two goats were selected for the offering. The first of these was sacrificed in the usual manner for the sins of the people; but the blood of this victim was then sprinkled inside the Holy of Holies, the place where Yahweh was believed to dwell. Next the high priest placed his hands on the remaining goat and transferred the sins and wickedness of the nation to the hapless creature. It was then driven out into the desert where it was forced to wander or possibly was killed by being thrown off a cliff to prevent it from returning to the city with its heavy burden of guilt.[27] By this cleansing Israel's sins were wiped away for another year and reconciliation with Yahweh, symbolised by the admission of the high priest into the Holy of Holies (this was the one day in the year when he - and he alone - was permitted to enter) was effected.

Bizarre and backwards as this ceremony may be to us today, it seems likely that it was influential in formulating very early Christian beliefs about the saving consequences of Jesus' death, particularly to Jewish rather than gentile Christians, so providing Christianity with one possible basis for its atonement doctrine today. We can tell this is the case because there's a particular document in the New Testament, the letter to the Hebrews, written in the closing decades of the 1st century, that specifically draws attention to this influence.

After explaining the procedure of the Day of Atonement ritual, the unknown author of this letter then asserts that as the mediator of a new covenant, Jesus is the new high priest permitted to enter the inner sanctuary 'taking with him not the blood of goats and bull calves, but his own blood.' Goat's blood is now deemed useless for taking away sins; only the blood of Jesus, who 'offered himself as the perfect sacrifice to God'[28] is considered effective in wiping out sins. It would appear then that the importance of a blood sacrifice in Christian theology can be traced back to ancient Jewish rituals and beliefs.

---

[27]The mechanics of the Day of Atonement ritual are set out in Leviticus 16:1-34. The term *scapegoat* derives from this custom.

[28]Hebrews 9:12, 14, 10:4.

Jesus The Meek And Innocent Lamb ?

Clearly the Christian redemption belief hinges primarily on Jesus' death being understood as a self-sacrifice. But was it really a sacrifice? If this interpretation is to be considered a valid one, two key requirements need to be evaluated and satisfied: firstly, that Jesus was an innocent victim and secondly, that despite his innocence he was still willing to die.

Obviously the Christian understanding is that Jesus was completely blameless of the trumped up charges against him but nevertheless, in total obedience to his father's will, allowed himself to be killed. So in the gospels we see him portrayed as unjustly condemned and offering neither defence nor resistance during the whole process of his arrest and trial. But we must remember that the traditions underlying these accounts came solely from Jesus' disciples and earliest followers, and these were supporters who would have put the most favourable gloss on everything preserved and handed down about him. And if at a very early stage in the development of Christianity they began to see Jesus as a contemporary fulfilment of Isaiah's Suffering Servant, we would expect them to understand and proclaim his death as some sort of willing martyrdom or sacrifice.

In turn these traditions were distilled through the theological reflection and political spin of the evangelists as well and would have been adapted to suit the needs of their communities. For these mixed or gentile communities, far removed from the culture and politics of Palestine and for whom the concept of a nationalistic deliverer would have been quite foreign, one of the more important of those needs was to make sense of the circumstances surrounding Jesus' death. Just as it was very testing for his Jewish supporters to accept that the one they believed to be the messiah had died before redeeming Israel, so it would have been equally galling and problematic for gentile Christians to come to terms with the fact that the figurehead of their new faith had been executed by the Romans for treason.

The problem would have been particularly acute for Mark as the first evangelist, whose task was to produce not an abstract theology in the manner of Paul, but a more accessible presentation of the faith based around the life and death of Jesus. However, the revolutionary new document that he wrote also has to be understood within the context of the time and situation from which it emerged.

As we've noted, there is a general consensus in scholarly opinion that Mark's gospel was written around the year 70 and that it probably originated from the Christian community at Rome. Written with the very recent persecution of Christians by Nero (in 64 CE)[29] and the brutal end of the Jewish revolt casting dark shadows over the community, Mark's gospel had to grapple with the enormous problem posed by Jesus' crucifixion, the fact that he'd been executed as a Jewish subversive, or at the very least as one who appeared to be a subversive, resisting Roman rule. This alone would have been highly embarrassing and awkward for the community. But at a time when Jews were generally seen as treacherous for having staged a fierce revolt against Rome, it may also have re-ignited and intensified the suspicions of the authorities about anything associated with Judaism.

So it was imperative for Mark not only somehow to explain Jesus' condemnation and death, but also to demonstrate unequivocally that the new religion posed no threat to the state so as to avoid future persecution. Distancing Jesus and the faith from the political fanaticism of the Jews therefore became a necessary priority. To achieve this Mark presented Jesus as the tragic victim of a miscarriage of justice with the actual offence of sedition written out of the account. And Pilate, the figure of Roman authority, is portrayed in the most favourable light possible, as an eminently fair and almost genial governor,[30] vehemently opposed to condemning a man whom he regarded as innocent. Later Christian apologists would even go so far as to proclaim that in his heart Pilate was already a Christian.[31]

To highlight the drama and the pathos Jesus offers no resistance at

---

[29]We can detect Mark's hand and the circumstances of this gospel's composition in comments ascribed to Jesus such as his warning that 'You will be hated by all men on account of my name' (13:13), written in to the text perhaps to bolster the faith of those who survived the persecution.

[30]In fact Pilate was a particularly bloody and heavy handed governor. Josephus records that after slaughtering a large number of protesting Jews some years after Jesus' death, Pilate was accused of murder and was ordered by Vitellius, the consul of Syria, to return to Rome to answer the charges before the emperor (*Antiquities* XVIII, iv, 1-2). Luke also alludes to Pilate's brutality with his remark about the 'Galileans whose blood Pilate had mingled with that of their sacrifices' (13:1).

[31]Brandon, *The Trial of Jesus of Nazareth*, p 155, citing Tertullian's *Apology* (xxi: 24). I am indebted to many of Professor Brandon's insights concerning the political dimension of Jesus' arrest and trial.

his arrest and virtually no defence at his trial; instead he stoically accepts his fate, so rousing a sense of admiration and pity and dissociating him from the violent and undignified conduct of the rebellious Jews. And lastly, and tragically, the Jews themselves (and not the Romans) are depicted as responsible for Jesus' death and become the contemptible and malicious villains of the whole affair.

Is this an accurate representation of the events surrounding the condemnation of Jesus? Well, if we're prepared to read the stories of the arrest and trial critically we can begin to see how contrived they are and can detect the little details that have slipped through to suggest that Jesus may not have been the wholly innocent and willing victim that Mark and the other evangelists would have their audiences believe.

To begin with, when he is arrested all four gospels record that the Jewish authorities met with armed resistance, with one of their number attacked with a sword, suggesting that Jesus had no intention of surrendering quietly to his enemies. Naturally the evangelists try to distance Jesus from this violent behaviour. Mark for instance records that it was an anonymous 'bystander' (and not even one of Jesus' followers) who attacked and wounded the high priest's servant. It seems very unlikely however, that a disinterested third party would get so embroiled in the altercation to take such drastic action, thereby risking being arrested himself, especially if Jesus and his followers remained peaceful and did not resist arrest. Moreover Mark's chronology indicates that the arrest took place very late at night (and outside the city as well) and so we have to wonder about the likelihood of suitably armed bystanders even being present at such a late hour.

In Matthew it is an unnamed follower of Jesus who injures the servant and in response Jesus issues the famous maxim 'all who draw the sword will die by the sword' to prevent further bloodshed. As with so many of Jesus' sayings in the gospels, we cannot know whether Jesus really said these words himself or whether they were put into his mouth subsequently by the writer. But as if to apologise for the whole incident and explain why it was that the confrontation was a violent one, Matthew resorts once again to his favourite ploy, the apparent fulfilment of 'the prophecies in scripture.' So according to Matthew there was a scuffle only because some ancient (and unspecified) writing said there should be, and not because Jesus and the disciples feared and resisted arrest.[32]

In reality it may be that Jesus never said these words at all and only allowed himself to be taken when it was clear that further resistance was useless. Luke resorts to the still less plausible miracle story to demonstrate Jesus' non-violent credentials with Jesus carrying out some sharp regenerative surgery to the injured man's ear. But this pacifism just doesn't reconcile to the fact that previously Jesus had advised his crew to sell their cloaks in order to buy swords. Moreover, we can tell that it wasn't just one particularly aggressive disciple who carried a weapon, for on seeing Jesus being arrested, Luke tells us that 'His followers . . . said "Lord, shall we use our swords?"' suggesting that a fair number of them were armed. And in the Fourth Gospel Jesus commands Simon-Peter to put his sword back in its 'scabbard' thus implying that at least one of the disciples regularly carried a sword. Why, we might wonder, was this sword-culture permitted by Jesus if his message was that his followers should always love their enemies and not resist evil?[33]

However, all this distracts us from the larger question: why might the Jewish authorities themselves have come armed to arrest Jesus and why might he have been charged with a capital offence in the first place? Mark unwittingly allows a crucial piece of information to slip out: an uprising had occurred in Jerusalem shortly before Jesus' arrest and there were riots and murders in the city at around the same time. Perhaps Jesus and his supporters (among whom was at least one Zealot, a Jewish resistance fighter) were not so blameless (and harmless) after all

---

[32]Matthew 26:47-56. Matthew didn't provide a source for his claim that 'all this happened to fulfil the prophecies in scripture.' However, it is usually understood that this is a further reference to Isaiah's Suffering Servant (53:12) 'he let himself be taken for a criminal.' But this still fails to explain the violence: if Jesus 'let himself be taken', why the swordfight?

[33]Luke 22:36, John 18:11. Christians find it so intolerable that Jesus might have resorted to or recommended violence that this unpalatable detail has to be explained away. Like Matthew, Luke turns to prophecy fulfilment to justify this detail, quoting Isaiah. Christian commentators today provide an extremely contrived and virtually meaningless gloss, for example: 'Since Luke narrates in his gospel that Jesus not only preached love of his enemies but also lived that preaching . . . he cannot mean by "sword" here a lethal weapon . . . Rather "sword" is a symbol for crisis' (*Jerome* 43:183). The writer doesn't explain why one might sell a cloak to buy a symbol, a crisis. As the Temple incident suggests, it seems that Jesus could be violent and aggressive when it suited him.

but were connected to this insurrection in some way? Having heard about Jesus' violent and intemperate behaviour in the Temple that had caused such a disturbance just a day or so beforehand, the Romans may have considered that this riot was part of the larger rebellion.

Certainly Jesus' unprovoked attack on the money changers and other legitimate Temple merchants could hardly have been an unaggressive incident, with the meek and gentle saviour politely asking these traders to move on. In the Fourth Gospel John actually records that Jesus used a whip to drive them out and this clearly unruly and violent act may have been regarded as a threat to social order.[34] The incident is usually referred to euphemistically as 'the cleansing of the Temple', but it seems quite similar to me to anti-capitalist protesters today smashing up branches of Mcdonalds on May Day, and mob violence might be a more appropriate way to describe the affair. In the highly charged atmosphere of an uprising occurring during the Passover festival, (which of course commemorated Jewish liberty from Egyptian slavery and which therefore was always a time of high tension for the Romans), Jesus' actions can only have been seen as dangerous and provocative by both the Jewish and Roman authorities alike.

So Jesus is arrested and arraigned before Pilate, 'as a political agitator' as Luke notes, and here the narratives begin to lose plausibility as they try to suppress the true nature of the offence with which Jesus was charged. Additionally all accounts of the trial try to persuade us that Pilate believed Jesus to be innocent of any charge whatsoever and that he did his utmost to save him. Indeed so much care has been taken by the four evangelists to emphasise this that the trial before Pilate comes across as a complete whitewash of both Jesus and the Roman governor.

In the Fourth Gospel for example, there are five separate occasions when Pilate expresses either his reluctance to condemn Jesus or his opinion that he is innocent: 'Take him yourselves and try him by your own Law . . . I find no case against him . . . I am going to bring him out to you to let you see that I find no case . . . Take him yourselves

---

[34]The *Catechism* can't ignore this awkward incident but skates over it with the very brief comment that Jesus was 'angered' that the outer court of the Temple had become a place of commerce (584). Interestingly, elsewhere it notes that anger is a mortal sin and that 'Everyone who is angry with his brother shall be liable to judgement' (2302). I hope that Jesus repented for his sin and apologised to the traders.

and crucify him: I can find no case against him . . . Pilate was anxious to set him free'[35]). However, there is no explanation at all as to how or why he came to this conclusion. In Matthew the artificiality is still more apparent with a further example of this evangelist's second favourite trick, the warning in a dream. This time it's Pilate's wife who advises the procurator to have nothing to do with Jesus on the basis of her night-time revelation. But if Pilate was so convinced of Jesus' innocence, why didn't he just release him?

Ostensibly it seems he was unwilling to do so because the Jews were baying for Jesus' blood and Pilate feared a riot if he didn't placate them. So as well as the real nature of the charge against Jesus being buried and the Roman governor exonerated of all culpability, the gospels ensure that it was the Jews who pulled the short straw and became responsible for Jesus' death. In Mark, in response to Pilate's incredible and unlikely question 'what am I to do with the man you call the king of the Jews?' the crowds shout back 'Crucify him.'[36] Would the governor of a province *really* ask the mob such a question? The sheer implausibility of this part of the story becomes clear when we consider one commentator's comparison from a review of Mel Gibson's controversial film *The Passion of the Christ*: 'Can you imagine Paul Bremer sticking his head out of the hotel window and asking the Iraqi crowd whether he should send some religious agitator to Guantanamo Bay or release him?'[37]

In Matthew the polemic against the Jews reaches its lowest point and we find the Jewish people incriminated as a whole and made culpable in perpetuity for the so-called murder of Christ, with the infamous curse supposedly voiced by those present at the trial clamouring that 'his blood be on us and on our children.'[38] It is of course an indication of the general nastiness of Christianity that it should have taken this obnoxious passage very literally and very

---

[35]John 18:31–19:12.

[36]Mark 15:12-13.

[37] The Rev Dr Fraser in *The Guardian* 7 February 2004.

[38]Matthew 27:25. This hate crime against the Jews was not officially abandoned by the Church until Vatican II in the 1960s. The Council document *Nostra Aetate* (1965) affirmed that 'neither all Jews indiscriminately at that time, nor Jews today, can be charged with the crimes committed during his Passion.' In Luke and John the anti-Jewish rhetoric is similar and their narratives imply that it was actually the Jews who were responsible for crucifying Jesus.

seriously for much of its history, so initiating nearly twenty centuries of prejudice and persecution, culminating in modern times with gas chambers disguised as showers.[39] In its shameful ill will towards the Jews it seems to have overlooked the fact that Jesus' death was theologically necessary for the faith, that it was part of the Father-god's plan and is frequently thought of as 'the source of eternal salvation' for all mankind.

We then come to the dubious story of Pilate releasing a prisoner, a custom that was apparently granted to the Jews at festival time.[40] Suddenly Pilate is reduced from being the supreme governor of the province who believed wholeheartedly in Jesus' innocence and who had the authority to set him free, to a feeble and almost powerless minor official who has to try to plead and bargain with the Jewish leaders to secure Jesus' release.

Like so many other gospel stories, this incident comes across as a literary device, in this instance again to drive home that it was the Jews who were responsible for Jesus' death; for according to the evangelists it is their demand that Pilate should release Barabbas rather than Jesus that ultimately seals Jesus' fate. Fearing that 'a riot was imminent' Pilate yields to the crowd's demands and agrees to release Barabbas, a man who already 'had committed murder during the uprising.' So we're asked to believe that at a time of great tension and social unrest, Pilate happily releases a dangerous man already known to and imprisoned by the Romans for 'rioting and murder'[41] (rioting that is, almost certainly against Roman rule and murder, probably of Roman soldiers) and sends a man he believes to be innocent to his death. Once again, the whole thing comes across as hopelessly implausible.

---

[39]In an article published in the *London Jewish Chronicle* in 1965, Hans Kung ventured that 'The monstrous crimes of Nazi anti-Semitism would have been impossible without the hidden, often Christian anti-Semitism of more than 1,500 years.' Cited from Gilbert, *The Vatican Council and the Jews*, p 24. *The Holocaust Encyclopedia* (p 111) maintains that the Church's 'need to validate Christian claims and to discredit the Jewish adversary . . . led to an easily transferable prejudice . . . long-held theological prejudices became interwoven with more rabid expressions of anti-Jewish hatred . . . Although Catholic anti-Judaism was not a necessary precondition for the Holocaust, it was clearly a contributing factor to Nazi anti-Semitism.' See also Kahl (*op cit*, pp 51-62) for a brief outline of Christianity's persecution of the Jews.

[40]Brandon (*op cit*, p 101) points out that this 'is not confirmed by any other evidence.'

[41]Matthew 27:24, Mark 15:8, Luke 23:25.

Finally we might note that the two men crucified alongside Jesus were themselves probably political rebels. Traditionally they are reported as being thieves or robbers, but theft or theft with violence were not capital offences under Roman law. The Greek word used by Mark to describe them - *lestai* - might better be translated as 'brigands' and this term was in use at the time to designate men convicted of insurrection.[42] It would appear then that there are grounds for believing that on that fateful day Jesus may simply have been one of a number of men executed by the Romans for treasonable offences in the aftermath of an unsuccessful uprising, which they put down with brutal and ruthless efficiency.

So perhaps after all Jesus was not arrested and led to his death like the willing, innocent lamb to the slaughter but was tried and duly convicted by the Romans for a secular offence which had nothing to do with the notion of a religious sacrifice at all. Whether he was genuinely guilty or, like millions of others throughout history, was the victim of a tragic miscarriage of justice, we cannot truly know. Even if it were the latter and Jesus was innocent, a miscarriage of justice is far from being the obedient self-sacrifice of Christian teaching.

Similarly we cannot know whether Jesus really was willing to die: it may be that the weight of evidence against him was overwhelming and he could offer no defence at his trial. Or perhaps Jesus' stoical silence is literary rather than actual - after all, it would probably have been seen as highly undignified if he was portrayed as pleading for his life. Perhaps the silence of Isaiah's Suffering Servant influenced the story-telling? And once a prisoner had been convicted and condemned to death, obedience and a willingness to die would have become redundant and meaningless concepts in the Roman judicial process.

What we can know is that calling Jesus' death a sacrifice is merely one particular interpretation of events and one that was supplied by writers who were opposed to any criticism either of Jesus' conduct or of Roman justice and who had their own ideological agenda to pursue. And that interpretation isn't necessarily the correct one, certainly not

---

[42]Lane, *The Gospel of Mark*, p 568. Lane points out that the word in question is constantly used by Josephus for the Zealots who were committed to armed resistance to Roman rule. In John (18:40) the word *lestes* is used to describe the man released by Pilate, Barabbas and is translated as *brigand*. As we've noted, Barabbas was probably an insurrectionalist.

an impartial one and probably not a realistic one.

Devilish Transactions And Cosmic War

Even if Jesus' death was a form of martyrdom, this is still a long way from a religious sacrifice offered to Yahweh. And we still have no understanding of precisely how the sacrifice of a goat (on which Jesus' apparent sacrifice may have been modelled) was able to take away sins as the ritual of Yom Kippur insisted. Neither the Old nor the New Testament provide any explanation as to how slitting an animal's throat and then splashing its blood over a slab of stone removes the sins, disobedience or guilt of an entire people.

Today we're more likely to consider such a ritual as superstitious nonsense, something most of us would find backwards and offensive. Somehow bloodlust just doesn't reconcile with the Christian conception of a benevolent god, a kind and gentle father or indeed with contemporary sensibilities and our regard for the welfare of animals. Perhaps Christians comfort themselves with the thought that Jesus' death obviated the need for this practice. But the very doctrine of Christian redemption is entirely based on and endorses the principle of a blood sacrifice. The letter to the Hebrews maintains that a death is absolutely necessary for a new covenant to be effected and that 'if there is no shedding of blood, there is no remission [of sins].'[43]

One might have thought that this ancient understanding would be quietly forgotten today by a faith trying to reach out and appeal to a more enlightened 21st century congregation. But it is actually confirmed by the Church with its savage blood and cross theology; for the prospect of being saved, we're told 'comes to us *above all* through the *blood* of his cross',[44] an understanding that is perpetuated through blood-drinking and re-enactment of the sacrifice at Christian services.[45]

---

[43]Hebrews 9:23

[44]*Catechism*, 517, my italics.

[45]Of course it's not *really* blood that Christians drink at mass, but a rather syrupy and sickly wine; however, according to Catholic theology, regardless of whether or not one believes, the oversweet plonk really has been turned into Jesus' blood: 'it has always been the conviction of the Church of God . . . that . . . there takes place a change . . . of the whole substance of the wine into the substance of his blood.' Naturally this magical transformation 'cannot be apprehended by the senses but only by faith'. The Church also regards the mass as a sacrifice itself: 'when the Church celebrates the Eucharist . . . the

And if anything the Christian teaching is even more deplorable than the Jewish Old Testament atonement belief, for in the final analysis Christianity is based on and celebrates a *human* sacrifice.

It is of course our instinctive horror of human sacrifice that makes the Church's teaching so abominable. A sacrifice by definition is something offered to a god and if accepted may be deemed to be pleasing to the god. The New Testament teaches that Jesus 'offered himself as the perfect sacrifice to God.'[46] If it is perfect there can be nothing reprehensible about it, especially since it was part of the Father-god's plan. But such is the horror associated with human sacrifice, even Christians recoil from it; consequently they soon discover that their sins are not so freely and easily absolved after all. The New Testament may proclaim that Jesus came to 'give' his life and that his 'perfect sacrifice' was a 'free gift';[47] but at the same time it's an appalling act which brought with it its own terrible price to be paid.

For today the Church teaches that the killing of Jesus was 'the greatest moral evil ever committed'[48] and that all sinners were and continue to be responsible for this ritual murder. So while Jesus' sacrifice is taught as having been made to take away sins, at the same time Christians are suddenly burdened with an even more crushing sense of guilt brought about by the greatest sin of all time in which everyone played a part. In the end, even if we accept Christian teaching, far from resolving or achieving anything, Jesus' so-called sacrifice is the same as the process that banks call 'debt restructuring'; it takes away the burden of interest or guilt or sins with one hand and then compounds the overall problem by imposing an even greater penalty to the total debt with the other. Ultimately it does nothing but add to the sum total of human guilt and misery. So why was Jesus' death so necessary for people to be saved? Why couldn't the Christian god simply have effected a reconciliation or have wiped out sins

---

sacrifice of Christ offered for all on the cross remains ever present . . . it *re-presents* (makes present) the sacrifice of the cross . . . the bloody sacrifice [is] . . . re-presented.' (*Ibid,* 1376, 1381, 1364-1366).

[46]Hebrews 9:14.

[47]Romans 3:24.

[48]*Catechism*, 312. To proclaim that Jesus' sacrifice is perfect and yet at the same time the greatest moral evil is of course a fine example of Christianity's use of doublethink and how it is used simultaneously to attract and to oppress its adherents.

without an act of such brutality and apparent injustice? Why did blood have to be shed?

Finding satisfactory answers to these rather obvious questions proves to be virtually impossible. By its very nature as a mystery of faith the doctrine of the redemption of mankind achieved through Jesus' sacrificial death is unintelligible and incapable of being reasonably explained or understood. Because it's a mystery we are to understand only that we should not expect to understand. So the Church line seems to follow Paul's lead which maintained that 'the crucifixion of Christ cannot be expressed' and that 'the language of the cross [is] illogical.' Only those who are on the way to salvation he says, presumably those whose faith asks no questions but simply accepts, can see its power to save.[49]

Consequently the *Catechism* fails to address the issue in any meaningful way and contents itself merely with tiresome, repetitive and wholly unsupported proclamations: 'Jesus' violent death . . . is part of the mystery of God's plan . . . Christ's death . . . accomplishes the definitive redemption of men through the Lamb of God who takes away the sin of the world . . . By his glorious Cross Christ has won salvation for all men'[50] and so on.

If we turn to the *New Catholic Encyclopedia* for guidance or explanation,[51] we're told that the New Testament provides no exposition of the redemption doctrine and that while many explanations have been put forward by Christian thinkers over the centuries, 'none of them can exhaust the mystery.' Perhaps an intellectually more honest response would have said that none of these attempted explanations can remove or overcome the sheer unintelligibility of the belief. It goes on to affirm that an integral theology of the redemption is a work that 'remains to be done satisfactorily – if, indeed, it can ever be accomplished satisfactorily', suggesting a vague (but inadmissible) awareness that the redemption doctrine makes no real sense at all and is – and always will be – beyond coherent and meaningful explanation.

---

[49] 1 Cor. 1:17-18.

[50] *Catechism*, 599, 613, 1741.

[51] The articles concerning *Redemption* and *Theology of Redemption*, from which subsequent quotes are taken are in Vol XII, pp 136-161.

However, the *Encyclopedia* does offer seven closely related *themes* which taken together apparently provide an answer to the question 'how and by what means man is delivered from the evil of sin and is restored to the grace of God.' It is through a combination of (1) the Incarnation, (2) the fact that Jesus gave his life as a ransom, (3) the suffering of Jesus, (4) the sacrifice of Jesus on the cross, (5) his victory over the Devil, (6) his obedience and finally (7) Jesus' resurrection that the redemption of mankind is achieved. There is of course a caveat: none of these themes provides a reasonable explanation nor even an insight to understand the matter, but only 'a clue for insight into various aspects of the mystery', so we're not really making any significant headway and shouldn't expect too much from this exposition. Even so, let's examine some of these themes briefly and see what the *Encyclopedia* has to say about them.

We've already considered Jesus' resurrection and the idea of his sacrifice on the cross; and the Incarnation is something I will be considering in greater detail in the next chapter. So the focus of this examination will be on the remaining clues.

The idea that Jesus offered his life as some sort of ransom (clue no. 2) goes back to the gospels themselves: 'the Son of man', Jesus is reported to have said 'did not come to be served but to serve, and to give his life as a ransom for the many.'[52] When we think of the term ransom today we usually associate it with kidnapping; the ransom is the price paid to ensure the victim's safe return. In the Old Testament the concept was broadly similar but was used on a national level to refer to the deliverance of Israel from Egyptian slavery. It is also used repeatedly in the book of Isaiah, undoubtedly influencing the earliest Christian messianic belief. It seems that the first Christians took this ancient understanding and developed it into an early and primitive theory of their own (known as the ransom theory) to explain how Jesus' death liberated the human race from sin.

According to Paul everyone has become a slave of sin, a point he makes very forcefully in his letter to the Romans. In the Graeco-Roman world of masters and slaves it was possible for a slave to obtain his freedom by paying a price for his redemption (the word redemption derives from the Latin verb *redemere* meaning to buy back)

---

[52]Mark 10:45.

and Paul uses this everyday understanding to explain that a price had been paid to release the world from the slavery of sin. According to the ransom theory Satan was the originator and master of all sin, the very embodiment of the foul pollution. Since everyone is a slave to sin, effectively everyone 'belongs' to Satan and hence the rights to the souls of all men, women and children are possessed by the Devil. To bring about the release of humanity, the Father-god entered into a bargain with Satan, offering the life of his son to redeem, to buy back all the human souls held by the Devil. With everyone in slavery to sin only Jesus, who of course as a god was free of sin, could act as the ransom. The Devil accepts the deal but on the third day he finds to his eternal consternation that he's been duped: the Son-god is far too powerful for him to hold and is able to escape by overcoming death.

A close variant of this is the theme of Jesus' victory over the Devil (clue for insight no. 5). This manages to avoid the somewhat unlikely and embarrassing idea of the Father-god (supposedly all powerful) having to resort to some shady dealing (clearly he had no intention of honouring his side of the bargain) and the payment of a ransom to the Prince of Darkness to obtain the release of human souls from captivity in hell after death.

Now the relationship between the god and the Devil is no longer a (less than respectable) business one but one of open warfare with Jesus' death paradoxically bringing about his unsurpassed and total victory. Jesus is considered to be triumphant and all-conquering because the Devil was simply unable to tempt him from his complete and unwavering obedience to the will of the Father (clue 6). And just as sin and the 'forces of evil' are vanquished through obedience, so through the resurrection, death - the ultimate price to be paid for sin and the clearest manifestation of its universality - is similarly overcome.

The final detail of this extraordinary theory adds a touch of the farcical to the whole process. Since the Devil hasn't volunteered to release the captive souls of those who have already died, a crucial part of Jesus' mission was a weekend trip to hell (a specific article in the Apostles' creed and mentioned in the first letter of Peter) to preach the gospel to the dead spirits imprisoned there, thereby giving the unjustly incarcerated souls the means to stage a mass break-out.

Clearly these clues for insight into the mystery present many problems for the modern mind which finds it difficult to take seriously the real existence of a supreme devil either in perpetual warfare with the Christian god or trading ownership of people's souls. Similarly the idea that people are in slavery to sin is just as absurd to us today. Apart from the fact that it derives only from the interpretation of the human condition of one person Paul, a man who was wholly and unhealthily obsessed by sin, there's nothing to support the understanding. Paul might have argued that since we're all subject to death we are all indisputably slaves of sin ('for the wages of sin is death'[53]) but this depends entirely on the somewhat implausible belief taught by Christianity that death is a specific punishment for sin (something which I consider at greater length in Chapter 10).

And even if we do accept the idea that there's some sort of cosmic battle going on between the Christian god and the Devil, why did Jesus have to be sacrificed to bring about that victory? Why couldn't the combatants have done something less harmful (such as arm wrestling for example) instead? Why did the Son-god even have to come to the earth and become a human? Surely as the son of an all powerful god he could have wiped out Satan without having to be crucified? And of course, if Jesus' victory over the Devil is so complete, why is it that there are no discernible practical results of that victory? If Satan is the cause of sin and death and he has been so utterly vanquished, why is it that Christians continue to sin and die?

Very little of the lengthy, meandering and often impenetrably dense article in the *Encyclopedia* adds to a clear understanding of the doctrine or explains why Jesus had to be sacrificed and how his death acquired redemptive qualities. For example the article asks the specific question 'why God required the sacrifice of Jesus as the price of redemption for all and did not simply forgive sin freely?' But the answer it gives just doesn't make any real sense. First it notes that in the Old Testament reparation for sins was taught and was required. It then says that humanity is so fallen as a result of its sins that it is completely helpless to provide adequate reparation. Only 'a new act of perfect obedience' could compensate for the offence caused to the god and Jesus' perfect obedience repairs the disorder caused, thereby rescuing mankind. And so it comes about that 'Objectively the sacrifice of Jesus, offered in the name of sinners, accomplishes total reparation

---

[53] Romans 6:23.

and redemption.'

Once again this passage comes across not as an intelligible explanation but as a series of rhetorical statements based on highly questionable assumptions. How can it be known for example that humanity is so helpless that it is unable to mend the relationship with the god? After all, the Jewish belief was that reconciliation could be and was effected regularly through the Day of Atonement ceremonies (albeit through the sacrifice of an animal). Why should this religious understanding be surpassed or swept aside by an arbitrary Christian assumption? Did Jesus himself indicate that these Jewish ceremonies were no longer valid or effective? Why is reparation for sins required in the first place? How can we be sure that only 'a new act of perfect obedience' can make up for humanity's sinfulness? And precisely how does Jesus' obedience and self-sacrifice provide that reparation and so rescue mankind? After all, if an arresting officer or crown prosecutor - or even the Judge's son - volunteered to go to prison or to be executed to serve the term or death penalty of a convicted murderer, neither the Judiciary nor the victim's family, nor society as a whole would ever think that this selfless, voluntary act provided just or meaningful or adequate reparation. Nor could it *ever remove* the convicted man's guilt.

Moreover if we turn to the gospels we can see that the whole concept of reparation seems to be contrary to what Jesus himself taught. Over and over again in Jesus' actions, teachings and parables we can see that he didn't teach that reparation or compensation for sins was needed. All that was required was that the sinner should offer genuine and sincere repentance. For example when one of the Scribes questions him about which was the greatest of all the commandments and adds that to love the Father-god and to love one's neighbour is 'far more important than any holocaust or *sacrifice*', Jesus tells him that he is 'not far from the kingdom of God.'[54] When Jesus heals the paralytic man, he tells him that his sins are forgiven but doesn't mention any requirement for reparation for his sins. And in the well known parable of the Prodigal son, the wayward son is instantly forgiven by his father upon his return and isn't required to make good the inheritance he had squandered.

---

[54]Mark 12:28-34.

If Jesus himself taught that reparation for sins wasn't required to be reconciled to the Father-god, how is it that after his death it was? If it's possible, as Jesus himself said, for people to be forgiven and reconciled through personal repentance, why does the Church insist that Jesus had to be sacrificed to bring about this reconciliation, to achieve our salvation?

The answer can only be that Jesus' death has to be regarded as having a redemptive value or purpose because to suppose otherwise renders it meaningless. And if Jesus' death isn't seen as a redeeming sacrifice but merely a judicial execution by a Roman governor, the very basis of the Incarnation and the reason why Jesus came to earth is critically undermined. At the same time however, the whole redemption belief is valid only if Jesus is a god in the first place; so let's move on now to consider the grounds for accepting Jesus as a god. Can any sense be made of the mystery of the Incarnation?

7

The Road To Divinity: Another Holy Ghost Mystery

Flash ! Aaahhh . . .
Saviour of the Universe.
Flash ! Aaahhh . . .
He'll save every one of us . . .
Just a man, with a man's courage,
You know he's nothing but a man . . .[1]

If there had been tabloid newspapers in the time of the late Roman Empire, one might have read the headline (in massive type) one summer morning in the year 325 - *It's Official: Jesus Is A God! Same Substance As The Father!* - and not thought too much more about it. For gods in the Graeco-Roman world were regularly declared in much the same way that Christianity churns out its saints today. It was a tradition for example that Roman emperors were deified either in their own lifetime (as in the case of the megalomaniac Caligula who in the 1st century proclaimed himself as a god) or, more usually after they had died. So at the beginning of the 4th century Constantine, the newly triumphant emperor who had recently united the whole of the Empire through a succession of military victories, had declared Constantius his deceased father to be divine. And with so many gods from various different beliefs and cults to worship, it would have been no great surprise to learn that yet another had been proclaimed.

A little more than a decade earlier, after centuries of sporadic and often brutal persecution, Christianity had been promoted to being almost the official religion of the Empire, so it would have seemed

---

[1]Queen, *Flash*.

only fitting that the person around whom the belief revolved should have been exalted to divine status. But this formal deification of Jesus was in an entirely different league from any other: it was to become one of the defining moments in the history of Christianity and was to have a monumental impact on the whole of western civilisation. For by declaring that Jesus was not just a god but was 'of the same substance as the Father', it was understood that he was being hailed as a deity above all others in a culture which, under the influence of Christianity, was gradually tending towards a belief in a single, supreme god. And as such, it was inevitable that the faith founded in his name would become a religion superior to all others.

And yet for all this, Jesus never claimed that he was a god and as a strict Jewish monotheist it is inconceivable that he would ever have believed he was the *equal* of the one god that he and his disciples worshipped. On the contrary there are passages in the New Testament which suggest that he actually rejected such an exaltation; and while his earliest followers may have regarded him as especially favoured, they certainly didn't worship him as a god. To the rich young man who flattered him by addressing him as 'Good master' and who sought from him the secret of how to inherit eternal life, Jesus said 'Why do you call me good? No one is good but God alone'. And even after the resurrection Peter acclaimed him merely as 'a man commended to you by God', adding that the miracles Jesus had supposedly worked were acts that 'God worked through him'[2] and not therefore a demonstration of his own divine powers.

So if he made no claim to divinity and had no awareness of having this status, how did so enormous and so important a transition occur? What are the grounds for accepting Jesus as a god? Is it reasonable for us today to continue to accept these grounds? And how did Christianity attempt to resolve the conceptual problems that arose as a consequence from this understanding?

The Incarnation Mystery

Even by the beginning of the 4th century the issue of Jesus' nature and status had long been problematic for the Church, a fact we can tell

---

[2] Mark 10:18, Acts 2:22.

from the various doctrines and definitions proposed by early Church fathers and theologians in the attempts to arrive at a satisfactory understanding. Strangely enough it was not the divinity of Jesus that first caused problems but his humanity. One of the earliest heresies was known as Docetism which maintained that Jesus was a spiritual being only and could not have had a human nature. At the other (slightly more realistic) end of the scale were the Ebionites who, we may recall, evolved from the less radical Jewish faction of the Church and who believed that while Jesus may have been the messiah and may have had an inspired and special relationship with the Father, he could not be seen as anything other than merely human.

In between were other beliefs trying to combine the two polarities. Sabellius, a 3rd century theologian from Libya, for example believed that the terms Father, Son and Holy Spirit were simply modes or personae of the one god; while Paul of Samosata, the bishop of Antioch, argued that divine status was conferred upon Jesus after the resurrection but wasn't his by nature. Both of these opinions were themselves to be condemned as heresies in due course. The orthodoxy eventually taken by the Church was formulated at the Council of Nicaea in 325 where the concept 'of the same substance as the Father' was first formally adopted. But it wasn't until the Council of Chalcedon in 451 that the final wording of this formula was established, decreeing that Jesus was 'perfect in divinity and perfect in humanity . . . to be acknowledged in two natures without confusion, change, division or separation . . . preserved as they came together in one person.'[3]

The Incarnation doctrine immediately throws up some significant problems. How for instance could Christians believe that Jesus was a god, distinct from the Father when everything in their religion taught that there was and could only ever be one god? This absolute commitment to only one god was a belief that Christianity could not easily relinquish since to do so would have been tantamount to admitting that everything in its history and Scriptures was wrong; and as we've seen, much of the appeal of Christianity and evidence of its truth lay in the apparent fulfilment of prophecies contained in these ancient writings. For the moment the faith was in a quandary as early

---

[3] *Catechism*, 467.

Church fathers grappled with the problem, and it wasn't until the 5ᵗʰ century that it was officially 'resolved' through the formulation of the Trinity, the mysterious belief that though there are three separate gods, they are at the same time all one god.

But for the moment the more pressing problem was the understanding that as well as being a god Jesus was at the same time a man. By this stage Christian teaching had long accepted Paul's doctrine of the redeeming nature of Jesus' death as its central teaching. But the fact that Jesus had saved humanity from its sins through his death meant that the sacrifice could not be regarded as a genuine one if there had been no actual loss to Jesus himself. If Jesus was merely a god his sacrifice would not have been meritorious since he would not have suffered as a man and there wouldn't have been anything actually forfeited.

It was fundamental then to believe that Jesus was fully human and therefore had actually sacrificed something of value, that is his human life, to save the world. On the other hand, at the same time he also had to be regarded as a god, otherwise again his sacrifice could never have been the world changing event that Christians believed it was. So it was essential that Jesus had to be preached and believed to be both a human and a god at the same time.

King Of The Impossible: A Few Conceptual Problems

An obvious and workable solution might have been to accept that Jesus was half human and half divine; perhaps if there had been a better understanding of human reproduction and an appreciation that each person was as much the product of the mother as of the father[4] this might have been adopted. However, Christianity insisted that Jesus was not six of one and half a dozen of the other but both *fully* human and *fully* divine despite the obvious incoherence of the belief. On this point the *Catechism* is emphatic: 'the unique and altogether singular event of the Incarnation of the Son of God does not mean that Jesus Christ is part God and part man, nor does it imply that he is the result of a confused mixture of the divine and human. He became truly man

---

[4]The understanding of the time was that all of the genetic material or spirit came from the father; the mother was merely an empty vessel to house the developing child.

while remaining truly God. Jesus Christ is true God and true man'[5] So Jesus had two natures at the same time, one fully human and one fully divine.

But this of course is logically absurd. It's not simply a matter of it being unverifiable or too difficult or too abstract to understand; it is actually logically impossible. We can see this if we approach the matter with the conceptual understanding that it's impossible for anything to have a 200% nature (that is 100% of human nature and 100% of divine nature - 100% being another way to express the concept 'fully' or 'truly').

A simple analogy to illustrate this principle would be the case of a water jug which has a certain maximum capacity. It is always impossible to fill the jug with an amount of water in excess of its maximum capacity. If the jug has a capacity of 2 litres, you'd never be able to fit 4 litres of water into it. Of course you might somehow be able to change the jug to double the amount of water it could hold. But even if you did this, the jug would still never be able to contain more than 100% of its capacity. So you would never be able to fill the jug to its full capacity with 'human water' and then at the same time fit in an equal amount of 'divine water'. It's simply impossible. So it is with a person's nature; no matter how hard one thinks, it's just not possible to conceive of a person being filled or endowed with more than 100% of his capacity or nature.

We can also see just how incoherent the principle of the doctrine is if we substitute the concept of 'divine' with some other, more everyday nature with which we are more familiar. For example, if someone were to argue that Jesus was at the same time *true man* and *true goat* we would see immediately that this proposition is self-evidently a nonsense. You only need to repeat part of the passage above from the *Catechism* 'He became true man while remaining truly God' and replace 'God' with 'goat' to appreciate that conceptually the proposition can't in any way be meaningful or tenable. For when we consider the attributes of each being we can see immediately the impossibility of combining them without loss, confusion or incoherence. For example humans have only two legs but goats have four legs. Self-evidently it's impossible for a creature to have only two

---

[5] *Catechism*, 464.

legs and four legs at the same time. If there were some horrible freak of nature or appalling scientific experiment that somehow combined the two, we might see a creature that had the lower body of a goat with four legs and the upper torso of a human, like the satyrs of Greek myth. But this creature couldn't have *all* the properties of a goat and *all* the properties of a human. And again we could hardly say that such a creature was fully human and fully goat.

Now let us apply the same principles back to the case of Jesus. If we found it impossible to conceive in the abstract of a being that could have a 200% nature, combining the full nature of two types of beings, why should this logical absurdity suddenly vanish and become acceptable in the case of Jesus being both fully human and fully divine? Likewise if we couldn't conceive of a being that had all the attributes of two different natures, how is it that Christians can accept that Jesus had all the attributes of two natures? In the instance of a man and a goat we can readily understand that self-evidently their natures can't fully combine in one being without the problems of loss, confusion or incoherence because many of their attributes are contradictory or mutually exclusive. Yet when we examine the nature and attributes of a god and compare them with those of a human we find that precisely the same problem arises.

It's impossible of course to know exactly what the attributes of a god are since we're unable to observe or verify them as we can do for real, earthly beings. So any such properties are a matter of speculation and depend on our understanding or interpretation of the idea of a god. But generally it's reckoned that the Christian god possesses (and has to possess) such qualities as omniscience, omnipotence, omnipresence and anything and everything else that is great (Samuel Beckett once amusingly referred to the Christian god as 'the omni-omni') including immortality, immutability and moral perfection. Yet these are qualities that a fully human being does not and cannot have. So a person combining the two natures of humanity and divinity would at the same time have to be omniscient and yet not omniscient, immortal and yet mortal. In other words it's the two legs and four legs problem all over again.

As is to be expected the Church doesn't actually address the problem; it simply hails the Incarnation as another mystery of faith which obviously we cannot and should not expect or even attempt to understand. Instead we must accept it as a truth divinely revealed. So it simply throws down a doctrine without providing any clarification or explanation, 'a from of words which as yet has no specified meaning' according to one leading commentator on the Incarnation.[6]

There have of course been various attempts by Christian thinkers to make the Incarnation a logically coherent belief, but their arguments have tended to fall at the first hurdle. The most basic response for example was to suggest that in becoming a human, Jesus divested himself of all his divine attributes but without losing the divine nature. As a man therefore he wasn't omnipotent or omni anything else which was incompatible with being human, yet at the same time he still had a divine nature alongside his human nature. Once he had ceased to be a normal human, presumably after the resurrection, he reacquired these divine attributes to take the form once again of an eternal and perfect god.

This is known as *kenosis*, taking its name from the Greek verb *kenoun* meaning 'to empty' and used in the early hymn recorded by Paul in his letter to the Philippians: 'His state was divine yet he did not cling to his equality with God but emptied himself to assume the condition of a slave and became as men are'.[7] There are hints in the *Catechism* that the Church endorses this idea, using it to explain how the gospel can affirm that Jesus could 'increase in wisdom and stature';[8] obviously if you're already omniscient it's impossible to become *more* knowledgeable.

But once you start removing all the key attributes of divinity, you have to wonder what's actually left of the divine nature. Removing attributes or qualities impacts and diminishes a nature as suggested by our normal everyday experience. For example when we encounter thugs or extremely callous individuals who have lost the qualities of compassion or kindness or mercy or who have no concern for the welfare of others, we often see them as somehow lacking in essential human qualities and call them animals or inhuman, as if their human nature is somehow diminished or lacking.

---

[6] Hick, *The Metaphor of God Incarnate* p 48. I am indebted to Hick's detailed commentary on the Incarnation (pp 47-79) for much of the following discussion on responses to the conceptual problems it poses.

[7] Philippians 2:5-7.

[8] Luke 2:52, *Catechism,* 472.

Thinking more conceptually, a square has certain properties such as four sides of equal length and four interior angles which total 360 degrees. But if you remove one or more of those properties (such as one of the sides), the square can no longer be thought of as a square. The same can be said with respect to the divine nature when stripped of all its attributes that are not compatible with a human nature (that is just about all of them). For what we understand by the concept of a god necessarily involves omniscience and omnipotence and to conceive of a god (or more specifically a Christian god) that doesn't have these qualities becomes a nonsense, a contradiction in terms. Furthermore our conception of a god normally considers that it is characterised by immutability; it's a being not subject to decay and is incapable of being changed or diminished in any way. So if a god is incapable of being changed or changing itself, how is it possible for it to rid itself of its qualities (which surely involves a diminution)?

Two Brains . . ?

Other theories are even more speculative. One of them, known as the two minds theory proposed that the Incarnation should be understood in terms of Jesus having two minds or consciousnesses to explain why he didn't appear to be omniscient in the gospels. You don't have to be Captain Kirk to work out the basic flaw with this theory, that in the entire experience of humanity every mind has always required a brain to be able to function. So if each and every mind requires a brain, it follows that two minds would require two brains. So far as we know there has never been a one brained person who has had two minds, with each mind able to act independently of the other at the same time. Nor do the gospels record Jesus being endowed with two brains or having an unusually large head.

Still, Jesus is a special case and naturally for the Christian god all things are possible. So advocates of this theory suggest (without having any evidence to substantiate their theories) that the human mind of Jesus was contained within but did not contain the divine mind of Jesus the Son-god using analogies such as the psychological condition of multiple personalities to illustrate the viability of this idea. Two or more personalities in one mind as a consequence of unusual or deficient brain chemistry or structure however is very different from two minds in one person; and such conditions don't permit the two personalities to have simultaneous, independent cognition as the theory suggests the two minds of Jesus would have.

Even supposing these difficulties could be overlooked this response still has its problems. For example, as a fully human person Jesus must have been free to sin and was liable to do so; but as a god he is morally perfect and therefore incapable of sinning. The solution posited by one proponent of the theory was that Jesus never sinned, not because he was not free to do so but because if he had been tempted to sin, the will of the divine mind of his person would have intervened and prevented such a lapse.[9] But this creates another problem because it suggests that Jesus was never truly free; if he had ever got fed up with being so damn holy and had ever really wanted to sin just once, he simply would not have been able to do so.

Moreover, even if we allow that the human Jesus had been outwardly perfect, how do we know that he never sinned in his mind? Jesus himself taught that some transgressions need not be fulfilled physically or in actuality in order to be sinful: 'if a man looks at a woman lustfully', he taught his followers 'he has already committed adultery with her.'[10] Merely thinking about illicit sex then is tantamount to going all the way so far as Jesus is concerned. Now if this teaching that certain sins can be committed in the mind is true, it follows that Jesus could very well have been sinful himself. In such instances the intervention of the divine will would have been too late to prevent such sins being committed since the improper thought must have been conceived in order to bring about the intervention. The only way that this type of sin could be prevented would be to control the thoughts of the human Jesus; but in such circumstances his human freewill would effectively have been removed and he could not therefore be fully human.

So could Jesus ever have had improper thoughts? It's impossible for anyone to know every detail of the workings of Jesus' mind, so it would be rather presumptuous to assert that he never had such inclinations. (This of course has not prevented the Church from

---

[9]Thomas Morris, *The Logic of God Incarnate,* as discussed by Hick, *op cit*, pp 47–60. A thoughtful and extensive critique of Morris' work is also provided by Martin, *The Case Against Christianity*, pp 125–161 to which I am similarly indebted.

[10]Matthew 5:28.

declaring that Jesus was sinless.[11]) Appealing to his human goodness isn't enough since even the most morally perfect people can have 'impure' thoughts. Indeed we can suggest that failure and moral imperfection are essential aspects of being human and if Jesus was never prone to such defects we may find it difficult to accept that he really was fully human, of the same nature as the rest of us and like us in every respect. It's possible therefore, perhaps highly probable that Jesus did sin in his mind.

If we're disinclined to accept this, what is there to suggest that Jesus *never* sinned either in his mind or outwardly in his actions? If anything the gospels suggest the contrary. We've already seen how the baptism of Jesus, 'a baptism of repentance for the forgiveness of sins' caused embarrassment to the evangelists; but the fact is Mark records that those who were baptised by John 'confessed their sins'[12] as they made their way into the river Jordan. Why would Jesus seek such a baptism if it were not to express a formal repentance?

So if we accept that it was likely that Jesus repented for having sinned, it becomes nonsensical to think of him as fully human and fully divine at the same time. As a god he could not have sinned and yet it seems highly probable that as a man he did sin. Once again we are back with the two legs, four legs problem but in a different, less tangible form.

The Road To Divinity

If the thinking behind the Incarnation makes no sense at all, how can it be defended? The only possible response available to the Church is to resort to the ploy of calling the belief a mystery. Hence it's able to dismiss the incoherence by pronouncing that the doctrine is not accessible to reason and should only be approached through faith. So once again it recommends a blind acceptance, to be believed without critical or reasonable scrutiny, thus helpfully obviating the need to provide any genuinely meaningful exposition. So the *Catechism*

---

[11]*Catechism*, 467: Jesus is 'like us in all things but sin.' In Chapter 9 I argue that Jesus' actual behaviour was not as perfect as the Church makes out; he showed considerable anger for example when confronting some of his opponents. Anger of course is one of the seven deadly sins.

[12]Mark 1:4–6.

contents itself merely with lazy and unexplained affirmations such as 'because human nature was assumed, not absorbed, in the mysterious union of the Incarnation, the Church was led over the course of centuries to confess the full reality of Christ's human soul . . . and of his human body.'[13] Not especially helpful except that it highlights the fact that it took the Church several centuries to fathom out and proclaim this mystery.

Why then did it take so long for this reality to be understood? Well, according to the Church this is because its god only communicates or reveals itself gradually to humankind; and while the full revelation of its plan was made through Jesus, 'it has not been made explicit.' Consequently 'it remains for the Christian faith to grasp its full significance over the course of the centuries.'[14] Effectively this is *carte blanche* for the Church to make up whatever beliefs and doctrines it likes (indeed, as we shall see, it continued even up to the mid 20th century to do so) and insist on their validity by appealing to the flimsy argument of gradual revelation. And so it was that three centuries or more after Jesus' life and death it could make proclamations about his nature that not even he was aware of and certainly never claimed for himself.

The transmission of revelation, which the Church calls Tradition, is 'accomplished in the Holy Spirit'[15] and so whenever the Church decides upon doctrines, it insists that it has been guided by the Holy Spirit. Consequently all such teaching must necessarily be true. According to the Church then, the Council of Nicaea in 325 was inspired by the Holy Spirit in its decision to proclaim the divinity of Jesus. But how do we know this? Was there a blinding light, as apparently there was at the conversion of Paul, experienced by any of the bishops who attended? Was there a voice from the sky, as the gospels record there was at Jesus' baptism, at the moment when the votes were cast?

Unfortunately none of these divine phenomena were reported; in fact the only thing we have to indicate that there was a divine inspiration guiding these Councils is this undemonstrable and

---

[13] *Catechism*, 470.

[14] *Ibid*, 66.

[15] *Ibid*, 78.

unverifiable claim of the Church. John Hick expresses the problem for Christian believers: 'There is an obvious circularity here: one believes the dogma to be true because ecumenical councils were divinely guided in declaring it, and one believes that they were divinely guided because one believes the dogma to be true.'[16]

If we find we can't take this self-proclaimed authority as seriously as the Church does, a more instructive way to understand how Jesus came to be declared a god is to look at the evolving beliefs concerning his status and the gradual historical process that led to his deification. Of course this more down to earth approach turns Christian teaching on its head – instead of trying to understand the impossible idea that Jesus was a god who became a human while retaining his divine nature, it assumes that Jesus was merely a man who over the course of time came to be regarded as a god. So how might this transformation have come about?

It begins some two centuries back from the Nicaea pronouncement with the increasing exaltation of Jesus in the gospels. Just as he was increasingly idealised in terms of moral goodness and miraculous abilities, so he is exalted in status progressing from the undeclared and secret messiah of Mark to being 'the Way, the Truth and the Life' in John. In fact by the time we get to the Fourth Gospel we see Jesus declaring that 'The father and I are one' and 'To have seen me is to have seen the father'[17] pointing very much towards the eventual doctrine of the Trinity. However, we should understand that it's extremely unlikely that these words were ever actually spoken by Jesus and they should be seen more as an expression of that evangelist's own theological beliefs; like so many of this gospel's claims concerning Jesus' status and relationship with the Father-god, they need to be taken with several (industrial-sized) packets of salt.

But one of the ways we can trace and understand the evolution of these beliefs and conjecture how Jesus might originally and genuinely have been thought of is to consider the titles his contemporaries gave him. Throughout the gospels Jesus is referred to by the crowds, his disciples and the evangelists themselves with a variety of different titles from the simple 'rabbi', or teacher through to 'son of God'. For our

---

[16]Hick, *op cit*, p 37.
[17]John 14:6, 10:30, 14:9.

purposes of understanding his proclaimed divinity however, the two that concern us most, featuring very prominently in the gospels, and which the *Catechism* comments on specifically are 'Lord' and 'son of God.'

What are we to make of these titles? Don't they hint that Jesus was recognised to be a god by his own generation or at least by those who wrote the gospels? Unfortunately our conception of these titles is so well conditioned by centuries of Christian teaching that we automatically associate them with a divine Jesus. But what would those people in 1st century Palestine who originally referred to Jesus as 'Lord' or 'son of God' have meant by them? What status did they confer at that time as opposed to the status conferred in later Christian times? To answer these questions once again we can turn to the valuable insights provided by Professor Vermes who has reviewed Jesus' titles in his book *Jesus the Jew*, a work based not on Christian beliefs about such titles, but on a historical understanding of 1st century Galilee and an extensive and careful examination of Jewish Scripture and Inter-testamental literature.[18]

Vermes concluded that while 'Lord' certainly referred to the Jewish god Yahweh (usually found in the form 'my lord' or 'lord of heaven' rather than 'the lord'), it was also used in a secular context to refer to a person of authority such as a king or a governor. On at least one occasion it was used to refer to a miracle worker and could often indicate a teacher who was more distinguished than the more common 'rabbi'. 'My lord' was also a form of address to venerable people. This evolved to 'the lord' and was used in deferential speech to address (in the third person) an influential teacher or a supernatural person.

For Vermes this title is applied to Jesus in Mark and Matthew mostly in connection with his being a miracle worker; in Luke it's also used to imply a teacher (although on two occasions it refers to the risen Jesus). On all these occasions then it might be more correct to translate the title as 'sir' or 'master.' Even so, Vermes notes that in John the title acquires additional significance when the doubting Thomas addresses the risen Jesus as 'my lord and my God.' But the more 'reliable' synoptic gospels wouldn't have used the term to imply or

---

[18]Vermes, *Jesus the Jew*, pp 64-186. The titles Vermes reviews are prophet, lord, messiah, son of man and son of god.

suggest that Jesus was a god, the equal of Yahweh. The *Catechism* of course teaches otherwise, maintaining that 'The title "Lord" indicates divine sovereignty. To confess or invoke Jesus as Lord is to believe in his divinity.'[19]

In the case of 'son of God' the origin of the title turns out to be less clear cut than one might have expected. In the Old Testament this title is used to refer to heavenly or angelic beings (Vermes believes this would have been the most obvious association for a 1st century Palestinian Jew), Israelites in general and the kings of Israel in particular. However, from the second association evolved the understanding that it could be used to denote a particularly holy man or more especially the messiah that was expected. Such a term might readily have been used then to address or refer to Jesus without implying that he was the only 'son of God' or that he was actually a divine being through his sonship.

When we learn that it was a characteristic of the Hasidim or holy men whom we have previously encountered (and of whom Vermes considers Jesus to be the leading example) to express their close relationship to Yahweh by addressing him as *abba* or father, we can begin to understand why his contemporaries may have thought of Jesus and hailed him as *a* 'son of God'. Most revealingly, Vermes points out that one such charismatic healer, Hanina was said to have been addressed as 'my son' by a heavenly voice, just as at his baptism Jesus was similarly acclaimed. So it's quite possible that Jesus may even have regarded himself as *a* son of god without claiming to be *the* 'son of God' in the Christian understanding of the term.

The earliest Christian beliefs about Jesus as 'Lord' and 'son of God' seem to have been that it was his resurrection that led to his elevation. This also appears to be the understanding that Paul had when he wrote that Jesus 'was proclaimed Son of God in all his power through his resurrection from the dead.'[20] However if this conferred on Jesus the right to be called 'Lord' or 'son of God', it was still a title or status that was conferred on him, not necessarily one he was born to, still less one that was his by nature. But what seems to have happened was a free association between the office or titles conferred on Jesus and his actual

---

[19] *Catechism*, 455.
[20] Romans 1:4.

nature.

We can see this happening most obviously in the way that Paul uses the Greek translation of the title of messiah (that is, Christ) to refer to Jesus as if this were his name, constantly referring to him as Jesus Christ or Christ Jesus or even just Christ. Gradually over the course of his letter writing period the historical name and person of Jesus (never one of Paul's concerns anyway) is virtually abandoned. In his first letter to the Thessalonians for example there are some 19 references to Jesus by name, of which 7 are either Jesus or Lord Jesus; the remaining 12 are Jesus Christ (or Christ Jesus) or Christ. But by the time we get to the later letter to the Philippians, written some five to six years later, of the 40 or so references to Jesus, only 2 are Jesus or Lord Jesus. The remainder are split roughly equally between Jesus Christ and Christ. With such frequent association then, for Paul's gentile audience, probably indifferent to or ignorant of the Jewish concept of the messiah, Christ is Jesus and Jesus is Christ. So we see Christ the title meaning simply 'anointed one' becoming first his name and then in due course his very identity or nature, something which can be preached and proclaimed, as Paul's own words make clear: 'Christ is proclaimed; and that makes me happy . . . Life to me, of course is Christ . . . All I want to know is Christ and the power of his resurrection'[21].

A similar process may also have happened with these other two titles of Jesus especially since at the same time there would have been a shift in their meaning as Christianity was removed further and further from its Jewish roots. As we've seen, following the suppression of the Jewish revolt and the destruction of the Temple in Jerusalem in the year 70, the Jerusalem faction of the Church lost its leading influence and Christianity became increasingly a religion spread in and influenced by the Hellenistic world. So 'Lord' and 'son of God' could easily have taken on the more esoteric Hellenistic connotations derived from Greek myth whose heroes were often the offspring of divine figures. It is pointed out by numerous commentators for example that both Plato and Alexander the Great were commonly believed to be of divine parentage with miraculous events attending their conceptions.

Moreover some of the terms associated with Jesus (son of god,

---

[21]Philippians 1:18, 21, 2:10.

saviour, lord, gospel) were also associated with rulers of the same era.[22] So if great men were readily seen as divine or divine offspring, it's quite plausible to suppose that a similar recognition was given to the new saviour king being proclaimed, a saviour so great that he had even risen from the dead. Meanwhile the original, more commonplace and down to earth Jewish meanings would have fallen by the wayside, soon to be forgotten completely. And so in the Hellenistic milieu in which gods were much more readily proclaimed (one story in Acts, well away from Palestine, has Paul and Barnabas hailed as gods after they healed a crippled man[23]) it may only have been a matter of time before these titles, now increasingly understood as signifying Jesus' nature, led to him being acclaimed and worshipped as a god.

The New Imperial God

By the end of the 2nd century then Jesus was generally believed by Christians to be a god, a fact that pagans were aware of as Celsus' tract suggested. As we've already seen this brought about a succession of disputes and controversies as various thinkers sought to provide some intellectual coherence to the belief. The greatest of these, and the one which provided the biggest threat to the already fragile unity of the Church, was the Arian controversy which erupted around the year 320.

The origin of this controversy lay in a quarrel between Arius, a priest from the Egyptian city of Alexandria and the bishop there, Alexander. Arius was puzzled by the relationship between the Father and Son gods; if Jesus was the 'son of God', did this mean that he was as great as the original Father-god? And if the Son had been begotten by the Father, as the concept of paternity implied, didn't it follow that there must have been a time when Jesus the Son did not exist? If this were the case the two could never be thought of as equal and Jesus couldn't be a god in the same sense as the Father-god.

---

[22]Both the Hellenistic and Jewish background of divine sonship are reviewed in detail in *Two Roots or a Tangled Mass?* by Frances Young, published in *The Myth of God Incarnate*, pp 64-121.

[23]Acts 14:11-12: 'When the crowd saw what Paul had done they shouted . . . "These people are gods who have come down to us disguised as men." They addressed Barnabas as Zeus, and since Paul was the principal speaker they called him Hermes.'

Alexander found such thinking intolerable since it made Jesus part of the creation rather than a being which existed prior to any act of creation and therefore a lesser or inferior god, possibly not even a god at all. Consequently he had Arius' doctrines condemned by a convocation of bishops. In response Arius turned to and received the support of another bishop, the powerful Eusebius of Nicomedia, then the capital of the Eastern Empire in northern Asia Minor. With his own synod of bishops Eusebius reaffirmed Arius' views, so turning what was originally a local dispute into a potential schism between two rival centres of Christianity. News of the growing controversy reached the Emperor, Constantine prompting him to write to Arius and Alexander to try to reconcile the two. When this had no effect, he resolved to settle the matter by convening a general council of the Church, at the town of Nicaea in 325, assembling as many of its bishops as possible to ensure that once a consensus was reached it would be accepted by all.

At this point we might wonder why a Roman emperor should concern himself with the apparently trivial bickerings of a religion which his predecessor, Diocletian just twenty years beforehand had tried to eradicate by unleashing a brutal persecution. Furthermore, how had it come about that the Christians, who had been persecuted to a very large extent because their loyalty to the emperor had always been suspect and who had managed to resist such hardships for so many years, now agreed to submit so willingly to his authority? Could this be the Holy Spirit at work, gradually but diligently influencing attitudes and events?

Christians might like to believe so, but understanding the change of heart, or more precisely the change of policy made by Constantine is better considered by looking back to the events that brought him to power and acknowledging his real political motivations. The former Emperor, Diocletian had abdicated in 305 perhaps as a result of illness or perhaps because after ruling for 21 years he was unable to face the impending conflicts that were to trouble the Empire for the best part of the next two decades.

Part of his legacy was to have left in place a co-emperor, Maximiam and two powerful deputies, Galerius and Constantius, appointed to help him meet the challenges of running an empire so extensive and so prone to crises. Naturally, once Diocletian abdicated this became the principal cause of the Empire's internal political turmoil, a problem that was only going to become more pronounced with the emergence of two power hungry sons, Maxentius and Constantine. Galerius had died without an heir in 311, Constantius in 306, while Maximian had been effectively out-manoeuvred by his son, leaving the two young upstarts as the remaining contenders for supreme control of the Western Empire.

The two finally met in 312 at the decisive battle of Milvian Bridge, some ten miles north of Rome. Despite being heavily outnumbered and attacking a defensive position, Constantine won an unlikely but resounding victory and here the Christian legends associated with Constantine begin. According to his later Christian biographer Eusebius (not the bishop of Nicomedia but the author of the *History of the Church*), at some point before the battle Constantine looked into the sky and 'a most marvellous sign appeared to him from heaven, the account of which it might have been hard to believe had it been related by any other person.' This sign of course was a cross and, even more amazingly it was accompanied by writing in the sky, providing Constantine with the heavenly instruction to 'conquer by this.'[24]

Once again Christians are up to their old tricks; it's remarkable how so many key moments or incidents in the Christian story seem to be accompanied by frankly implausible signs or visions or miracles. Even if in this instance there was a sign, given as an indication of divine favour or approval, it's somewhat distressing to consider that the Christian god had to resort to conquest and bloodshed to get people to believe in him, a course of action that goes completely against the grain of Jesus' teaching.

Still, we aren't supposed to understand the mysterious ways of the Father-god and if a Christian writer records this sign as a genuine historical event, then it really must be true. We are fortunate therefore to have had a person so trustworthy as Constantine[25] to provide the testimony for this 'marvellous sign', for as Eusebius indicates, had it been anyone else claiming to see writing in the sky, it would hardly

---

[24] Eusebius, *The Life of Constantine* I: 28. Quoted from Kee, *Constantine versus Christ,* p 15.

[25] Constantine was prone to having divine visions; in his earlier years for example at a time when his patron gods were pagan, he was reported to have been visited by the god Apollo. See Grant, *The Emperor Constantine,* pp 131-134.

have been taken seriously at all. Perhaps aware that he's undermining the event somewhat, he goes on to record that a company of Constantine's army was likewise struck with amazement since it too 'witnessed the miracle.' Unfortunately no independent testimony of the army was ever recorded.

Whether or not there was such a sign in the sky, it seems that Constantine believed that he had indeed conquered by transferring his allegiance to the evidently more powerful Christian god and this is often seen as the point that marks his conversion to Christianity. So in the following years Christians found that not only were they tolerated, they were also provided with unprecedented support and privileges. Those entering the priesthood were exempt from public duties, Church lands were no longer taxed, confiscated property where possible was restored and material and labour grants were made to enable the building of new churches. More importantly bishops were given positions of judicial authority and some were invited to become advisers at the imperial court.[26] Of course there's no such a thing as a free lunch even for one so bounteous as Constantine and for this patronage there was a price to be paid, namely the recognition and acceptance of the emperor as the supreme earthly authority, even in matters of faith.

Now we may begin to understand what it was that probably determined Constantine's motives in convening the Council. Constantine is often thought of as being the first Christian emperor and for some historians he was a true Christian profoundly involved with the development of the Church's theology and doctrines as well as a benevolent patron who nurtured its growing influence.

But he wasn't the sort of Christian we would recognise today. In reality he seems to have had very little concern for the message and teachings of Jesus which might have encouraged him at least to try to show some concern for his enemies rather than slaughter them. For Constantine the Christian god was more a god of conquest whose patronage simply helped to secure military victories[27] and who proved to be more powerful than his former pagan gods. To the person of

---

[26] *Ibid*, pp 159-160.

[27] Not much changes. War-pig politicians today continue to make use of the Christian god to persuade themselves and their supporters that the wars they enter are just wars and that the victories they win are indicative of divine approval.

Jesus he was at best indifferent, hardly ever referring to him in his letters and edicts. And in his personal morality he seems not to have had the least interest in the values espoused by the gospels. He was still willing to accept crucifixion as an appropriate punishment for slaves convicted of treason for example;[28] and most notoriously he had his son executed and his second wife, Fausta murdered – if the most gruesome accounts are to be believed – by having her immersed in a bath of scalding hot water.[29]

Nor was Constantine excessively concerned with points of theology as we can see from his response to the Arian dispute; in his letter to Arius and Alexander he refers to the matter in dismissive terms over and over again, suggesting that he didn't really appreciate the issue and cared about it still less. 'When I examined the origin and cause of all this, I found the pretext for it far too trifling and unworthy of such contentiousness as this' he wrote, almost contemptuous of what he saw as a 'very silly question' which had arisen only as a consequence of too much 'useless leisure'.[30]

What he did care about however was Imperial unity. In 324, after a protracted campaign lasting nearly two decades he finally succeeded in unifying the whole Empire by defeating the Eastern co-emperor Licinius. But now at the very moment when his cherished objective, to be the sole ruler of a Roman world free from internal division, had been achieved a tiresome and pointless dispute over nothing, a 'foolish verbal disagreement' as he put it, was threatening that hard won peace. And once it became clear that Arius and Alexander hadn't been reconciled by the mild chastisement of his letter, Constantine must have understood that the only way to impose his authority would be in person.

Even so, as an astute politician he would have appreciated the former resilience of Christians under persecution and the threat of compulsion. So he may well have calculated that rather than trying to coerce the bishops into a uniform belief, his interests might be better served by giving them the impression that they would be permitted to

---

[28]Kee, *op cit*, p 97.

[29]Grant *op cit*, pp 110-114.

[30]Letter from Constantine to Alexander and Arius, c. 324, quoted from Keresztes, *Constantine - A Great Christian Monarch & Apostle*, pp 119-122.

reach a consensus of their own making, with just a little guidance from the Imperial throne.

Even before the Council opened however, it was clear that Constantine was pulling all the strings. His presence alone with all the grandeur of majesty might have been enough to generate a feeling of reverence among the assembled bishops; but it's likely that he would already have secured their deference and goodwill having shrewdly incurred their travelling expenses and provided hospitality throughout the proceedings. Moreover, having expressed the need for unity in his opening address, it was clearly understood that any defiance of the consensus reached (that is, defiance of his will) would mean banishment. Few among the delegates would have wanted to stand up to him, especially since of the three hundred or so bishops attending, the majority probably had no real concern about the somewhat perplexing and speculative theology at the heart of the debate.

Still, they knew and cared enough to consider that Arius' views were wrong and these were rejected early in the Council proceedings. A mediating position submitted earlier by one of his supporters was declared by the Emperor to be consistent with his own beliefs. But this statement of belief still affirmed that Jesus was 'first born of all creation' and therefore implied that he was inferior to the Father. So to placate Arius' opponents, Constantine himself (if Eusebius, his biographer is to be believed) proposed that the formula 'of the same substance' should be inserted into the creed.

Quite why the Emperor sided with the Alexandrians against Arius is unclear. Perhaps he was influenced by his ecclesiastical secretary Hosius, a western bishop who was himself opposed to Arius. Or it may have been that he saw Arius as a trouble-maker who had caused the whole controversy in the first place and whose opinions could not therefore be allowed to prevail. Whatever it was, Constantine's point of view was the decisive factor and only Arius' most loyal supporters were brave enough to refuse to sign up to the official creed. That the Emperor used his fearsome authority to intimidate the bishops to accept his preferred creed can be seen from a letter that Eusebius of Nicomedia, one of the potential dissenters, later wrote expressing regret for haven been cajoled into a position against his conscience.[31]

---

[31] I. Wilson, *op cit*, p 142.

Naturally the two who did dissent, along with Arius himself were immediately banished while the compliant majority continued to enjoy Constantine's goodwill and hospitality in the form of a lavish banquet to celebrate the twentieth anniversary of his rule.

Jesus - A New God Or Just A Man ?

Can we conclude then that it's reasonable to accept that Jesus is a god, a being who existed before the creation of the universe and who was able to take the form of a man while simultaneously retaining his divine being? It's a very demanding belief and there seem to be too many obstacles in the way to allow it to be considered a valid or tenable doctrine. In his book *The Case Against Christianity*, Michael Martin neatly summarises the nature of the difficulty to be overcome: 'there is a strong presumption that a theory that has no empirical support should not be believed. However, when a theory lacks such support *and* has serious conceptual problems - including a prima facie incoherency - there is a very strong presumption that it should not be believed.'[32] We would normally apply such stringent and cautious criteria to theories in other walks of life, so why is it that as soon as a theory or belief takes on religious connotations such prudence and thoughtfulness is happily abandoned?

The Incarnation belief - that Jesus could be a god and a man at the same time is clearly logically incoherent if not impossible, a fact that the Church seems tacitly to acknowledge by teaching that it is a mystery. By this it specifically means that the belief is beyond rational or human comprehension and that it can only be approached and accepted (but not understood) through faith. Essentially it requires the suspension of all reasonable judgement.

It would be more honest of the Church however to admit that such a belief is beyond understanding because, like other 'mysteries of faith', it is a doctrine of doublethink, obliging one to hold two contradictory beliefs at the same time, and therefore is something of a fudge made for ideological purposes. What might those purposes be? As we noted earlier, if Jesus isn't human, his sacrifice is not a real one. On the other hand, if he isn't a god, what's the big deal about him

---

[32]Martin, *op cit*, p 157.

dying on a cross anyway? Lots of other Jewish men were executed in similar circumstances under the Romans, so why should humanity have been redeemed by this one particular execution if Jesus isn't a god? So for Christians Jesus has to be a god and a man at the same time because to suppose otherwise means that Christian theology simply does not compute and no one can be saved.

Let us suppose however that we can ignore or overcome the conceptual difficulties posed by the Incarnation; do we have any grounds for accepting this belief as a truth divinely revealed, under the guidance of the Holy Spirit? To accept this proposition means acknowledging upfront the existence of the threefold Christian god and the validity of the Christian revelation. But again this involves a circular reasoning: how do we know that Jesus is a god? From the revelation of the Holy Spirit. How do we know about the Holy Spirit and the Christian god? From the teachings of Jesus. How do we know that the teachings of Jesus are true? Because Jesus is a god. But how do we know that Jesus is a god? And so on.[33]

But even ignoring this stumbling block, do we have any evidence for the operation of the Holy Spirit inspiring the decision of the Council of Nicaea? Even if we should choose to believe in the highly implausible sign given to Constantine, it's still hard to see him as a chosen instrument of revelation. In any case it will always be a matter of interpretation rather than indisputable historical fact. While one historian may regard Constantine (as the title of his book indicates) as a true Christian and apostle,[34] another sees him as a military dictator who used Christianity to achieve his own political objectives and whose values replaced those of Jesus in its unfolding development.[35] The Emperor himself may well have proclaimed that the Council of Nicaea was guided by the Holy Spirit; but as we've seen, Constantine's over-riding concern was the uniform acceptance of a creed rather than its

---

[33] The circularity of the argument is easily spotted in the *Catechism*: 'Now God's Spirit, who reveals God, makes known to us Christ his Word . . . it is Christ who is seen . . . but it is the Spirit who reveals him' (i.e. Jesus is revealed as a god by the Holy Spirit). 'Before his Passover, Jesus announced the sending of "another Paraclete (Advocate), the Holy Spirit" . . . thus revealed as another divine person with Jesus and the Father' (i.e. Jesus reveals the Holy Spirit to be a god). 687, 689, 243.

[34] Keresztes, *op cit.*

[35] Kee, *op cit*, pp 1-4.

theological content.

Finally we might ask the most basic and obvious question: where in Jesus' life and career is there evidence to support the Christian claim that he is a god? One might cite his miracles, but apart from the fact that their historicity is far from certain, they can be considered more plausibly in non-miraculous terms. Moreover, if one uses miracles as a basis to determine divinity, why does Christianity not recognise other men who were recorded as having performed miracles as gods?

Similar observations might be made about his resurrection; the fact that Jesus was believed to have risen from the dead would not in itself mean that he is a god. In fact his earliest and closest followers who believed most fervently in the reality of that event did not accord him divine status as a consequence. And again we've observed that the evidence for so extraordinary an event falls far short of being persuasive let alone conclusive.

So what else might be used to support the notion that Jesus is a god? We can consider the possibility that Jesus was morally perfect, something that we've already touched on and which doesn't hold too much promise. And it's worth looking closely at that old chestnut which is often used to argue that Jesus was the 'son of God' and therefore divine in his own right, the doctrine of the virgin birth.[36]

---

[36]'The Fathers see in the virginal conception the sign that it truly was the Son of God who came in a humanity like our own' (*Catechism*, 496).

8

Mysteries Of The Burning Bush

But if you really want me, move it slow
There's things about me you just have to know . . .[1]

It may come as something of a surprise to the reader of the gospels to note just how little they have to say about Mary, the mother of Jesus. In Mark she is of no consequence to the narrative at all, mentioned only twice and both times merely in passing. Matthew includes her in his opening chapters which tell the stories of the conception and birth of Jesus. Yet even these stories are constructed more around the person of Joseph than around Mary and she's not permitted to speak a single word. In John there's no birth narrative but Mary appears in two other vignettes, at the wedding at Cana where Jesus turns water into wine and at the crucifixion. On both occasions however, she seems to be there more to fulfil a literary or theological purpose. Only in Luke is there an extended story about Mary concerning the conception of Jesus and her subsequent visit to Elizabeth, the mother of John the Baptist and, according to Luke, her kinswoman (or possibly her cousin). She then features briefly in two further incidents following on from this (her involvement in Jesus' birth and upbringing); but effectively, with Luke's annunciation being her one and only star moment, from the evangelists' point of view Mary is almost irrelevant to the Christian message.

It's astonishing then to reflect on how so much secondary material, so many teachings and, most remarkably, so much veneration have evolved around this figure. After Jesus Mary is (and by an almost unimaginable margin) the most important person in Christianity,

---

[1] Britney Spears, *Sometimes*.

almost something of a saviour figure herself. Yet in the gospels she's not much more than an occasionally necessary, but vague figure hovering in the background, brought into play when required and then exited when no longer needed. And were it not for just one apparently unique but utterly improbable accomplishment, the fact that she 'conceived what is in her by the Holy Spirit'[2] she would doubtless have remained that bit part player in the drama of the life of Jesus. But these key words are there and they change everything; and so much controversy, so much unjustifiable elaboration and fabrication have come about as a consequence that it's worth looking at the Christian mysteries and doctrines that revolve around Mary in some detail.

Holy Fecundation !

The virgin conception of Jesus (not to be confused with the virgin birth which, as we shall see, is another matter altogether and no less extraordinary) is one of the best known yet most erroneous of all Christian beliefs. Through this mystery (another one which naturally 'surpasses all human understanding and possibility') Christians are required to accept two basic principles: first, there was no human sperm which caused fertilisation in Mary's womb and second, Mary conceived yet remained physically intact and hence there could not have been any sexual experience in the conception of the saviour. Each element is crucial to the belief, the former to confer divine status upon Jesus and the latter to ensure that he was not subject to original sin which Christianity later taught to be transmitted through sex.

These two beliefs go hand in hand to form the basis for the subsequent glorification of Mary. From her humble origins as a simple, undistinguished Jewish mother she has become, according to the Church, 'Queen of all things . . . the new Eve . . . the seat of Wisdom . . . the masterwork of the mission of the Son and the Spirit in the fullness of time . . . the burning bush of the definitive theophany.' In other words, the greatest and holiest woman in the universe, ever. But this exaltation has come about not through any great achievement (nor indeed through *any* achievement) by Mary in her own right, but merely through the agency of the Holy Spirit which, in the equally

---

[2]Matthew 1:20.

wonderful and memorable words of the *Catechism* was 'sent to sanctify the womb of the virgin Mary and divinely fecundate it.'[3] Fecundated by a ghost! Feck! Whatever next? What on earth are we to make of such a bizarre and frankly comical idea?

We know of the virgin conception from only two of the gospels, Matthew and Luke; but they tell very different stories suggesting that the virginity of Mary emerged as a late belief. It is not even mentioned in any of the earlier Christian writings despite being so extraordinary an event. Just as Paul knew nothing of Jesus' miracles, so he was unaware of any unusual goings-on here, recording only that Jesus was 'born of a woman.' This isn't especially illuminating since everyone is born of a woman; it may be that in the Hellenistic milieu in which Paul's mission took place this served to emphasise the humanity of Jesus before his death. For Paul it was the resurrection which proclaimed Jesus as 'Son of God', not his birth.[4] And although Mark mentions Jesus' mother twice and knows that she is called Mary, he doesn't refer to her as a virgin. So the story of the virginity of Mary seems likely to have emerged only in the closing decades of the 1st century, probably with or just prior to the appearance of Matthew's gospel, around the year 80 CE.

The Church concedes that this presents something of a problem, with the *Catechism* acknowledging that 'People are sometimes troubled by the silence of St Mark's gospel and the New Testament epistles about Jesus' virginal conception.' However, instead of actually addressing the problem in any meaningful way, it simply assumes the ostrich position. First it ducks the issue by introducing a secondary concern, the fact that some people think that it is a legendary and not a historical belief. It then moves away from addressing the original and real problem, the ignorance of the earliest Christian writers of this story and its omission from their writings, by responding only to this secondary issue. The virgin conception it says, could not have been invented for theological purposes since the very idea was unknown, not understood and ridiculed by both Jewish and pagan non-believers.[5]

---

[3] *Catechism*, 497, 966, 726, 721, 724, 488.

[4] Gal. 4:4; Paul also affirmed that Jesus 'was a descendant of David . . . proclaimed Son of God in all his power through his resurrection from the dead (Romans 1:4-5).

[5] This isn't strictly true. Bultmann for example (*op cit*, p 292) observes 'in Hellenism . . . the idea of the generation of a king or hero from a virgin by the godhead was

So therefore the evangelists would never have made up such a story. So it must be historically true. Not ok, but even if this were the case, why don't Mark and Paul refer to it?

By now we should begin to suspect that we're not going to get a coherent answer. And sure enough, instead of providing a clear response the *Catechism* goes into churchspeak overkill and succeeds only in baffling the reader with its preposterous and incomprehensible mystery talk: 'The meaning of this event' it says, 'is accessible only to faith, which understands in it the connection of these mysteries with one another in the totality of Christ's mysteries . . . Mary's virginity and giving birth, and even the Lord's death escaped the notice of the prince of this world: these three mysteries worthy of proclamation were accomplished in God's silence.'[6] Unfortunately the meaning of this passage is accessible only to churchy swots and it's very difficult to make any real sense of it. What is clear however is that it provides no intelligible explanation for the ignorance of Mark and Paul and the reader is simply left totally bewildered.

So to try to understand what's going on, let's look at the original gospel stories. In Luke Mary is presented as 'a virgin betrothed to a man named Joseph.' One day she's visited by an angel, Gabriel who tells her that she is highly favoured and will conceive and give birth to a son who will be great and will rule for ever and ever. Mary wonders about this but Gabriel reassures her, telling her that the Holy Spirit will come upon her. As a sign, the angel informs her that her kinswoman Elizabeth, thought by everyone to be barren (i.e. post-menopausal) had herself conceived and was now six months pregnant. Immediately afterwards Mary sets out to visit Elizabeth to share the happy news whereupon the embryonic John the Baptist leaps for joy inside his mother's womb to acknowledge Mary's newly conferred holiness.

In the general excitement Mary then recites a strangely inappropriate and disturbingly militant hymn in which she praises the Almighty not so much with joy at the prospect of having a baby, nor in thanks for her apparently miraculous conception as you might

---

widespread.' And Warner notes in her study of Mary, *Alone of All Her Sex* (p 35) that 'The historical fact remains that the virgin birth of heroes and sages was a widespread formula in the Hellenistic world: Pythagoras, Plato, Alexander were all believed to be born of women by the power of a holy spirit.'

[6] *Catechism*, 498.

expect in the circumstances, but because

> He has shown the power of his arm,
> He has routed the proud of heart.
> He has pulled down princes from their thrones.[7]

We can see straight away that this hardly forms compelling evidence for so extraordinary a miracle, indeed it is so vague that if we didn't have the accompanying story in Matthew, it would be very difficult to suppose that there had ever been a virgin conception. The text simply tells us that an unmarried woman is visited by an angel who informed her that she would become pregnant and that her son would grow up to assume great significance in the history of Israel.

The initial use of the word virgin certainly highlights her condition; but as a betrothed and as yet unmarried woman, this wouldn't have been anything out of the ordinary. The angel says merely 'You will conceive'; many other virgin women betrothed to be married have also gone on to conceive children. It doesn't tell her that she has already done so despite her virginal state, nor is there any indication that this was the point of conception as Christian commentators sometimes argue. Mary protests and asks how this can come about since at this point she hadn't slept with Joseph. Apart from this single question, at no point in Luke's account is there any hint that a miracle has occurred, is occurring or is about to occur. So the whole of the narrative from the doctrinal point of view hinges on an interpretation of this simple response given by Mary: 'How can this be since I do not know a man?' We'll return to this shortly.

Matthew's account is completely different (although strictly speaking not inconsistent with Luke's), with Joseph being the one who receives the fantastic news from heaven. It's much briefer and more precise, and it's here that we find the specific statement that Joseph 'knew her not (i.e. didn't have sex with her) until she had borne a

---

[7]Luke 1:26-38 details the annunciation, verses 39-56 Mary's visit to Elizabeth. The words of the hymn, the Magnificat, as it is known, are clearly not those of the historical Mary. Even the Catholic scholar R. E. Brown declares that 'Virtually no serious scholar would argue today that the Magnificat was composed by Mary' (*The Birth of the Messiah*, p 340). We should be very wary therefore of any words put into her mouth, particularly her question to the angel.

son'.[8] We have no indication as to how Matthew acquired this intimate knowledge. As in Luke, Mary is betrothed but before the marriage takes place she is unexpectedly found to be pregnant and so Joseph decides to cancel the betrothal. Being an honourable man, he decides not to make a public show of this so as to spare Mary from the likely shame that would have ensued. But he is persuaded not to take this course through a personal revelation from the angel of the Lord (not named as Gabriel in this instance) which advises him of the heavenly origins of her conception. The angel goes on to prophesy that the son born to him will be the one to save people from their sins. And to provide the conclusive proof that this definitely occurred, sure enough Matthew informs us that 'all this took place to fulfil the words of the Lord spoken through the prophet'.[9]

As we've already noted, Matthew is very fond of citing prophecies to demonstrate that Jesus was the messiah and in this instance also we should be wary of accepting the prophecy at face value. In fact this is probably the most controversial of all his prophecy fulfilments because it has been so distorted and because it seems as if the event has given rise to the prophecy rather than being its actual fulfilment. The prophecy itself, if indeed we can call it that – 'The virgin will conceive and give birth to a son and they will call him Immanuel' – is taken from Isaiah, written over 700 years before Jesus' birth and is wholly inappropriate to the circumstances of Mary. But the most problematic issue is that no such prophecy was ever actually made.

Matthew was written originally in Greek and whoever wrote it was a Greek speaker, possibly unfamiliar with the Hebrew language. Accordingly, his use of Hebrew Scriptures is derived from their Greek translation, a work known as the Septuagint (or LXX)[10] so called because it was believed that seventy translators were employed to complete the mammoth task. In this Greek version of the Jewish Scriptures the word for 'virgin' used in this passage is *parthenos*, a word that denotes a woman who has had no sexual experience. However, in the original Hebrew the word used is *almah* which means simply a

---

[8]Matthew 1:25 (RSV).

[9]Matthew 1:18-25.

[10]Wells notes for instance *(Who was Jesus*, p 101) that in Jesus' encounter with the Devil all of the scriptural rebukes made by Jesus agree to the LXX, not to the Hebrew Old Testament.

young woman. If the writer of Isaiah had wanted to refer to a sexually inexperienced woman, he would most likely have used the Hebrew word *bethulah*.[11]

But even if he had meant a virgin in the technical or biological sense, there was nothing in his prophecy to suggest that such a woman would have remained a virgin after conceiving. If one says 'this little girl will get married' for example, it doesn't follow that the girl will always remain a child or will be a young girl when she does marry. It is hugely speculative then to suppose that when Isaiah made this prophecy he was thinking that its fulfilment would be found in a woman who conceives a child and yet remains a virgin. There's simply nothing in his text to justify this interpretation.

Moreover, when we consider the context of Isaiah, it's clear that the prophecy doesn't refer to the birth of a messiah at all. At the time of Isaiah's prophecy the armies of Syria and Israel had invaded Judah to force its king, Ahaz into a coalition against Assyria, the dominant military power of the region at that time.[12] According to Isaiah, Ahaz was told by Yahweh, speaking through the prophet, to ask for a sign to reassure him that his kingdom would be safe. But Ahaz was unwilling to put Yahweh to the test and declined to do so. So Isaiah told him that 'the Lord himself shall give you a sign.' This sign was in the form of a prophecy which promised that 'the young woman' (the use of the definite article suggests that the identity of the woman, perhaps one of Ahaz's wives was known[13]) would become pregnant and give birth to a son. The child would be called Immanuel (not Jesus) and by the time he reached a certain age, his father's enemies would be destroyed.[14]

The prophecy therefore focuses on the birth and age of a child and not on the manner of his conception. Furthermore it's clear that the fulfilment of this prophecy would occur at that time and not several hundred years in the future, for according to Isaiah the sign was volunteered by Yahweh for 'you', that is for Ahaz. It is quite wrong therefore to suppose that the prophet intended that the sign would be

---

[11]Vermes, *op cit*, p 191. The *Catechism* (497) ignores the problem of the mistranslation altogether, once again adopting the ostrich strategy.

[12]*Jerome*, 15:2, 18.

[13]*Ibid*, 15:19: '*Ha'alma* is not the technical term for a virgin. This is best understood as a wife of Ahaz.'

[14]Isaiah 7:1-16.

fulfilled by an event hundreds of years later.[15] After all, what possible use to Ahaz would be a sign which could not be discerned in his own lifetime? Why would the prophet even inform him of such a sign? Once again then, it seems as if we can't place any reliance at all on Matthew's interpretation of Old Testament prophecies; and at the end of the day, an interpretation – and a very poor one at that – based on a mistranslation is all that it is. So this can hardly provide the basis or evidence for the virgin conception that any reasonable person could accept.

But what of the rest of Matthew's narrative, can this be considered any more reliable? As we've noted, the rest of it revolves around the angelic message given to Joseph; but once again Matthew makes use of his familiar and highly questionable ploy of having the revelation made through a dream. Just as in Luke the only witness to the angelic annunciation is Mary herself, so here too there is a single witness. Neither piece of testimony therefore could ever have been verified, but at least Mary had the advantage of being awake. We've already seen how suspect Matthew's narrative becomes when he has to resort to dreams to convey information and to carry the storyline forward; so if we felt previously that we couldn't trust those parts of his story which are based on dreams (the warnings to the astrologers and to Joseph after Jesus' birth and later on to Pilate's wife), then we should dismiss the whole of Matthew's testimony concerning the virgin conception since all of it takes place entirely within a dream.

So what about Luke's annunciation narrative; should we regard this as any less suspect? Can we accept that it really was the case that an angel visited Mary to tell her of her conception and that her response to the angel is correctly recorded? This is crucial because if we're disinclined to accept Matthew's dreamy testimony and dodgy prophecy, the validity of the whole virgin conception doctrine (and all its improbable consequences) depend on this story in Luke.

We left off with Mary's question to Gabriel 'How can this come about since I do not know a man?' In the circumstances this question just isn't plausible. We're told plainly that Mary is betrothed to be

---

[15]Brown (*op cit*, p 146) remarks that the notion of prophecy 'as prediction of the distant future has disappeared from most serious scholarship today and it is widely recognised that the NT "fulfilment" of the OT involved much that the OT writers did not foresee at all.'

married, a status that presumably she is aware of. So it's obvious that at some point in the near future she would expect to enter into a sexual relationship with Joseph resulting (most probably) in due course in the conception and birth of a child. In this respect then the angel is providing no great revelation since it merely tells her that at some unspecified point she would indeed have a child. Unless Mary had doubts about either her own or Joseph's fertility she would've had no reason to suppose otherwise.

So why would she question or show surprise at only this part of the angel's prophecy, an aspect that's not at all improbable? Even *The Catholic Encyclopedia* concedes that 'these words can hardly be understood unless we assume that Mary had made a vow of virginity'.[16] But there's nothing in any of the gospels to suggest that this vow was ever made. It goes on to speculate that 'The most opportune occasion for such a vow was her presentation in the Temple.' However, we don't know if this event ever occurred either. The only information we have about Mary's childhood comes from a gospel outside the New Testament, *The Proto-evangelium of James* and its derivatives which the *Encyclopaedia* refers to.[17]

This work, written to fill in the gaps in the story of Jesus' birth and to glorify Mary, first tells the story of Mary's own birth and upbringing in its opening chapters. Many of the episodes of her childhood are quaint and charming yet slightly disturbing: from the age of three for example, Mary was thought to be so holy that she was separated from her parents and had to live with the priests in the Temple where she was fed each day by an angel.

So in this wildly extravagant and speculative pre-gospel we see Mary presented in the Temple at the very tender age of three. It seems then that the argument for the virgin conception is founded either on a dream, a mistranslation or on the speculation that a three year old girl made a vow to virginity (based on a work written at least 800 years

---

[16]*The Catholic Encyclopedia*, Vol XV (online version, sourced from www.new advent.org). Just to confuse things, *The New Catholic Encyclopedia* takes exactly the opposite point of view: 'the thought in Lk 1:34 does not refer to a "vow" of virginity Mary would have already made' (Vol IX, p 339).

[17]Mary's childhood is also known through the *Gospel of Pseudo Matthew* or the *Historia de Nativitate Mariae*, written much later than the *Proto-evangelium of James* (on which it is based), possibly in the 8th or 9th century (Elliot, *op cit*, p 86). The vow of virginity appears only in *Pseudo Matthew* and is therefore a *very* late belief.

later). It's very difficult to accept this as a valid or reasonable basis for a belief which itself is so extraordinary. Why would Mary make such a pledge? How many toddlers are there that can even understand the meaning of the word virginity?[18] And if she had made such a vow, why on earth did she acquiesce to her betrothal? Merely considering questions such as these shows just how flimsy this conjecture is.

Let us assume then that no such vow was made. We still have the situation that there is no plausible explanation for Mary's question. Furthermore, given that Gabriel has just informed Mary completely out of the blue that her child will inherit 'the throne of his ancestor David' and that 'his reign will have no end', it is *very* strange that her only concern is with something that is insignificant relative to the overall intelligence that the angel brings. Surely she would have been more surprised to learn that her child will become not only a king but an *eternal* king? So why doesn't her protest question this aspect of the angel's message? It can only be because her question is not a genuine one and can only be seen as a literary device to continue the dialogue and to enable Luke's angel to deliver the rest of his message. That this is so becomes clear when we look at the rest of this story which is constructed according to the form or pattern typical for an angelic visitation and which contains a number of elements which are clearly literary rather than historical in origin.

We can tell that this is the case if we compare this visitation with the one which immediately precedes it. Here Gabriel appears in the Temple before Zechariah, the father of John the Baptist to announce that his old and apparently barren wife will herself have a child. Each of these annunciations is constructed in an almost identical way, following the same pattern and with similar diction. In both cases the encounter begins with the sudden and unexpected appearance of the angel quickly followed by the initial fear of the beholder. The angel reassures them and then gives the reason for his appearance, the announcement that a child will be born, what he is to be called and his significance for the history of Israel. Then both Zechariah and Mary make an almost identical protest, both questioning in amazement how

---

[18] *The Catholic Encyclopedia* overcomes this slight difficulty by speculating further that just as 'some of the Fathers admit that the faculties of St John the Baptist were prematurely developed by a special intervention of God's power, [so] we may admit a similar grace for the child of Joachim and Anna' (i.e. Mary). I am not convinced by this.

such things will happen. In both instances the question adds nothing, other than a touch of drama. The angel provides further assurance (without directly answering the question) and finally a sign to show that what he says really is true. In the first story Zechariah is struck dumb whereas Mary was spared such punishment and was advised instead about Elizabeth's pregnancy.[19] Both of these angelic visitations therefore come across as artificial and contrived and there's precious little, if anything to persuade us that there are genuinely historical events underlying either of these stories.

That the annunciation to Mary never *really* took place is confirmed by an incident related by Luke later on in Jesus' childhood when he is lost after the Passover festival. Mary and Joseph search desperately for him and eventually find him discoursing with the doctors in the Temple. When they chide him for having gone missing, he tells them that he is busy 'with my Father's affairs'; yet they were unable to understand what he meant. But how could Mary not understand his words having experienced what she has? Having been advised by an angel of her son's destiny and knowing of the unique manner of his conception, how on earth could she be so uncomprehending or so forgetful, especially since later, at Jesus' birth we're told that she 'treasured all these things and pondered them in her heart'?[20] It is very difficult therefore to see the Mary of Luke's annunciation as a real person who had experienced a real event; she comes across simply as a literary character written in to carry and proclaim the theological beliefs of its author.

If we agree that we can only see these narratives as literary, motivated by theological concerns and that consequently the virgin

---

[19]The appearance to Mary: 'She was deeply disturbed . . . but the angel said to her "Mary do not be afraid . . . you are to conceive and bear a son, and you must name him Jesus. He will be great". . . . Mary said to the angel "But how can this come about since I do not know a man?" . . . the angel answered . . . "Know this . . ." (Luke 1:26-38). The appearance to Zechariah: 'The sight disturbed Zechariah . . . but the angel said to him "Zechariah, do not be afraid . . . your wife Elizabeth is to bear you a son and you must name him John . . . he will be great" . . . Zechariah said to the angel "How can I be sure of this? I am an old man" . . . The angel replied . . . "Listen . . . you will be silenced"' (Luke 1:11-25). Luke's annunciations are also almost identical in form to the angelic annunciations of the conceptions of Ishmael and Isaac in the book of Genesis. Brown observes that they 'are nearly perfect examples of the genre' (*op cit*, p 157), suggesting that their origin was literary and not historical.

[20] Luke 2:41-50, 2:19.

conception has no actual or historical foundation, the questions remain, why did the belief arise and how did these accounts come about in the first place? In the case of Luke the story may have arisen as a consequence of his including a story about the conception and birth of John the Baptist. Given that this is a detailed and colourful narrative, it must have seemed imperative that the conception of Jesus should have had a similar story or even a more fancy one to demonstrate how much greater he was than John. In the story about the conception of John the power of the Holy Spirit is manifested in its intervention in bringing about a pregnancy in a woman considered too old to conceive. As Geoffrey Parrinder suggests in a rare book about Joseph's paternity claims, perhaps the story of Mary arose as a demonstration of that power at the other end of the biological spectrum, in a woman normally considered too young to conceive.[21] And just as there's nothing to suggest that Elizabeth was divinely impregnated, so there's nothing that actually indicates that Mary's conception was anything but human in origin.

With Matthew's account no such easy explanation is possible. It's often thought that the basis of the virgin conception belief lies in the mistranslation of Isaiah's prophecy. But with his specific statement that Mary gave birth to a son but hadn't slept with Joseph, it seems almost as if Matthew had already made up his mind about the matter and then searched for and found a scriptural prophecy which appeared to justify it. For some reason then he must have had a compelling reason to want to attribute a miracle to Jesus' conception. It's unlikely that this would have been to attribute divine paternity to Jesus for as we've just seen, it was only much later that Jesus was thought of and declared to be a god. And in his birth narrative Matthew has at least three other prophecies to persuade us that Jesus was the messiah making this one, with its stretched interpretation, somewhat superfluous. What then might have been his motive?

---

[21]Parrinder, *Son of Joseph - The Parentage of Jesus*, p 30. It's also worth noting his remark (p 11) that the original Greek doesn't give the definite article or capital letters to 'the Holy Spirit' which Christians took to indicate the third person or god of the Trinity. The more accurate rendition of Matthew's narrative would therefore be 'she has conceived what is in her by holy spirit' or possibly, as Schaberg suggests 'by a spirit which is holy' (*The Illegitimacy of Jesus*, p 62). Vermes points out that a girl could be married before reaching puberty and that a girl betrothed could be as young as twelve years and six months, *op cit*, pp 192, 194.

We've seen how the execution of Jesus would have been regarded as a scandal, particularly when the new religion was being spread in other parts of the Roman Empire. As well as imposing the greatest suffering on the convicted man, crucifixion conferred the greatest shame and the evangelists and other early supporters of Jesus had to work hard to give this event a positive spin. And with the birth of Jesus here too we see Matthew having to bring into play numerous ploys (dream, dodgy prophecy) to convince us of the virgin conception, suggesting that he's trying to distract attention from or is responding to some other matter. And this other matter might be the fact that 'before they came to live together she was found to be with child (through the Holy Spirit).'[22]

If you omit the words in brackets, it becomes possible to see what the real concern might have been. It has been alleged almost from the earliest days of Christianity that Jesus was actually the illegitimate son of Mary and that the virgin conception story was fabricated to try to hide his dishonourable birth.[23] The earliest explicit articulation of this charge is found in Celsus' critique, written before the end of the 2nd century. Drawing possibly on Jewish sources, Celsus alleged that Jesus was the son of a Roman soldier called Panthera and that he 'fabricated the story of his birth from a virgin [who] . . . was driven out by her husband . . . as she was convicted of adultery . . . and while she was wandering about in a disgraceful way she secretly gave birth to Jesus.'[24] The story is also known in some Jewish writings of the 2nd and 3rd centuries although the references are vague and in none of these sources is the charge substantiated.[25]

More importantly, there are indications in the gospels themselves that some of Jesus' contemporaries may have believed him to be illegitimate. The most obvious of these is the ugly confrontation between Jesus and his opponents (derisorily labelled 'the Jews' by the Fourth Gospel - as if Jesus himself wasn't a Jew) who mock him by

---

[22]Matthew 1:18.

[23]See Ludemann, *Virgin Birth? The Real Story of Mary and Her Son Jesus*, who argues that Matthew and Luke used the virgin conception stories to cover up the fact that Mary was probably raped; and Schaberg (*op cit*) who believes that the two evangelists were arguing a case for Jesus' messiahship *despite* his illegitimacy.

[24]Origen, *Contra Celsum* 1:32, 28.

[25]Schaberg, *op cit*, pp 170-177.

saying 'We were not born of fornication.'[26] In the original Greek there is emphasis on the word 'we'[27] implying that you, Jesus were conceived or born outside of marriage. This seems to have been a very sore point for Jesus - in response to this taunt he accuses the crowd of being sons of the Devil and of doing the Devil's work. Elsewhere we see Jesus hailed by some of the crowds from his hometown, Nazareth (people who might have been privy to any local gossip or scandal) as 'the son of Mary.' Since a man was normally identified by his father's name there is a suggestion that his father was unknown and that Jesus was therefore illegitimate.[28]

Of course this could also mean that Joseph was no longer alive; but the changes that both Matthew and Luke made to this phrase (they changed it to 'the carpenter's son' or 'Joseph's son'[29]) suggest a certain unease or embarrassment felt about this means of identification. If there was dirt going around that Jesus was illegitimate, once he had been proclaimed messiah, nothing could be allowed to sully his reputation; damaging rumours would simply have to be answered or edited out, no matter how improbable the spin. And so as a response the idea of the virgin conception, an idea typical of its time, may have come into being. None of this can be proven, but ask yourself which is more likely, a biologically impossible conception attested by a dream, a nonsensical 'prophecy' and possibly by a clearly fictitious angelic encounter; or the possibility that Jesus, like hundreds of thousands, millions of others throughout history, was conceived by his mother before she was married?

Circus Freak

Circus freaks are those unfortunate people whose anatomy is in some way so unusual or so disfigured that they are exploited and are

---

[26]John 8:41(RSV).

[27]Schaberg, *op cit*, p 157.

[28]*Ibid*, p 161. Schaberg argues that the phrase 'son of Mary' (Mark 6:3) was a slur reflecting on the doubt of the identity of Jesus' father. Although she concedes that there is no evidence in 1st century Judaism that an illegitimate son was identified by the name of his mother, 'it is a later Jewish legal principle that a man is illegitimate when he is called by his mother's name, for a bastard has no father.'

[29]Matthew 13:55, Luke 4:23.

turned into perverse attractions for heartless and unenlightened people to gawp at. To their shame the early Christians turned Mary into a freak of nature wholly without justification simply to propagate their doctrines, a mean and shabby abuse that continues to this day.

We noted above that the term virgin birth, the one which is more familiar, expresses a belief distinct from the virgin conception which we've just considered. The virgin birth arose as a consequence of the Church's later belief in the perpetual virginity of Mary. This strange doctrine has three separate aspects: first the virgin conception, next the virgin birth which maintains that even in the act of giving birth Mary remained a virgin in the strictly technical sense (that is her hymen remained unbroken) and finally her continued and complete sexual abstinence after Jesus' birth until her death.

However bizarre and implausible we may find these ideas (particularly the virgin birth) the perpetual virginity of Mary is a dogma that the Church proclaims today with no sense of unease or of the ridiculous. According to the *Catechism*, 'The deepening faith in the virginal motherhood led the Church to confess Mary's real and perpetual virginity even in the act of giving birth to the Son of God made man. In fact Christ's birth did not diminish his mother's virginal integrity but sanctified it.'[30]

No justification for or explanation of this belief is offered by the *Catechism*. What then was the basis for its adoption by the Church? The dogma wasn't formally declared until the Lateran Council of 649 CE,[31] some 600 years after the lives of Jesus, Mary and anyone who ever knew them. One presumes then that personal testimony to substantiate the claim was never submitted to the Council. Nor was anything available from the New Testament to confirm or even suggest this understanding of the circumstances surrounding Jesus' entry into the world. But the idea of a virgin birth does appear in a non-canonical book written towards the end of the 2nd century, the

---

[30]*Catechism*, 499.

[31]The formal decree declared 'If anyone does not confess in harmony with the Holy Fathers that the holy and ever virgin and immaculate Mary is really and verily the mother of God inasmuch as she in the last times and without semen by the Holy Spirit conceived God the Word himself . . . and she bore him incorrupted and after his birth her virginity remaining indissoluble, let him be condemned.' Quoted from Benko, *Protestants, Catholics, and Mary*, p 30.

Book of James, also known as the *Proto-evangelium of James*, mentioned above and this is generally accepted as the earliest (written) source of the belief.

In this gospel's version of the nativity story (clearly, written by somebody with a lively imagination) having given birth to Jesus, Mary is approached by an unknown woman, Salome. Salome has learnt from the midwife present at the delivery that 'a virgin has brought forth, a thing which her condition does not allow.' Here then for the first time we see the virgin conception expanded into a virgin birth. Understandably she doesn't believe this astonishing news and therefore decides to check for herself whether or not Mary has remained intact. Accordingly, she goes into the cave where Mary is resting and sticks her finger inside her vagina. It was a bad move for as soon as she discovers her error she is punished for her unbelief and wickedness by having her hand consumed by fire.[32]

So if we accept this account (and there is no other earlier record of this idea), we're required to believe that having just given birth Mary was willing to allow a complete stranger to finger her intimately to check that she was indeed this biological impossibility. Unfortunately no concern for the feelings of Mary, the humiliated and vulnerable young mother (remember, she may have been little more than a child herself), is ever expressed. Mary may have been subsequently exalted and glorified by the Church, but she had first to be publicly dishonoured and shamelessly turned into a freak of nature for Christians, with their love of childish and offensive miracles, to drool over in stupefied amazement or obsequious and unquestioning veneration.

So was there really a virgin birth? Given the legendary nature of the source material to support the belief one can't help thinking the whole thing is nothing but a flight of fancy of later generations of over-enthusiastic Christians. And when we read the gospels - which for the Church obviously have a greater authority than any non-

---

[32]'And Salome said "As the Lord my God lives, unless I insert my finger and test her condition, I will not believe that a virgin has given birth." And the midwife went in and said to Mary: "Make yourself ready for there is no small contention concerning you" . . . And Salome inserted her finger to test her condition', *Proto-evangelium of James* 19:3-20:1, Elliot, *op cit*, p 64. One suspects that it was the story of Moses' first encounter with Yahweh in the desert rather than this unpleasant incident that inspired the Church to hail Mary as 'the burning bush.'

canonical work - we find that they suggest that from the biological point of view Jesus' actual birth was entirely normal. Luke tells us for instance that at the appropriate time (i.e. 40 days after the birth) Mary presented herself and her child for the Jewish purification rites in the Temple. Mary is not recorded as having made any extraordinary claims about a virgin birth at this ceremony (despite the fact that two people, Simeon, an upright and devout man and Anna, an ancient prophetess, hail Jesus as a wonder-child), nor did she act in any way that suggested that the birth was other than normal.[33] It seems then that she herself had no awareness of this miracle; and if she didn't know anything about it, how on earth could anyone else have thought or known otherwise?

It really is very difficult to acknowledge and understand that Jesus came into the world while his mother's 'integrity' (as the Church likes to call it) was preserved; should Christians accept *The Catholic Encyclopedia*'s quirky explanation which proclaims that by the 'power of the most high [he] passed through the barriers of nature without injuring them'? Or is it more plausible to suppose that there was a rupture but almost simultaneously it was repaired? Clearly Jesus was capable of regenerating bodily parts since he healed the high priest's servant's ear at the time of his arrest. So perhaps just milli-seconds after his birth he was able to perform the necessary reconstructive surgery on his mother in a similar fashion. Or should Christians reject the whole doctrine as a complete nonsense? Quite how Mary's integrity was preserved remains a mystery of course; but it is an even greater mystery as to how the Church can continue to proclaim this manifestly absurd and untrue doctrine.

Perplexing and amusing though this may be, it's actually quite disturbing to reflect on the *men* who formulated this belief and who are responsible for its continued promulgation. Why we might legitimately ask, should they have become so obsessed with the condition of one woman's sexual parts? Why is it that they have such hang-ups with

---

[33]Luke 2:22-38. The reaction of Mary to this acclamation is recorded - 'the child's father and mother stood there wondering at the things that were being said about him.' Mary seems overwhelmed by the praise suggesting that it's all news to her which in turn suggests that she didn't know anything about a virgin conception or a virgin birth. Moreover if the birth was a divinely worked miracle, there would hardly have been any need for Mary to have been purified.

normal human sexual and reproductive activity? And isn't it just rather sad to note that it's the Catholic Church, none of whose officials are allowed to marry or have a sexual relationship, that seems to have the strongest fixation with what may or may not have happened between Mary's legs?

Brothers & Sisters: Joseph & Mary Made It Together

If the early Church had gone to such trouble to ensure that Mary's integrity was preserved, it certainly wasn't going to let her ruin things by having sex or children after this spectacular miracle, even if the evangelists suggested or recorded that she did so. So despite numerous references in the gospels to Jesus' brothers and sisters the Church still teaches that Mary remained a virgin. Of course it can't edit out such details from the gospels; so instead it has to rely on the hopeless argument that the word brothers doesn't mean brothers in the biological or familial sense, even though it is repeatedly used in a context which suggests an immediate family.

Early on in Mark's gospel we discover Jesus' family to be very concerned about him, convinced he was mad and it's here that we're first introduced to his siblings: 'His mother and his brothers now arrived and, standing outside, sent in a message asking for him. A crowd was sitting round him at the time the message was passed to him, "Your mother and brothers and sisters are outside asking for you."' A little later a different crowd, hostile to Jesus, wonders about him: 'this is the carpenter, surely the son of Mary, the brother of James and Joset and Jude and Simeon? His sisters, too are they not here with us?'[34]

In the first passage both the writer and the characters in the crowd recognise the people looking for Jesus as his mother and his brothers while in the second passage the identity of Jesus' brothers (again mentioned alongside his mother and sisters) is so distinct that they can even be named by the crowd. Over the centuries the Church's response to these and other references in the New Testament to Jesus' siblings has changed as it struggled to maintain its belief in Mary's perpetual virginity. Initially Jesus' brothers were taken to be half-

---

[34]Mark 3:31-32, 6:3.

brothers, fathered by Joseph from a previous marriage. However this understanding had the non-canonical and hence 'unofficial' *Book of James* as its sole authority and was soon abandoned.

In the 4th century the biblical scholar and translator Jerome proposed a novel solution. Jerome lived in an age when Christianity had become obsessed with virginity and he thought it quite in keeping with the spirit of his religion that Joseph, as well as Mary, should also have been a lifelong virgin. So, based on a highly speculative interpretation of some minor details in the gospels, he argued in his tract *Against Helvidius* in 383 CE that Jesus' brothers were not even half brothers but cousins.[35]

According to Jerome the disciple James, son of Alphaeus was the same person as James, the brother of Jesus. His argument depended on the identity of a certain woman also called Mary who was present at the crucifixion. Mark reported that 'Mary of Magdala, *Mary who was the mother of James* the younger and Joset, and Salome' witnessed the execution of Jesus from a distance. The gospel of John however records that 'Near the cross stood his mother and *his mother's sister, Mary the wife of Clopas* and Mary of Magdala.'[36] Jerome understood that Mary the mother of James (from Mark's gospel) was the same woman as Mary the sister of Jesus' mother (from John's gospel). Accordingly, James was Jesus' cousin on the maternal side.

It's not hard to spot the many flaws in this argument. Apart from the fact that the whole argument is based on a coincidence (Mary was a very common name for Jewish women) arising from otherwise inconsistent accounts, it depends also on the understanding that there were three women present at the crucifixion from the gospel of John: Mary, the mother of Jesus, her sister, also called Mary (and the wife of Clopas) and a third Mary, of Magdala.[37] But a more plausible reading would suggest that there were actually four women: Mary the mother

---

[35] I am indebted to the critical evaluation of Jerome's argument given by Bernheim (*James, Brother of Jesus*, pp 15-29) for much of the material in this section.

[36] Mark 15:40; John 19:25, my italics.

[37] The reliability of John's testimony concerning the witnesses to the crucifixion is suspect: if Jesus' mother really had been present, as John records, it's unthinkable that this fact would have escaped the attention of the other evangelists. Moreover John seems to have written her into his crucifixion scene for dramatic purposes, to associate her with the beloved disciple.

of Jesus, her sister *as well as* Mary the wife of Clopas and Mary of Magdala. This actually makes more sense since if we accept the first reading we have the ridiculous situation that the parents of Mary (the mother of Jesus) had two daughters both of whom were given the same name! Moreover, how can Mary the wife of Clopas from the gospel of John be the same woman as the mother of James if James' father (and hence Mary's husband) is Alphaeus? Responding to this objection Jerome simply insisted that Mary of Clopas (usually understood as the wife of Clopas) actually meant that Mary was the daughter of Clopas.

Even if we overlook these objections, why is James called the brother of Jesus rather than his cousin? Commentators defending Mary's perpetual virginity point out that the Hebrew language had no word for cousin and that the word brother was used as a substitute. When the oral traditions in Hebrew or Aramaic were passed down to the Greek speaking evangelists (who of course wrote their gospels in Greek), this mistaken relationship was overlooked.[38]

However Paul, who knew James personally and who therefore must have been aware of his true relationship to Jesus, also called him 'the brother of the Lord.' But Paul was writing in Greek, and the passages in his letters that mention James were not dependant on Hebrew traditions; hence the argument that brothers meant cousins, owing to the deficiencies of the Hebrew language, cannot apply to Paul's letters. If James had really been Jesus' cousin, Paul would almost certainly have used the word *anepsios* (meaning cousin); that he used the word *adelphos* (meaning brother) to refer to him suggests that he can't have regarded James as anything other than Jesus' actual brother.[39]

Today it seems that the Church has quietly dropped this highly contrived interpretation. However, it still insists that Mary remained a virgin and so it resorts to another argument which under examination is no less flimsy. Now the official line is that 'The Church has always

---

[38]See for example *The New Catholic Encyclopedia* (Vol IX, p 337). It points out that the Greek words used 'have the meaning of full blood brother and sister' but nevertheless follows Jerome's argument that the evangelists understood brothers to be cousins. It's mildly vexing to note that the Church is willing to recognise mistranslations when it suits its purposes, but not otherwise (i.e. *almah / parthenos*).

[39]Bernheim, *op cit*, p 29. Paul refers to James as brother in his letter to the Galatians (2:19).

understood these passages (i.e. those which mention Jesus' brothers and sisters) as not referring to other children of the Virgin Mary. In fact James and Joseph, "brothers of Jesus", are sons of another Mary, a disciple of Christ whom St Matthew significantly calls "the other Mary."'[40] So we have two possible interpretations. First, that the brothers are 'close relations' as the *Catechism* explicitly affirms and second, that they are no more than followers of Jesus.

It's difficult to understand the basis of the Church's affirmation that the brothers are 'close relations'. If they are the sons of 'another Mary' who herself is not actually related to Jesus, but is merely 'a disciple of Christ', how on earth can they be related to Jesus at all? Even if we're willing to accept the argument that they are 'close relations', what exactly is the relationship? The only possible way to regard them as related by blood is to follow Jerome's argument that we considered above and which we have seen is a no-brainer.

Accordingly, no argument is offered to affirm that any such relationship existed. Instead the *Catechism* simply says that the brothers are 'close relations of Jesus, according to an Old Testament expression'; that is, it falls back on the deficiencies of the Hebrew language approach. To support its contention, it refers us to a number of Old Testament passages where the word brother is used to inform us of non-sibling relationships. But in each of the examples cited, the surrounding passage makes the nature of the relationship absolutely clear and explicit. So for example we're referred to the relationships between Abraham and Lot, and Laban and Jacob who are all described as 'kinsmen' or brothers. But in both instances, prior to the passage cited, the relationship is made crystal clear: 'Abram took his wife Sarai and his brother's son Lot' while Rebakah, Jacob's mother tells him to 'Flee at once to Haran, to my brother Laban.'[41]

If on the other hand 'the other Mary' is not related to Jesus, but is merely one of his disciples, as the *Catechism* affirms, then her sons too can only be followers of Jesus; so is this reading any more tenable? Unfortunately this too is desperately poor reasoning. At no point do the gospels suggest that the sons of another Mary are meant by the crowd. And it would be a remarkable coincidence if on two separate

---

[40] *Catechism*, 500.
[41] Genesis 12:5, 27:43.

264

occasions different crowds referred to followers of Jesus as his brothers and sisters, especially when they are with his actual mother or are referred to in the same context as Mary.

Furthermore, if the brothers are understood to be followers, Jesus' response to the news that his mother and brothers are looking for him ('"Who are my mother and brothers?" And looking round at those sitting in a circle about him, he said, "Here are my mother and brothers"') loses its impact and becomes almost nonsensical.[42] For what can he mean by emphasising 'these are my brothers' (i.e. followers) if he is merely contrasting one set of followers sat before him with another set who, for some bizarre reason, are trooping around with his mother? Why would he call the followers sitting at his feet 'brothers' if he were not comparing them to his actual blood brothers?

Finally we can tell that Jesus' brothers are distinct from his followers when we read in the Fourth Gospel (which is ignorant of or indifferent to the virginity of Mary) that 'his *brothers* said to him "Why not leave this place and go to Judaea and let *your disciples* see the works you are doing."' If brothers means followers, then we have to accept that Jesus had some followers who seemed to be closer to him (to the extent that they felt they could advise him behind his disciples' backs) than the twelve men whom he appointed as his core disciples. But these would have been very unusual (and quite useless) followers indeed, for if we read on we're told that 'Not even his brothers, in fact had faith in him.'[43] How on earth could such men be followers of Jesus if they didn't even believe in him?

If this were not enough to refute the belief that Mary had no other children, we should consider references to the matter outside the gospels. Josephus also refers to James as 'the brother of Jesus called the Christ'[44] as does the Christian historian Eusebius.[45] Furthermore, we haven't yet addressed the one obvious human point: are we to suppose that having just married, Joseph and Mary never consummated their union? If not, why not? Neither Gabriel nor the angel in Matthew

---

[42] Mark 3:34. To appreciate just how nonsensical this argument is, read the quote again but replace 'brothers' with 'followers'.

[43] John 7:2, 5, my italics.

[44] *Antiquities of the Jews* XX, ix, 1. Like Paul, Josephus also wrote in Greek and would not have had problems expressing the precise nature of the relationship.

[45] Eusebius, *History of the Church* 2:1.

delivers any instruction to the couple to remain celibate so what possible reason could they have had for such drastic behaviour? Can we really accept that they would've remained celibate for the rest of their lives for no apparent reason in a culture that had none of the hang-ups about sex that Christianity later developed and which regarded children as a blessing?[46]

It seems unlikely that they would've taken such a path and here too if we look at the gospels closely we find suggestions that the couple's alleged lifelong abstinence is simply wishful thinking by later Christians. Luke records that Jesus was Mary's 'first born'[47] implying that she may have had further children; while in Matthew we find that after Joseph received his dream message, he 'did as the angel of the Lord commanded him; he took his wife. And he knew her not until she had borne a son'.[48] While this may try to persuade us that no man was involved in the conception of Jesus, it also suggests that once he had been born, the marriage of Joseph and Mary followed the normal course and was therefore fully and properly consummated

The Spotless Queen Of Heaven

What, we may wonder, is the point of this fixation and all the fervour with which it is championed? Although the dogma of Mary's perpetual virginity was formally declared in the 7th century, it seems that by the end of the 4th century belief in Mary's ever-virgin status was already firmly established.[49] To understand the attention this belief received we need to consider the context out of which it arose.

---

[46]Vermes points out that 'the Hebrew Bible, though it prescribes temporary sexual abstinence in certain circumstances, never orders a life of total celibacy', *op cit* p 79.

[47]Luke 2:7. Interestingly in other gospel stories where it was understood that the character in question had no siblings Luke refers to 'the only son' (7:12) or 'the only daughter' (8:42). That he didn't refer to Jesus in this way adds weight to the argument that he understood that Mary had more than one child.

[48]Matthew 1:25. *The New Catholic Encyclopedia* claims that in this passage the word 'until' 'is not a term of chronological intent' (Vol IX, p 338) – i.e. it doesn't mean 'until'. The flimsiness of this argument is more apparent if one replaces the Jewish euphemism 'he did not know her' with its modern equivalent 'he did not sleep with her' or 'he did not have sex with her'. By now it should be clear to the reader that doctrines about Mary's virginity are sustainable only through mistranslations or a wilful refusal to accept the normal meaning of words.

[49]Miegge, *The Virgin Mary: The Roman Catholic Marian Doctrine*, p 47.

First of all we've seen that Jesus was formally pronounced to be a god by the early part of the 4th century at the Council of Nicaea. A hundred years later at the Council of Ephesus in 431 CE Mary was formally acclaimed to be *Theokotos*, or *Mother of God*, a title that arose in response to another controversy, the belief that Jesus was two beings, one human and one divine, both of which were squeezed into the same body. This understanding did not prevail and was condemned by the Council as a heresy (known subsequently as the Nestorian heresy after the bishop, Nestorius who preached it). Now if the official line taught that Jesus united both the divine and the human in one being, it followed that Mary could not be regarded only as the mother of the human Jesus (as opposed to the mother of the pre-existing god) without this being inconsistent with the new formulation. So her resultant elevation and status as *Theokotos* came about not as an intentional glorification of her person but as a logical though secondary consequence of the rejection of a heresy.[50]

A consequence of this elevation was the need to distance Mary as much as possible from any suggestion of sinfulness and pollution. It simply wasn't fitting that the god-mother should be thought of as sinful in any way, especially since by association this could carry through to the saviour himself. This was the age that was dominated by some of the heaviest heavyweight Christian thinkers of all time, in particular Augustine and Jerome, both of whom had an almost neurotic loathing of sex and in Jerome's case at least, a disgust for the female.[51]

He wasn't alone in his misogyny; writing about Christianity's attitudes towards women and sexuality in this Patristic age, Kim Power observes that 'all the physical sexual processes of women were associated with corruption. Defloration corrupted the body initially and childbirth even more . . . women's reproductive organs were considered foul . . . birthgiving was considered polluting.'[52] That such activity was considered dirty and polluting was perhaps a continuation and grotesque expansion of the Jewish principle under the Law that menstruating and childbearing women were regarded as ritually

---

[50] *Ibid*, pp 53-67.

[51] Jerome was unperturbed for instance to believe and declare that 'Woman is the gate of the devil, the way of evil, the sting of the scorpion'. Quoted from Kahl, *op cit*, p 77.

[52] Power, *Veiled Desire: Augustine's Writing on Women*, p 44.

unclean.[53] So if Mary could have remained intact at the birth of Jesus, without the passing of blood, neither Jesus nor *Theokotos* would have been sullied in any way.

More importantly, under the influence of Augustine, sex itself was increasingly regarded as something shameful and offensive. It was Augustine who formulated and championed the doctrine of original sin, the horrible idea that the whole of humanity is infected by the sin of disobedience committed by Adam; and tragically for so many people for so many centuries, he taught that this sin was transmitted from one generation to the next through sex. With sexual pleasure associated with sin, the effect of Augustine's appalling doctrine was, in Power's words, the depressing scenario in which men were 'taught to hold women in contempt for their very desirability. And women . . . to hold men in contempt for desiring them, and to hold themselves in contempt for desiring to be desired.'[54]

Accordingly chastity and virginity were seen increasingly as great Christian virtues. Hence to provide a way out of the guilt and shame of human sexuality that Christianity was espousing, the response of the Church was to promote monasticism and the ascetic life. In this context Mary's virginity before, during and after the birth of Jesus took on an even greater significance and came to be seen as an ideal, an inspiring example rather than a human impossibility.

The dogma of the Immaculate Conception (sometimes confused with the virgin conception) takes this idealisation further into the clouds. If original sin was transmitted through sex, this meant that Mary herself, like every other member of the human race, was conceived in sin. This was deemed to be so unfitting for her glorified status and so potentially damaging to Jesus' own sinless nature that almost 1,900 years after the event, the Church decided formally to declare that from the moment when she herself was conceived 'by a singular grace and privilege granted by Almighty God . . . [Mary] was preserved free from all stain of original sin'. Furthermore it was also declared that 'she committed no sin of any kind during her whole

---

[53]Leviticus 12:1-8: 'If a woman conceives and bears a child, then she shall be unclean seven days; as at the time of her menstruation, she shall be unclean.' Quite why childbirth should render a woman unclean is not explained although it appears to be related to the discharge of blood which is referred to three times in this passage.
[54]Power, *op cit*, p 161.

earthly life.'[55] The belief was pronounced by Pius IX in 1854 through the papal bull *Ineffabilis Deus* thus anticipating the doctrine of papal infallibility which was to follow less than twenty years later.[56]

Ineffabilis Deus is truly a masterpiece of grandiose Vatican nonsense, with page after page of rhetorical gush in praise of Mary giving us an idea of just how pompous and deranged Christianity had become. It starts off by reminding us of 'the lamentable wretchedness of the entire human race'; rising above this rotten humanity however emerges the Virgin who somehow achieved a 'renowned victory over the most foul enemy of the human race'. One doesn't normally think of Mary as a belligerent person or as a warrior queen, but clearly this viewpoint is a mistaken one; for we're told that she was 'eternally at enmity with the evil serpent and most completely triumphed over him, and thus crushed his head with her immaculate foot.' It goes on and on like this over the course of several thousand words, repeating itself over and over again presumably because 'to praise her all the tongues of heaven and earth do not suffice.' So we're told 23 times that Mary was preserved from all stain of sin and there are 9 references to her apparent triumph over 'the serpent' with the much maligned reptile being pilloried with a variety of colourful adjectives ('ancient', 'deceitful', 'evil', 'treacherous', 'poisonous', 'cruel') to emphasise just what a complete rotter the Prince of Darkness is.

It culminates in eulogising Mary as 'more beautiful than beauty, more lovely than loveliness; more holy than holiness . . . the one who surpassed all integrity and virginity . . . more excellent than all'. One might understand such lavish and fulsome praise if it were in respect of a real woman known to the writer, a woman who had actually distinguished herself in some way. But given that virtually nothing about Mary is *actually known*, this comes across more as empty, formulaic nonsense. How does the writer know that she was beautiful in either appearance, demeanour or character for example? And how can anyone 'surpass' virginity? Either one is a virgin or one is not; it simply doesn't make sense to claim that a woman exceeds or can go

---

[55] *Catechism*, 411. Once again nothing is offered by the *Catechism* to justify this claim.

[56] A number of commentators note that the papal declaration of this dogma led as much to the exaltation of the pope as to that of Mary and that it helped the Church in its struggle against the emerging ideologies of Marxism and communism. See Perry / Echeverria, *Under the Heel of Mary*, pp 115–118, Cornwell, *Hitler's Pope*, p 344.

beyond this state.

Ultimately this wonderful, lunatic document is unintentionally a piece of writing of high comedy climaxing with the megalomaniac bishop of Rome making you an offer you can't refuse: 'dare to think otherwise than as has been defined by us' about the conception of the god-mother and you'll find yourself forever excluded from the kingdom in the sky, condemned, according to the Vatican, by the errors of your own judgement.

A hundred years later we come to the final dogma concerning Mary. In 1950, at the beginning of the decade of Sputnik, the discovery of the double helix of the DNA molecule and, of course, Elvis, the Church's contribution to progress and to the mood of the age was to declare the Assumption of Mary. Under this doctrine, again pronounced through a papal bull, *Munificentissimus Deus*, it was proclaimed that when Mary's life was over, instead of being subject to the universal law of physical decomposition, she was 'taken up body and soul into heavenly glory'.

To a certain extent this teaching is a 'logical' consequence of the Immaculate Conception and of Mary's perpetual virginity: 'as he kept you a virgin in childbirth', the bull affirms, 'so he has kept your body incorrupt in the tomb and has glorified it by his divine act of transferring it from the tomb'. If Christians accept the Church's teaching that death came into the world as a punishment for Adam's first sin and that Mary had been declared free of that transmitted original sin and indeed of any other sin, it follows that she should not have been subject to the consequences. In other words, in theory she should never have died. Indeed even in the 1950s when the dogma of the Assumption was announced there was still a hardcore of Mariologists who believed that Mary had never actually died but had been taken up to heaven beforehand.[57] This was a belief that was not discouraged by the ambivalent wording of the bull itself which makes no reference to her death but proclaims that the Assumption occurred 'upon the completion of her earthly sojourn'. So if Mary's body hadn't been subject to decay and if she had always been free from sin, in the bizarre logic of the Catholic Church it was only natural to pronounce that her body had actually been taken up to heaven.

---

[57]Benko, *op cit*, p 39.

That this had really occurred was based primarily on the principle that it was fitting and appropriate that Mary should've been granted this privilege. The bull of course can provide no personal testimony that this event took place and there is no scriptural justification either. Instead there's merely a series of lame arguments such as the fact that it was impossible to think of Mary as being separated from Jesus; and a tiresome litany of convictions and teachings of 'the holy fathers and the great Doctors' of the later (8th century) Church. Some of the arguments advanced are absurd beyond belief. For example the bull claims that 'since the Church has never looked for the bodily relics of the Blessed Virgin . . . we have a *proof* that the Assumption genuinely took place. Clearly the Vatican boys from the class of 1950 would never have made it past day one at detective school.

Elsewhere it seems that the Church is so desperate to add weight to its argument that it is prepared to accept a mass of acknowledged nonsense to support its case. So it recognises even the interpretation of Scripture of those great doctors who have been 'rather free in their use of events and expression taken from Sacred Scripture to explain their belief in the Assumption.' Thus we find that the words of the Psalm (131) 'Arise O Lord, into your resting place; you and the ark, which you have sanctified' are accepted as an Old Testament pre-figuring of the Assumption in which the 'incorruptible wood' of the Ark of the Covenant corresponds to the body of Mary 'preserved and exempt from the corruption of the tomb.'[58] It's very ingenious but unfortunately it all sounds far too much like Indiana Jones to me to be in the least bit plausible.

And let's keep in mind that however fervent and edifying the testimony of the saints and early Church fathers cited by the bull, it's being used to justify something that is so problematic that it's tempting to dismiss the whole belief without further consideration. A woman's corpse (the bull doesn't define whether Mary was re-animated before being received in heaven) is lifted clear of the earth: how was it possible that Mary's body could overcome the force of gravity? Sputnik was only a tiny satellite, weighing some 80 kilos, yet it required an enormously powerful rocket to enable it to escape the

---

[58]*Munificentissimus Deus*, paras. 44, 18, 20, 33, 26, my italics. Sourced from www. catholicforum.com.

earth's gravitational pull. How then was Mary's body lifted up? Why did nobody see this event? Furthermore, the logical implication of an actual body being taken up to heaven is that heaven itself must be a physical place. So if this happened exactly where did the body go to? Could we ever discover this place for ourselves without having to die beforehand? If only we had a spaceship with enough coal, surely we could get to heaven under our own steam without having to bother to go to church every week? You can begin to see just how stupid and pointless it is to consider the doctrine of the Assumption any further.

One could go on and on asking such questions but none of this matters to the Church and as one might expect the language and character of the bull are more inscrutable than explanatory. As with all the mysteries concerning Mary, ultimately reason and common sense count for nothing and in the words of one prominent Marian scholar, Professor Miegge, this dogma 'has as its sole foundation the infallibility of the Roman Catholic Church.'[59] *Munificentissimus Deus* we should note, has the distinction of being the only vehicle ever used to exercise papal infallibility. And when we're told that ultimately it is from the Church's teaching authority 'under the protection of the Spirit of Truth and therefore absolutely without error' that we have 'certain and firm proof . . . [of] the Blessed Virgin Mary's bodily Assumption into heaven' and that it 'must be firmly and faithfully believed by all children of the Church',[60] we can begin to appreciate the necessary but menacing association between mystery and authority and how they are mutually reinforcing. It is to the latter of these, the teaching authority of both Jesus and the Church that we now turn.

---

[59] Miegge, *op cit*, p 106.

[60] *Munificentissimus Deus*, para. 12. Predictably this bull also closes with the threat of 'the wrath of Almighty God' to anyone who opposes it (para. 47).

9

Authority

You say you want a revolution
Well you know
We all want to change the world . . .
But when you talk about destruction
Don't you know that you can count me out [1]

Jesus is often thought of - even by non Christians - as a remarkable and revolutionary ethical teacher, one who gave us one of the most enlightened of all moral codes; a man who with great humility preached and personified nothing but love, goodness and infinite kindness. Stories of Jesus' forgiveness such as that given to the adulterous woman whom the over-zealous Scribes and Pharisees wanted to stone to death, or the father's unconditional pardon recounted in the parable of the prodigal son are moving and powerful tales that stick long in the mind. His love of small children and his high-minded concern for the welfare of the poor and the needy rouse our admiration and inspire us to imitate his example. Not surprisingly then, we tend to think of compassion, tenderness and mercy when we think about Jesus and recall only how benevolent and humane he was.

But reading the gospels closely and critically reveals that this rose-tinted vision is all part of the Christian spin; many of Jesus' stories and sayings reflect the opposite of these qualities and some come across to us today as brutal and morally abhorrent. Jesus may have prevented the adulterous woman from being stoned with his admirable maxim that whoever was without sin should throw the first stone; but elsewhere he reiterated with apparent approval that anyone convicted of breaking Moses' law even for trivial offences (in the case in point the transgression was merely to curse one's parents) should be put to death.

---

[1] The Beatles, *Revolution.*

Later on, in one of his stories he endorses the threat and use of torture to bring about compliance with his requirement for brotherly forgiveness. And seemingly unable to deal with rejection, he promises with the chilling intensity of an uncompromising fanatic that there will be severe punishment for all those who spurn his teaching.

A critical reading of the gospels would also suggest that Jesus was not the embodiment of moral perfection he is generally believed by Christians to have been; he may well have preached love, temperance and forgiveness but he didn't hesitate to reprimand and curse his own opponents and he even condemned his entire generation as 'evil' for doubting him. Perhaps it would've been helpful if he had applied one of his more celebrated and positive maxims - 'Take the plank out of your own eye first, and then you will see clearly enough to take the splinter out of your brother's eye'[2] to his own conduct and person.

From the testimony of the evangelists themselves then, it seems very unlikely that Jesus' moral teachings and personal conduct were all sweetness and light, as they are commonly supposed to be. So it's appropriate that these aspects of his mission and his example should also be considered and evaluated to determine whether they provide the basis of a sensible, humane and workable ethical code and a model of exemplary conduct; or whether they simply provide us with further reasons to reject Christianity.

Carrots and Sticks: The Basis Of Christian Morality

The whole basis of Christian morality is founded not on conduct and attitudes that are to be followed because they are demonstrably good or right in themselves or conducive to human happiness, but on certain principles that are held to be the revealed will of its god. In response to this will, men and women are not to consider and evaluate the moral law handed down, based on conscience and their ability to make reasoned, ethical judgements; their role is simply to accept and to comply. This inflexible iron will is expressed in a variety of forms, but in most instances the manner of its expression is essentially authoritarian. The clearest example of this authoritarianism is found in

---

[2]Matthew 7:5; Jesus called the people evil and unfaithful when some of them not unreasonably ask him for a sign to validate his claim to authority (Matthew 12:39).

the ten commandments which Jesus makes the foundation of much of his teaching.

As the word commandments suggests, these are precepts formulated not in terms of guiding standards or arguments of moral persuasion, but are absolute and exceptionless decrees which, according to Jesus, must be followed without question. This underlying principle is upheld by the Church today absolutely: in all matters of faith *and morals* it maintains that a Christian has a 'duty of observing the constitutions and decrees conveyed by the legitimate authority of the Church.' If this were not severe and legalistic enough, it goes on to declare that '*personal conscience* and *reason* should not be set in opposition to the moral law or the Magisterium of the Church.'[3] So you can reason and argue with your priest until blue in the face; but in the end if you're a Christian you're simply not permitted to act against the Church's rules, not even when the issue at stake is a private one concerning personal happiness or the avoidance of suffering.[4]

Just how inappropriate this high-handed approach is as the basis of a moral code can be understood by considering the first commandment. According to Jesus 'you *must* love the Lord your God with all your heart, with all your soul and with all your mind.'[5] This he says is the greatest of the commandments, to be obeyed without question. But, we may ask, how can love be commanded? Love is a voluntary emotion given freely; love chooses its own objects of affection and devotion without external pressure or interference. Loving the glorious leader simply because it is decreed that one must do so can hardly be thought of as love at all. And Jesus never explains *why* you have to love the god; he simply turns this most fulfilling and most joyous human emotion into an austere ideological duty, an obligation.

Fulfilment or neglect of this obligation, and indeed of all the commandments, has some pretty serious consequences either way. All

---

[3] *Catechism,* 2037, 2039, my italics.

[4] Recently for example the Vatican condemned the use of the 'morning-after' pill taken by a number of Kosovan women who had been gang-raped by Serbian soldiers. As the commentator Joan Smith pointed out, 'it is a perplexing form of morality that condemns traumatised women, who are already the victims of war crimes, to the further torment of bearing their rapists' children.' *The Independent on Sunday,* May 16 1999.

[5] Mark 12:30, my italics.

of Jesus' teachings concerning personal conduct and behaviour are enforced by a very simplistic and primitive system of punishment and reward. This is the method used to train laboratory rats: only, instead of electric shocks and pellets of food, Jesus uses the threat of hell and the promise of the kingdom of heaven to control the minds and actions of his followers. Assertions such as 'if a man calls his brother. . . "Renegade" he will answer for it in hell fire' or 'your almsgiving must be in secret and your Father who sees all that is done in secret will reward you'[6] are typical of Jesus' teaching. Being virtuous for its own sake however, or for the good of the community isn't something that is especially urged or even considered by Jesus. What counts is pleasing the Father-god and by doing so one can add valuable bonus points to one's personal account in the divine reward programme. At the other end of the scale, in some of his stories and exhortations Jesus urged the crowds to 'fear him who, after he has killed, has the power to cast into hell.'[7] Effectively then at the heart of Jesus' ethical system (if indeed it can be called that) is an elaborate but rather distasteful racket of bribery and intimidation appealing to and relying on nothing more than self-interest and self-concern.

The problem however for those who regard Jesus as a champion of virtue is that bribery and intimidation are usually considered to be unethical and unacceptable actions themselves when applied to adult conduct and decisions. For this reason alone the whole of his 'ethical' teaching can be regarded as unsound.

More importantly men and women can reason for themselves and enlightened teachers should encourage them to do so. Value judgements are often formed by questioning and challenging rather than blindly following established rules and the use of individual conscience and evaluation is far more likely to lead to a more valid and more meaningful ethic than enforced or induced compliance. Most of us would accept for instance that a person who declines to drink at a new year's eve party because he considers that to drink may have extremely harmful consequences as he drives home is more responsible

---

[6]Matthew 5:22, 6:4.

[7]Luke 12:5. This theme is reiterated in a later parable about those who reject or fail to respond positively to Jesus' message about the kingdom. It concludes with the king ranting 'as for my enemies who did not want me for their king, bring them here and *execute them* in my presence.'(Luke 19:11-27, my italics).

and has a higher ethic than one who doesn't drink because he knows that the police are out in significant numbers at that time of year and that he risks being caught and punished.

But this doesn't matter to Jesus. People whose dignity and sense of self-worth leads them to value their intellect and their ability to make informed, 'grown up' judgements for themselves are doomed forever to remain on the wrong side of the pearly gates. Not surprisingly then he warns that 'anyone who does not welcome the kingdom of God like a little child will never enter it.'[8] Jesus wants us all to respond to him like little children precisely because young children are highly impressionable, because they tend to accept things with a naive trust and are often unable to challenge or respond critically to what they are taught.

Nowhere is this primitive justice more clearly depicted than in Jesus' teaching about the Day of Judgement. Sitting on his 'throne of glory' and attended by hosts of subservient angels, Jesus proclaims that he will be sitting in judgement of all people: 'all the nations will be assembled before him and he will separate men from one another as the shepherd separates sheep from goats. He will place the sheep on his right hand and the goats on his left.' The meek and obedient sheep are given the glory of the kingdom but for the unfortunate goats there's only condemnation 'to the eternal fire prepared for the devil and his angels.'

This same point is repeatedly made throughout Jesus' preaching, strongly emphasising that judgement, punishment and reward were fundamental to his mission. In the earlier parable of the dragnet for instance he explains that just as fishermen trawling for fish with a net separate and throw away the smaller fish which are inedible or which can't be sold, the fish which are of 'no use', so at the end of time 'the angels will appear and separate the wicked from the just to throw them into the blazing furnace where there will be weeping and grinding of teeth.'[9] As I've already pointed out, the Christian idea of evil - which includes remarriage after divorce - is not one that many people would happily endorse.[10]

---

[8] Luke 18:17.

[9] Matthew 25:31-46, 12:47-50.

[10] See pp 24-25. Remarriage (or indeed any sexual relationship) after divorce constitutes

277

Sadly this ghastly selection procedure brings to mind the terrible fate to which millions of Europe's Jews were subjected as they got out of cattle trucks and perhaps for the first time grasped the full horror of the Final Solution. Those to the right are permitted to live; those to the left have no such hope. So Jesus too seems to have proposed his own Final Solution for those he considered not sufficiently deserving, the ones who are 'no use'; and with an unhealthy enthusiasm for retribution (as opposed to constructive rehabilitation) his solution was just as grim. Instead of extermination Jesus' victims must suffer eternal punishment, the nature of which is hinted at in the book of Revelation: the damned it proclaims 'will be tortured in the presence of the holy angels and the Lamb and the smoke of their torture will go up for ever and ever.'[11] It's a horrible scene to contemplate - Jesus, the holy and compassionate lamb looking on with quiet satisfaction as men and women - and who knows, perhaps even children - suffer unspeakable pain for no good reason.[12]

Many Christians don't like to dwell too much on these disturbing and unsavoury aspects of Christian teaching and sweep them to one side maintaining that they don't subscribe to this type of hellfire Christianity. Certainly it's very difficult to reconcile this teaching with the understanding that the Christian god is a kind and loving father; after all, what sort of responsible parent would treat his or her own child, even a completely rebellious one, in such a manner? But does the Church today repudiate this teaching? Unfortunately not. It's worth reminding ourselves that it teaches that 'In Sacred Scripture the Church finds her nourishment and her strength.'[13] Sacred Scripture of

---

adultery, considered to be a mortal sin which can bring about one's eternal damnation.

[11] Revelation 14:10-11.

[12] Among the Church's more dismal principles is the understanding that infant children who die without being baptised may not be eligible for salvation (i.e. they are given the same punishment as the truly wicked). Despite being incapable of any moral wrong, the fact remains that 'as regards children who have died without Baptism, the Church can only entrust them to the mercy of God.' It is this 'mercy' rather than any principle of justice which 'allows us to hope that there is a way of salvation for [these] children' (*Catechism*, 1261).

[13] *Catechism*, 105, 104. It continues with the observation (107) that since 'all that the inspired authors or sacred writers affirm should be regarded as affirmed by the Holy Spirit, we must acknowledge that the books of Scripture firmly, faithfully, and without error teach that truth that God, for the sake of our salvation wished to see confided to Sacred Scripture.'

course includes the book of Revelation and the gospel of Matthew in which Jesus' pronunciations about the Day of Judgement are to be found. It would seem then that the unpleasantries of this last day and its aftermath receives the Church's endorsement.

Indeed it must do for it is unthinkable for Christians to suppose that Jesus ever told a lie. The *Catechism* affirms that 'God . . . can neither deceive nor be deceived . . . God is the source of all truth. His word is truth . . . In Jesus Christ, the whole of God's truth has been made manifest' and that 'A lie consists in speaking a falsehood with the intention of deceiving.'[14] So when Jesus talks about sheep and goats and eternal punishment or when he concludes his parable of the unforgiving slave by pointing out that 'in his anger the master handed him over to the *torturers . . . And that is how my heavenly father will deal with you* unless you forgive your brother from your heart'[15] it seems that Christians must take him at his word and accept that he's giving us the real deal.

So the Day of Judgement and the subsequent pain for the ungodly, the unrepentant and the wicked would appear to be part of the Christian god's plan. While the *Catechism* (wisely) declines to comment specifically on both the saviour's and Revelation's ideas of 'justice' (that is violent punishment for those who don't tow the party line) so clearly articulated in these passages, it does reaffirm them and reminds us that 'The way of Christ leads to life; a contrary way leads to *destruction* . . . There are two ways, the one of life, the other of death.'[16] And as we've previously noted it reaffirms the existence of hell and the reality of its 'eternal fire.' It would appear then that the basic principle of Christian morality amounts to little more than a totalitarian diktat that decrees that everyone must do as the Church says, or otherwise suffer the consequences.

---

[14] *Ibid,* 156, 2465, 2466, 2482. As previously pointed out, the *Catechism* also declares (126) that the gospels 'faithfully hand on what Jesus, the Son of God, while he lived among men, *really did and taught*' (my italics).

[15] Matthew 18:34-35, my italics. Many people understand that confessions made under torture or the threat of torture cannot be deemed valid in a responsible and humane judicial system. Genuine forgiveness is (and can only be) freely given, a truth that Jesus seems to be completely unaware of. The *Catechism* (215) affirms that 'God's promises always come true'; the gospel doesn't indicate that Jesus' conclusion to the parable is an actual 'promise' but he certainly appears to be speaking in earnest.

[16] *Catechism,* 678, 1696, my italics.

Given that such an unhappy end will be the lot of unrepentant sinners, one can imagine that the question of greatest concern for Christians is 'what must I do to be saved?' *Obey* would be the one word answer, but for those looking for more substantial advice a careful reading of the gospels reveals the supreme importance of several key 'virtues' (or perhaps more appropriately, key 'requirements') to be followed: purity, humility, love for all people, pacifism and poverty.

These requirements crop up over and over again in various stories, sermons and instances of private advice given to certain individuals such as the rich man who posed this very question. So it is these values that I will be exploring in greater detail. Although Jesus' teaching is quite unsystematic to the point that it often seems like a random selection of disparate ideas, these ideas can be usefully categorised under the headings 'personal morality', 'family values' and 'social conduct'. So let's consider Jesus' core values (and some related Church doctrines which derive from them) under these headings to assess the overall merit of his moral teaching.

Personal Morality

Apart from obedience the two most important concerns of personal morality for Jesus were purity and humility. Jesus seems to have loathed the self-righteous and ostentatious who paraded their virtue, those whom the gospels identify as the Scribes and the Pharisees. Perhaps in reaction to their ways, Jesus taught his followers to adopt the opposite attitude, to be humble.

Humility, according to Jesus was pleasing to the Father-god. So we see him continually exhorting his disciples and followers to pray and fast in secret, to regard themselves as the servants of all and to allow their opponents to walk all over them. Why? The whole point of making oneself so subservient is revealed in Jesus' parable of the Pharisee and the tax collector which concludes with the understanding that 'everyone who exalts himself will be humbled, but the man who humbles himself will be exalted.'[17]

Whether or not this role reversal will occur we cannot determine; but we can ask whether there are any practical advantages or benefits

---

[17]Luke 18:14.

in humbling oneself in the life and world that we do know. Like Jesus, most of us tend to dislike arrogant and self-important people and a degree of humility in behaviour and attitude is often regarded as a desirable trait. We may even think it a good thing for the high and mighty to be brought down to earth by a degree of misfortune from time to time. Perhaps it's this entirely human disdain for the proud and self-satisfied that influenced Jesus' thinking.

But his ideas of humbling oneself go far beyond a common and everyday response to smugness. According to Jesus it seems to be wrong ever to seek to gain the respect, admiration or even approval either of friends, adversaries or society as a whole, for any virtuous acts must be kept secret: 'Be careful not to parade your good deeds before men to attract their notice; by doing this you will lose all reward from your Father in heaven.'[18] But he seems to have overlooked not only the entirely human need to feel esteemed by one's friends and neighbours but also the rather obvious fact that if good examples are seen to bring recognition and admiration from society in general they can motivate one to continue to act virtuously or inspire virtuous behaviour in others, thus bringing about a greater good.

He then goes on to say that one must behave in a lowly and submissive manner, one must volunteer oneself to become the servant or lackey of all and one should never presume to make a single judgement of other people. But again Jesus seems to have had a poor understanding of human psychology and character: all this excessive humility he recommended might come to be regarded as affected or sanctimonious and could actually (and later *did*) become that self-righteousness that he so despised in the first place. Surely it would be far more profitable and rewarding for all parties simply to engage socially or professionally with neither arrogance nor an excessive show of humility?

Nor did he appreciate that to humble oneself continually can bring many disadvantages and can cause psychological damage. It may, for instance, lead to low self-esteem and a low sense of self-worth; it's still more likely to encourage unfair or even cruel exploitation by more dominant or unscrupulous members of society. Indeed throughout much of its history the Church seems to have used this precept very

---

[18]Matthew 6:1.

much to its own advantage as a means of social control. And in some cases it may lead to the formation and repression of resentful and angry feelings in a person who feels obliged by his religion or upbringing always to be humble. Jesus recommended for example that the humble person should   tolerate being slapped in the face by anyone and everyone; effectively this is simply inviting and heaping up anguish and frustration for oneself, leading to bitterness and pointless emotional suffering.

The worst effect of continually making oneself humble however is to erode and perhaps even destroy one's self-confidence and self-belief. Such a person is then likely to become vulnerable and helpless, dependent not on his or her interior mental resources but on external help and support. Needless to say, this is precisely how the Church wants you to regard yourself. Of course it's far too inappropriate today to declare this explicitly and at first it seems that there is no especial emphasis on the need for total and permanent humility nor on the general wretchedness or lowliness of humanity that Christianity was once so fond of proclaiming.[19] Instead the Church stresses the absolute necessity of *grace* for salvation.

Grace is defined as that 'favour, the free and undeserved help that God gives us to respond to his call.'[20] Without grace it's impossible for any of us to be saved: we are too useless, too helpless to redeem ourselves. Like Wayne and Garth in *Wayne's World*, prostrating themselves before Alice Cooper, we are to understand that 'we're not worthy', no matter how good we are or how hard we try.[21] Christians then are taught to accept that they are wholly dependent on the god's grace; as Jesus himself said 'I am the vine, you are the branches . . . cut

---

[19]However the *Catechism* (2540, 520, 544) does specify that 'the baptised person should train himself to live in humility', that 'In humbling himself, he (Jesus) has given us an example to imitate' and that 'the kingdom belongs to the poor and the lowly.' As we've seen, the Church's former contempt for humanity is clearly expressed in pronouncements such as the bull *Ineffabilis Deus* (p 269).

[20]*Ibid*, 1996.

[21]'We cannot . . . rely on our feelings or our works to conclude that we are justified and saved.' *Ibid*, 2005. At the Catholic mass, in the final prayer before the congregation lines up to eat Jesus, it confesses 'Lord, I am not worthy to receive you, but only say the word and I shall be healed.' At this important moment then, Christians are obliged to acknowledge publicly that they are unworthy, that they can never be good enough. It is almost unthinkable to suppose that the Church would ever let its members claim 'Lord, you know what, I'm really not that bad a person, in fact I reckon *I am worthy*.'

off from me you can do nothing.'[22]

As a consequence of being dependant on grace Christians become conditioned to remain servile, to see and accept themselves as inadequate and worthless, unable to bring about their own salvation; and, because the Church is the Father-god's representative on earth and administers his grace (through the sacraments), they are manoeuvred into being dependent on the Church for their ultimate spiritual or psychological well-being. As we shall see in the next chapter, so crucial is this dependency for the Church that when certain Christian reformers (such as the 5th century moral campaigner Pelagius) tried to assert the moral worthiness and goodness of mankind, they were swiftly denounced and their teachings were condemned as heresy.

So the Church subtly reaffirms the very first thing taught by Jesus at the beginning of the Sermon on the Mount: 'Blessed are the poor in spirit for they shall inherit the kingdom of heaven.'[23] At face value this can be taken as a well meaning message of hope to the down-trodden and distressed; perhaps that's all that Jesus meant by it. But unfortunately the saying has been transformed into one of Christianity's guiding maxims to persuade us that acceptance of lowliness is a great virtue, thus becoming a dangerous and harmful precept. For if it is the poor in spirit who will inherit the kingdom and possibly even *only* the poor in spirit who will do so, then misery, suffering, self-denial, renunciation of the world and material poverty - everything that is associated with unhappiness, everything that is contrary to living a positive and fulfilling life - become aspirational for committed Christians.

Effectively then Christianity wants and encourages its adherents to live depressing, emotionally and materially impoverished lives. Suffering for the sake of the gospel becomes a mark of virtue and the Christian community is urged to follow the path that Jesus took, the path of 'poverty and obedience, of service and self-sacrifice.'[24] Most of us would agree that a degree of humility is no bad thing; but Jesus'

---

[22]John 15:5.

[23]Matthew 5:3.

[24]*Catechism*, 852. The point is made more forcefully in the New Testament: 'Think of what Christ suffered in this life, and then arm yourselves with the same resolution that he had . . . If you can share in the sufferings of Christ, be glad' (1 Peter 4:1, 13).

recommendation of lowliness has turned out to be little short of disastrous.

In order to exceed the virtue of the Scribes and Pharisees Jesus also insisted on purity of heart and mind. The best known example of this teaching focuses on his strict concerns about sexual desire. Actual adultery was considered a sin by the Jews, contravening the sixth commandment, but Jesus took a much more extreme stance. If it is the case that Jesus was illegitimate, as we've discussed, it may be that fornication, sex outside of marriage was a particularly sore point for him, possibly helping to explain the severe position he took. According to Jesus even having illicit thoughts about sex was contrary to the moral law and was tantamount to the sin of adultery itself: 'You have heard how it was said: You must not commit adultery. But I say this to you: if a man looks at a woman lustfully, he has already committed adultery with her in his heart.'[25]

There are significant problems with this teaching, not least that the very idea of 'sins of the heart' probably strikes us as unnecessarily harsh if not morally repugnant. Since no offence outside the mind or the heart is actually committed, effectively Jesus is proclaiming that one can sin (and hence one can be punished) merely for having certain thoughts or feelings. Feelings and desires themselves are therefore judged to be intrinsically reprehensible. Aside from the fact that generally we instinctively recoil from any ideology which overtly seeks to control thoughts and feelings (Orwell called it *thoughtcrime*) and that the supremely nasty effect of this injunction is to induce self-imposed guilt, the teaching itself just seems plain daft.

Quite how absurd it is can be understood if we apply a different sin to the same principle that Jesus announced. Suppose for example that some burger scoffing bloke passes by a cake shop and then begins to think about tucking in to the pastries and the flans; do his fantasises about cream cakes and iced buns mean that he has committed the (apparently deadly) sin of gluttony? Do they even mean that he has committed gluttony in the heart or mind? Should we really think that he's done something morally wrong – or something contrary to the god's law simply by having had such seemingly wicked thoughts about a couple of cakes? Should he be punished for having these thoughts?

---

[25]Matthew 5:27-28.

According to this principle of Jesus' teaching the answer to these questions would appear to be 'yes'.

Then there are some major practical difficulties with this doctrine. Adultery is defined as a sexual relationship or encounter between a married man or woman with a partner other than the legal spouse. But what about single people? Are they permitted to have lustful thoughts or to eye up the talent? If so, it seems that a single man can only lust after a single woman (or vice versa); if the woman is married, she's off limits and he commits adultery in his heart (that is, although unmarried himself, he fantasises about a situation in which an adulterous act takes place).

But what happens if the marital status of the woman is unknown? How then does he know if he has committed a sin or not? Should he enquire beforehand? Further difficulties arise when we consider that the Church decrees that all sex *before* marriage is also a sin; by the same principle therefore if a single man looks lustfully at a single woman he has committed the sin of fornication in his heart. The logic of Jesus' teaching therefore would seem to dictate, quite preposterously, that outside of marriage no thoughts of sexual desire are ever permitted. In everyday terms then, if we accept that Jesus' principle is valid, it would seem that it's not permissible to flirt with or fancy any member of the opposite sex prior to being married; and once married you can only give the glad-eye to your spouse.

The real problem however is that thoughts or feelings concerning appetites - whether for food or sex - are frequently involuntary; one just can't help having them and it's often impossible to shut them out. Continually trying to repress or obliterate one's natural emotions and responses to the surrounding world and then feeling guilt (or even punishing oneself) for having had them in the first place again is likely to lead to serious and lasting psychological damage. This teaching that Jesus espouses seems then to be particularly harmful and undesirable for the individual.

And if this isn't damaging enough, his remedy for these sins of the heart is even more drastic. If you can't help yourself from sinning, if you can't control your lust, then you should make yourself incapable of committing such a sin in the first place: 'If your right eye should cause you to sin, tear it out and throw it away; for it will do you less harm to lose one part of you than to have your whole body thrown into hell.'[26]

We cannot know of course whether Jesus intended this to be taken literally or not; certainly it seems that his teaching about the physical punishments and fires of hell was meant to be (and was) accepted at face value so there's no reason to doubt his earnestness.[27] Most Christians however prefer to believe that Jesus was exaggerating here for rhetorical effect, to make his teaching more memorable. Needless to say this interpretation is almost obligatory for Christians, since to think otherwise would mean that Jesus, the mild and gentle saviour, had recommended that sinners should mutilate themselves if they were unable otherwise to change their wicked ways.

Family Values

From adultery and thoughtcrime Jesus moves swiftly on to the related issue of divorce and here too we find a blanket prohibition. But we also see that Jesus is rather slippery when it comes to arguing his case and that his argument has no solid foundation. When the Pharisees specifically ask him 'Is it against the law for a man to divorce his wife?'[28] instead of offering a direct and honest response Jesus refers his adversaries to Scripture: 'What did Moses command you?' he asks, suggesting that Moses is to be regarded as the highest authority on the matter and that his teaching should be followed.

Unfortunately for the saviour the well-versed Pharisees were among the intellectual elite of the day and they confound Jesus by informing him that well, actually Moses *did* allow them to divorce. Jesus is caught out, but instead of accepting the legal and moral position adopted by mainstream Judaism with good grace, he insists that his teaching on this issue, based on his interpretation of an entirely different scriptural passage, supersedes that of Moses. Accordingly he

---

[26]Matthew 5:29.

[27]Later on Jesus mentions (without any hint of disapproval) the 'eunuchs who have made themselves that way for the kingdom of heaven' (Matthew 19:12) suggesting that self-mutilation for religious reasons was not unknown at that time. The 2nd century scholar Origen is famous for having castrated himself to rid himself of his sexual desire and the abysmal practice of self-mortification through scourging was to become a well known and common enough practice: see Knight, *Honest to Man: Christian Ethics Re-examined*, pp 71-76.

[28]Mark 10:2-9.

proclaims that divorce is not permitted at all.[29]

Of course Jesus couldn't openly reject the authority of Moses, especially since elsewhere he used it to rebuke and chastise his opponents. At one point he even said that he had no intention of replacing the law of Moses.[30] So instead he insists that Moses only allowed divorce as a concession, 'because you were so unteachable.' Now, Jesus declares, this concession is withdrawn, presumably since he has arrived on the scene to re-educate everyone. He then goes on to prohibit divorce absolutely since he believes that Scripture revealed that permanent union was the creator's original intention. And so we get to Jesus' formula used at countless Christian wedding ceremonies throughout the world: 'what God has united, man must not divide.'

The Church's anti-divorce stance therefore derives from Jesus' own prohibition and this in turn is based on the book of Genesis which he quoted to support his teaching: 'God made them male and female . . . and the two become one body.'[31] But it's actually quite difficult to read this as a specific prohibition of divorce; in fact it seems to be more of a celebratory poetic expression to portray the loving and sexual union of men and women with each other.

Furthermore it is equally difficult to accept Genesis as some sort of unsurpassable and unimpeachable moral authority. In Genesis we also find the story of Abraham sleeping with Hagar, his wife's Egyptian slave-girl for instance. If Genesis is accepted as a valid moral authority to justify a prohibition on divorce, then it's just as appropriate to use it as a justification *in favour of* adultery and perhaps even in favour of the sexual abuse of slaves. After all, Abraham, held out to be the greatest of Jewish patriarchs and a model of Christian faith and obedience, is never rebuked or required to repent by Yahweh for his sexual misdemeanours.[32]

---

[29]Jesus declares that divorcees who remarry commit adultery; however, in Matthew (5:32 and 19:9) there's an exception: men who remarry after divorcing wives who have themselves had an extra-marital affair do not commit adultery suggesting that divorce is recognised in these circumstances.

[30]See for example Mark 7:10, 12:26, Matthew 5:17.

[31]Mark 10:5-7, quoting Genesis 1:27, 2:24.

[32]Genesis 16:1-16. In fact it is Hagar who's rebuked (by an angel) after she ran away; Hagar is told to return to her mistress and submit to her ill treatment. Abraham was 85 years old at the time of his adultery. We cannot tell from the text whether Hagar had sex with Abraham willingly or whether she was raped.

Jesus' intransigence concerning divorce is the policy of the Catholic Church today (other Christian denominations are not quite so rigid): it is prohibited absolutely. There appear to be three key reasons for this hard and fast rule. Divorce is prohibited first of all because Jesus said so (as we've just observed) and since Jesus is a god, (a) he must be right and (b) he cannot be disobeyed. This suggests that all of Jesus' teachings must be true and must be followed to the letter; in no circumstances can any of them be overridden.

However, elsewhere we see that some of Jesus' teaching wasn't correct and find some that is clearly rejected by the Church. For example, Jesus repeatedly prophesied that he would return in glory with lots of angels within the lifetime of his contemporaries.[33] This main event has yet to happen and in this instance Jesus really was wrong. And in the Sermon on the Mount he said without any ambiguity 'offer the wicked man no resistance' and 'if anyone hits you on the right cheek, offer him the other as well.'[34] We'll come to consider the wisdom (or lack thereof) of this teaching later, but for the moment the point is this instruction has been over-ruled by the Church today, with the *Catechism* declaring that 'armed *resistance*' to evil in certain circumstances *is* permitted.[35] If the Church can ignore or override this express command, then clearly it doesn't regard Jesus' teaching as being infallible and therefore it can be disobeyed. If this is so the argument that divorce must always be prohibited merely because Jesus said so is just not tenable.

Secondly, marriage is regarded as a covenant between the married partners sealed in the presence of the Father-god; it is therefore sinful to break this covenant since to do so means breaking a promise made before the god. Behind this difficult understanding there are numerous vague and esoteric assertions (they cannot be called arguments) which don't seem to be based on any reasonable premises at all.

---

[33] Matthew 16:27-28: 'I tell you solemnly, there are some of these standing here who will not taste death before they see the Son of Man coming with his kingdom.' When it became clear that the second coming wasn't going to happen within the foreseeable future as Jesus predicted, New Testament writers sought to explain the delay with flimsy excuses such as 'with the Lord, 'a day' can mean a thousand years, and a thousand years is like a day' (2 Peter 3:8).

[34] Matthew 5:39.

[35] *Catechism*, 2243, my italics.

The understanding begins with the recognition that it often seems to be an impossible demand to insist on marriage being indissoluble, a recognition that a lifelong commitment can place a heavy burden on spouses. Initially this demand seems to be much more onerous than that of the law of Moses which did permit divorce. But in prohibiting divorce Jesus didn't actually make this burden heavier; on the contrary he lightened it. This is because those who are married under the law of Jesus are given a special inner strength to help them cope with the extra demands placed on spouses by an indissoluble union; for as part of his mission, we're told that Jesus came to give married couples 'the strength and grace to live marriage in the new dimension of the Reign of God.'

How do we know this? The Church interprets Jesus' attendance at the wedding at Cana as a revelation that marriage is 'an efficacious sign of Christ's presence.' Consequently couples joined together in Christian marriage are strengthened by this presence throughout their married lives through the special sacrament of marriage; and in turn it seems that this sacrament confers divine aid, or grace on the couple. This grace originates from Jesus' own sacrifice (or, as the *Catechism* puts it somewhat more fancifully, 'this grace of Christian marriage is a fruit of Christ's cross'); and just as Jesus was unwaveringly faithful in his covenant to the Church, despite the suffering he endured, so spouses must follow his example and remain faithful in their own covenant to each other. So it comes about that 'the covenant between spouses is integrated into God's covenant with man' and 'thus the marriage bond . . . established by God himself . . . can never be dissolved.'[36]

It's impossible of course to refute or argue against any of this since it is founded on a series of arbitrary assertions, none of which are demonstrable; nor can they be subject to reasonable scrutiny or critical evaluation. Consequently it is essentially so incoherent as to be virtually meaningless. How can it be known for example that special divine aid is given to married couples? What does it consist of? If it consists of strength of character or depth of love, how do we know such traits are divine blessings given only on one's wedding day as opposed to innate personal characteristics?

And what should we make of the Church's interpretation that

---

[36] *Ibid*, 1613, 1615, 1638–40, 1647, 1648.

Jesus' presence at the wedding at Cana is a sign of this benevolence? Reading the story from the Fourth Gospel, it's clear that there is no especial endorsement of marriage given by Jesus at all. The story simply concerns Jesus' ability to turn water into wine; the fact that this utterly fantastic party trick took place at a wedding is purely incidental, for Jesus says nothing about the good of marriage and doesn't even give his blessing to the happy couple. One might more reasonably conclude that this is more a story that endorses binge drinking.[37]

Even if divine aid is given to married couples, one might justly argue that when a marriage breaks down and there are irreconcilable differences between the couple, this aid would appear to have been prematurely exhausted or withdrawn. And if this is so, then the god has gone back on its side of the bargain. One could then quite legitimately say that the deal's off and that no further obligation to the Father-god is due from either spouse.

Nor does this argument seem to have any practical value. We can easily imagine the priests and cardinals who wrote the relevant passages in the *Catechism* (men who have never experienced the pain and distress of a broken marriage firsthand for themselves) feeling pleased with themselves for having composed an ingenuous, pseudo-intellectual justification for the prohibition of divorce. It's not so easy however to imagine a desperately unhappy Catholic couple, whose marriage has broken down to the extent that they can no longer bear the sight or sound of each other, thinking to themselves: 'nevermind, we must stay together because our marriage has been blessed with "an efficacious sign of Christ's presence."'

What's so disturbing about this 'argument' however is that it's based on obliging or persuading people to continue to accept unhappiness and suffering willingly rather than encouraging them or even permitting them to do something about it. Reading between the lines it seems to be saying that since Jesus happily embraced suffering for our sake and was faithful in his covenant with all mankind, it is

---

[37]The story of the miracle at Cana is told in John 2:1-10. The names of the married couple and details of the ceremony are not mentioned. Later, when the evangelist refers to Cana again, he says it is where 'he had changed the water into wine' (4:46) rather than the place where he had witnessed and had given his blessing to a marriage. Jesus turns six stone jars of water, each with a capacity of 20-30 *gallons* into wine; that's between 750 and 1,150 bottles of wine. We're not told how many guests are present at the reception.

entirely fitting (perhaps even desirable?) that unhappily married couples should suffer for the sake of their own covenant rather than break it.

So we have the heartbreaking situation that instead of allowing these unfortunate people to move on from their personal unhappiness, the Church prefers them and indeed requires them to follow the depressing example of Jesus and make a personal and painful sacrifice: 'It is by following Christ, by renouncing themselves, *by taking up their crosses* that spouses will be able to "receive" the original meaning of marriage and live it with the help of Christ.'[38] Put into plain English, this seems to be saying that by giving up any hopes for personal happiness, by accepting suffering and by accepting that suffering is a good thing (because Jesus' whole mission was based on suffering), those in desperately unhappy marriages will be able to come to terms with their unhappy state and find a compensatory comfort in the understanding that they're doing the Christian god's will by continuing to live together, by continuing to suffer. Christians therefore are required to put the god's happiness and satisfaction ahead of their own.

The third reason for the prohibition of divorce is much more down to earth. Divorce is immoral because 'it introduces disorder into the family' and brings 'grave harm to the deserted spouse, to children traumatised by the separation of their parents.'[39] It's certainly true that divorce can severely distress or even damage young children and if it's the case that one spouse is unfairly abandoned either emotionally, physically or financially, grave harm may indeed be caused.

However, it's also the case that forcing a couple to continue to live together can also bring about these harmful effects, both to the children (who continue to witness the ongoing trauma between their parents) and to the spouses (who needlessly add to each other's distress by their enforced proximity). Why isn't it possible to judge each case on its own merits rather than have a total prohibition? Why can't the spouses themselves use their own judgement to reach an agreed outcome?

Moreover it seems that the Church is only capable of seeing divorce as a negative and injurious process; it's sometimes the case that a divorce is mutually agreed by spouses and that there are no children

---

[38] *Catechism*, 1615, my italics.

[39] *Ibid*, 2385.

involved or the children are adults themselves. Why then is divorce prohibited and considered so immoral in these circumstances?

The most deplorable thing about the Church's reasoning in this area however is the fact that it exercises such double standards. For if we read the *Catechism* closely we discover that it does specifically permit separation of spouses in certain circumstances.[40] Prolonged separation which evolves into permanent separation for all practical purposes is essentially the same as divorce; but even in cases of permanent separation Christian spouses can't divorce and so are not free to remarry. Nor are they permitted to have a loving and sexual relationship outside of marriage since 'the sexual act must take place exclusively within marriage.'[41] If the Church is really so concerned about the emotional well-being of children and the deserted spouse, why in cases of permanent separation doesn't it allow a new parent-figure and partner to be brought into the family's life, to provide love and emotional support for all concerned? No answer is provided to this question other than the dogmatic formulations outlined above.

Aside from divorce Jesus doesn't seem to have had too high a regard for the family. In his public teaching he emphasised that one should honour one's parents, at one point even maintaining that 'Anyone who curses father or mother must be put to death.' But in his own life he seemed to care very little about his own family. His relationship with his mother in particular is characterised by resentment or even open hostility. When Jesus is told that his mother and brothers are concerned for his well-being and want to see him, he openly snubs them: 'who are my mother and my brothers?' he asks. 'And looking around at those sitting in a circle about him, he said, "Here are my mother and my brothers."'[42] We're not told what Mary's reaction to this was, but we can scarcely feel that she felt honoured by his sharp and humiliating rebuke.

---

[40] Where Catholic couples do wish to separate, for example when one partner has committed adultery, the *Code of Canon Law* specifies that 'the innocent spouse is to bring a case for separation to the competent ecclesiastical authority' (*Codex Iuris Canonici*, 1152). Hence such couples don't simply go their separate ways; they must petition the Church which either agrees or doesn't agree to the separation. Effectively then it grants separations just as civil authorities grant divorces.

[41] *Catechism*, 2390.

[42] Mark 7:10, 3:33-34.

Jesus foresees that his teaching, like that of many fanatics, will lead to family break-ups and will cause brothers to betray each other, children to rebel against their parents and parents to hate their children, yet he does nothing to try to prevent this situation from ever happening. If anything he seems to have endorsed it by praising and encouraging his followers to turn their backs on their family, just as he had done. Now that Jesus has come to proclaim the good news, family bonds, family love and loyalty are irrelevant to the true disciple. Anyone who prefers his father or mother or his children to Jesus is not worthy of him he declares, with small regard, sympathy or understanding for the emotional distress this might cause. In Luke's gospel he even says 'If any man comes to me without hating his father, mother, wife, children, brothers, sisters . . . he cannot be my disciple.' Clearly this is at odds with his earlier teaching about honouring one's parents.

If this were not insensitive enough, shortly afterwards he tells his disciples that those who have 'left house, wife, brothers, parents or children for the sake of the kingdom of God'[43] will be appropriately rewarded many times over. So while he doesn't permit deeply unhappy spouses to end their mutual torment through divorce, it seems that it's perfectly acceptable to abandon one's husband or wife, parents and even children for the selfish desire to follow him and to gain a greater reward in his kingdom of the hereafter.

Social Conduct

Just as Jesus sought to cultivate inner purity and humility in the private morality of his followers, so in practical, public acts he and his later proclaimers taught that their behaviour should be governed by a sense of helplessness, resignation and self-imposed vulnerability. Purity is translated socially into neighbour-love and then into love for enemies and those who persecute minorities or society's weaker members; while humility was to be reflected publicly in such 'virtues' as obedience, a resigned tolerance of any injustice and even acceptance of criminal acts through complete non-resistance to wickedness. In the first letter of Peter the writer declares that 'slaves must be respectful

---

[43]Luke 14:26, 18:29.

and obedient to their masters, not only when they are kind and gentle *but also when they are unfair*' because 'there is some merit in putting up with the pains of unearned punishment if it is done for the sake of God.'

It's true that Jesus himself makes no comments on slavery; but if his closest disciple gave such extreme advice one suspects that the master himself may not have held wildly different opinions.[44] In fact we see Jesus giving his followers similar advice about submission to ill-treatment when he tells them to 'rejoice and be glad' when they are abused and persecuted.[45] And to ensure that his followers would achieve these lowly ideals, he taught that they should aspire to being the poorest members of society in material terms, surviving as beggars, to be wholly dependant on the work and goodwill of other people.

Jesus' starting point in his guide for everyday living begins with the exhortation to love one's neighbours. This golden rule is admirable enough, but rather unclear: does it mean that one should simply show consideration and concern for one's neighbours or does it oblige one to love them as one might love one's closest family or friends? If it's the latter it is highly idealistic and in practical terms probably achieved only very rarely. It's often thought that this is one of the more original and 'Christian' aspects of Jesus' teachings; the reality however is that this precept was formulated not by Jesus himself but was lifted straight from the Old Testament book of Leviticus.

Of course Jesus has to add his own personal twist to this formula; and in doing so he turns a worthy basic principle into a set of completely impractical and nonsensical doctrines. So far as Jesus is concerned, loving your neighbour is no longer good enough; followers are now required to love their enemies as well and to 'offer the wicked man no resistance.'

Furthermore, they must now willingly and happily collaborate with (or even over indulge) occupying powers ('if anyone orders you to go

---

[44] 1 Peter 2:18-19, my italics. Authorship of this letter however is disputed, the writer not universally believed by scholars to be the actual disciple (see Kummel, *op cit*, pp 421-424). Catholic scholars are inclined to regard Peter as the true author (see for example *Jerome*, 57:2). Even though he endorses such abhorrent morality, condoning both slavery and undeserved (and therefore unfair) punishment, Peter has always been and continues to be revered as one of the Church's greatest saints.

[45] Matthew 5:11-12.

one mile, go two miles with him') and shouldn't seek to obtain justice through the law courts. Instead of fighting your case, even if you are convinced you're right, you must submit to your opponent's claim and then *over compensate* him for his trouble ('if a man takes you to law and would have your tunic, let him have your cloak as well'). In the gospel of Luke Jesus even forbids his followers to seek redress when they are robbed ('do not ask for your property back from the man who robs you').[46]

It's difficult to see how any society would survive or be able to organise itself if it seriously attempted to put all or any of these silly ideas into practice. Disagreements, disputes and injustices always arise between individuals, that's why courts of law came into being in the first place, to seek to resolve such matters as fairly as possible. But Jesus says that Christians shouldn't bother with well thought out judicial systems; instead they should always yield to those with whom they have a dispute. If genuinely practised the effect of this would simply be to encourage unscrupulous non-Christians to exploit and abuse the easy-prey Christians; eventually it would bring about a state of chaos and great injustice.

As for non-resistance and loving one's enemies, what would happen to a Christian community, or more disastrously to a truly Christian nation, if it was never prepared to defend itself against outside aggressors or to stand up to manifestly wicked practices? Should Britain have refused to defend itself against the Nazis in 1940? Should police forces throughout the world today not bother to pursue terrorists or not seek to prevent their attacks? If you're being bullied at work or at school should you refuse to do anything about it other than submit to and encourage your tormentor? Simply thinking about Jesus' teachings and applying them to one's own life or to today's world shows how absurd they are; indeed they are so impractical and so nonsensical that in 'real life' application they have been all but abandoned by the Church today.[47]

Given that these precepts are so extreme and so impractical, why might Jesus have taught them in the first place? It may be that he

---

[46]Matthew 5:39-41, Luke 6:30.

[47]The *Catechism* affirms that war (2308) and armed resistance (and therefore presumably unarmed resistance) are permissible (2242-43) as is recourse to civil authorities (2498).

recognised the political reality of the day, that the Jews were under an occupying power and were too weak to oppose such an enemy in practical ways. So perhaps he made a virtue out of necessity: non-resistance and collaboration were the safest or most practical options. Or it may be that the urgency of his eschatological hopes and expectations made social and political considerations or injustices irrelevant. If the world was going to end in the very near future, why waste time pursuing matters in court? If the kingdom was about to become a reality, why get uptight about helping a Roman soldier who was probably soon going to be vaporised in the eternal fire anyway?

However, a close reading of the Sermon on the Mount suggests an alternative explanation. After exhorting the assembled crowds to love their enemies Jesus asks them 'if you love [only] those who love you, what right have you to claim any credit? . . . are you doing anything exceptional?' From this it seems that Jesus required his followers to love their enemies simply because he wanted them to stand out, to be exceptional, to be distinguished or *better* in some way than the pagans and tax collectors or possibly the Scribes and Pharisees whose standards he had previously noted ('if your virtue goes no deeper than that of the Scribes and Pharisees, you will never get into the kingdom of heaven'[48]). If this is the case, it may be that here Jesus' teaching is motivated simply by a rather silly and superficial spiritual pride, a biblical equivalent of keeping up with the Joneses perhaps, or rather, trying to beat them at their own game; and that love for enemies in reality amounts to little more than self-importance and self-love.[49]

Jesus seems to have had a great contempt for wealth but it's not entirely clear why. At times it seems his opposition to riches is based on an underlying egalitarianism: money might be put to better use if it were distributed among the many poor rather than remain in the hands of a few wealthy individuals. Perhaps it was the luxurious lifestyle of the rich in full view of the poor, the hungry and the destitute that

---

[48]Matthew 5:46-47, 20.

[49]This is confirmed in Paul's letter to the Romans (12:17, 20): 'Never repay evil with evil but *let everyone see* that you are interested only in the highest ideals.' It seems then that non-retaliation is recommended not out of genuine love for enemies but to exhibit moral superiority motivated by spiritual pride. And from a practical point of view this behaviour is intended more to shame one's opponents rather than to express love for them: 'If your enemy is hungry you should give him food, and if he is thirsty, let him drink. Thus you heap red-hot coals on his head.'

offended the sensibilities of both Jesus and the crowds he taught. Accordingly it seems he had a very low regard for those who were rich, to the extent that he taught that wealthy people weren't capable of being saved, regardless of whether they were otherwise virtuous people.

We see this most obviously in his advice to a wealthy man who, desperate to inherit eternal life, asks Jesus what he must do to secure his passage. Jesus responds by telling him that although he has kept the commandments, this won't suffice: he must sell all his possessions. To make the point more forcefully, he later tells the story of the rich man and Lazarus. Here the rich man is crassly depicted as a fat cat who 'used to dress in purple and fine linen and feast magnificently everyday.' Even before we know anything of his character and circumstances then, we are persuaded to despise him for being rich. The portrayal of Lazarus on the other hand is designed to evoke our compassion and pity; a beggar who used to live off the rich man's scraps, he is right at the bottom of the pile, so much so that 'Dogs even came and licked his sores.' As the story unfolds it seems that the rich man is condemned to hell merely for having money, for there's no mention of any of his sins or wickedness as he suffers the eternal torments; while Lazarus is 'carried away by the angels to the bosom of Abraham'[50] simply because he is a beggar. In other words: poor good, rich bad.

So those who prosper and do well in life, whether it be through hard work, good fortune or prudence are denounced by Jesus: 'alas for you who are rich: you are having your consolation now.'[51] Once again we see how negative Jesus' teaching is. For instead of using wealth to maintain their self-reliance (and possibly help other people to be self-reliant), Jesus teaches that the rich should sell all they have and thus turn themselves into homeless beggars. On other occasions the charitable outcome of material renunciation isn't mentioned and seems to be irrelevant - Jesus simply required his followers, both rich and poor, to give up their possessions simply for the sake of making such a sacrifice so as to be considered worthy of him. 'None of you can be my disciple' he declares, 'unless he gives up all his possessions.'

---

[50]Luke 16:19-31.

[51]Luke 6:24.

This suggests that worldliness and material comfort or well-being are things that are inherently wrong. But when his disciples protest that they've given up everything for his sake and get concerned about what they're going to get in return, it is purely in worldly and material terms that their reward is described: they're going to sit on thrones and, like the rich man of his story, will eat and drink magnificently with Jesus at the top table in his kingdom. And those who have abandoned their livelihoods and homes will be appropriately recompensed; they will be 'repaid a hundred times over, [with] houses . . . and land, now in this present time and in the world to come, eternal life.'[52]

Still more disturbingly Jesus urged his followers to show no concern for the future or for one's basic needs; birds don't work, he argues and flowers don't wear clothes, so why should they worry about such matters? Instead of providing for themselves and their children, Jesus' followers should spend their time praying and setting their hearts on (or day-dreaming about) the celestial paradise; if they do this the heavenly father won't fail to provide for all their needs. But what would happen if people followed his advice today?

Here too we can see how foolhardy and how potentially harmful Jesus' teaching is for it's simply not the case that the religiously minded poor have their needs entirely provided for by a benevolent Christian god. Tragically hundreds of thousands, if not millions die each year because they have insufficient food, contaminated water, inadequate shelter or too few medical supplies.

But rather than admit that Jesus was wrong or naïve or irresponsible to give such advice or that his teaching was only appropriate in an apocalyptic context, the Church today seems to go along with this thinking with a shocking and shameful insensitivity to poverty and suffering in the real world: 'Abandonment to the providence of the Father in heaven' it says, commenting on the relevant verses of Matthew's gospel, 'frees us from anxiety about tomorrow. Trust in God is a preparation for the blessedness of the poor . . . the Father who gives us life cannot but give us the nourishment that life requires.'[53] Unfortunately the tragedy of repeated crop failures and recurrent famine in Africa and other regions of the

---

[52]Luke 14:33, Matthew 19:29.

[53]*Catechism*, 2547, 2830.

world might suggest that the loving Father is not so bounteous as the Church would have us think.

Practising What You Preach

If Jesus were alive today or had somehow returned to the world, there's no way he would ever get invited round to a dinner party at my place. It just wouldn't happen, not even if (instead of bringing a bottle) he promised to turn my tap water into an unending flow of wine. In one of only a small number of social occasions in the gospels we see him invited to dine at the house of a Pharisee. But on this occasion Jesus proved himself to be so rude and so thoroughly obnoxious that the whole evening was probably ruined.

To begin with he seems happy enough to accept the hospitality and the free food. But when his host politely remarks that he hadn't observed the customary and socially desirable rituals of hygiene (he hadn't washed before sitting at the table), instead of offering an apology or explanation for his oversight or lack of manners, Jesus launches into a fierce and excessive denunciation of him and the other guests. 'Oh you Pharisees!' he snarls, 'You clean the outside of cup and plate, while inside yourselves you are filled with extortion and wickedness. Fools!'[54] He was very angry.

Despite having been berated so unnecessarily, to his credit his host has the decency to hear out Jesus' petulant tirade with courtesy and good grace, qualities so obviously lacking in Jesus, and without returning the insults. A fellow guest however, a lawyer is unable to show such restraint and speaks out, again very politely informing Jesus (he addresses him as 'Master') that everyone present feels insulted (and one imagines deeply embarrassed as well) by his outburst.

But instead of trying to diffuse the situation, instead of seeking a reconciliation (as earlier he had exhorted his followers to do in such circumstances) Jesus decides to cause further offence by insulting the lawyer too: 'Alas for you lawyers also because you load on men burdens that are unendurable.' He seems to have conveniently forgotten however that previously he himself had placed the burden of a much stricter moral code on his followers; their virtue, it may be

---

[54]Luke 11:39-43.

recalled, had to be 'deeper than that of the Scribes and Pharisees' if they were to meet his exacting standards for entry into the kingdom. [55]

Later on, in Jerusalem Jesus attacks the Pharisees with even greater venom, cursing them as hypocrites seven times. What seems particularly to have offended his sensibilities was that 'they do not practise what they preach'; we can assume then that to practise what you preach was very important to Jesus, as indeed it is to most of us today. But Jesus seems to have been completely oblivious to the fact that this same accusation could be laid at his feet; in fact instead of having any doubt at all about his own righteousness or any genuine self-awareness, he holds himself out to be a model of virtuous conduct: 'Learn from me for I am gentle and humble in heart'[56] he boasts.

Down the centuries the imitation of Jesus' example (especially in terms of obedience) has been a cherished ideal for Christians. Indeed we're told that 'In all of his life Jesus presents himself as our model. He is the perfect man.'[57] But critical scrutiny of the gospels reveals that Jesus' moral perfection is an idealisation, not a fact: Jesus simply didn't practise his own standards in his personal conduct and he can't be taken as that paragon of virtue that the Church proclaims him to be. In short, of all the biblical hypocrites, the biblical Jesus is perhaps the greatest and undoubtedly the least recognised.

We see this duplicity in a variety of situations in which Jesus' actions contravene many aspects of his earlier teaching. He talked the talk magnificently when preaching the need to be humble and pure in heart, to love both neighbours and enemies. But in later incidents his fine words and lofty sentiments were quickly forgotten. He was capable of great compassion to the poor and needy, to the downtrodden and desperate, people who would've shown enormous gratitude to him for his attentions. (Admirable as this is, according to Jesus' very own words this behaviour in itself was not especially meritorious, for as we've noted, he asks 'if you love those who love you, what right have you to claim any credit?')

But when he was doubted and taken to task by the more self-reliant and those who were not so readily enthralled by him, his

---

[55]Luke 11:46, Matthew 5:20.

[56]Matthew 23:3, 11:29.

[57]*Catechism*, 520.

tenderness soon fell by the wayside. He showed little or no love for his opponents for example when he cursed the Pharisees over and over again. What did Jesus say at the Sermon on the Mount? 'Anyone who is angry with his brother will answer for it before the court; if a man calls his brother "Fool" he will answer for it before the Sanhedrin . . . be reconciled with your brother . . . Come to terms with your opponent.' But then what does Jesus go and do? He calls the Pharisees 'Fools' and many other more offensive names besides ('hypocrites', 'blind men', 'sons of murderers' and best of all, 'serpents, brood of vipers'). The text doesn't record Jesus' actual emotions during this protracted and indignant outburst, but with such bitter insults being repeatedly expressed, one's inclined to suppose that his feelings were much closer to real hatred than to brotherly love.

And despite saying to the crowds 'Do not judge and you will not be judged' it seems as if Jesus hands down a guilty verdict to the Pharisees with his disdainful rhetorical question 'how can you escape being condemned to hell?'[58] There's not much of the spirit of reconciliation being shown by the gentle and humble saviour here. If a man who insults his fellow man will have to 'answer for it before the Sanhedrin' one can't help feeling that there was a certain poetic justice in that council's apparent condemnation of Jesus.

Jesus also preached humility and specifically took exception to the Pharisees for acting so ostentatiously: 'Everything they do is done to attract attention, like wearing broader phylacteries and longer tassels.' But frequently Jesus himself comes across as arrogant and self-important; he tells his followers to listen to no one but himself 'for you have only one Teacher, the Christ', he boasts that his testimony is greater than John the Baptist's, he calls himself the 'light of the world' and says that anyone who refuses to honour him refuses to honour the Father-god.[59] And if he condemned the Pharisees so vehemently for drawing attention to themselves, why is it that when he entered Jerusalem, he did so with such great fanfare and carefully orchestrated triumphalism, happy to proceed with the crowds greeting him like a

---

[58]Matthew 5:22-25, 7:1, 23:33. Since there's no indication that the Pharisees asked Jesus for forgiveness and since it is Jesus who will be doing all the judging on that fateful day at the end of time, we can only presume that these wicked sinners will be cast into the blazing furnace.

[59]Matthew 23:10, John 5:36, 7:12, 5:23.

king, spreading their cloaks and palm leaves on the path before him?[60]

Similarly Jesus seems not to have practised some of the social values he preached. He insists that a life of poverty is the ideal and advises people many times to sell all they have, to give the proceeds to the poor and to reject worldly materialism. But a later incident suggests that here too Jesus had double standards. Shortly before his betrayal a woman anoints his head with a very expensive ointment. Seeing this the disciples (who have renounced their former livelihoods and have been obliged to endure poverty themselves) are somewhat indignant. Surely they argue, in keeping with his teaching Jesus should have advised the woman to sell the oil and give the money to the poor rather than have allowed himself to be so indulged? Jesus' curt and dismissive response is to observe that the poor will always be around whereas he won't be around for much longer and therefore he is more deserving.[61]

But if this is a valid argument for Jesus, then it's reasonable to assume that it's valid for anyone and everyone. No one's going to be around for ever, no one knows the hour of his death, everyone values the life they have and most people enjoy 'the things of this world'. It seems then that Jesus has one principle or standard for himself and a harsher one for everyone else.

That this episode was embarrassing for very early Christianity can be seen in the differing ways in which it was reported. Matthew records that it was the group of the disciples as a whole who could see Jesus' hypocrisy and who objected; Luke declines to record the protest while in the later gospel of John the story has been modified and it is only Judas, the traitor, who complained so as to lessen the impact of the criticism. And just in case we have too much respect for Judas' altruism, the evangelist writes in a quick and dirty character assassination: Judas protested, he says 'not because he cared about the poor but because he was a thief'[62] and would've helped himself to the

---

[60]Luke tells us that before reaching Jerusalem 'he sent messengers ahead of him' (9:52) to prepare for his arrival; the fact that so many people were on the streets to greet him suggests that the disciples must have told people about his imminent arrival and importance. We're also told that on entering the city the Pharisees pleaded with Jesus to moderate his disciples' enthusiasm, but he refused to do so (19:39-40).

[61]Matthew 26:6-13.

[62]John 12:6.

proceeds.

It's possible to find many more examples of Jesus' double standards – he preached that one should honour one's mother and father but as we've seen, he showed a callous disdain for his own mother; he taught that everyone should be treated as a neighbour but likened a Gentile woman to a dog and initially refused to help her. And he said that one should not resist wicked men, thereby implying that one should never use force or violent actions, but conveniently forgot this absolute commitment to pacifism when clearing the Temple of the money changers and merchants.[63]

In his sevenfold curse of the Pharisees, Jesus condemned them because they 'appear to people from the outside like good honest men, but inside . . . are full of hypocrisy and lawlessness.'[64] Perhaps he should have taken a good look at himself before making such a rash and sweeping condemnation. And as for the supposedly noble and perfect example he set, one can only conclude that it's a nonsense for the Church to have idealised and placed Jesus on a pedestal to be admired and imitated when he himself thought so little of his own moral code, so little in fact that he abandoned many of its principles as soon as and whenever it suited him.

The Whitewashed Tomb

Just as Jesus deviated from his own standards, so we find the Church today preaching one standard but practising another. It's beyond the scope of this book to consider every incidence of Christianity's double standards over the centuries; but highlighting one or two of the most glaring cases will give an insight into the problem.

In its section on social justice, to which of course the Church professes to be fully committed the *Catechism* provides us with an indication of its understanding of 'respect for the human person.'

---

[63]Jesus condemned the Temple merchants but it seems he may have made use of their services. He tells his disciples Peter and John to 'make the preparations for us to eat the Passover' (Luke 22:8), a ritual meal consisting of a 'Passover lamb [that] was *sacrificed*' (Mark 14:12, my italics). The chances are the sacrificial victim, an unblemished lamb, would have been acquired from one of these merchants (John records them as selling 'cattle, sheep and pigeons'- 2:14) and then killed within the Temple walls.

[64]Matthew 23:28.

Social justice is necessarily dependent on such respect and in turn this respect entails respect for the rights of the person. These rights 'are the basis of the moral legitimacy of every authority: by flouting them or refusing to recognise them . . . a society undermines it own moral legitimacy.'

Respect for the human person proceeds on acknowledging and practising the principle that Christians should look upon their neighbour (without any exceptions) as another 'self'. 'This same duty', it continues is owed and 'extends to those who think or act differently from us.' Consequently any form of prejudice or discrimination is intolerable: 'Every form of social or cultural discrimination in fundamental personal rights on the grounds of sex, race, colour, social conditions, language or religion must be curbed and eradicated.'[65]

So far so good, and at first glance this seems like a fairly comprehensive and laudable affirmation of human rights similar to those professed by governments, organisations and even multi-nationals throughout the world. But respect for one fundamental right which in the contemporary world is increasingly recognised (at least by non-religious entities) is missing: the respect for sexual orientation.

Even though the Church specifically proclaims that Christians must respect and treat fairly those people 'who think or act differently from us' it just can't bring itself round to accepting that gay men and women have a right to seek and enjoy loving sexual relationships in the way that heterosexual people have. In the eyes of the Church 'homosexual acts' can never be seen as expressions of love; instead they're condemned unequivocally as acts of 'grave depravity', they are 'intrinsically disordered'[66] and cannot be permitted in any circumstances.

Denying people the opportunity of love, happiness and emotional and sexual fulfilment is surely a denial of one of the most fundamental of all personal rights that the Church professes to care about so deeply. So why are gay sexual relationships or expressions of love not permitted? The *Catechism* declines to provide any argument or justification for this blanket prohibition and merely refers the reader to the Church's sense of tradition and to its ultimate authority, the Bible.

---

[65] *Catechism*, 1930, 1931, 1933, 1935.
[66] *Ibid*, 2357.

Appeals to a sense of tradition don't normally provide a reasonable basis for a particular law or practice, whether moral or otherwise, particularly when it is recognised that over the years such a tradition has unfairly discriminated against a certain interest or group. We would laugh at or consider absurd (or offensive), for example the argument that women shouldn't be allowed to vote simply because (until the beginning of the 20th century) by tradition women had never been permitted to vote. So what about the biblical justifications? Let's consider these very briefly.

First of all the *Catechism* refers us to Chapter 19 of the book of Genesis and its quaint but dark story of Lot, the undistinguished nephew of Abraham. Unfortunately Lot's town, Sodom has been earmarked for destruction by the Lord on account of its great but unspecified wickedness. However two angels arrive one evening, seemingly to warn Lot of the terrorist attack that is to come. Soon enough word gets round that a couple of angelic lads are hanging out at Lot's place. Next thing, all the men of the town, both young and old, gather around Lot's house and then quite astonishingly demand that the angels be brought out 'so that we can have intercourse with them.' No, no my friends, says Lot, 'do not be so wicked.'

And that's it. From this bizarre and improbable story (sex with spirits?[67]), from this single personal entreaty we are to infer and accept that all 'homosexual acts' are wicked and that every gay relationship should be prohibited. Arguments or justifications don't come much more flimsy than this and it's very difficult to take the Church seriously as a credible and respectable authority if it has to resort to using this sort of story to justify an important part of its moral code. It doesn't even amount to a divine prohibition or condemnation.

Moreover in a subsequent remark Lot urges the men not to touch the angels not so much because 'homosexual acts' are 'intrinsically disordered' but simply because they're his guests and he's looking out for them. It seems quite inappropriate therefore for the Church to use a story about an attempt to prevent possible sexual abuse to condemn consensual gay sex. After all if the angels had been female, the likely

---

[67]The *Catechism* declares that angels are 'non-corporeal beings . . . purely *spiritual* creatures' (328, 330). It is impossible to conceive how one might have 'intercourse' with a being that has no body.

moral to be drawn from the story would have been that it is rape that's wrong, not consensual sex between men and women.

And who is Lot anyway? Is he an exceptionally holy man or some figure of great moral authority whose wisdom we should unquestioningly respect? Actually in terms of morals Lot comes down to us today as not much higher than pondlife. So anxious is he to protect the two angels that he offers up his two virgin daughters to be gang-raped by the mob instead: 'let me bring them out to you', he pleads with the crowd 'and you can do what you like with them.' And if we read on we discover that soon after the promised fire and brimstone are rained down on the doomed city, in a drunken stupor Lot ends up having sex with his daughters himself.[68] Clearly this is not an authority for which we can have much respect, moral or otherwise.

Next we're directed to various comments made by the apostle Paul. The denunciation of homosexuality is made most fiercely in his letter to the Romans, in his venomous attack on the pagans where he speaks of 'degrading passions' arising from 'women [who] have turned from natural intercourse to unnatural practices' and of men 'doing shameless things with men.'[69] This, it would appear, seals the matter once and for all: the Christian god just doesn't like gays and doesn't approve of their base and unnatural passions. Well, not quite.

The problem is when Paul speaks about sexual matters he's usually expressing his own opinions rather than communicating divine fiats. So once again the authority that the *Catechism* cites to support its pronouncement has no divine status. We can tell that this is the case because in another, earlier letter (to the community in Corinth), when responding to questions about virginity and marriage, Paul explicitly points out that he has only one specific decree 'from the Lord', this being the prohibition of divorce. Any other regulations concerning sexual morality originate from his mind, as he openly admits: 'the rest is from me and not from the Lord.'[70]

It's not certain why the personal opinions of one man should be thought of as being the final authority concerning issues of sexual conduct nor why any of his views should be taken as being binding on

---

[68]Genesis 19:1-36.

[69]Romans 1:26, 27.

[70]1 Cor. 7:10, 12.

all humanity. Nor does there appear to be any reason even to consider these opinions as legitimate; no reasoning or arguments are presented by Paul to back them up and his views come across as being little more than expressions of a distasteful and almost neurotic loathing rather than the result of a carefully considered and enlightened moral stance.

Moreover many of Paul's opinions on other matters are not thought of as being necessarily valid or correct. The Church adopts a highly selective approach to Paul, taking on board those aspects of his teaching which suit its purposes and happily jettisoning those which are too extreme, even for Christianity.

Paul also recommended for instance that 'it is a good thing for a man not to touch a woman,' and hinted that marriage was not an expression of love and commitment but merely a means to provide a legitimate outlet for sexual frustration. He even recommended that if a woman refused to wear a veil when praying she 'ought to have her hair cut off.' [71] And at the end of his frenzied outburst against the pagans and their wicked and intolerable behaviour he concludes that they 'deserve to die.' Does the Church today proclaim that sinners and non-Christians deserve to die? Of course not. So if it can cast aside these unsavoury opinions and recommendations, why does it have to maintain his condemnation of homosexuality? One can't help feeling that the Catholic Church (all of whose officials have celibacy imposed on them) just doesn't like people *enjoying* sex for its own sake[72] and that sex between two men or two women is a thousand times more abhorrent than heterosexual sex within marriage. Needless to say the *Catechism* provides no further comment on the matter.

Moving on from gay sex we might next observe that the Church is opposed to 'discrimination on the grounds of sex'; any such discrimination it says 'must be curbed and eradicated.' Since the 'moral legitimacy of every authority' is based on the fundamental rights of the person, not to respect those rights or to discriminate against the individual on these or other grounds undermines that legitimacy. But

---

[71] 1 Cor. 7:1-2: 'it is a good thing for a man not to touch a woman; but since sex is always a danger, let each man have his own wife and each woman her own husband.' The remark about shaving off women's hair is made in the same letter (11:6).

[72] Perhaps at this point it's worth reflecting on a line from Blake's poem *The Marriage of Heaven and Hell*: 'Those who restrain desire do so because theirs is weak enough to be restrained'.

here too, once again we find contemporary Christianity to be like the Pharisees whom Jesus condemned, 'whitewashed tombs that look handsome on the outside' but in reality 'full of hypocrisy and lawlessness.'[73]

It's all very well for the Church make fine declarations and to preach at the rest of the world, but what is it doing to put its own house in order? Effectively the (Catholic) Church is a closed shop, a men's club which absolutely prohibits entry to women to positions of genuine authority.

Throughout its history every one of its 400 or so leaders - the popes - has been a man; all of its senior directors - the cardinals - are men and its entire middle management - the bishops - are also all men, as are all of its lesser officials, the priests. Women - in the Catholic Church at least - can't even aspire to this lowest level of Church officialdom, still less can they have any say or vote in the determination of its policy or the election of a new leader. Why?

The reality is the Church is simply too unwilling to give up its own 'discrimination on the grounds of sex.'[74] And once again there's no real or satisfactory attempt to provide an explanation or justification for this overt discrimination; the *Catechism* simply says that women can't be ordained as priests because they're not men. The reason for this? When Jesus chose his twelve apostles he chose men and in turn these men chose other men to succeed them. As a result 'the Church recognises herself to be bound by this choice made by the Lord himself. For this reason the ordination of women is not possible.'[75] It's not much of a reason for so great and offensive a prejudice - but then prejudices are usually founded not on reason but on some deeper emotional insecurity.

---

[73]Matthew 23:27-28.

[74]Canon Law even specifies that women shouldn't serve at the altar: Canon 813, para 2 stipulates 'The mass server should not be a woman, unless no man can be found and there is a good reason, and then on this understanding that the woman responds from a distance and does in no way approach the altar.' And Canon 1262, para 1 still declares that 'It is desirable that, in harmony with ancient Church order, the women in Church be separated from the men.' I am indebted to www.womenpriests.org for these observations.

[75]*Catechism*, 1577. We might observe that the twelve disciples chosen by Jesus were also all Jews: if we accept the 'logic' of the Church's selection procedure shouldn't all Christian clergy be Jews or at least of Jewish origin?

Still, the outlook is not entirely negative for female Christians who might wish to offer a life of service to the Lord. Such women can console themselves by becoming nuns if they want. Or if they find the celibate and contemplative life too unappealing and seek a greater degree of involvement in Church affairs, like the irrepressible Mrs Doyle they can always become housekeepers for priests.[76] Perhaps the Church thinks that in this capacity women can find the religious fulfilment they seek, spiritually content with the understanding that they also serve who cook and clean the church.

---

[76]The *Catechism* (371, 1605) affirms that the first woman was created from Adam's spare rib and was 'given to him (i.e. man) as a helpmate.' Paul decided that being created second meant that women should forever have a secondary status: 'I am not giving permission for a woman to teach or to tell a man what to do. A woman ought not to speak, because Adam was formed first and Eve afterwards.' He then observes that it was Eve who fell into sin but concludes that it's not all doom and gloom for women for 'she will be saved by childbearing, provided she lives a modest life.' (1 Tim 2:12-15).

10

War

When I look back upon my life
It's always with a sense of shame
I've always been the one to blame
For everything I long to do
No matter when or where or who
Has one thing in common too
It's a sin.[1]

In George Orwell's *1984* the whole drama of Winston Smith's life
- his work at the Ministry of Truth, his affair with Julia, his hatred of
the Party and his brief rebellion against it - is played out with the
menace and the horror of a vague but ever-present war in the
background. Winston can scarcely remember a time when there was
no war; yet despite its being part of his daily life, he has little
understanding about why it is being waged. But his ignorance soon
changes once he believes he has made contact with the rebellious
Brotherhood, a shadowy and elusive movement committed to bringing
down the Party and opposing its entire ideology. 'To understand the
nature of the present war', he reads in Goldstein's forbidden book, *The
Theory and Practice of Oligarchical Collectivism*, 'one must realise in the
first place that it is impossible for it to be decisive.'

Appalled, Winston reads on to learn some of the central truths
about the incessant conflict that Oceania is waging variously but
continuously against Eurasia or Eastasia. The essential and most
depressing fact about the war, as he discovers, is not so much that there
is no possibility of it ever ending, but that the Party's real war aim is
simply to perpetuate the conflict, as meaningless and as futile as it is.

---

[1]Pet Shop Boys, *It's a Sin.*

According to Goldstein the three superstates know and accept that the war is unwinable, that they can never conquer one of their opponents; they even understand that there would be no advantage to them to do so. Yet despite this, a blind fanaticism drives the Party's prosecution of the war: 'no inner Party member wavers for an instant in his mystical belief that the war *is* real, and that it is bound to end victoriously, with Oceania the undisputed master of the entire world.' And just as Christians believe wholeheartedly in Jesus' glorious second coming, so 'all members of the inner Party believe in this coming conquest as an article of faith.'

Far removed from the horror of Orwell's nightmare world, the whole scenario comes across to us as both criminal and absurd, without any apparent humanity or rationality behind it. Orwell may well have been responding to the advent of the Cold War following on almost immediately from the Second World War in which the former ally is transformed almost overnight into the new evil enemy. But a darker insight of Orwell's vision was that extreme ideologies have a positive interest in maintaining a state of war and enhance themselves or even survive by this method.

The twisted logic of the Party is most fully articulated in *the book* (which, of course, turns out to have been written by the Party itself), but it's an obvious strategy apparent to any half astute observer. Winston's lover, Julia for example, although almost indifferent to the Party's intrigues, possesses this insight even before she has read a page of the outlawed book. The war she casually remarks to Winston is something that originates from the Party which probably fires rocket bombs on its own cities 'just to keep people frightened.' And similarly tales about Goldstein and the mysterious Brotherhood 'were simply a lot of rubbish which the Party had invented for its own purposes' and which one had to pretend to believe in.[2]

The set up in the Christian ideology is remarkably similar. Christianity of course has had its own bloodthirsty wars throughout much of its history and has been responsible for the suffering and deaths of millions, perhaps even tens of millions of people. But its real war is a spiritual one, one that has been waged over its entire history and will continue so long as Christianity exists. This war is its war

---

[2]Orwell, *op cit,* pp 164, 169, 135.

against sin. For hundreds of years the Church has used sin - or more precisely the consequences of committing sins - as one of the most effective means of social control ever known, thereby maintaining throughout most of its history the wealth, authority and privilege of a powerful elite. And in our own times, while the Church no longer has any real or absolute political power, it continues to use sin as a means to govern the thoughts and minds of millions of people and dictate how they should live their lives (consider the Church's peremptory teachings on issues of personal morality such as sex, contraception and divorce for example).

It's not difficult to understand how those faithful to the Church have in fact become its victims and Julia's suspicions about the Party's manipulations can just as easily be levelled against Christianity. Doctrines about hell and the fiery punishments that await the damned for their sins serve merely 'to keep people frightened' and frightened people of course can be more easily controlled.[3]

Likewise old wives tales and official teachings about Satan suit Christianity's purposes very well, providing a bogey-man figure whom one can legitimately hate and whose existence as a common and reviled and still dangerous enemy increases loyalty to the god. It is little wonder then that the struggle against sin should be forever perpetuated and that it is conceived of as a struggle that can never be resolved until some impossible point in the future, at the end of time when, according to the Church's rapturous and somewhat over-excited proclamation, 'The kingdom will be fulfilled . . . by God's victory over the final unleashing of evil, which will cause his Bride to come down from heaven.'[4]

The Adversary

The war begins with and focuses around a mythical enemy. In *1984* Ingsoc is obsessed with its 'enemy of the people', Goldstein.

---

[3] The *Catechism* declares 'anyone who fears God . . . has been acceptable to him' (781); contrition for one's sins (i.e. a willingness to conform to the rules) is born of 'the fear of eternal damnation and the other penalties threatening the sinner' (1453); and fear of the Lord is considered to be one of the seven 'gifts' of the Holy Spirit which help to 'make the faithful docile in readily obeying' (1831).

[4] *Catechism*, 677.

Goldstein's history is that of a one-time leading member of the Party, 'almost on a level with Big Brother himself'; but having engaged in 'counter-revolutionary activities' his fall from grace was as swift as it was complete, earning him the Party's total condemnation. Somehow managing to escape death, he continued, or was allowed to continue his subversive activities and acquired the notoriety of being 'the primal traitor, the earliest defiler of the Party's purity.' Reconciliation and dialogue with this personification of evil are impossible. Whatever he does only adds to his error and compounds his criminality, so much so that 'all subsequent crimes against the Party, all treacheries, acts of sabotage, heresies, deviations' are understood and accepted as originating with his teaching and initial act of rebellion.

Over the years the fear and loathing of this enemy have been carefully cultivated by the Party to such rabid proportions that its regular public assemblies, the 'Two Minutes Hate' lead readily to mass hysteria, calmed only by the soothing image of Big Brother. Just how absurd and irrational the whole set up is can be seen in the fact that Goldstein's message seems to be an eminently reasonable and fair one, calling only for an end to the war and for the freedom of the individual. But years of relentless indoctrination means that the demonising forces of the Party have turned a man of apparent common sense into a monster, always to be feared and despised.

While Christianity doesn't have, at the present time at least, such venomous rituals, the on-going hatred for its own foe, the 'enemy of the entire human race' is no less insidious. The enemy of the Christian ideology, Satan, whose name simply means *the adversary*, has a history that is almost identical. Like Goldstein he was once one of the brightest and most favoured ministers, but having rebelled out of pride he 'radically and irrevocably rejected God and his reign.'[5] However, instead of actually defeating the rebellious crew or seeking a rapprochement, the Christian god inexplicably allowed Satan to continue with his supposedly evil designs. Acting out of malice and spite (so we are told), Satan engineers the fall of humanity by tempting the first humans to disobey the god's sole command.

As a result the world is plunged into everlasting war against the forces of evil, a war that, so far as the Church is concerned, dominates

---

[5] *Ibid*, 392.

the whole of human history. Using militaristic imagery, it insists with a touch of melodrama that the 'dramatic situation of the whole world which is in the power of the evil one makes man's life a battle'; and with the whole world turned into a giant battlefield, 'the whole of man's history has been the story of dour combat with the powers of evil stretching . . . from the very dawn of history until the last day.'

Indeed so consumed is the Church with this conflict and so aroused and carried away is it with the thought of victory that once again the language of the *Catechism* descends into histrionics: 'Victory over the prince of this world was won once for all at the Hour when Jesus freely gave himself up to death . . . the prince of this world is cast out. He pursued the woman but had no hold on her; the new Eve, full of grace of the Holy Spirit, is preserved from sin and the corruption of death . . . Then the dragon was angry with the woman, and went off to make war on the rest of her offspring.'[6]

Satan's chief weapon in this war is sin and sin necessarily dominates Christianity. Christians are taught to accept Jesus as the saviour of the world and for most believers salvation is the whole point of the Christian religion. But if this is a valid teaching, it must be the case, as I've already pointed out, that Jesus saves people *from something*. This something of course is hell and earlier we saw how obsessed Christianity is with punishment. But one wonders, why do we have to be threatened with damnation in the first place?

The real answer is that without the threat of punishment, Christianity becomes pointless. For if we don't need to be saved from hell, or from our sins which may lead us there, we have no need for Jesus as a saviour, and the claim that he is *the saviour* of mankind becomes more or less unintelligible. Salvation depends on there being a hell (or some other form of punishment) from which we are saved and hell, in turn, depends on there being sins for which we must and will be punished if we fail to repent. And if Jesus isn't a saviour and if his death and (supposed) resurrection have no redeeming consequences or saving qualities, ultimately all this stuff about being sacrificed on a cross becomes redundant and meaningless, just so much empty rhetoric.

Effectively therefore the whole of the Christian religion depends on sin for its very existence; and so we have the unhappy situation that

---

[6] *Ibid,* 409, 2853.

the Church has a vested interest in perpetuating the belief in the sinfulness - or rottenness - of humanity. Amazingly enough, this is something that it seems willing to concede: 'The Church . . . knows very well that we cannot tamper with the revelation of original sin without undermining the mystery of Christ.'[7] Lose the churchy language and what this seems to be saying is that if the doctrine about mankind's innate sinfulness is modified or abandoned, the very purpose of Jesus' life and death are called into question; in other words, without sin the validity and essential purpose of the Christian religion simply vanish into thin air.

The mission of the Church is a universal one and Jesus is preached as having died and risen to save all mankind. Since all mankind needs to be saved, all mankind has to be sinful. Even if one leads an exemplary life, following the example and teachings of Jesus to the letter, one is still considered by the Church to be sinful. To suppose otherwise would mean that Jesus' death wasn't necessary to save that person, that such a person could escape punishment and get into heaven without having to rely on his sacrifice. This is a situation that the Church necessarily finds intolerable. As *The New Catholic Encyclopedia* duly notes 'the Church reacted by seeing in the assertion of man's autonomy in self-determination, both for good and evil, a direct challenge to the saviourship of Jesus Christ.'[8]

This reaction of the Church was made in response to the 5th century heresy known as Pelagianism (which is considered below) and resulted in the formulation and official acceptance of the doctrine of original sin.

Original sin is one of Christianity's most austere, pessimistic doctrines, teaching that every member of the human race has been conceived in and born in sin. What this means is that from the moment of our conception, even before we've come into the world, our nature is inherently flawed. Essentially we are born bad and the only way we can rid ourselves of this blight, to make good our deficiency is to be baptised, to become Christians and to submit to the Church's teaching and authority.

Many people have great difficulty in accepting a belief so severe

---

[7] *Ibid*, 389.

[8] *The New Catholic Encyclopedia*, Vol X, p 779.

and negative as this. Many find the whole doctrine incomprehensible and without foundation. So much of this chapter will be to assess whether or not the doctrine of original sin can be considered to be true in any way and to observe how it was that Christianity got to so bleak and depressing a position in the first place.

What Is Sin ?

A sin is often thought of as some moral transgression. If Jesus came to save people from their sins and hell was the place of punishment for sinners, it would seem that to sin is to do something wicked or wrong which, without proper repentance, is deserving of punishment. The reality however is that sins don't actually have that much to do with morality as we generally understand the term. A sin is primarily an act of disobedience to the laws of the Christian god.

So when Yahweh commanded Abraham to sacrifice his son to him, it would have been a sin for Abraham to have protested and refused outright to kill Isaac; yet bizarrely by obeying Yahweh, he did not sin, even though his obedience consisted of a willingness to murder a child. Indeed, it was this unquestioning trust and obedience that earned him Yahweh's favour concerning the promised land; far from sinning, Abraham became celebrated as a model of faith. So just as faith is ultimately a matter of obedience, so sin, in the final analysis is nothing other than disobedience.

In trying to convey the significance of this, the Church's teaching today, like the disturbing story of Abraham, comes across as equally deranged to the enlightened sensibility: 'Sin is an offence against God: "Against you, you alone have I sinned, and done that which is evil in your sight" . . . Like the first sin, it is disobedience, a revolt against God through the will to become like gods . . . In this proud self-exaltation, sin is diametrically opposed to the obedience of Jesus, which achieves our salvation.'[9]

It's hard to read this without laughing at, or at least being struck by its pomposity and absurdity, especially when we consider what types of behaviour or attitude fall within the scope of sin. 'There are a great many kinds of sins' the *Catechism* continues, helpfully providing us

---

[9] *Catechism*, 1850.

with some of the juiciest examples: fornication (of course), that is any sex outside marriage, is the first in its unholy list, followed by impurity, anger, selfishness, dissension, drunkenness, and carousing. All of these are considered to be sinful activities or attitudes.[10]

It seems then that in the eyes of the Church, being angry (a natural and important human emotion, one which even Jesus himself exhibited), considering one's personal interests before those of other people (which everyone does on a regular basis), having an argument, presumably with your priest, but – given Paul's authoritarian streak – quite possibly with any authority, such as the government or the police, getting oneself seriously or mildly inebriated or having a one night stand are all acts of rebellion and, quite bizarrely, are tantamount to trying to become like a god. For this reason such conduct has to be punished if proper repentance isn't offered.

Christianity's obsession with sin can be seen in the number of different ways sins can be categorised: there are mortal sins and venial sins (which can be either grave or not grave in nature), capital sins (the new, more user-friendly name for the seven deadly sins), personal or social sins and even sins that cry to heaven (such as 'the sin of the Sodomites'). Furthermore sins can also be distinguished according to the virtues they oppose, by excess or defect; they can be classed 'according to whether they concern God, neighbour or oneself' and then can be further subdivided into 'spiritual and carnal sins, or again as sins in thought, word, deed or omission.'[11]

Phew! This seems to be pretty much a 'catch all' categorisation and it seems as if almost anything, except loving and obeying the gods (all three of them) and singing hymns could, in some way or other, be construed as a sin. With such a plethora of different types of sins, one

---

[10] *Ibid*, 1852. The list of sins is from Paul's letter to the Galatians. Paul warned this community that those who committed such sins wouldn't 'inherit the Kingdom of God'.

[11] *Ibid*, 1852-1867. Mortal sin is a grave violation of the god's law, deliberately and knowingly committed and which turns man away from the god. Venial sin only offends and wounds the charity of the heart and is not opposed to love of the god or love of one's neighbour. The *Catechism* then gives some examples of venial sin – 'thoughtless chatter or immoderate laughter and the like' (1856) and confirms that 'it merits temporal punishment' (1863). Excessive laughter, according to the *Catechism,* therefore deserves to be punished by earthly authorities. Grave matter is specified by the 10 commandments. Capital or deadly sins (pride, avarice, envy, wrath, lust, gluttony and sloth) are so called because they 'engender other sins, other vices.'

cannot envy the task of Jesus who apparently will have sole responsibility on the Day of Judgement for assessing the individual sins (presumably according to the types outlined above) and degrees of repentance of the thousands of millions of people who *ever* existed. That's a lot of judging. Perhaps on that final day, he will be assisted by the unknown and possibly limitless number of angels, 'servants and messengers of God'[12] who, in a Kafkaesque-like bureaucracy might already be preparing and submitting our cases for that final verdict? Or perhaps, being omniscient, Jesus already knows all the answers?

So where did all this start and how did Christianity develop such a negative and unhealthy obsession? To discover the source of sin we need to go back to the very beginning of all things, to the book of Genesis and its story of Adam and Eve. Here we find the first fault (it is never actually called a sin, the word *sin* is first used in the story of Cain and Abel) clearly presented as an act of disobedience but one which also has no ethical consequences. Once this occurred, the floodgates are opened and the rest of human history, so far as the Church sees it, is inundated by sin. Soon after the initial transgression, Genesis records the first murder (Cain kills his brother Abel) after which there is a general and continual propensity to evil. As we've already seen, by the time we get to Noah, living ten generations after Adam, the world is so sinful and so loathsome to Yahweh Elohim, the Lord God that it decides that it has simply had enough of the wickedness of mankind and decides to drown everyone except Noah and his family.

Much later, when we get to the age of Jesus, the universality of sin is once again almost overwhelming. This readiness to see sin everywhere and in everything may in part have been due to Israel's tendency to regard certain historical processes as a consequence of the extent of sin, with the Roman occupation, like the Babylonian captivity some six centuries previously, being seen as a divine punishment for the sinfulness of the nation. Yahweh was, after all, first and foremost a territorial god who would reward his chosen people with the promised land so long as they kept to their side of the deal and obeyed his law. If obedience brought the possibility of fulfilment

---

[12] *Ibid* 329. Angels really exist as personal, non-corporeal and immortal creatures (328, 330). Apparently there are four orders of angels - Thrones, Dominions, Principalities and Authorities, all of whom 'belong' to Jesus (331). At the last judgement 'Christ will come in glory, and all the angels with him' (1038).

of that promise, then disobedience might just as easily bring set backs or even catastrophe.

Whether or not this influenced Jesus' own sentiments we do not know, but he seems to have been especially conscious of sin and, according to the gospels, was continually engaged in a cosmic struggle against Satan and other, lesser devils. He speaks of his generation as 'adulterous and sinful' (in fact throughout the gospels there's only one reported case of adultery,[13] so based on the evidence available, one can't help thinking that Jesus was being a little over-zealous in his condemnation) and the very first words we hear him say in the earliest gospel urge the crowds to address this drastic situation: '"The time has come" he said "and the kingdom of God is close at hand. Repent. . ."'

This is a theme he returns to over and over again throughout the gospels either in parables such as that of the prodigal son or the barren fig tree, or sometimes in more explicit terms. Sin, he believes has reached epidemic proportions and the whole of Israel is infected: 'It is not those who are well who need the doctor, but the sick. I have not come to call the virtuous, but sinners to repentance.'[14] If Jesus came to call the sick and if, as the Church insists, the whole of humanity has need of Jesus to be saved, it would seem that Christianity necessarily regards all mankind as sick, a point that Nietzsche was to reflect upon with the full measure of his contempt: 'Christianity', he wrote in *The Anti-Christ* 'needs sickness . . . making sick is the true hidden objective of the Church's whole system of salvation . . . one is not "converted" to Christianity - one must be sufficiently sick for it . . .'[15]

If there was an epidemic of sin in Jesus' time, shortly after his death his most vocal and forceful supporter, Paul saw that it had become a fatal contagion. Paul's sense of sin, if anything, was even more morbid: 'the wages of sin is death' is now the downbeat message not just for the Jews but for the whole of mankind. This pessimism seems to have derived very much from his own experience and inner spiritual turmoil, for Paul appears from his letters to have had an overwhelming and lugubrious obsession with sin. He often refers to 'sin' in the

---

[13]John 8:3-11. If it was the case that Jesus was illegitimate, as previously discussed, his sensitivity to adultery becomes understandable.

[14]Mark 1:15, Luke 5:31-32.

[15]Nietzsche, *op cit*, 51.

singular (this contrasts with the gospels where Jesus tends to talk about either a 'sin' in particular or 'sins' in general - that is as individual and identifiable transgressions) suggesting that it is like some sort of metaphysical force, an ugly, black spectre that is forever hounding and haunting him rather than a specific breach of the Law. In fact sin for Paul, prior to his Damascus trip, comes across almost as something of an alien being living within him, paralysing every aspect of his life: 'I am a slave to sin', he laments in a personal and revealing confession, 'I fail to carry out the things I want to do, and I find myself doing the very things I hate . . . the thing behaving in that way is not my self but sin living in me'. And inevitably such a mortifying sense of failure leads him only to a guilt-ridden despair and self-loathing: 'The fact is, I know of nothing good living in me . . . What a wretched man I am!'[16]

Original Sin

Paul's personal experience was that he had somehow been released from his enormous burden of guilt and misery by faith in the resurrection of Jesus; and after this dramatic revelation, preaching 'Christ crucified' became the over-riding purpose of his entire missionary career. But such an intense mystical feeling, an experience so powerful that it changed his life, was not something that could be easily conveyed to others. Indeed those who to Paul's mind should have responded most readily to this teaching of an unmerited gift from Yahweh, the Jews, resisted the notion that Jesus was the instrument of a new covenant which would free them from the onerous burdens of the Law and save them from their sins.

Ultimately all of Paul's evangelising work can be seen as an extended attempt to formulate a theological justification for his own highly idiosyncratic religious convictions and to persuade others to understand and follow his inner spiritual experience. It was in his letter to the Romans, written around the year 57 that Paul articulated his most extensive and developed theology to argue his case and explain how redemption or salvation might be gained by faith in Jesus' resurrection. In part he found his explanation in the story of Adam: by using an analogy, in which Jesus became a reversed 'type' of Adam, he

---

[16]Romans 6:23, 7:15-24.

offered an argument to 'prove' how the resurrection provided mankind with the undeserved gift of redemption. For just as sin and therefore death came into the world through one man, Adam, so through one man, Jesus, the new Adam, sin and death had been conquered.

Since 'the wages of sin is death' our universal mortality proves that everyone is sinful; but just as we all share in the fault and punishment of Adam, so we can all share the possibility of eternal life in Christ by faith. While the intention behind this was to try to provide a theological basis to persuade Jews and Gentiles alike to share in his unshakeable conviction about the redeeming nature of Jesus' death and resurrection, the disastrous effect of this analogy was also to dump on humanity the basis of the doctrine of original sin like some filthy, toxic by-product. For his rhetoric only 'works' if the 'one man' thesis and antithesis are maintained; and in his eagerness to drive home the overwhelming goodness and merit of one man's obedient sacrifice, he brought into relief the notion that the sinfulness of humanity originated with one man and one man alone: 'as one man's fall brought condemnation on everyone, so the good act of one man brings everyone life and makes them justified. As by one man's disobedience many were made sinners, so by one man's obedience many will be made righteous'.[17]

This theme has passed down virtually unchanged to the Church's teaching today. Unfortunately it is taken at face value and is espoused no less harshly: 'the Church has always taught that the overwhelming misery which oppresses men and their inclination towards evil and death cannot be understood apart from their connection with Adam's sin and the fact that he has transmitted to us a sin with which we are all born afflicted'[18] is the present day teaching on original sin. So a personal transgression of a distant and uncertain ancestor, an act of disobedience of 'our first parents' has somehow affected the whole of human nature and is passed down as 'a fallen state' to each and every one of us. From the Christian point of view then, from the moment of our conception we are all marked by a universal guilt.

Traditionally the Church calls this condition 'concupiscence', an

---

[17]Romans 5:18-19.

[18]*Catechism*, 403.

ever present contamination, active in every one of us. Essentially concupiscence is 'any intense form of human desire' that inclines us to take greater pleasure and delight in the things of this world rather than in the Christian god, a willingness to respond to what we desire rather than to what the god wills.[19] Even newly born infants are subject to this blight, despite being entirely incapable of having either an inclination to evil or any possible awareness of a god. So for Christians today, the worst of Paul's pessimism has been retained and further distilled to produce an even more noxious and deplorable doctrine: sin is not merely a fatal contagion, it is now part of our genetic inheritance.

To a certain extent this defilement can be washed away by the cleansing properties of Christian baptism; unfortunately baptism doesn't have the qualities of today's biological washing powders and is unable to eradicate the stain completely for 'the consequences for nature, weakened and inclined to evil, persist' and 'certain temporal consequences for sin remain . . . such as suffering, illness, death'.[20] Broadly speaking, this is the Christian explanation for all pain, suffering and evil in the world: if we experience illness or suffering in life, it's part of the Christian god's punishment.

While Paul may have inadvertently sketched the broad outline of this horrible doctrine, it wasn't until the 5th century that it was more fully formulated in the work of that other great doctor of the Church, Augustine. Augustine was a north African bishop of immense learning and influence and the author of many theological works, the best known of which is his *Confessions*. By the time he died in 430 CE he was considered to be a figure of enormous stature by the Church and after Paul he is often acknowledged to be its greatest and most

---

[19] *The New Catholic Encyclopedia* explains concupiscence as a form of selfishness which prevents one from leading a truly human life. To overcome this selfishness 'requires at times a recognition and acceptance of the fact that sacrifice of personal convenience and preference is required for the glory of God'. In the same article it also declares that 'without Christ . . . [one] is incapable of living an entire life worthy of a human being' (Vol X, p 780). Non-Christians, in other words, are thought of as unworthy or even sub-human.

[20] *Catechism*, 2515, 1264. In presenting its teaching about concupiscence, once again the *Catechism* descends into meaningless gobbledygook: 'since concupiscence "is left for us to wrestle with, it cannot harm those who do not consent but manfully resist it by the grace of Jesus Christ". Indeed, "an athlete is not crowned unless he competes according to the rules."'

influential theologian. 'Anyone who wants to understand the Catholic Church', says the contemporary Catholic theologian, Hans Kung, 'has to understand Augustine.'[21]

Like Paul, Augustine underwent a deeply traumatic conversion, an experience which today we might be more inclined to regard as something approaching a nervous breakdown. His own words recounting the event in *Confessions* certainly suggest so: 'I tore my hair and hammered my forehead with my fists; I locked my fingers and hugged my knees . . . a great storm broke within me, bringing with it a great deluge of tears . . . I gave way to the tears which now streamed from my eyes.' And according to one of his modern biographers, in the period leading up to this dramatic event 'it is more than probable that . . . Augustine had come to develop the physical manifestations of a nervous breakdown.'[22]

Augustine also felt himself to be enslaved by sin as did Paul, although in Augustine's case it was specifically manifested in what he felt to be his uncontrollable sexual desire. Against such an irrepressible urge, Augustine found the human will to be powerless and so sin, or more precisely, the inclination to sin became for him not so much a weakness in personal conduct or morality but an irresistible impulse, a defect of the will. We've seen how Paul used his own experience, his inner trauma and his recovery from it to provide him with a basis to argue that Jesus' death and resurrection provided a gateway to salvation for all; effectively he made his own personal problem, his obsession with sin, a universal one.

Similarly Augustine believed that his problem, his over-powering sex drive, what he was to call a 'diabolical excitement of the genitals'[23] and his inability to deal with it, was a condition that afflicted the whole of mankind. Brought up in an age in which abstinence was the ideal, rather than accept any personal responsibility or sense of weakness, he argued that this defect was something inherited, a consequence of Adam's initial disobedience. According to Augustine when Adam sinned, divine justice ensured that the punishment for his sin was

---

[21]Kung, *op cit*, p 53.

[22]Brown, *Augustine of Hippo* , p 102. Augustine's own recollection of his conversion is detailed in his *Confessions*, VIII vii, quoted in Brown, p 99.

[23]I owe this reference to Pagels, *Adam, Eve and the Serpent*, p 140.

entirely fitting to the offence. In his first sin Adam 'conceived a desire for freedom' and so for this one transgression his fate was to be subject to 'a life of cruel and wretched slavery'.[24] Hence for his disobedience he was to be forever punished by the disobedience of the mind and the body to his will.

This disobedience or lust exhibits itself in many forms, but for Augustine it was most apparent in the uncontrollable nature of sexual desire for 'it convulses all of a man when the emotion in his mind combines and mingles with the carnal drive to produce a pleasure unsurpassed . . . at the very moment of its climax there is almost total eclipse of acumen and, as it were sentinel alertness.'[25] So an instinctive and necessary biological drive and the unsurpassed pleasure it gives now become, as a consequence of one man's neuroses, morally reprehensible, a manifestation of our innate sinfulness.

The proof of all this, Augustine believed, was to be found in the shame that men and women feel for their sexual parts. It is reasonable, he asserted that we should feel ashamed of lust (because it was the punishment justly imposed for Adam's disobedience) and since the sexual organs are the most visible indicators of lust and are not themselves subject to the control of the will, these too are considered shameful. So when Adam and Eve understood that they had sinned, their first impulse was to cover themselves so as to hide their embarrassment.

Now just as the other punishments meted out for the first sin are passed by Adam to his posterity, so this defect of the will, or what Augustine calls 'our congenital conflict' is transmitted to the entire human race. Today the Church maintains that 'the transmission of original sin is a mystery that we cannot fully understand'[26] but for Augustine there was no such mystery and the blight is passed from parent to child like some sort of sexually transmitted disease through the semen of one's father: 'Man . . . engendered corrupt and condemned offspring. For we were all in that one man . . . we did not have yet individually created and apportioned shapes in which to live

---

[24]Augustine, *City of God,* XIV, xv. Few people today, other than despotic dictators, would go along with Augustine's notion that 'a desire for freedom' should be punished by a life of slavery.

[25]*Ibid,* XIV, xvi.

[26]*Catechism,* 404.

as individuals; what already existed was the seminal substance from which we were to be generated.'[27] Since we are all conceived as a consequence of sexual desire and since that desire is both sinful and a punishment for sin, it follows that for Augustine we are all conceived in sin and are born as a result of sin.[28] Today it would be far too offensive for the Church to maintain that original sin is transmitted from parent to child like HIV or some other venereal disease and so this aspect of Augustine's teaching seems to have been quietly dropped.[29] But the substance of the doctrine remains and original sin continues to afflict us all.

The Pelagian Controversy

Augustine's views came to dominate Christian thinking and within a hundred years of his death his teaching on original sin was formally adopted by the Church as part of the faith. But why was it that the Church took this particular course? Was this the Holy Spirit at work again, revealing sacred mysteries? Or was this doctrine of more human origin, the consequences of Augustine's sexual aversion, and one which just happened to suit the Church's purposes at that time? Certainly Augustine's psychological turmoil had much to do with it but the explanation also lies in historical circumstances. For just as the debate over the status and divinity of Jesus was escalated and eventually settled as a consequence of the Arian controversy, so the prominence given to Augustine's teaching in this matter seems to have come about to a large extent as a result of another dispute, known as the Pelagian controversy.

Pelagius was a Briton who was vehemently opposed to this aspect of Augustine's teachings. Not much is known about his background,

---

[27]Augustine, *op cit*, XIII, xiv.

[28]Jesus, of course was the noble exception since the virginity of Mary meant that there was no human semen involved in his conception and no sexual act to contaminate his being. As we've already noted, much later by the dogma of the Immaculate Conception Mary was also proclaimed free from original sin.

[29]However, in the papal encyclical *Humani Generis*, released by Pius XII in 1950 it was affirmed that 'original sin . . . proceeds from a sin actually committed by an individual Adam and which, *through generation*, is passed on to all' (my italics). Generation is the Church's preferred word for sex. It would appear that the Church is too embarrassed today to state openly that original sin is transmitted sexually.

but he seems to have been an ascetic or possibly a monk whose main concern was with the conduct and ethical behaviour of his fellow men and women. Having arrived in Rome around the year 380, he became distinguished as a practical moral reformer, impressing on his followers the need to return to the virtuous life appropriate for a true Christian. Both he and his close followers preached their case forcefully and with some success, attracting large numbers of supporters, many of whom were educated and influential people.

In his understanding of sin and of the biblical story of Adam and Eve, Pelagius was much more down to earth and closer to the modern consciousness than Augustine.[30] He taught that people were not helplessly enslaved to sin, as Augustine maintained, but were completely free either to be obedient or to sin. Man didn't have the luxury of such an excuse and was personally responsible for all of his transgressions. How else could a sin be a sin if it didn't involve the absolutely free choice of the individual? Consequently each person was more reliant on his or her own free will to achieve salvation than on divine grace. Sins had to be understood as voluntary imitations of Adam's bad example rather than as the consequences of an inherent and irresistible predisposition to sin. As such, these imitations of a bad example could be made good by imitating Jesus in his obedience and moral purity.

So while baptism had the power to wash away sins, it wasn't needed to eradicate some original stain, for human nature wasn't flawed in the first place by any such transmitted sin or hereditary guilt. Death therefore could not be regarded as a punishment for sin but was simply part of the natural order of things. Ultimately Augustine's view was very much more pessimistic, seeing humanity as helpless and wholly dependant on grace (so leading inevitably to a doctrine of arbitrary predestination - grace might be given to some, but it might just as easily be withheld from others). Pelagius, on the other hand, believed that mankind was created good and could still achieve that original state of perfection through its own merit.

---

[30]Pelagius' emphasis on choice and personal responsibility is similar to the thought and values of 20th century existentialism. See for example Sartre's essay *Existentialism and Humanism* (pp 28-29): 'Man is nothing else but that which he makes of himself. That is the first principle of existentialism . . . [it] places the entire responsibility for his existence squarely upon his own shoulders'.

Pelagius' views attracted attention but were declared to be orthodox by an Eastern synod in 415. The African bishops however, headed by Augustine who seemed to be acting like some early inquisitor, were incensed and distrusted the verdict. Determined to have Pelagius' teachings condemned, they appealed to a higher authority, to the Pope, Innocent.

Initially Innocent agreed with them and excommunicated Pelagius in the following year. Pelagius was given the opportunity to appeal but before his response by letter arrived at Rome, Innocent died. His successor, Zosimus took the opposite point of view and at first sided with Pelagius, reversing the earlier decision, unable to find fault with him. But after riots in Rome supposedly caused by his supporters, he and his followers were banished from the city by an Imperial edict and the Pope's stance was severely compromised. Augustine and his supporters seized their moment and courted the Imperial authorities, urging them to apply pressure on the Pope. Knowing how to achieve political influence, their case was undoubtedly assisted by a bribe of 80 of the finest African stallions to the Imperial court.[31] Eventually Zosimus caved in to the pressure exerted and declared Pelagius' views to be heretical.

Emerging as the champion of one of the major controversies of the day, Augustine became acclaimed as a leading Church figure whose views, no matter how contrary to existing traditions, became immensely influential in the development of mainstream Christianity. And if Pelagius' opinions were now heretical, the effect in due course was to make their opposite, Augustine's teachings on the necessity of grace and the hereditary nature of original sin, orthodox doctrines. But aside from the clever lobbying and political pressure, why did the Church hierarchy come to favour Augustine's stance over that of Pelagius?

In part the forces ranged against Pelagius were too powerful and he was effectively shot down by the big guns of Christianity. For as well as Augustine, the other heavyweight of the age, Jerome was also obsessed with discrediting Pelagius' teaching, perhaps because in this instance the two were old and bitter adversaries whose differences went back some two decades. In seeking to have Pelagius declared a

---

[31]Brown, *op cit*, p 364.

heretic, it seems that Jerome was as much interested in settling old scores as he was in defining true Christian teaching. Against two of the most forceful personalities of the established Church of the time, a troublesome outsider such as Pelagius stood little chance.

Moreover in his criticism of the lax moral standards in Rome, he saw the Church itself as culpable for doing little to remedy the situation and can hardly have been an endearing figure to its leaders and authorities. But more fundamentally his teaching did not fit in with the increasingly authoritarian nature of the Church. Christianity had once been an illegal and persecuted sect but by now, a century after Constantine's union of Church and state, it was part of the very machinery of the Empire and was becoming increasingly repressive. One of the more drastic and unpalatable consequences of that union was the fact that by the late 4th century heresy, choosing to believe teachings contrary to the official party line, had become not only a sin against faith but also an offence against the state.

Furthermore, if it was understood that man was inclined to sin by his very nature and was helpless to prevent himself from doing so, as Augustine insisted, his only recourse was to depend on divine grace and to submit himself entirely to the Father-god's mercy. And since the Church was the institution supposedly founded by Jesus and which therefore represented the divine will at work on earth, that mercy (and power) could be arrogated by the Church. Hence the control and authority of the Church itself could be (and was) vastly enhanced by officially embracing such an understanding. Indeed, when Augustine petitioned the Pope against Pelagius, his letters specifically pointed out that appeasement of Pelagius' views would severely undermine the authority of the bishops and of the Church.[32]

Events outside the Church also played their part. The Empire was on its last legs and in the West at least, was unable to sustain or defend itself. In 410 the spiritual home of Christianity, Rome the eternal and supposedly impregnable city, fell to Alaric the Visigoth and was sacked by his marauding armies. In such a climate internal unity, long regarded by many, especially Augustine, as fundamental to the well-being of the Church, became its overriding concern. Talk that espoused man's freewill as superior to the mediation and discipline of

---

[32] *Ibid*, p 359.

the Church and which suggested that its intervention might not be necessary for salvation now came to be seen as potentially dangerous and would have to be rooted out, if necessary by force.

Pelagius in fact was fortunate. Far away from Rome when the controversy was at its height, he survived the heavy hand of the papacy and lived out his days in Egypt having been banished previously from Palestine. An earlier ascetic campaigner, Priscillian who preached similar moral reform in Spain was not so lucky; declared to be a heretic, he became the first Christian to be tried and then executed by the state in 386 for holding opinions in the faith which his fellow Christians judged to be incorrect and intolerable. As Hans Kung points out, 'in less than a century the persecuted church had become a persecuting church.'[33]

All This Fuss Over A Mere Apple . . .

Naturally anyone considering the doctrine of original sin will understand that it is based on certain assumptions which can only be seen as wildly implausible or highly problematic. Let's consider the main issues to see whether the idea of a hereditary original sin is well supported. First of all Augustine's understanding was based on Paul's teaching that all sin came into the world from one man; and this in turn was based on Paul's interpretation of the biblical story of the fall recounted in the third chapter of the book of Genesis. Ultimately then the very concept of original sin depends on whether or not the narrative of the fall in Genesis can be deemed a reliable history or a valid source of some other form of truth concerning the human condition.

The story is known well enough and is one with which most of us are vaguely familiar. According to Genesis, at the very beginning of time when there was nothing but darkness and an empty void, the earth and all its life forms were created by the apparently limitless will of a supreme creator, 'the Lord God'. The god's work culminates on the sixth day with the creation of Adam, the first man, who is instructed to be fruitful and increase his kind, to rule over 'every living thing that moves upon the earth.' Less well known is the fact that there

---

[33]Kung, *op cit*, p 45.

are actually two different versions of the creation of humanity in this book; in the better known version, Eve is created some time after Adam in response to his sense of loneliness and is fashioned from his rib while he sleeps.[34] Both man and woman are created good, not inclined to evil and live for some time in a harmonious paradise, the garden of Eden.

But the harmony is disturbed with the appearance of the serpent, 'more crafty than any wild creature', a creature able to talk and reason.[35] For unknown reasons (only much later was the serpent identified as Satan) it seeks to tempt Eve to disobey the god's command not to pick and eat the fruit of a particular tree, 'the tree of the knowledge of good and evil'. The serpent succeeds in persuading her to take the forbidden fruit, promising her that by eating it 'your eyes will be opened and you will be like gods knowing both good and evil.'

Delighted with the effects of the fruit, Eve shares it with Adam; but suddenly both discover and feel the shame of their nakedness and cover themselves with fig leaves. Eventually, the god, while taking an evening stroll in the garden, becomes aware of the transgression and as a result curses all parties. The snake is forever reviled and condemned to crawl on its belly (so did snakes have a more dignified form of locomotion prior to this unhappy episode?); intense pain in labour and childbirth along with subjection to the mastery of her husband becomes Eve's lot, while Adam's existence is destined to be one of continual toil and struggle in a world that he now finds is hostile and resistant to his labours. Finally, according to the Christian understanding of the story, Adam and Eve, created as non-mortal are now doomed to die.

What are we to make of the Genesis narrative? Did the events recounted really happen or is it just a story to convey some other

---

[34] Genesis 2:18-25. In the other version both sexes are created at the same time (1:27). The reason for there being two stories is explained by the fact that Genesis is not the work of a single author. Scholars believe that there were three different (unknown) authors or sources of this work, commonly referred to as J, E and P. The *Catechism*'s understanding is self-contradictory. It maintains that 'God created man and woman together' (371), strongly suggesting that they were created at the same time. But it then goes on to reaffirm the story of Adam feeling lonely and states that Eve is created from his rib. Adam must therefore have existed prior to Eve.

[35] The story of the fall is told in Genesis 3:1-24.

elemental truth? Most scholarly commentators treat the opening chapters of this book as mythical rather than factual in nature and agree that it should not be read as a literal version of events concerning either the formation of the earth or the first moments of human history. Of course there are biblical fundamentalists who continue to maintain that everything in the Bible is literally true and who therefore believe that the Genesis stories of creation and fall should be taken as such. More dangerously, Creationists, while not always insisting on a literal reading, use Genesis to refute Darwinian theories of evolution, maintaining that humanity is a separately created species rather than one that evolved from an earlier, proto-human form. This essentially is the position adopted by mainstream Christianity.[36] However, clearly there are severe problems with accepting this narrative either as factually true or as a myth which reveals genuine truths about the origin and nature of humanity.

That we should be extremely sceptical about the reliability and validity of Genesis is urged by the text itself. For example, less well known than the creation story, Genesis also records the existence of a race of giants, the *Nephilim*, which came into being because 'the sons of gods had intercourse with the daughters of men and got children by them.'[37] And it asks us to believe that the earliest patriarchs of the chosen people - Adam, his son Seth and then his son, Enosh and so on for ten generations - all lived to impossibly old ages. Methuselah, the oldest of them all is reported to have lived for 969 years while Noah still had the vigour to father his sons when he was over 500 years old.

But there's nothing to support these unlikely and extravagant claims and common sense and experience should be sufficient for a reasonable person to dismiss them as flights of fancy. Few people indeed would be willing to accept these details as part of a realistic,

---

[36] *Humani Generis* was written to refute 'some false opinions which threaten to undermine the foundations of Catholic doctrine', one of which was the Darwinian theory of evolution. The Church permitted research and discussion of evolution 'provided that all are prepared to submit to the judgement of the Church' (para 36). In keeping with the spirit of the age when the encyclical was released (1950) it proclaimed that 'Communists gladly subscribe to this opinion [i.e. that evolution explains the origins of all things] so that they may the more efficaciously defend and propagate their dialectical materialism' (para 5). Capitalists, who also subscribed to theories of evolution, were spared a similar political censure.

[37] Genesis 6:1-4.

factual history and literalists have a hard time defending them. It is much more appropriate and plausible to consider them merely as colourful aspects of a story myth of an ancient and imaginative, but essentially unknowledgeable people, recounted by their story-tellers and poets to give them answers to their fundamental questions and sense of wonder about the world and their origins.

Now if we consider these particular details of Genesis as myth or folklore, what is it that persuades us to accept its account of the creation of the world and fall of humanity, which is no less incredible, as actually true? Are these stories in any way more realistic or credible? Do we possess anything to corroborate these narratives? Unfortunately not. There's no reason at all to believe literally in the claims of a book that in any other context would be read as a story and nothing more. The fact is the creation story in Genesis is not a factual chronicle but a poetic myth, and one of many such creation myths at that; as the biologist Richard Dawkins dryly observed, 'Nearly all peoples have developed their own creation myth, and the Genesis story is just the one that happened to have been adopted by one particular tribe of Middle Eastern herders. It has no more special status than the belief of a particular West African tribe that the world was created from the excrement of ants.'[38]

For much of its history the Church taught that Genesis was essentially true; but it has had to adapt its teaching in this area perhaps because it understands that it would be exposed to enormous ridicule if it continued to affirm that the story of Adam and Eve and a talking snake was literally true. However, it does so by presenting its teaching and its understanding so enigmatically and so vaguely that it is still able to retain the doctrine of an original sin committed by 'our first parents'. So even though effectively it adopts a mythical reading (it is unable to bring itself round to using the 'm' word however), the Church still insists that there was some real, underlying event which caused the world to be subject to suffering and evil: 'The account of the fall in Genesis [Chapter] 3 uses figurative language but affirms a primeval event, a deed that took place *at the beginning of the history of man*.'[39]

---

[38]Dawkins, *The Blind Watchmaker*, p 316.

[39] *Catechism*, 390. But in *Humani Generis* (para 38) Pius XII insisted that Chapters 1-11 of

What was this primeval event? If it was an 'event', it must have taken place at some point in time and at some specific place; when therefore, and where did it take place? What was its nature and whom did it affect? And how did the writer (or writers) of Genesis know about it? None of these questions are answered or even specifically addressed by the *Catechism* and its response to these concerns – 'Revelation gives us the certainty of faith that the whole of human history is marked by the original fault freely committed by our first parents'[40] – is both intellectually lazy and without any real meaning.

The *Catechism* states specifically that 'Genesis [Chapter] 3 uses figurative language'. If this is so then there wasn't *really* or literally a tree of knowledge or forbidden fruit, there was no talking snake and no evening stroll taken by the god in the garden. But what about Adam and Eve? Did they really exist? While the *Catechism* never explicitly claims that the story of the creation in Genesis is literally true, it does quote from it frequently and proceeds as if Genesis provides a broad and correct understanding of how the world came into being (that is, by specific acts of creation by its god), particularly in respect of humanity being a separately created species.[41] So should we accept the somewhat implausible and otherwise unsubstantiated and uncorroborated claim that there was a time when there really were only two humans on the entire planet? And is it the case that every human being descended from this first couple?

This is important because without this understanding of only two first humans, the doctrine of original sin starts to fall into great difficulties. Not surprisingly then the Church finds it impossible to abandon its literal belief in Adam and Eve. On the one hand, they are part of Genesis Chapter 3 and therefore we should, by the Church's own teaching, regard them as 'figurative' rather than actual people. If we take this approach then Adam becomes a type of 'Everyman' and Eve a representative for all women.

Genesis 'do pertain to history in the true sense and must not be considered on a par with other myths'.

[40] *Catechism*, 390.

[41] The *Catechism* (337, 343, 356) concedes that 'Scripture presents the work of the Creator *symbolically* [my italics] as a succession of six days of divine work' but specifically affirms that 'Man is the summit of the Creator's work . . . the only creature on earth that God has willed for its own sake' and is distinguished in creation from all other creatures.

But if the Church's understanding is that they are 'figurative' or representative of humanity, there's nothing in the *Catechism* to indicate that this is its teaching. On the contrary, it soon forgets this figurative understanding and starts to speak of them as if they were real and individual people. They are frequently referred to, for example, as 'our first parents', which is suggestive of two individuals from whom we are all descended; and there are numerous references to 'the first man' and 'one man's disobedience'[42] (as opposed to the first men and man(kind)'s disobedience) as if it really were the case that there was, at the very beginning of time, just one male human in the whole world. In fact if we refer back to the 1950 encyclical *Humani Generis* (which the *Catechism* cites) we can see what the Church really believes in this respect: 'Christ's faithful', it declares, 'cannot embrace that opinion which maintains either that after Adam there existed on this earth true men who did not take their origin through natural generation from him as from the first parent of all, or that Adam represents a certain number of first parents.'[43]

Why is the Church so insistent on this point despite its obvious stupidity? The answer is that it has to maintain this literal belief in order to preserve the coherence and validity of its doctrine of original sin, as indeed *Humani Generis* makes clear. Christians are not permitted to believe that Adam and Eve represent a certain number of first parents because 'it is no way apparent how such an opinion can be reconciled with that which the sources of revealed truth and the documents of the Teaching Authority of the Church propose with regard to original sin.'[44]

For if there were more than two humans before the fall, then it would have to be the case that all humans committed the original sin. To suppose otherwise would mean we would have the hugely unjust scenario that the god punished all people who were then alive for the disobedience of just one couple. And if only some people sinned, then the teaching that the fallen state (which is transmitted by sex) was passed on to *all* their offspring is impossible to sustain since there would have been some couples who were not tainted in the first place.

---

[42] *Ibid*, 375, 371, 374, 402.

[43] *Humani Generis*, 37.

[44] *Ibid*.

On the other hand, if all these original people did commit the original sin, they would have to have done so simultaneously. Since one of the consequences or punishments for this initial transgression is being subject to death, if this first sin was not committed by all humans *at exactly the same instant*, we would have the ridiculous and impossible situation that there were at the same time some humans who were mortal and some humans who were immortal and for whom death, in any form, could not and did not exist.

So if Adam and Eve are generic rather than individual, in order for the doctrine of the fall to be valid and intelligible, all people committed an original sin at exactly the same moment as if there was a precisely synchronised disobedience *en masse* either by chance or by design. Clearly any such scenario is highly implausible. Finally, if there were more than two first humans through whom sin came into the world, then Paul's typology, that just as we are all condemned by *one man's* disobedience, so we are all redeemed by *one man's* obedience, no longer holds. And if this no longer holds, then his ideas about the redeeming nature of Jesus' death are significantly undermined.

Consequently the Church has to fall back on and maintain its initial formulation of only two people.[45] But then we're back to the original problem of accepting that the entire human race came into being from just one couple; obviously it could only have increased through recourse to marriages between brother and sister (unless we accept the story about the sons of gods having sex with the 'daughters of men') and this is not capable of explaining such problems as racial diversity as well as the matter of the enormous geographical dispersion of the human race.

The next major difficulty of accepting the biblical story of the fall is the problem of death. As we've noted, according to Christian teaching, before the fall there was no such thing as death with Adam and Eve created as non-mortal beings. Death then is not part of the natural order but is a specific punishment for disobedience to the Christian

---

[45]Augustine's own reading of this aspect of Genesis was literal: 'when he created these animals, he did not propagate both kinds from single specimens, but ordered more than one to take up existence at the same time. In the case of man however, he proceeded differently . . . God created man one and alone . . . he created [Eve] out of that man in order that the human race might derive entirely from one man' (*op cit*, XII xxii). Clearly his doctrine of original sin (especially its transmission from one man's semen) depends entirely on this understanding.

god. This is not just some Old Testament myth but something that the *Catechism* affirms and which Christians today are expected to believe: 'Scripture portrays the tragic consequences of this first disobedience. . . the consequence explicitly foretold for this disobedience will come true . . . *Death makes its entrance into human history.*' At no point does it comment that death in this context is meant in a figurative sense and it points out that 'as long as he remained in the divine intimacy, man would not have to suffer or die.'[46]

The point is confirmed by *The New Catholic Encyclopedia* which declares: 'As to death, this much is . . . certain from the teaching of the Church: the death that man now dies he undergoes because of the sin of Adam.'[47] It is of course very difficult to take this teaching seriously and there is nothing to justify this understanding other than the text of Genesis itself (which as we have seen contains other wildly extravagant claims which are simply not believable). Furthermore, it is never explicitly affirmed in Genesis that Adam and Eve were created as non-mortal and such an understanding is merely one particular interpretation of the story.[48]

Just how implausible this interpretation is can be understood by considering the implications. For example if there was no death before Adam and Eve transgressed, it's reasonable to assume that no other non-human animal ever died before the god imposed the penalty of death for the first sin. But this necessarily means that species that have long been extinct, most obviously dinosaurs, for whose existence we have definite and reliable evidence, can't have died out prior to the appearance of humans. They can't have done so because there was no such thing as death before that fateful day when Adam and Eve ate the illicit and apparently deadly fruit. It follows therefore that if dinosaurs existed, they must have done so alongside humans. But apart from the fact that the Bible has no record of such gigantic and ferocious creatures, we have very good reason to believe that such species were

---

[46]*Catechism,* 376.

[47]*The New Catholic Encyclopedia,* Vol X, p 779.

[48]The Christian case for humanity being created immortal is based on the warning the god gives to Adam about the tree of knowledge: 'for on the day that you eat [from] it, you will certainly die' (2:17). This however may be just as easily interpreted as a warning or threat of immediate punishment (which was not actually carried out, for Adam and Eve did not die on that day) rather than an indication that their nature would change.

just not contemporaneous with even the earliest humanity.

This is just a brief consideration of some aspects of the story giving rise to the doctrine of original sin; but it's enough to show that it is very difficult for a reasonable person to take the Christian teaching about the fall seriously. It is simply stretching credulity too far to suppose that at the very beginning of history there were only two humans (who from the very start must have had complex and perfectly developed linguistic skills - presumably of the Hebrew language - in order to understand the prohibition) who were initially immortal and from whom we are all descended. And if we feel that these details are untenable, then we have to concede that the teaching of original sin itself is just not sustainable. Lastly, given that Christianity maintains that the fallen state has been inherited by every person who has *ever* lived (except of course Jesus and his mum), one would've thought that Jesus might have said something about it. But Jesus knew nothing about original sin. Of course he didn't, since the doctrine was formulated, invented hundreds of years after his death.

It Does Not Compute

If the evidence from Scripture to support the doctrine is less than compelling,[49] what about the coherence and validity of the teaching itself? Does this fare any better when subjected to critical scrutiny? Does it make sense to think of punishment and guilt to be passed from one generation to the next in perpetuity? And given that the Church understands that original sin is the ultimate cause of all suffering and evil in the world, does it provide a valid and intelligible explanation for the state of the human condition?

To consider and respond to these concerns again will show how untenable and unreasonable the teaching is. Firstly, the very notion of inherited guilt is one that in any other circumstances we would reject out of hand. It's simply not the case that guilt is passed down from one generation to the next, from parent to child. Likewise punishment for

---

[49] *The New Catholic Encyclopedia* (Vol X, pp 776-777) concedes that 'The OT makes no explicit or formal statement regarding the transmission of hereditary guilt from the first man to the entire human race' while 'the NT seldom, if ever, formulates theological definitions [concerning original sin] such as are currently used' and only 'hints at the universality of sin'.

those who had nothing to do with the initial disobedience of 'our first parents' can only be thought of as grossly unfair. Even the Bible itself rejects this idea.[50]

The closest example of a universal guilt that we might accept was the collective guilt imposed on the German people for the war crimes and crimes against humanity of the Nazis after World War II. We may or may not agree with this judgement. But we would be very reluctant to accept that infant children born in the final years of the war could be considered blameworthy; and we would automatically dismiss as preposterous the idea that people born after the end of the war could be considered equally responsible and deserving of punishment or moral censure. It goes against all our notions of what justice is and can't be reasonably defended. But this is precisely what the doctrine of original sin does propound. If we accept the concept of hereditary guilt it would mean that we would find it justifiable and right in principle at least, to consider that young children in Germany today share the responsibility for Nazi atrocities or should be punished for them. It's inconceivable to suppose that any person in his or her right mind would be willing to accept this; why then does it suddenly become an acceptable principle when the context is changed to the Christian one?

Next we might consider the relationship between the punishment and the offence. The only offence was one of disobedience so it's difficult to accept that this was an act of great evil as the Church would have us believe. *The New Catholic Encyclopedia* for example speaks of 'Adam's evil influence' and of the 'evil introduced into the world' but doesn't explain why Adam's disobedience is judged to be so utterly execrable.

Usually we associate evil with acts of great wickedness which cause irreparable harm to other people, acts such as torture, murder, rape or child abuse for example. Clearly there were no such actions or consequences in this instance. The nature of the punishment therefore comes across as harsh and excessive. Jesus taught that we should regard the god as a kind and loving father; but what sort of responsible parent would punish his or her children so severely for an offence so minor and inconsequential? Indeed the Christian god emerges from the

---

[50]Deuteronomy 24:16: 'Parents shall not be put to death for children, nor children be put to death for parents: a person shall be put to death only for his own crime.'

whole episode like a petulant and sulky child who simply can't deal with the fact that he's been disobeyed; one feels like slapping him in the face and telling him to move on, get over it. Unfortunately for the world the only way that our loving Father was able to deal with the situation was to impose an excessive and unnecessary punishment in perpetuity and then to send another god, his son to be sacrificed, a move that just doesn't make any sense at all; and, because the killing of Jesus is considered to be 'the greatest moral evil ever committed', the death simply compounds the problem by adding to the burden of guilt humanity must bear.

We ought also to consider that disobedience is not always necessarily wrong; in the Christian ideology, obsessed as it is with controlling people, it's true that obedience is the greatest virtue,[51] disobedience the most appalling and unacceptable fault. But in all ideologies it's possible that the highest authority can be wrong or corrupt and in such circumstances disobedience can become a desirable or almost heroic act. Oscar Wilde even ventured that 'disobedience. . . is our original virtue, it is through disobedience that progress has been made, through disobedience and rebellion.'

If we return to the Nazi war crimes again, most of the accused at the Nuremberg trials based their defence on the fact that they were following orders; they were being obedient. Being obedient however was not accepted as a mitigating factor; disobedience on the other hand, would have been deemed commendable, virtuous or even heroic conduct. And how many of us would *really* accept that the obedience of Abraham, a willingness to murder his own child for no reason, was an example of truly virtuous behaviour? If such a man as Abraham were alive today, his readiness to carry out the ghastly command of a voice in his head would more likely result in his being committed to the psychiatric wing; while a public institution that praised or sought to defend such conduct would be thought of as dangerously irresponsible.

In the case of Christianity we don't know what precisely the first disobedience consisted of; traditionally it is taught as the disobedience to the god's prohibition to acquire knowledge of good and evil, a

---

[51]In the *Catechism* the first topic to be presented about Christian faith is entitled 'The obedience of faith', considered to be 'our first obligation' (144, 2087).

prohibition which in itself seems irrational and immoral. However as if it recognises just how out of date and offensive to human dignity this prohibition is, the *Catechism* now teaches that the tree of knowledge is symbolic of the 'insurmountable limits that man must freely recognise.' What it seems to be saying is that man was not content with being human and wanted to be like a god. Apart from the fact that there's nothing to support this argument other than a few words spoken by an unusually gifted snake in an ancient storybook,[52] there's nothing intrinsically wrong with wanting to improve your condition or status. Recognition of our limits may involve disappointment or injury, but punishment for such aspiration (and such severe punishment at that) hardly seems to be just or appropriate.

Again, to consider the problem in the context of a loving parent and child relationship, one might have a clumsy daughter who wanted to be a ballerina when she grew up. A decent and responsible parent might either encourage or gently dissuade her from pursuing this; but one would be appalled or disgusted by a parent who punished the child merely for having such ambitions or for trying to realise them.

But in the story of the fall, none of this reasoning matters and ultimately the precise nature of the initial disobedience is irrelevant for Christian purposes. The prohibition could just as easily have been against picking your nose or scratching your bum; the only thing that matters is that man has to be portrayed as disobedient and therefore deserving of punishment.

And what of the belief that the whole of humanity, being subject to concupiscence, is 'inclined towards evil and death'? It's not at all certain that every individual person in the world is so inclined and if they were to give it any serious consideration, most people would take issue with this objectionable smear against their nature. Consider your own family and friends: according to the Church *all* these people are inclined towards evil. Do you really accept that this is the case? Evil is never explicitly defined by the *Catechism*, despite the extensive

---

[52]*Catechism*, 396. It should be noted that again this is simply one interpretation of the story and one which is ill supported by the text itself. A close reading of Genesis 3:1-7 shows that Eve was motivated to eat the fruit because it 'was good to eat, and . . . it was pleasing to the eye and tempting to contemplate.' Adam eats the fruit offered to him by Eve without any thought or reflection at all. Neither of them appear to show any interest in becoming like a god.

treatment it receives, so in the absence of a specific definition we might proceed with the general understanding of the term that I outlined above.

Immediately we can see that to allege that 'every man experiences evil . . . within himself'[53] (i.e. we're *all* inclined to cause irreparable harm or suffering to other people) is an offensive and irresponsible slander. If we consider that evil is made up of lesser offences such as brutality or unfair exploitation of others, it's clear that while there may be some or many individuals who are so inclined, the charge can't be held against every single person. And even if evil is nothing more than a basic human selfishness (a definition that few people would endorse), why is it so wrong to put one's own interests before those of other people? According to this understanding, it's evil to buy yourself an ice cream or a new pair of shoes and not extend the same munificence to everyone else in the neighbourhood. Furthermore, even if all people are inclined to selfishness, it's also the case that many people frequently show kindness and generosity towards others; people can and do care for and co-operate with each other – so why focus on the wholly negative aspect of human behaviour and insist that it has corrupted our entire nature?

War Without End

Why then does Christianity persist with its obsession with original sin and sin in general? In *1984* as Winston reads *the book* he learns more about the nature of the war of his times and, crucially, its ideological root causes. Foremost among the threats to Ingsoc's power and authority is the economic well-being of its people. The Party understands that if comfort, leisure and security were enjoyed by the majority of people, then 'the great mass of human beings who are normally stupefied by poverty would become literate and would learn to think for themselves.' The consequences of education and independent thought of course are disastrous for any authoritarian regime; once people learned to think for themselves 'they would soon realise that the privileged minority had no function, and they would sweep it away.'

---

[53]*Ibid*, 1606.

So the Party's real war aim isn't conquest of territory nor actual defeat of its external enemies. Rather, it is the general destruction of material well-being in order to impoverish its own people, to deprive them of their security, so limiting their potential and preventing them from ever becoming aware of and realising their freedom. Ultimately therefore, as *the book* concludes, 'the war is waged by each ruling group against its own subjects'; and with war hysteria stirring up a fearful population 'the consciousness of being at war, and therefore in danger, makes the handing-over of all power to a small caste seem the natural unavoidable condition of survival.'[54]

With Christianity the game-plan is broadly similar but is based primarily on the destruction of the *emotional well-being* of its flock. In his work *The Case Against God* the American philosopher George Smith concluded that 'Christianity has nothing to offer a happy man living in a natural, intelligible universe. If Christianity is to gain a motivational foothold, it must declare war on earthly pleasure and happiness, and this, historically, has been its precise course of action. . . *Just as Christianity must destroy reason before it can introduce faith, so it must destroy happiness before it can introduce salvation.*'[55]

Why might this drastic path be part of the Christian way? In part it's because theologically the whole religion is founded on suffering, its highest and most cherished expression being the suffering and the cruel and agonising death of Jesus. Consequently suffering (rather than pleasure or joy or having fun) for the sake of the Lord is elevated to being a great virtue, an ideal: 'Christ suffered for you and left an example for you to follow the way he took . . . think of what Christ suffered in this life. . . if you can have some share in the sufferings of Christ, be glad'.[56]

But the more fundamental reason is the fact that Christianity's only real attraction, its true prize and purpose is salvation. And for the prospect of salvation to have any meaningful value Christians need to be convinced that there's something from which they need to be saved. So the faith necessarily revolves around the idea that all of us need to be saved from hell and from our sins that might lead us there.

---

[54] Orwell, *op cit*, pp 167, 173, 168. Cf. the zeal with which the war on terror is preached.
[55] Smith, *op cit*, p 308.
[56] 1 Peter 2:21, 4:1, 13.

Consequently the faithful must be led to believe and must accept that they are sinful in the first place, that they are bad and unworthy people, that they will always be liable to sin: 'All members of the Church . . . must acknowledge that they are sinners . . . Conversion requires convincing of sin.'[57]

So Christianity needs *everyone* to be convinced of their sinfulness for its claim that Jesus is the saviour of the world to be valid and intelligible. Hence it makes the human condition itself an expression of sinfulness and the very nature of being human sinful. This is accomplished firstly through the doctrine of original sin which insists that everyone is conceived in sin and born corrupted, as a consequence of sin; and secondly - and much more destructively - by teaching that healthy, natural and human instincts and longings - enjoying sex, seeking love and emotional fulfilment,[58] delighting in the pleasures that the world has to offer, even feeling certain very human desires or emotions such as pride or anger - are sins.

So 'it is not accidental', Smith continues, 'that Christianity is profoundly anti-pleasure, especially in the area of sex; this bias serves a specific function.' For once Christian believers can be manipulated into rejecting the pleasures and joys of this life through the persuasion that these things are sinful, the compensatory hope of perfect happiness - *any happiness* in fact - in a life after death becomes all the more attractive and intense, perhaps the only thing worth living for. And if these unfortunate people - the 'poor in spirit' - can be hooked to this prospect and taught that the only way they can secure it for themselves is through obedience, then a culture of dependency and submission is established and the authority of the 'fishers of men' and their institution is maintained and enhanced. Not surprisingly an assault on earthly happiness and pleasure becomes a key priority for Christianity. 'As the caterpiller chooses the fairest leaves to lay her eggs on, so the priest lays his curse on the fairest joys.'[59] Desires can only be thought of

---

[57] *Catechism* 827, 1847

[58] Lust is one of the seven deadly sins and is defined by the Church as a 'disordered desire for inordinate enjoyment of sexual pleasure' (*Ibid*, 2351). As we've noted (see above, p 291) unhappily married Catholic couples are required to suffer and endure the anguish of their unions rather than be permitted to divorce and seek emotional and loving fulfilment in another relationship. Pride and anger are *deadly* sins.

[59] Blake, *The Marriage of Heaven and Hell.*

as being 'disordered' and everything one longs to do becomes forbidden. It's a sin.

Of course Christianity can never completely wipe out the natural human instinct for gratification and pleasure, nor could the Church ever openly teach that its members should seek to deny themselves the opportunities for earthly happiness, that they should live joyless, unfulfilling lives. Instead, like the Party in *1984* it 'accomplishes the necessary destruction . . . in a psychologically acceptable way' by introducing and insisting on the concept of *sacrifice*. Just as Jesus had to suffer and offer himself up in sacrifice, so Christians are encouraged to respond in a similar fashion, to make their own personal sacrifices in this life for the sake of the Lord: 'the sacrifice acceptable to God is a *broken spirit* . . . by uniting ourselves with his sacrifice *we can make our lives a sacrifice* to God . . . *the more we renounce ourselves*, the more we walk by the Spirit . . . There is no holiness without *renunciation* . . . Spiritual progress entails *ascesis and mortification*.'[60]

Without salvation Christianity has no purpose and without the threat of punishment for sins, salvation has no meaning. Hence Christianity absolutely needs a sense of sin to be of any use, to survive. Accordingly an everlasting, mutually reinforcing conflict between sin and salvation is established at the very heart of the ideology. Sin ensures that the fundamental reason for Christianity - salvation - survives as an attractive, compelling and urgent ideal; in return Christianity makes sure that sin - and the feeling of guilt that it brings - is forever perpetuated, a condition facilitated and universalised by the doctrine of original sin. Like the warring powers in *1984*, 'so long as they remain in conflict they prop each other up.'[61]

But the price to be paid by Christianity's victims, that is its own believers against whom the war is really waged, is a heavy one. Obliged to accept that they're born corrupted or flawed, that enjoying the pleasures that life has to offer is wrong and that guilt is the required response for such indulgence, like Augustine these unfortunate people also have to accept that they cannot help themselves, that they have to turn to their god - and hence to the control of the Church - to make their lives worthwhile, to be saved.

---

[60] *Catechism*, 2100, 736, 2015, my italics.

[61] Orwell, *op cit*, pp 171.

A Brief Conclusion

*There's a stake in your fat black heart
And the villagers never liked you.
They are dancing and stamping on you.
They always knew it was you.
Daddy, daddy, you bastard, I'm through.*[1]

For all its fanciful and elaborately constructed doctrines built up over the past 2,000 years like some massively imposing yet ill-conceived and structurally unsound medieval cathedral, essentially Christianity revolves around and depends upon an acceptance of two core propositions. Firstly, that a Jewish man called Jesus who lived and preached at the eastern edge of the Roman Empire twenty centuries ago was a god; and secondly, that by accepting him as such and by believing wholeheartedly in him, his teachings and above all in the sacrificial value of his death and the reality of his resurrection, one can be *saved* from punishment of some form after one's own death.

What should we make of these propositions? Are they valid? Should we accept them as true, as meaningful and as commendable? Do they form a worthy and sensible response to our deepest need to find some meaning and purpose for our lives?

Let's recap on why we should think that Jesus was a god. Although he never explicitly claimed to be divine, one might venture that Jesus was thought to be so because he was born of a virgin, because he worked spectacular miracles, because he had great moral authority and because he came back from the dead. However these accomplishments do not necessarily demonstrate or prove his divinity.

More importantly, there are good and ultimately more persuasive reasons to conclude that these dramatic exploits never really happened as the gospels depict. Christianity may regard the Bible as the perfect and infallible source of truth, but it has yet to make a reasonable and compelling case to support its contention that whatever is recorded in

---

[1]Sylvia Plath, *Daddy*.

345

the gospels *must be* true. In fact when we consider the gospels critically and without the bias of Christian faith, it's clear that their theologically minded and ideologically motivated authors can't be trusted as reliable and impartial reporters of the events in Jesus' life.

Finally, gods by their very nature are generally thought of as being immortal. They don't die. They can't die. Yet Jesus definitely did die. Consequently a Christian must accept Jesus not only as a god, but also at the same time as a mortal, a man. But then we have the conceptual problem of the Church's claim that two natures existed in one being, a proposition which common sense tells us simply makes no sense at all.

What should we make of the second proposition, that by having faith in Jesus and in his death and supposed resurrection one can be saved? Obviously if Jesus wasn't a god it's hard to understand why he of all men should be regarded as the saviour of the world. And apart from the sheer unintelligibility of the belief (despite the valiant efforts of the best minds of Christendom, 'none of them', we may recall, have been able to 'exhaust the mystery' - that is, offer a coherent explanation as to how Jesus' death brings about mankind's redemption), it is very difficult for enlightened people today to feel comfortable with its underlying principle. For how many of us would truly accept that the *best* way that a person or being - divine or otherwise - could express love and commitment to us and thereby bring about a meaningful reconciliation would be by conceiving and then fulfilling a plan which involved killing a beloved son?

However, of greater concern is the fairness and morality of the belief. For the implication would appear to be that those who don't have faith won't be saved, a consequence apparently confirmed by Jesus himself: 'whoever refuses to believe is condemned already.'[2] If we translate this formulation - that unbelievers will not be saved - into *dissidents will be subject to punishment*, we can begin to appreciate just how abhorrent Christianity's scheme of salvation really is. Why should millions of people, why indeed should anyone be punished simply for having a difference of opinion or belief? What sort of god or loving father is it that would make such a harsh and unfair judgement? Why should it even be that the whole of humanity is condemned in the first place?

---

[2] John 3:18.

Christianity endorses this brutal scheme partly because, as I hope should be clear by now, without the threat of punishment ultimately it has no meaning or purpose. If there's no hell or other punishment after death, then we have no need to be saved; if we have no need to be saved then Jesus can't be our saviour and the religion revolving around his gruesome death on a cross becomes more or less redundant and unintelligible.

But Christianity's dismal and unpalatable fixation with punishment – or the threat of punishment – exists also because like all ideologies it recognises that this provides the most effective means to control and exact obedience from people. Throughout history totalitarian regimes have understood and made use of the fact that people fearing inhumane and arbitrary punishment can be controlled and repressed much more easily than those who are not so intimidated; and whether one cares to admit it or not, intimidation is at the dark heart of the Christian religion. As the *Catechism* openly proclaims, *fear* of the Lord – apparently one of the seven 'gifts' of the Holy Spirit – helps to 'make the faithful docile in readily obeying' and 'fear of eternal damnation and the other penalties threatening the sinner' is paramount in governing the behaviour of these faithful.[3] If such punishment could potentially be everlasting, without any hope of remission, then the threat is all the more effective; while those who can be induced to *condemn themselves* through self-imposed guilt are just as malleable for Christianity's authoritarian proclivities.

Why then has Christianity thrived so spectacularly and for so long? Ignoring the fact that for much of its history it was forced, often brutally, on generally uneducated people (the practice continues today – albeit without the brutality – with the Christian indoctrination in schools of young children who are barely able to resist or challenge its teachings) we might venture that there are a number of key factors that go some way to explain its success. Our fear of death, Hamlet's 'undiscover'd country' from which 'no traveller returns', together with the intense need to find some purpose for our lives are universal human concerns which Christianity exploits in a comforting and enticing way. People find solace and consolation in the belief or hope that we will survive death, that we will be reunited with our loved

---

[3] *Catechism*, 1831, 1453.

ones, that there will be a perfect world of everlasting happiness awaiting us, where everything will be - quite literally - all right. Throw in Jesus' assurance that his god is not a fierce and remote deity but a merciful and compassionate father figure who loves us dearly and who will comfort and reward us, his children with his protection and blessing if only we would open our hearts and lives to him, and we get a potent and very tempting spiritual cocktail.

But the price to be paid for this comfort is a heavy one. In order to participate in Christianity's reward programme (the fulfilment of which of course can never be ascertained or guaranteed) one must conform to its requirements, which as we've seen focus primarily on unquestioning obedience, a surrender of moral and intellectual freedom and a life of submission and self-denial. Effectively Christians must fight against and overcome many of their natural and healthy instincts, thereby sacrificing much of the potential for fulfilment and happiness in their lives.

In his essay *Summer in Algiers*, Camus suggested that 'if there is a sin against life, it consists perhaps not so much in despairing of life as in hoping for another life.' If this is a valid observation, then ultimately Christianity is a religion of despair with its teaching that we should be living for and setting our hearts not upon this life, but the next, as if to say that this life, the only life we know, is not to be valued or lived for its own sake. And with its emphasis on personal sacrifice and to 'love not the world nor those things which are in this world'[4] the pleasures and joys of our world must be resisted to prove one's worthiness, to secure one's admission to the unknown kingdom beyond the pearly gates.

In *1984* some time after he emerges from the horribly named Ministry of Love, in a gin induced stupor Winston Smith reflects upon his predicament; and in one of the bleakest and most depressing endings in the whole canon of English literature, he finally yields his spirit to the mastery of Big Brother:

> He looked up again at the portrait of Big Brother. The colossus that bestrode the world! . . . He gazed up at the enormous face. Forty years it had taken him to learn what kind of smile was hidden beneath the dark moustache . . . Two gin-scented tears trickled

---

[4] 1 John 2:15.

down the sides of his nose. But it was all right, everything was all right, the struggle was finished. He had won the victory over himself. He loved Big Brother.[5]

Bleak as this ending is, it is still more depressing to consider that this principle of love for the glorious leader (which of course entails perfect obedience) forms the very basis of the Christian faith. For according to Jesus, of all its commandments the greatest is that 'you must love the Lord your God with all your heart, with all your soul, with all your mind and with all your strength.'[6] Christianity may trumpet that love is at the heart and soul of its own ministry; but tragically such love has burdened the world with a joyless, pessimistic religion that is obsessed with suffering, punishment and controlling and repressing the human spirit. No wonder John Lennon urged us to try to imagine a world without it, without its hell, without its heaven, to

Imagine all the people
Living for today.

[5]Orwell, *op cit*, p 258.
[6]Mark 12:30.

Bibliography

Ancient Sources

Augustine	*City of God*
Elliott, J (ed)	*The Apocryphal New Testament*, 1993
Eusebius	*The History of the Church*
The New Testament	*The Jerusalem Bible*
The Torah	*The Masoretic Text*, The Jewish Publication Society of America, 1962
Josephus	*Antiquities of the Jews*, trans. Whiston, 1883
Origen	*Contra Celsum*
Philostratus	*Apollonius of Tyana*
Stevenson, J (ed)	*A New Eusebius,* 1957
Tacitus	*The Histories*
	Annals

Commentaries, Dictionaries and Encyclopedias

Barrett, D et al (ed)	*World Christian Encyclopedia 2000*, 2001
Brandon, S G F (ed)	*A Dictionary of Comparative Religion*, 1970
Brown, R E et al (ed)	*The New Jerome Biblical Commentary*, 1989
Fuller, R C (ed)	*A Catholic Commentary on Holy Scripture*, 1969
Herbermann, C et al (ed)	*The Catholic Encyclopedia*, 1914
Hinnells, J (ed)	*A New Dictionary of Religions*, 1984
Konstant, D (ed)	*Catechism of the Catholic Church*, 1994
Laqueur, W (ed)	*The Holocaust Encyclopedia*, 2001
McDonald, J et al (ed)	*The New Catholic Encyclopedia*, 1967
Murray, D (ed)	*Oxford Companion to Christian Art & Architecture*, 1996
Office for National Statistics	*Official Yearbook of the United Kingdom, 2001*
Thomson, W A R (ed)	*Black's Medical Dictionary*, 1984

Secondary Sources

Angus, S	*The Mystery Religions and Christianity*, 1925
Armstrong, K	*A History of God*, 1993
Arnheim, M	*Is Christianity True?* 1984
Baker, G P	*Constantine the Great and the Christian Revolution*, 1931
Barnes, T D	*Constantine and Eusebius*, 1981

Barr, J	*The Garden of Eden and The Hope of Immortality*, 1992
Benko, S	*Protestants, Catholics and Mary*, 1968
Bernheim, P A	*James, Brother of Jesus*, 1997
Brandon, S G F	*The Fall of Jerusalem and the Christian Church*, 1957
	Jesus and The Zealots, 1967
	The Trial of Jesus of Nazareth, 1968
Brown, P	*Augustine of Hippo*, 1968
Brown, R E	*The Birth of the Messiah*, 1977
Bruce, S	*Religion in Modern Britain*, 1995
Bultmann, R	*The History of the Synoptic Tradition*, 1919 (1963)
Burkett, W	*Ancient Mystery Cults*, 1987
Burrows (ed) et al	*International Handbook of Clinical Hypnosis*, 2001
Chadwick, H	*The Early Church*, 1967
Cromwell, R S	*David Friedrich Strauss and His Place in Modern Thought*, 1974
Davies, S L	*Jesus the Healer*, 1995
Dibelius, M	*From Tradition to Gospel*, 1919 (1971)
Fox, R L	*The Unauthorised Version: Truth and Fiction in The Bible*, 1991
Frazer, G	*The Golden Bough*, 1922
Frend, W H C	*The Early Church: From the Beginnings to 461*, 1965
Fuller, R H	*The Formation of the Resurrection Narratives*, 1972
Gilbert, A	*The Vatican Council And The Jews*, 1968
Grant, M	*The Emperor Constantine*, 1993
Hatch, E	*The Influence of Greek Ideas on Christianity*, 1889
Helms, R	*Gospel Fictions*, 1988
Hengel, M	*The Atonement*, 1981
Hick, J (ed)	*The Myth of God Incarnate*, 1977
Hick, J	*The Metaphor of God Incarnate*, 1993
James, E O	*Origins of Sacrifice: A Study in Comparative Religion* 1933
Kahl, J	*The Misery of Christianity*, 1971
Kee, A	*Constantine Versus Christ*, 1982
Kelly, J N D	*Early Christian Creeds*, 1950
Kennedy, H A A	*St Paul and the Mystery Religions*, 1913
Kennedy, L	*All In The Mind - A Farewell To God*, 1999
Kingston, A R	*God in One - The Case for Non-Incarnational Christianity*, 1993
Klausner, J	*From Jesus to Paul*, 1939 (1944)
Knight, M	*Honest to Man: Christian Ethics Re-examined*, 1974
Kummel, W G	*An Introduction to the New Testament*, 1951 (1975)
	The New Testament - The History of the Investigation of its Problems, 1957
	The Theology of the New Testament, 1974
Kung, H	*The Catholic Church*, 2001
Lane, W	*The Gospel According to Mark*, 1974

Leed, E	*No Man's Land: Combat And Identity in World War I*, 1979
Ludemann, G	*The Resurrection of Jesus: History, Experience, Theology*, 1994
	Virgin Birth ? The Real Story of Mary and Her Son Jesus, 1998
Maccoby, H	*The Sacred Executioner - Human Sacrifice And The Legacy of Guilt*, 1982
	The Myth Maker - Paul and the Invention of Christianity, 1986
	Paul And Hellenism, 1991
Martin, M	*The Case Against Christianity*, 1991
Marxsen, W	*Introduction To The New Testament*, 1964 (1968)
	The Resurrection of Jesus of Nazareth, 1970
Miegge, G	*The Virgin Mary: The Roman Catholic Marian Doctrine*, 1950
Nietzsche	*The Anti-Christ*, 1889 (1968)
Nineham, D	*The Gospel of St Mark*, 1963
Orwell, G	*1984*, 1949
Pagels, E	*Adam, Eve and The Serpent*, 1988
Parrinder, G	*Son of Joseph: The Parentage of Jesus*, 1992
Power, K	*Veiled Desire - Augustine's Writing on Women*, 1995
Rees, B R	*Pelagius - A Reluctant Heretic*, 1988
Reimarus, H S (ed Talbert, C H)	*Fragments Concerning the Intention of Jesus and his Teaching*, 1774 (1971)
Robinson, R	*An Atheist's Values*, 1964
Schaberg, J	*The Illegitimacy of Jesus*, 1995
Schonfield, H J	*The Jew of Tarsus: An Unorthodox Portrait of Paul*, 1946
	Those Incredible Christians, 1968
Schweitzer, A	*The Quest of the Historical Jesus*, 1906 (2000)
Smith, G H	*Atheism: The Case Against God*, 1989
Smith, M	*Jesus the Magician*, 1978
Stanford, P	*The Devil: A Biography*, 1998
Strauss, D F	*The Life of Jesus Critically Examined*, 1835
Streeter, B H	*The Four Gospels - A Study of Origins*, 1926
Taylor, V	*The Gospel According to Mark*, 1952
Vermes, G	*Jesus The Jew*, 1973
	The Changing Faces of Jesus, 2001
Warner, M	*Alone of All Her Sex*, 1976
Wells, G A	*The Historical Evidence for Jesus*, 1982
	Who Was Jesus? 1989
Wenham, D (ed)	*Gospel Perspectives: The Miracles of Jesus*, 1986
Wilson, A N	*Jesus*, 1993
Wilson, I	*Jesus: The Evidence*, 1984
Winter, M	*The Atonement*, 1995
Wolman, B	*Psychosomatic Disorders*, 1988

Index